Professional and Development Issues in Leisure, Sport and Education

Edited by

Lesley Lawrence

Elizabeth Murdoch

Stan Parker

LSA
Publication No 56

First published in 1995 by
Leisure Studies Association

A catalogue record for this book
is available from the British Library.

ISBN: 0 906337 67 4

Layout design and typesetting by Myrene L. McFee
Reproduction by University of Brighton
Binding by Kensett Ltd., Hove

Contents

Introduction

This collection of papers — by educators and practitioners from a variety of leisure studies perspectives — ranges widely over significant professional and development issues which are currently being worked through in the related fields of leisure, sport and education.

The papers in this volume are presented in five sections: *gender, morality and deviance*; *provision for play*; *protection and safety issues in sport environments*; *leisure education*; and *young people, games and sport*. It should be understood, however, that the themes and issues dealt with in these five sections are extensively interrelated.

There are five contributions in Section I on GENDER, MORALITY AND DEVIANCE. In his paper 'Conformity and Deviance in Sport: a sociological approach', **Chas Critcher** discusses kinds of deviance in sport, the relationships between sport and morality, and sociological theories of deviance applied to sport. Questioning the traditional association of sport with the moral, he argues that the relationship between sport and morality is "contingent, arbitrary and ideological": to think otherwise is to place on sport a moral burden "not imposed on other areas of cultural life". For Critcher, there is no clear relationship between moral behaviour on the sportsfield and its equivalent in everyday life, as concrete examples and research studies illustrate. Yet (typically) gender-segregated activities such as sport are readily constructed around ideals of masculinity. In this vein, Critcher tackles the thorny question of what can be done to control deviance in sport and thus strengthen its moral order.

Jennifer Hargreaves, in 'Gender, Morality and the National Physical Education Curriculum', argues that stereotyped and reactionary attitudes to gender lie at the heart of John Major's pronouncement — "putting competitive team games back at the heart of school life" — and at the centre of the 1995 National Heritage publication of *Sport: Raising the Game*. She is critical of those who are in power to make decisions and accuses them of ignorance over the development of Physical Education, and the nature of the subject and debates within the subject. The lost opportunity to produce a National Curriculum which would question and transform traditional gender inequities and stereotypes is regretted. She fears that problems arising from gender stereotyping will be accentuated as a result of this failure.

Stereotyping is prevalent in the world of sport and education, with various groups suffering discrimination as a result of it. **Gill Clarke** gives voice to one such group in her paper 'Outlaws in Sport and Education? Exploring the sporting and education experiences of lesbian physical education teachers'. She focuses upon the interface of their 'private' worlds and the public worlds of education and sport, with illustrations of some of the identity management strategies employed to conceal their lesbianism.

Bob Carroll considers an equal opportunities issue in his paper 'Examinations in Physical Education and Sport: gender differences and influences on subject choice'. He discusses a study that looks at the reasons for, and factors influencing, subject choice, advice received and career aspirations of GCSE and 'A' level candidates, identifying gender differences. Determinants identified are personal preferences, people who influence the choice, the subject, how it is offered, and career aspirations.

Concentrating on one area of the secondary school curriculum, **Lynda Measor**, **Coralie Tiffin** and **Katrina Fry** discuss the provision of appropriate and effective sex education in a range of settings in 'Gender and Adolescent Sexual Cultures: the view from some boys'. They focus upon the pupils themselves and their reactions and responses to the education they receive, highlighting differences in behaviour between boys and girls. They suggest the need to develop sex education provision which is more closely tailored to expressed needs.

The needs of children feature in the first contribution in Section II of this volume — PROVISION FOR PLAY. In her paper 'Politically Correct Play', **Barbara Hendricks** explores urban playground provision in terms of adult perceptions of how and why children play. She claims that children's right to play is often ill-served by providers' misconceptions of the value and purposes of play, and by provision which is all too often merely trend-following — the current fashion being for so-called 'nature playgrounds'. She urges in a persuasive style that what is provided for children's play should be guided by child needs and not by adult societal goals such as 'environmental' and other 'educational' aims.

In a more political vein, **Caroline Jackson** considers the use of strategic processes in offering a practical solution to the future of play provision. She asks, 'Play Strategies: the vision or the reality?'. There appear to be a number of approaches to strategic management of play within local authorities which are focused either on a vision leading to aims and policies or on a pragmatic approach. She contends that much more research needs to be done to persuade and show local authorities what could be achieved by a mixture of both.

In another paper questioning current practice, **Stephen Williams**, in 'Urban Playgrounds: rethinking the city as an environment for children's play', contends that one of the primary interfaces between education and leisure is the experiential learning, through outdoor play, of children. He questions several of the key presumptions on which limitations of play are based. Recovering the full educational value of play will require both the development of a coherent and effective play policy and a revision in basic attitudes towards the urban environment and the position of children within it.

In Section III — PROTECTION AND SAFETY ISSUES IN SPORT ENVIRONMENTS — the first paper is 'The Commercialisation of Outdoor Education — profit and loss in adventure'. **Barbara Humberstone** examines the effects of government policies on the provision of outdoor education in England and Wales since 1988. She notes the reduced public funding and developing commercial interests in the provision of outdoor activities and believes that accidents raise questions concerning qualifications, safety and compulsory legislation.

The next two papers consider issues within the voluntary sector. In 'Safety at their Leisure — a study of youth sport courses', **Jenny Anderson** explores the attitudes of parents and children towards organised sport with particular emphasis on perceptions of safety. She reviews child sport motivation theory and research on safety in sport, and proposes a youth safety policy for working with young children in the voluntary sector.

In 'Educating for Child Protection in Sport', **Celia Brackenridge**, **Diana Summers** and **Diana Woodward** discuss the demonstrable lack of awareness, knowledge and recognition of child protection issues in sport. They investigate why an apparently 'taboo' subject — child sexual abuse in sport — has been rendered invisible in our voluntary sport system and has not been incorporated effectively into coach education. They propose mechanisms that might be adapted in the voluntary sector and set out an educational agenda for child protection in sport.

Another emotive subject, namely, steroid usage by athletes, is taken further when **Dan Christmas**, **P. Holmes**, **G. Nutt** and **D. Woodward** argue the case for steroid specific health promotion work within education, exploring the role of the PE professional as a key player. In 'Anabolic Steroids in Education — the role of the Physical Education professional', it is proposed that the role of the physical educator could be very significant in countering the effects of media portrayals of distorted body images by reinforcing a positive alternative to this through practical training.

The role of the physical education professional features in the first of four contributions in Section IV on LEISURE EDUCATION. In 'The Leisure and Education Interface Explored', **Lesley Lawrence** asks "in what 'places' within the school are leisure and education seen as meeting?". She considers the prominence of PE and within this, curricular and extracurricular roles, before examining the potential of other curriculum subjects. The inconsistency and differing views of teachers is noteworthy.

Two contributions address the thorny issue of the introduction of qualifications in the leisure industry. First, **John Hunter-Jones**, **Bob Carroll** and **Bob Jones,** in 'Knowledge or Competence? The changing face of qualifications in the leisure industry', outline the main types of courses and qualifications at sub degree level. They then focus upon General National Vocational Qualifications (GNVQs) and National Vocational Qualifications (NVQs) and discuss the implications of the change to competence-based assessment in the workplace.

David Smith and **Sue Eccles**, in 'Leisure Education and Training — competence approaches and quality issues', also address the present education environment and the emphasis on the new vocational qualifications and associated competence-based assessment. They discuss Further Education and its present context in relation to vocationalism before proposing a vocational partnership model between Higher Education, Further Education and employers for the implementation of an NVQ in Higher Education.

On a slightly different tack, **Bob Lentell** demonstrates in 'Missing Services: leisure management textbooks and the concept of services management' how an examination of leisure studies textbooks reveals a lack of recognition of developments within services operations management and services marketing over the last twenty years. He proposes the operation of more dynamic intellectual perspectives.

Section V focuses upon issues relating to YOUNG PEOPLE, GAMES AND SPORT. In 'Team Games in the National Curriculum: the relevance of Rugby Union football', **Andrew White** responds to the policy of extending, compulsorily, participation in team games of all 14-16 year olds, with particular reference to Rugby Union football. An overview of the social development of rugby assists in identifying the values embedded in the sport through the amateur ethos. He advocates a 'reflexive' attitude by PE professionals.

Widening the scope to youth sport in general, **Bill Tancred,** in his paper on 'Youth Sport: motivational approaches for coaches', recommends that coaches acquire understanding of why young people wish to participate in their chosen sport. On the basis of "actual procedures that have been followed" by practising coaches, he presents a comprehensive collection of motivational approaches by which coaches can maintain and enhance this interest, and suggests that the use of such approaches may result in less 'dropping out of sport' by young people.

What is deemed to be suitable and acceptable physical activity for young people is explored by **Sarah Gilroy**, in 'Setting the Boundaries: a critique of recent Government initiatives affecting sport and leisure'. She examines the discourse surrounding one particular government initiative — *Sport: Raising the Game* (DNH, 1995) — and assesses the assumptions underpinning this policy. She considers that the government-approved form of sport has been embraced not only in *Sport; Raising the Game*, but also in the 'new orders' (DES, 1995) for Physical Education in the National Curriculum.

The theme of what should be included in a national curriculum continues in the next contribution in this section. **Zinaida Kuznetsova** and **Alexandre Kuznetsov,** in 'The Educational Meaning of Tatar Folk Games in Physical Education', characterise folk games pedagogically and according to age, and argue for their inclusion in a Tatar national curriculum similar to that in the UK. Folk games, they argue, will both preserve national traditions and promote motor competencies and skills in children and young people.

Rounding off both the contributions in this section and in the volume, **Ken Roberts**, in his paper 'School Children and Sport', discusses findings from a large-scale survey conducted in 1995 of young people's involvement in sport and other types of leisure. He notes levels and patterns of participation alongside trends with age and gender differences, drawing conclusions about the significance of sport in young people's lifestyles and the overall influence of school education.

The over-arching themes from this volume are those prioritised in its title: professional and developmental matters. So there is a concern both with the professions (and the professionals) who 'deliver' sport, education and leisure activities, and with the development of the areas themselves. In particular, the educational contribution (in its widest sense) of physical activity — both in and out of schools — is shown to be both more problematic, more political and more contested than might have been supposed: there is still room to debate *what* should go on in education, and *why*. Moreover, the question of how (if at all) achievement should be recognised through qualifications is perennial. And similar issues arise outside the context of formal education — questions both of safety and of rationale. This volume makes a significant contribution to the clarification of such issues; and perhaps to their resolution.

Lesley Lawrence *(University of Luton)*
Elizabeth Murdoch *(University of Brighton)*
Stan Parker *(University of Brighton)*

November, 1995

Note: Versions of the papers contained in this volume were originally presented at the Leisure Studies Association Annual Conference on "Leisure, Sport and Education: The Interfaces", held at the Chelsea School, University of Brighton, Eastbourne, 12-14 September, 1995. Two other volumes arising from that event are *Policy and Politics in Sport, Physical Education and Leisure* edited by Scott Fleming, Margaret Talbot and Alan Tomlinson; and *Leisure Cultures: Values, Genders, Lifestyles* edited by Graham McFee, Wilf Murphy and Garry Whannel.

Part I

Gender, Morality and Deviance

Conformity and Deviance in Sport: A Sociological Approach

Chas Critcher

Sheffield Hallam University

Introduction

The aim of this paper is to evaluate the relevance of a sociological approach to the problem of deviance in sport. This is not a novel enterprise but there would seem room for further consolidation and exploration of what has often been a fragmented and specialised discussion. Sociology should in principle be of some relevance, since its fundamental task is the explanation of in society as a whole and its constituent processes and institutions. It should therefore provide some models and concepts with which to analyse order and disorder, conformity and deviance, in sport.

Already we encounter the problem of definition, since the meaning of none of these terms can be taken as self-evident. However, I intend to side-step the problem. I shall adopt a working definition of sport as physical goal-directed behaviour which is competitive and rule governed. Conformity is behaviour which is supportive of the social order and deviance behaviour which is disruptive of it. It would be naive to think that order and disorder, conformity and deviance are mutually exclusive opposites. Rather each situation may be (often finely) balanced between order and disorder. Each individual may at different times exhibit both conformist and deviant behaviour: there are acts which are clearly conformist, those which are clearly deviant and those which are in an arena of ambiguity. Our aim is to explain deviance rather than deviants.

It could be argued that any attempt to explain deviance as a whole is as suspect in sport as it is in society. No one theory can possibly encompass the whole range of social deviance or even the whole range of crimes. Thus to begin from the position that it is possible to have one framework to explain the great varieties of deviance in sport is bound to fail. However, we can at least provisionally accept the argument that, because sport is such a precisely rule-bound activity and because the forms of deviance it produces are much narrower than those in society as

3

a whole, then it may at least be worth exploring the viability of a framework which can encompass the whole or most of deviance in sport. It has, for example, been argued that explanations of drug-taking in sport have a wider application:

> The spread of doping is here regarded as closely connected with the development of sports at the top level, especially international development.... [It] does not differ in principle from ... violence in sport. (Johansson, 1987: p. 83)

However, deviance in sport is a complex category. The apparently precise nature of the rules governing sport might lead us to expect that we could define deviance fairly straightforwardly as any act which is in breach of the codified rules. In fact, as a moment's thought will reveal, it is not that easy. Codified rules are often only a loose framework which cannot cover every ~~contingency and which requires interpretation. Much of the activity~~ ~~involved with sport ... interpretation ... one reason why~~ umpiring is such a thankless task. As those who have studied the rules of sport have revealed, the formal rules are only one part of what constitutes the framework of conformity in sport. There are different kinds of concepts available to describe the understandings which necessarily underpin the framework of rules and I shall refer briefly to an exploration of the problem later on. For the moment, I am (though others may not be) content to use terms derived from functionalist sociology and accept that in sport, as in society as a whole, there is a basic distinction to be made between rules, norms and values.

No sociologist that I am aware of believes that social order can be maintained by rules and formal punishments alone. Even the most vicious dictatorship will at least try to achieve a wider legitimacy for itself. It is not enough to provide prescriptions for specific behaviour: these need to be supported by conventions about how to behave, which in turn require some adherence to a set of moral values which legitimise the social order as a whole:

- *rules* are simply the laws of any group, frequently written down.
- *norms* are a much looser set of expectations about how people ought to behave: they are prescriptions which stop short of being formal rules.
- *values* are the key moral principles on which rules and norms are based.

We can in principle have:

- *deviance from the rules*, clearly observable (in principle at least);
- *deviance from the norms*, behaviour which is not expressly forbidden by the rules but which breaches established expectations;
- *deviance from values*, in which the whole purpose of the activity is denied.

These three conceptually distinct kinds of deviance may be illustrated from cricket:

- a no-ball is deviance from the rules;

- short-pitched bowling is deviance from the norms (despite attempts to outlaw it);

- spurious appealing is deviance from the values of cricket, since it attempts to intimidate umpires and invalidates the whole point of the game to win by outappealing rather than outplaying the opposition.

Thus we have in principle three kinds of deviance: those which infringe the rules, those which breach the norms, and those which deny the values. It is of course possible for an act to be in all three categories but it is equally possible for an act to be deviant in only one of these senses. And, as I shall try to argue all the way through, the obverse of what is true for deviance is true for conformity. There can be conformity to all three categories, there can be conformity to one category but not another ('there's nothing against it in the rules') or conformity to one category can override the others ('it may not be against the rules but it violates the spirit of the game').

As will become evident, these terms are related to but distinct from the concepts of constitutive rules, normative rules and the ethos or values of the sport.

The level of deviance is only part of the complexity for deviance in sport also varies in its behavioural forms and apparent motivations. If we are to discuss deviance in sport as a whole (and some would say such complexities vitiate the whole effort) then we have to look for a theoretical framework which can encompass those acts which have a quite obvious goal (physical obstruction of an opponent, drug-taking etc.) and those where the goal is less obvious or even absent altogether, of which the most obvious example is dissent from referees' decisions. This activity achieves very little (though even here there is sometimes an ulterior motive of intimidating the official); it is more likely to attract punishment than gain advantage. The conventional (again structural functionalist derived) distinction here is between instrumental behaviour, aimed to achieve an identifiable advantage in the game, and expressive behaviour, in which the player gives vent to an emotional outburst of anger or frustration. The former would appear to be more explicable in sociological terms that the latter, which might need a more psychological approach. Sociologists would then not be obliged to explain the personality characteristics of Eric Cantona, which would be a blessed relief to us all.

The problem is further complicated by the great variations in the levels and types of deviant behaviour in sport. Some sports have acquired a greater toleration of deviant behaviour (e.g. ice hockey) than others where behaviour is very minutely circumscribed (e.g. golf). Even within the same sport, the levels and styles of deviance are quite different between the amateur and professional levels (e.g. tennis).

We are left with quite a task. We cannot easily define deviance; we are unsure what is being deviated from; insofar as we can identify it, the forms it takes are myriad and in any case levels and types vary between sports and between the different levels of any one sport. But here is a good test case for sociology: if we can't explain the nature of the social order in sport, then we certainly shouldn't try it for society as a whole.

In the rest of the paper, I shall firstly deal with the confusing place of morals and ethics in sport, examine the applicability of various sociological schools to deviance in sport, discuss the key problem of masculinity and briefly review the kinds of measures which might lessen deviance in sport. I shall be arguing three basic theses:

1) That sport is less an occasion for the realisation of moral values than a structured opportunity for deviant behaviour;

2) That sociological theories of deviance do offer a useful set of explanations for most of the dominant forms of deviance in sport;

3) That many of the most obvious and least resolved issues about the causes and styles of deviance in sport are quite clearly related to competing forms of masculinity.

Sport and morality

Much discussion of sport's contribution to the common good proceeds on the assumption that there is something inherently moral in sport and that as a consequence morality is a defining characteristic of sport. I want to dissent from this view. The connections between sport and morality should rather be seen as contingent, arbitrary and ideological. They are *contingent* because they stem from a particular historical conjuncture in British history when an emergent class seized upon sport as expressive of its manly ideals. There seems no particular reason why this contingent relationship should be perpetuated in the twentieth century.

They are *arbitrary* because this burden of morality is not imposed on other areas of cultural life. It is possible but sounds faintly absurd to make equivalent claims for the moral lessons to be learned from, for example, music, whether classical, folk or popular. Perhaps there is a musicologist somewhere who believes that playing or listening will induce in those involved discipline, teamwork, fortitude in the face of adversity and all the other myriad moral lessons which sport is supposed to induce. That sport has formal rules, while music does not, is no reason to suppose that sport has a more inherently moral character.

The relationships between sport and morality are *ideological* because they attempt to infuse sport with a set of cultural meanings derived from a constellation of interests outside of it, which concentrate on a highly restricted set of possible meanings which are ultimately reflections of nineteenth century male bourgeois ideals.

Let us consider the opposite case: that sport is not a moral but an immoral or at least amoral activity, that:

> ...competitive sport is an inherently self-interested activity, the purpose of which is to demonstrate superiority over others accord-ing to an agreed set of rules. (Lee, 1995: p. 57)

If we consider some of the most prevalent behaviours in sport we en-counter a repertoire which would not be tolerated in the rest of life. Even at the humblest levels, we may encounter verbal abuse (of the self, referees, opponents), physical damage (to the self, opponents or equipment), and a general perception of rules as something to get round rather than adhere to. Indeed, there are few activities in life as a whole which offer what I earlier referred to as structured opportunities for deviant behaviour. The only other activity I can think of where otherwise law-abiding people con-sistently flout the rules, behave as if only their interests have to be taken into account and feel victimised when apprehended, is driving a motor car. Driving shares with sport this characteristic of permitting behaviour which if exhibited elsewhere in life (at least outside the family) would attract immediate disapproval from the rest of society.

This claim does not have to rest on mere assertion. Those who have studied moral behaviour in sport have consistently come up with only the most tenuous evidence that sport teaches or endorses any moral lessons at all. Here are two such examples:

> Far away from being a channel for the harmless abreaction of aggression and violence, today's sport of high competition legi-timates, requires and promotes violence and aggression. Aggression and violence seems to be a usual or normal, indispensable, irrevo-cable, inevitable behaviour necessary for success in highly skilled sportsmen and sportswomen in general. (Pilz, 1979: p. 23)

> On the basis of this study, we suggest that involvement in sport characterised by a relatively high degree of physical contact may be developmentally counterproductive for most preadolescent chil-dren. The types of social interactions fostered by relatively high contact sports may provide little stimulus for — and may even impede — moral growth. (Bredemeier *et al.*, 1986: p. 136)

In fact, people appear to operate in sport with much lower levels of morality than they do in society as a whole. Lee (1995), for example, has sum-marised some of the main findings about moral attitudes in sport. Lower levels of sports morality are associated with contact rather than non-contact sports, with older rather than younger players, with men rather than women and with competitive rather than recreational participants. Though Lee argues that morality may lie more in underlying values than in surface attitudes, the argument could still be made that sport presents us not on our best but on our worst behaviour.

In a series of studies of the moral judgements made by children and adult athletes, Bredemeier and Shields (1986b) have developed a more complex argument. They suggest that, just as sport is separated off from the rest of social conduct, so sports morality is different in kind from that operative in the rest of social life. In sport, the very existence of detailed regulation of behaviour and direct supervision by agents of enforcement absolves participants from the responsibility to make moral judgements which take account of the interest of others, resulting in what they term egocentric judgements. There is a morality in sport, but more limited in scope and sensitivity than normal moral judgements, which they describe as "a situationally operative morality that is bracketed within broader morality" (Bredemeier and Shields, 1986b: p.22). As their empirical research demonstrates, sportspeople do make moral judgements about aggressive behaviour which is and is not acceptable, but the grounds on which they make those judgements are much narrower and more self-serving than equivalent judgements in everyday life.

So the best that can be said about morality in sport is that, insofar as it exists at all, it is at a very primitive level. Far from being a model for the rest of our lives, it is a separate insulated sphere where we are permitted to think and behave in ways which would soon lead to disorder and chaos if applied to the rest of social life.

All this seems to point to the need to abandon the idea that sport is a school for morality; rather it is the opportunity for us all to behave, for a while, like delinquents. The ultimate pleasure of sport lies in its otherness: its a capacity to move into another realm, beyond the mundane, the everyday — and the moral. In that literal sense, sport is a romance: that is what it shares with literature and music. Rules, morals, ethics are a means to that end: they are not themselves the ends. Systematic cheating robs us not of our moral fibre but of the aura of romance. Thus understanding of what encourages conformity and what discourages deviance in sport (and analysis of such related evils as multi-national sponsorship and Rupert Murdoch) is necessary in order to protect the romance: illusion cannot bear too much intrusion of reality.

So we should not mistake the moral means for the amoral ends in sport or indeed in leisure as a whole. There are plenty of other areas of our public and private lives where morality needs to be restored as a goal without infusing sport with a spurious moral duty. Again, this has been recognised by others:

> ...[before] sport is further overloaded and misused by an unending number of social functions, one should consider how many losers, deviants and victims of discipline it has produced, how many wrong models it has already presented and in whose true interests in has acted. (Weiss, 1976 cited in Pilz, 1979: p. 24)

So by all means let us value sport, in or out of school, but as an arena of human expressivity and pleasure: not as an extension of religious education or social and life skills. Let us say that equality of the conditions of performance — and thus adherence to rules and codes — is an essential precondition of its successful accomplishment. But let us not say that there is anything special about the moral attributes of sport or sports heroes. If we admire Linford Christie, Ian Botham or Paul Gascoigne, let us not set them up as moral icons, expecting their conduct in and out of competition to provide us all with lessons on how to conduct ourselves. They, and sport itself, will rarely repay our moral expectations. We should do better to abandon such expectations and not be disppointed if, in and out of sport, they exhibit signs of moral primitivism. We should value them for their abilities to express and achieve what we ourselves cannot. That should be enough.

Sociological theories of deviance applied to sport

The application of sociological theories of deviance to sport is hardly original but existing reviews (e.g. Lueschen, 1993) seem far from comprehensive. Such theories will be grouped into four clusters with the ideas of each being outlined and then applied to sport.

Configurational sociology will be largely absent from the discussion, which may seem a curious omission in a discussion of deviance in sport. The rationale for this is that configurational sociology does not seem designed to offer anything like an adequate theory of deviance in sport. This is so for two main reasons. Firstly, virtually all of the analysis is confined to violence in sport, thus omitting many other forms of deviance (dissent, non-violent rule infraction, drug-taking etc.). It thus remains unclear how the approach of configurational sociology could or should be extended to such non-violent forms of deviance. Secondly, the analysis is restricted to combat team sports, thus omitting the very great numbers of sports played by individuals or not involving physical contact.

Unless or until the approach incorporates the full range of both sporting deviance and sporting forms, it cannot be regarded as comprehensive. However, this is not to underestimate the other achievements of the perspective relevant to any discussion of deviance in sport, especially the detailed unmasking of fair play as an aspect of a class-bound amateur ideology; their explanation of the progressively lesser tolerance of overt violence in contact sports; and their emphasis of the links between masculinity, violence and sporting subcultures. These considerable achievements will be given due weight at appropriate points in the discussion, which will begin with consideration of structural theories of the social order, conformity and deviance,

1.   Deviance and social structure

Otherwise divergent theories of the social order nevertheless have in common the idea that behaviour is a derivative of the social structure. Thus social order, conformity and deviance are to be explained in terms of the way the social structure is organised and cultural prescriptions are formulated.

Marxism or critical theory holds such a position, though its capacity to explain deviance is limited. Its emphasis on class issues leads it to see most deviance as a diversion from the revolutionary struggle which divides the working class and enables repressive measures by the ruling class, an analysis which can hardly be transposed to sport. Alternatively, sport and deviance within it, are seen as manifestations of the political economy of mass culture under capitalism, involving such terms as alienation, mass- ification and commodification. Such concepts seem limited in their useful- ness as explanations of deviance in sport (e.g. Eitzen, 1988).

The most useful observation of a critical perspective may be that often those who are supposed to uphold law and order themselves habitually break it and that the forces charged with the enforcement of the law are themselves frequently corrupt. Applying the latter proposition to sport leads to some awkward questions about the extent to which ruling bodies in sport are institutionally corrupt. Examples might include the difficulties in getting all countries to test consistently for drugs or a refusal to act against habitually violent conduct. More transparent would be the questions to be asked about such bodies as the International Olympic Committee and FIFA (the world body governing soccer) when deciding where to hold major championships, a procedure which seems to involve inducements which elsewhere might be called corruption. It may also be that whole events have become so institutionally corrupted that they are irredeemable and should be abandoned as proper sports. Lueschen (1993), for example, suggest that this might be the case for drug-taking in cycling, weightlifting and power events in athletics.

Much more useful in general terms is the approach to deviance developed by the theory of structural functionalism, especially in the work of Robert Merton (1978). In Merton's view, all normative behaviour is a balance between culturally prescribed means and socially approved ends. The 'conformist' is one who accepts and abides by the prescription of means and ends. But this is only one of five possible adaptations. The 'retreatist' withdraws from ends and means and becomes an outsider. The 'rebel' challenges means and ends, seeking to replace them with alternative versions. The 'ritualist' becomes highly committed to the means but loses sight of the ends — a characteristic of bureaucratic behaviour everywhere, including in the administration and officiating of sport.

The fifth adaptation is that of the 'deviant'. He or (less likely) she accepts the ends but rejects the means because they are regarded as unavailable. Hence other illegitimate means are adopted to realise con- formist ends. Rather confusingly, Merton terms this response 'innovation' but for our purposes it is equivalent to deviance.

What interested Merton is why a society, in his case America in the 1930s, reached a point where it appeared to generate systematic deviance, especially criminal behaviour. Merton argued that the fault was in the social structure. What had happened was that a disequilibrium had emerged between ends and means in society as a whole, which he termed (following Durkheim) *anomie*. For Merton, American society had come to place too great and too exclusive a stress on materialism, unqualified by any other objectives. At the same time, the access to the means of achieving material success, through education or entrepreneurial activity, was in practice confined to a very few, especially those from already privileged backgrounds. Hence, argued Merton, an escalating rate of deviant behaviour, especially property crime, is explicable in terms of an excessive emphasis on narrowly defined goals and a set of institutionalised means which systematically exclude particular groups. The solutions he proposed were liberal and reformist, if rather vague: a reformulation of societal goals away from excessive materialism and a programme of equal opportunities to open up institutionalised means to otherwise excluded groups.

In sociology and criminology, Merton's theory has been vigorously criticised for *inter alia* its mechanistic determinism, failure to take account of group behaviour and subcultural values and inability to account for deviant behaviour outside property crime. Few would now defend it, though Downes and Rock (1988: p.112), amongst others, have emphasised its value as the one theory which consistently explains why, as societies become richer, they invariably experience spiralling crime rates:

> Anomie theory deserves recovery. Among its strengths are a focus on the implications for deviance one of the defining features of capitalist societies, that is, the fostering of the propensity to consume irrespective of the material possibilities of such a course, a meta theory which is capable of application to societies other than those of the capitalist world; and the capacity ... of addressing the conditions that may suffice to determine the breakdown of social order. (Downes and Rock, 1988: p. 112)

Merton's basic idea is disarmingly simple and has much potential for explaining deviance, at least of the instrumental kind, in contemporary sport. His basic idea is that the more emphasis there is on success and the fewer who have the opportunity to attain it, the more we can expect deviant conduct to arise. On this basis it could be said that sport institutionalises the preconditions for deviance, the more so the higher the level at which it is played:

> The current factual increase in sports-related violence is primarily attributable to the growing cultural centrality of sport, to the fact that sport in modern society has become a phenomenon which can be described as quasi-religious. This has led people to pursue their sports seriously and to place an increasing emphasis on success. In its turn this has led to a growth in the competitiveness of sports, contributing to an increase in the rate and intensity of sporting interactions, in that way leading to a growth in violence, both intentional and unintentional. (Dunning and Sheard, 1979: p. 277)

Winning is the main objective, only slightly — especially at higher levels — qualified by the pleasures of participation. Moreover, competitions are so structured that material and symbolic rewards are conferred mainly on the (one) winner, although there may be consolation prizes for second and third. Conversely, the failure to win is punished: losers are expelled from knock-out competitions and relegated in a league system:

> The more sport becomes professionalized, the more winning, as opposed to the means by which it is achieved, is emphasised as the goal of sports aspirations and, finally, the more significant the economic as others consequences of victory are, the greater is the possibility that the rules of sport will be violated in favour of other interests. Whenever victory and success are the highest goals, the end will legitimise illegitimate means. (Weiss, 1976 cited in Johansson, 1987: p. 95)

An important qualification here is that sport, unlike society, formally endorses equality of opportunity: all are free to compete under the same conditions. Some sports even have handicapping systems to ensure equality of starting points amongst otherwise unequally matched opponents. However, as in society, perfect equality of opportunity is virtually impossible to achieve:

> The concept of fairness is relative. There is a great deal of injustice in the fact that the competing countries in the Olympic Games have so different economic and social resources and in the fact that these Games include events that are more frequently represented in some countries that others. Persons from the same country have also varying possibilities to train and compete owing to sex, race, social position, etc. (Johansson, 1987: p. 96)

Some have more natural talent than others, some have more material resources (scholarships, sponsorship, coaching) than others. So there is always the temptation to seek compensation for national or social disadvantages by adopting deviant means to beat opponents who are more gifted and skilled (the almost permanent state of England's national football team).

Thus sport is predisposed to create a high rate of anomie amongst participants and, if its ends are narrowly prescribed and its means unevenly distributed, then deviance may well become endemic. However, such a view tends to undervalue the importance of group beliefs in deviance, which has been redressed by subcultural theory.

2.   Deviance and subcultures

Dissatisfaction with the highly individualistic nature of Merton's theory and its inability to explain expressive deviance led to the development of theories which transferred the idea of 'strain' in the social system but saw this as being experienced and reacted to by social groups.

A very early version of this theory attributed deviance to 'differential association'. Whether a person was led to commit deviant acts depended on the values of the (reference) groups to which they were exposed. This claimed to explain why people in the same circumstances differed in their propensity for deviance. It also helped to explain white collar crime such as fraud, as the outcome of a situation where the occupational or social group endorsed and encouraged deviant behaviour:

> Differential association theory holds that criminal behaviour is learned in interaction with other people... [involving] techniques of committing the crime and the direction of drives, motives, attitudes, and definitions of the law. It is argued that a person will become criminal if he or she is exposed to an excess of definitions favourable to the violation of the law over definitions unfavourable to violation of the law, the process itself being described as differential association. (Downes and Rock, 1988: p.79)

Such approaches were developed into subcultural theory which suggested that working class boys in particular were disaffected from the conventional values presented to them at school. They therefore generated their own set of cultural values, many of which contradicted the conventional values. One list of the deviant working class subculture's focal concerns enumerated then as: trouble, toughness, smartness, excitement, fate and autonomy. In later versions, working class subcultures were explained as an amalgam of values drawn from the dominant and mainstream working class cultures.

Much of this work concentrated explicitly on the working class and implicitly on boys. It had narrowed the broader question of deviance to one of working class juvenile delinquency and in so doing lost much of its more general applicability. However, some of its ideas remain potentially useful in the analysis of deviance in sport. Firstly, there is the idea that deviance is a form of behaviour learned in peer groups:

> Through socialisation, a generalised expectancy is developed that essentially legitimises illegal behaviour in particular situations ... a player is willing to exhibit an illegal act ... because it is normative, legitimised and can provide personal and social reinforcement that far outweighs any punishment that presently exists in the constitutive rules. It has also been demonstrated that behaviour such as fighting and other forms of illegal aggression elicits minimal guilt feelings in the offender. Thus internal prohibitions against such behaviour in sport appear to have been unlearned or have never been learned at all. (Silva, 1981: p. 13)

> ... much of the violence in sport is the product of socialisation. Owing to the widespread approval of violence in sport, together with the prevalence of violent role models, violent techniques and

attitudes are socially learned, reinforced and legitimated. (Smith, 1972, cited in Pilz, 1979: p. 22)

Applying this to sport would emphasise how sports peer groups, teams, clubs etc., can actually approve of behaviour which the governing bodies would disapprove of. The achievement of status in such a peer group might appear more important than the possibility of being apprehended by the authorities. Thus are generated sporting subcultures in which deviant conduct becomes normative (e.g. psyching out opponents, habitual foul play, drug-taking), so that the sporting system contains several subcultures with variable relationships to conformist conduct in sport.

Secondly, there is the possibility that such groups may justify their approval of deviant behaviour by generating a set of values quite distinct from those of the dominant sports culture. The list cited above, for example, would certainly fit the subculture of professional soccer players, suggesting that sporting experience has more in common with delinquent subcultures than the supposed norms of respectable society. Coakley (1995) suggests that over-conformity to sports culture produces deviance:

> ... the most dangerous forms of deviance in many sports actually involve extreme over-conformity among athletes rather than a rejection of norms. (p. 16)

> .... much deviance in sports occurs when athletes care too much for, accept too completely and over-conform to what has become the basic value system in many sports and sport groups across a wide range of participation levels. If athletes never question that value system grounded in the sport ethic, even though the sport ethic consists of what most people would consider to be positive values, problems of deviance are likely. This is especially true for high performance athletes, although it's certainly not limited to them. (p. 16)

> It is the athlete's vulnerability to group demands, combined with the desire to gain or reaffirm group membership through over-conforming to those demands, that is a critical factor in the incidence of positive deviance.(p. 18)

Within this perspective, deviance in sport would be seen less as an individual activity than a group ethos and any attempt to control deviance aimed simply at isolated individuals would be bound to fail. Another cluster of theories sees the individual rather than the group as the focus of attention and the rational calculation of self-interest to be more important a cause of deviance than membership of peer groups.

3.   Deviance and opportunity

This cluster contains a number of otherwise disparate theories linked by the idea that the potential for deviance is present wherever there are humans seeking to maximise their self interest. Social causes and psychological motivations are less important than ensuring that conformity is assessed as more rational than deviance and that the opportunity for deviant acts is decreased:

> The immediate stress of situational control theories — is on the purely technical, cost-benefit — ratio aspects of crime: the opportunities for crime available in the environment, and the risks attached to criminal activity. (Downes and Rock, 1988: p. 228)

In one version— control theories — deviance is seen as most likely to occur where social situations are so structured that surveillance and intervention are insufficient. The design or inadequate supervision of city centres and problem estates are seen as inviting crime. The solution is greater surveillance by CCTV, private security guards, neighbourhood watch schemes and the like. The equivalent in sport would be to make the conduct of players subject to much closer scrutiny. At the top levels of sport, the use of video evidence increases the likelihood of detecting transgressions which would otherwise go unpunished. An unexplored implication would also be the increase in the number, training and (possibly) youth of officials, so that any temptation to deviate would be deterred by systematic surveillance.

In another version — game theories — people are portrayed as constantly making calculations about how to maximise their interests at the expense of others. In sport, participants make calculations about their chances in the game by assessing the likely conduct of others involved. They may conclude that it is in their interests to deviate, either because they will lose out to those who do deviate or because deviance will give them an advantage over conformists:

> Game theory is a formal theory making suppositions about consistency of preferences and rationality of choices that are hard to find in real life situations. On the other hand top level sport is probably a field where actors are more rational and utility-maximising in their behaviour than in most other areas of life. The goals are clearly defined and a means limited. A rational manipulation of various means will have predictable consequences. (Breivik, 1992: p. 249)

Hence top level athletes may be attracted to drug-taking because they believe they cannot compete with those who do take drugs or because they will gain an advantage over those who do not. In this scenario, the least rational decision is that not to take drugs because the result will almost certainly be disadvantage in competition. Only the likelihood of getting caught will deter the potential deviant, though the longer-term solution is to make values over and above those of self-interest a more attractive source of satisfaction.

4.   Deviance and social construction

Under this heading are grouped a number of approaches, again often quite differently slanted (symbolic interactionism, labelling theory, phenomeno-logy, ethnomethodology), which nevertheless share a view of the nature of the social order which contradicts the assumptions of structural theories. This is that the social order, and thus conformity to and deviance from it, are socially constructed. Each social situation requires the interpretation and re-making of rules to enable it to happen. Social order is not a product but a process in which meanings are continuously re-created and affirmed.

Thus sport is not a social institution in the structural sense but a set of meanings which have to be recognised and understood through social practices. What applies to sport as a whole applies to the individual con-test. The meaning and nature of the game have to be created by the partici-pants, players and umpires. What constitutes and realises order is not just (or even mainly) the set of codified rules which appear to govern the activity but the set of meanings and understandings the participants bring to the event, which are then negotiated in the course of constructing the game. The grudge match or the local derby will have particular built-in tensions which may or may not be realised in the course of the contest. In that sense, the production of order is a process of negotiation between those involved:

> During a sport contest, moral balances about athletic aggression are often negotiated among athletes through subtle variations in the intensity, frequency and rule-boundedness of physical contact. (Bredemeier and Shields, 1986: p. 20)

This has particular implications for the analysis of rules and their relation-ship to order. Kew (1987, 1992) for instance, has used an ethnomethod-ological approach to show how the implementation of and changes in rules depend upon confirmations of and breaches in the common understand-ings:

> Formalist accounts of games implicitly condone a Parsonian theory of social action and depict players ... as merely acting in com-pliance with pre-established rules as *given* rather than recognising the skilful practical reasoning through which the social order of games is *achieved* .... (Garfinkel) argues that the formulation of game rules is based upon a tacit assumption that players will poss-ess 'common-sense understandings of what is expected in games-playing generally'. (Kew, 1992: p. 30)

Unfortunately, he declines to analyse how conformity and deviance emerge. Since deviance is not a product but a process, causal explanation is es-chewed in favour of analysis of the process of construction.

This position is similar to that taken by labelling theory. This argues that deviance is a quality attributed by an audience and what matters is understanding the conditions and processes by which acts come to be designated as deviant. The definition of and application of sanctions to deviance are arbitrary, often affected less by the quality of the act than by the sensibilities and prejudices of enforcers. Not the least of its insights is that, since the powerful are (generally) white, male and middle class, it is their definitions of deviance which hold most sway. It also has links to the proposition that middle class deviance is handled in quite different ways from that of the working class. The main relevance of this perspective to sport is the recognition that high profile performers may be less likely to be penalised than lesser known ones, or that some players may acquire a reputation for deviance and are thus monitored more closely.

The analysis so far identifies circumstances where deviance is most likely to occur in sport where there is:

- institutionalised corruption

- an imbalance between ends and means

- any group subculture which endorses deviant behaviour

- inadequate surveillance of behaviour

- rational calculations that cheating will pay

- a breakdown in the common understandings of participants.

In short, we have here a football match between Arsenal and Wimbledon. Yet that example may remind us of two aspects we have so far insufficiently considered, which may be linked. First, that much deviance in sport is expressive rather than instrumental and the theories so far considered are generally more applicable to instrumental behaviour. Second, that both instrumental and expressive behaviour appear to be more commonly engaged in by men than women.

Expressive deviance and the sociology of emotions: a note

Of the sociological theories so far outlined, only that of subcultures, with its emphasis on alternative sets of values, seems to offer any potential for the analysis of expressive deviance, inside or outside sport. It seems fairly obvious that much of expressive behaviour is rooted in such psychological mechanisms as frustration, tension, motivation and aggression. My limited encounter with the psychological literature on sport suggests that such psychological conditions have been studied for their effects upon performance but not for their effects upon deviance.

This does seem to be a problem best tackled by social psychology, but in its apparent absence we may have to substitute a sociology of the emotions. Sociologically, as Elias and Dunning (1988) have emphasised, sport is one of the few remaining arenas in modern society where excitement can be habitually experienced and openly expressed. Excitement here is taken to encompass a wide range of emotions, from total elation to utter despair. Yet this fact is rarely acknowledged in the rules or norms of sport, which may even expressly forbid emotional outbursts. So we have a social situation in which people experience emotional extremes (and in professional sport are surrounded by spectators giving vent to them), yet are supposed not to give them spontaneous expression, at least in such conventional ways as shouting, swearing, throwing things — though laughter and tears, if not encouraged, are at least not forbidden.

The higher the level of competition, the more such a contradiction is experienced, since the level of tension is greater and more is at stake in terms of material and symbolic reward and even self-identity. The result is behaviour which is not primarily rational, in which displaced targets are chosen for the expression of undischarged tension:

> ... the social and personality structure that have given rise to the modern game have simultaneously increased the incidence of instrumental violence ... The growing competitive pressure that leads to the increasing covert use of rational violence is simultaneously conducive to overt violence, namely that which occurs when sportsmen and women momentarily lose their self-control and strike an opponent in retaliation. The fact that the tactical use of instrumental violence often forms a trigger leading to such a loss of self-control shows again how one kind of violence can be rapidly transformed into another. (Dunning, in Elias and Dunning, 1986: p. 232)

This would repay some serious psychological study. This brief consideration of it has raised a question with which sociology may feel more comfortable. The experiencing and handling of tension seem to be highly gendered. In contradistinction to the sexist stereotype that women are more emotional and men more rational, in sport we seem to have the opposite. It is women who remain calm in a crisis and men who lose control. This is part of a general problem of the centrality of gendered identity to conformity and deviance in sport.

Gender identity, deviance and conformity in sport

That men are more consistently deviant in sport would be expected, given their general propensity for deviance in society as a whole. Downes and Rock (1988) remind us that before they reach 28, 30 per cent of men in England and Wales will have appeared in court. By contrast, as Barbara Wootton once remarked, if men behaved like women, all the courts would close and all the prisons would be empty.

This pattern of gender difference would appear to be reproduced in sport. Men seem more likely to indulge in systematic or occasional deviance of both an instrumental and expressive kind. There are some minor qualifications to make. Some women at the highest levels have adopted male forms of deviance, such as drug-taking in athletics. If physical contact sports induce more deviance, then women's general exclusion from them helps explain their lower rates of deviance. It could thus be argued that if women are more involved in highly competitive levels of sport and if they continue to take up physical contact sports, then they may behave more like men:

> Impelled by the increasing importance of winning and as the value-climate in sport subtly changes in the direction of the legitimisation of female violence, together with the appearance of appropriate reference groups for the social learning of violence, female sport may be moving toward the male. (Smith, 1972 cited in Pilz, 1979: p. 19)

As against that, there is a convincing case that where women compete at equivalent levels of competition and reward as men, it is still the men who exhibit more deviant behaviours, professional tennis being the most obvious example. At the moment, it seems reasonable to argue that men are more prone to deviance in sport and that this fact should therefore be encompassed in any sociological consideration of the reasons for deviance in sport.

Configurational sociology has tackled the problem of gender identity in sport, insofar as displaced forms of masculinity are used to explain football hooliganism, resistance to the long-term evolution of the civilising trend and the cultural atmosphere of particular male sports clubs:

> Our norms of manliness still show signs of their origins in the pre-industrial division of labour when men were warriors and protect-ors of their families ... our norms of masculinity have not changed commensurately with these wider social changes. The result is that a sphere of social life is needed where traditional ideals of mascu-linity can be developed and expressed ... Contact sports, with their stress in strength, toughness and physical courage, are an ideal medium in this regard though ... the reverse is also true; namely that contact sports have helped to perpetuate traditional standards of masculinity. (Dunning and Sheard, 1979: p. 281)

However, the narrow range of sports involved and a generally exclusive preoccupation with violence has tended to limit its generalisability to deviance. Indeed, when touching upon the problem of violence on the pitch in professional soccer, one recent essay from the Leicester group appears to give up on the whole problem (Murphy, Williams and Dunning, 1990) as here defined, reverting to arguments about the long-term trends of the civilising process. But due credit should be given to configurational sociolo-gists for being some of the first to have emphasised the importance of masculinity to the sporting experience and difficulties which arise within it.

The first wave of feminism in sport sociology quite properly and under-standably concentrated on the position of women in sport: their exclusion, marginalisation and denigration (Hall, 1993; for sports psychology see Krane, 1994). Deviance in sport, especially that of men, was some way down the agenda. It was later given more prominence (Theberge, 1987), especially by male feminists (Messner and Sabo in the USA, Kidd in Canada). They recognised the nature of masculinity to be at the heart of many of the problems of sport. Hence aggression and violence at least were explained in terms of the need to *achieve*, if necessary by deviant and violent means, which characterises the male presence in society more generally.

But there is something of a contradiction here. for example in some of the work by Messner (1990). Much of the discussion of violence seems to fall prey to a kind of essentialism: since men are or have learned to be competitive, aggressive and violent, such characteristics will be reproduced and even exaggerated in the sporting context. On the other hand, there is recognition of the more complex arguments involved in gender studies that there is no one monolithic masculinity (or femininity either) in what is now called the gender order. Rather, at any one time, there are competing versions of masculinity, even if they share some common assumptions. This seems to contradict the position taken over violence, that it is the product of an observably uniform masculine style.

Part of the problem may lie in the underlying assumption that sport is a derivative of society as a whole. If we want to know about masculinity in sport, we take what we know about masculinity in society as a whole and look for signs of it in sport, as in the following example:

> Probably the main implication of the present analysis is the fact that sport appears to be only of secondary importance with respect to the production and reproduction of masculine identity. Of far greater significance in this regard, it seems are those features of the wider social structure that affect the relative power chances of the sexes and the degree of sexual segregation that exists within the necessary interdependence of men and women. All that sport appears to do in this connection is to play a secondary and reinforcing role. As such, however, it is nevertheless crucial in sustaining more modified and controlled forms of macho aggressiveness. (Dunning in Elias and Dunning, 1986: p. 283)

We may need a more complex model in which sport is both the reflection and the articulation of particular models of masculinity. (Think for example of the male hero figure: sport is now arguably the most powerful non-fictional embodiment of male heroism. It makes no sense of think of the male hero as something sport reflects: rather sport is one of the ways it is constituted.)

If we conceive of sports conduct as articulating different possibilities of masculine style, this may help to understand why some sports experience expressive deviance more than others. There are sports without instrumental or expressive deviance (golf), sports with instrumental deviance but comparatively little expressive deviance (rugby), sports with more expressive than instrumental deviance (tennis) and sports with high levels of both (soccer). The existence of distinctive codes of behaviour in each sport does not explain away the factor of gender, since such codes are themselves embodiments of masculinity: versions of what a man does or does not do in given circumstances. Thus swearing, arguing with match officials, throwing equipment about, physical retaliation against an opponent, may in one sport be regarded as the normal (i.e. normative) response — how a man should react; while in another sport they will be regarded as a deviant response — how a man should not react.

Thus we need to operate with a more complex model in which sport does not simply reflect but reproduces and articulates masculinities. There may well be a dominant form of masculinity which is more prevalent in sport than in other cultural forms, such as popular music. However, there may be sufficient variations in prescriptions about appropriate male conduct for us to recognise that there are several masculinities articulated within sport, albeit within a restricted range. Hargreaves (1985) has argued for the use of the concept of hegemony to explain both the dominant forms and the existence of some alternatives. "The dominant image of masculinity may still prevail but sport is, nevertheless a contested zone" (p.116).

The general proposition remains, even with these qualifications: men are habitually more deviant in sport than women. This is because male sport, some would say all sport, has as one of its essential cultural functions the expression of masculinity.

This is not necessarily incompatible with some of the more general and often gender-blind sociological theories of deviance discussed earlier. Men may be more materialist, more opportunistic and more likely to be members of deviant subcultures. They are also likely to socially construct gender segregated activities such as sport around ideals of masculinity.

We have here the beginnings of an explanation of why men are more prone to deviance in sport than women. There remains the obverse to explain: why women are more conformist. Again, the most straightforward explanation suggests that women's conforming behaviour in sport is a reproduction of their more conformist behaviour in society as a whole. Feminist criminologists and developmental psychologists have looked at this issue. The key factors are those of gender socialisation and the consequent cultural position of women, They learn to be more submissive and have a greater fear of sanctions which will denigrate their sexuality. Women have a prescribed commitment to maintaining domestic and public order, often against the potential threat posed by men.

Such conventional gender identities are reproduced and articulated through sport. In her study of moral judgements in sport made by high school and college athletes, Duquin (1990) argued that women tended to employ an ethic of caring whilst men emphasised an orientation to self-interest. If women are indeed altruistic in sport whilst men are egotistical, that is a remarkable testimony to the durability of female gender identity for what we have is the importation into a highly self-interested activity of altruistic ideals. This could be read in two different ways: either it demonstrates that the self-interest of sport can be tempered by a wider based morality or that women may have difficulty in achieving the requisite level of egotism for sustained involvement in serious sport. Dubois (1990) studied 8-10 year old boys and girls in a soccer programme and argued that the experience confirmed boys' initial emphasis on the goal of success whilst girls became less interested in this aspect. This, he suggested, was because sport sensitised girls to its incompatibility with their developing consciousness of the conventional female gender identity.

The importance of gender identity in sport may have wider implications. It could be argued (and has been by Coakley, 1995) that men's identities are more bound up with success in the public sphere, such as on the sportsfield, and that this may predispose them to protect that identity, if necessary by deviant behaviour. By contrast, the conventional identity of women rests in the private rather than the public sphere:

> ...athletes whose identities or future chances for material success are exclusively tied to sports are most likely to engage in deviance grounded in over-conformity to the sport ethic.... [This] would be more characteristic among men than women since men are more likely to use sport as an exclusive identity and/or mobility source, among low income minority athletes in revenue producing sports... and among those whose relationships with significant others have been based exclusively on continued involvement and success in sport. (Coakley, 1995: pp. 17-18)

We must, however, remain aware of the problems of essentialism about women as well as men and consequently allow for competing femininities as well as masculinities. Thus sport could articulate other kinds of femininity, one in which sporting success was not incompatible with conventional gender identity, or another in which sporting success is used as a challenge to conventional gender identity.

Whatever the reasons, there are lessons for sport to be learnt from the conduct of women. If we want to increase the level of conformity and decrease the level of deviance, then we need an approach to sport which is more like women's than men's in which sport is NOT seen as the opportunity for cheating, violence, misplaced assertiveness and the expression and validation of gender identity. We need to take the maleness out of sport, or, to follow the earlier argument, to have sport articulate different kinds of masculinities from those which now appear dominant.

So we have added a second set of prescriptions for the maintenance of social (moral) order in sport:

- the need to curb, control, or allow outlets for, emotional expression

- not to confuse sporting success with the validation of self-identity

- to develop kinds of masculinities which can cope with tension and the fear of failure.

The prospects for reform

Sociology is quite often accused of lacking policy prescriptions. Such criticism is often justified: many problems are too complex for simple solutions to be formulated. Yet often the accusation is unjustified, for what is actually being said is that the solutions suggested by sociologists are not liked because they are too complicated, too radical and, above all, too expensive. Nor can there be any guarantee that they will work.

All that notwithstanding, I am not going to duck the challenge to indicate what might be done to control (because it would be possible to eliminate) deviance in sport and thus to strengthen its moral order. I shall assume that, even if we would want to encourage new kinds of sport which might not have some of the inherent predispositions to encourage deviant behaviour which I have outlined, that there would still be a need to maintain order.

The current dilemma about the social order, conformity and deviance in sport has been well formulated by Johansson:

> Sport must be restored to a kind of order that will be positive for individuals, for the sports movement and for society as a whole. The question is, what kind of order and what ideas are to be advocated. (1987,: p.84)

Bredemeier and Shields are more specific about the means by which aggression in sport can be controlled:

> A more broadly shared consensus about such [aggressive] acts awaits a time when (a) moral reflection and discourse, rather than being viewed as obstacles to efficient play, are encouraged amongst athletes, (b) aggression terminology is classified to provided a sharp distinction between assertive play and intentionally injurious acts, and (c) constitutive rules and penalties are amended to more clearly convey acceptable behaviour. (Bredemeier and Shields, 1986: p. 24)

This can be tackled at the three levels identified in the introduction of rules or constitutive rules, norms or normative rules and values or ethos. I shall take the catholic view that most of the theories discussed have some merit and that what is needed is an approach which reflects the multi-layered nature of the problem.

In terms of *formal rules*, we have encountered a need to clarify rules in order to outlaw specific behaviour; to introduce stiffer penalties for transgression and to ensure, through increased surveillance, that deviance will not go undetected. Such measures would have — indeed in some sports, such as the professional foul in football already have had — an effect upon calculated instrumental deviance. This might involve such draconian measures as the banning for life of any athlete found to have knowingly used banned substances.

In terms of *norms*, such sanctions are irrelevant. For we are talking about understandings and expectations. It has been noted how weak are moral ideals in sport: we have to find some way of reintroducing a less obviously ideological notion of fairness. We have to tackle the groups who perpetuate deviant values and challenge the assumption that cheating is acceptable and normal. A balance has to be struck between recognising the emotional expressivity of sport and its illegitimate outlets. In all these matters, both the grass roots and the higher levels of sport need to undergo a cultural change but that can only be achieved if there is also an alteration in underlying values.

In terms of *values*, there has to be more emphasis on means and less on ends, so that the sport itself is understood to be the ultimate end. There needs to be an end to institutional corruption. It is not clear that the sports order can carry the burden of endorsing personal identities which should be rooted elsewhere. Finally, we have to develop more flexible gender identities, so that participation and success in sport is not perceived as the validation of masculine identity and the invalidation of feminine identity.

Such a programme is, to put it mildly, utopian. It is tempting to believe that society gets the sport, like the politicians, that it deserves. The only way out of fatalism is to identify who are the key players in this attempted reformation. Schools ought to play a part, though their lesser role in junior sport and the new sports curriculum may limit their effectiveness. Much junior sport is now run in the voluntary sector by those whose training is technical, if they have any at all. So it may be that coaching programmes have a role to play. Then there are the sports organisers and administrators who often pay lip service to the idea of sports morals but lack the will or the means to define and realise them. Some of the more responsible sections of the media might actually take some sustained and intelligent interest in the problem.

Just as the focus of action needs to be multi-layered, so do the actors need to be drawn from all sectors. In the galvanisation of such groups, there may be a modest role for those who teach and analyse sport and leisure. But I wouldn't like to bet on the outcome.

References

Bredemeier, B. J. (1985) 'Moral reasoning and the perceived legitimacy of intentionally injurious sports acts', *Journal of Sport Psychology*, Vol. 7, No. 2: pp. 110-124.

Bredemeier, B. J. and Shields, D. L. (1986) 'Athletic aggression: An issue of contextual morality', *Sociology of Sport Journal*, Vol. 3, No. 1: pp. 15-28.

Bredemeier, B. J., Weiss M. R., Shields, D. L. and Cooper, B. A. B. (1986) 'The relationship of sport involvement with children's moral reasoning and aggression tendencies', *Journal of Sport Psychology*, Vol. 8, No. 4: pp. 304-318.

Breivek, G. (1992) 'Doping games — a game theoretical analysis of doping', *International Journal of Sport*, Vol. 27, No. 3: pp. 235-256.

Coakley, J. L. (1995) 'Ethics, deviance and sports: a critical look at crucial issues' in A. Tomlinson and S. Fleming (eds) *Ethics, sport and leisure: Crises and critiques*. Chelsea School Topic Report 5. Brighton: University of Brighton, pp. 3-24.

Critcher, C. (1995) 'Running the rule over sport: a sociologist's view of ethics', in A. Tomlinson and S. Fleming (eds) *Ethics, sport and leisure: Crises and critiques*. Chelsea School Topic Report 5. Brighton: University of Brighton, pp. 25-36.

Downes, D. and Rock, P (1 988) *Understanding deviance*. Oxford: Oxford University Press.

Dubois, P. (1 990) 'Gender differences in value orientation towards sports: a longitudinal analysis', *Journal of Sport Behaviour*, Vol. 13, No. 1: pp. 3-14.

Dunning, E. (1986) 'Social bonding and violence in sport' in N. Elias and E. Dunning (eds) *Quest for excitement*. Oxford: Basil Blackwell, pp. 224-244.

Dunning, E. and Sheard, K. (1979) *Barbarians, gentlemen and players*. Oxford: Martin Robertson.

Duquin, M. (1984) 'Power and authority: moral consensus and conformity in sport', *International Review for the Sociology of Sport*, Vol. 19, No. 3/4: pp. 295-304.

Eitzen, S. D. (1988) 'Conflict theory and deviance in sport', *International Review for the Sociology of Sport* Vol. 3, No. 3: pp. 193-204.

Hall, M. A. (1990)'Gender and sport in the 1990s: feminism, culture and politics', *Social Science Review*, Vol. 2, No. 1: pp. 48-68.

Hargreaves, J. (1986) 'Where's the virtue? Where's the grace? A discussion of the social production of gender relations in and through sport', *Theory, Culture and Society*, Vol. 3, No. 1: pp. 109-121.

Johansson, M. (1987) 'Doping as a threat against sport and society: the case of Sweden', *International Review for the Sociology of Sport*, Vol. 22, No. 2: pp. 83-97.

Kew, F. C. (1987) 'Contested rules: an explanation of how games change', *International Review for the Sociology of Sport*, Vol. 22, No. 2: pp. 124-134.

——— (1992) 'Game rules and social theory', *International Review for the Sociology of Sport,* Vol. 27, No. 4.

Krane, V. (1 994) 'A feminist perspective on contemporary sport psychology research', *The Sports Psychologist,* Vol. 8: pp. 393-410.

Lee, M. (1995) 'Value foundations of ethical decisions in children's sport', in A. Tomlinson and S. Fleming (eds) *Ethics, sport and leisure: Crises and critiques.* Chelsea School Topic Report 5. Brighton: University of Brighton, pp. 55-78.

Lueschen, G. (1993) 'Doping in sport: the social structure of a deviant subculture', *Social Science Review,* Vol. 2, No. 1: pp. 92-106.

Merton, R. (1978) 'Anomie and social structure', in P. Worsley *et al.* (eds) *Modern sociology.* Harmondsworth: Penguin.

Messner, M. A. (1990) 'When bodies are weapons: masculinity and violence in sport', *International Review for the Sociology of Sport,* Vol. 25, No. 3: pp. 203-220.

Messner, M. A. and Sabo, D. (1990) *Sport, men and the gender order: Critical feminist perspectives.* Champaign IL: Human Kinetics.

Murphy, P. , Williams, J. and Dunning, E. (1990) *Football on trial.* London: Routledge.

Pilz, G. A. (1979) 'Attitudes toward different forms of aggressive and violent behaviour in competitive sports: two empirical studies', *Journal of Sport Behaviour,* Vol. 2: pp. 3-26.

Silva, J. (1981) 'Normative compliance and rule-violating behaviour in sport', *International Journal of Sport Psychology,* Vol. 12: pp. 10-18.

Theberge, N. (1987) 'A feminist analysis of responses to sports violence: Media coverage of the 1987 World Junior Hockey Championship', *Sociology of Sport Journal,* Vol. 6, No. 3: pp. 247-256.

Gender, Morality and the National Physical Education Curriculum

Jennifer Hargreaves

Roehampton Institute, London

"I don't regard sport", declared John Major at the Conservative Party Conference in October 1994, "especially team sport, as a trivial 'add-on' to education". He continued:

> "It is part of the British instinct; it is part of our character. Sport is fun, but it deserves a proper place in the life of all our children. Sport, of course, can't supersede Maths or English, but how I longed for it to do so while I was at school! But it must take its proper place alongside them. We are therefore changing the National Curriculum to put competitive games back at the heart of school life. Sport will be played by children in every school from 5 to 16 and more time must be devoted to team games. Many schools already offer at least two hours a week for sport and physical education. That should be the minimum and I hope schools will offer more. Schools should establish links with local clubs and national sports bodies to help do this. They must open up their facilities out of school hours and harness the willing help that I know is out there. There are sports coaches, parents and other volunteers by the hundreds and hundreds and hundreds who will willingly come in outside school hours to help our youngsters have a better grounding in sport and all it means to the rest of their lives. So while we're about it, I don't want Councils selling off school playing fields they may need. I want those playing fields kept and I want those playing fields used." (Transcript of John Major's speech on Sport in Schools — Conservative Party Conference, 14 Oct. 1994)

This speech on Sport in Schools was given an uncharacteristically impassioned delivery by our Prime Minister at the Conservative Party Conference on 14 October 1994. In this paper I argue that it highlights the changing face of physical education, and that at its heart lie stereotyped and reactionary attitudes to gender.

But John Major's homage to sport (and especially competitive team games) is only one of a string of recent public and political pronouncements about the revival of school sport in the National Physical Education Curriculum, culminating in the government's Major Sport Policy Statement *Sport: Raising the Game* (Department of National Heritage, 1995). They are all part of a huge escalation of state intervention into the affairs of the school and their cumulative effect has been to shift ideas — inside and outside the physical education profession — about the relationship between physical education and sport, one aspect of which has been to legitimise old and gendered dogmas about the values of sport.

In 1990 in its *Education Reform fact sheet for Governing Bodies of Sport and Local Sports Organisations*, the Sports Council stated unequivocally that 'physical education is not the same as sport', and that looking to schools for future sports stars 'would not be a major objective of the physical education programme'. But in today's establishment rhetoric, *physical education* (PE) *has come to mean sport*, and even although in most schools PE is still used as an umbrella term to encompass a range of activities, it is generally understood that the most important of these are competitive team games. John Major (Department of National Heritage 1995: p. 2) describes sport as "one of the great pillars of education alongside the academic, the vocational and the moral" and he declares that he is "determined to see that our great national sports — cricket, hockey, swimming, athletics, football, netball, rugby, tennis and the like — are put firmly centre stage" (*ibid*: p. 3). His posturing has given credibility and power to a small minority of the physical education profession — almost exclusively male — who for the last few years have been arguing that sports education should replace physical education, and that dance and other 'non-sports-activities' should be the business of the performing arts department (if there is one), or be dropped from the curriculum altogether. The majority of women in the profession oppose this gendered viewpoint and want physical education to continue to encompass a range of activities (all equally valued and to include dance).

The shift to sport from PE is symbolized in the latest edition of the Sports Council *Sportsnews* publication (Sports Council [London Region], August 1995) by the bold heading *Sport rather than physical education*. It signals a report on the Government's Sports Policy Document:

> Schools will be accountable for their commitment to sport as for any other aspect of school life. Schools will be required to include details in annual prospectuses of their sporting aims and provision for sport and record in their governors' annual report how they have met these aims and record their sporting achievements. (unnumbered pages)

Upgrading sport in schools in this way embodies the ideology of competition, and the government has made it impossible for schools to ignore the directive, or without losing public approval and patronage, to oppose it. The new Sports Mark and Gold Star Awards have been set up to recognise those schools that are promoting sport effectively and those with outstanding sporting achievements. All schools applying for the awards will be expected to offer a minimum of two hours each week of formal PE lessons and at least four hours each week of formal structured sports outside formal lessons — at lunchtimes, evenings and weekends; they will be required to devote at least half the time spent on PE both inside and outside of formal lessons to sports; secondary schools will have to ensure that pupils of all ages have the opportunity to take part in competition, and that competition is promoted within the school and against other schools (Stewart, 1995). In *Sport: Raising the Game* (Department of National Heritage, 1995) it is also laid down that, in all schools, inspectors will be responsible for monitoring the provision and standards of games; the National Coaching Foundation will receive £1 million from the Sports Council to help non-specialist teachers get coaching qualifications; more sports scholarships will be given; rules to prevent the further loss of playing fields will be applied; and £100 million will come out of lottery funds for a British Academy of Sport to nurture talented performers. It has even been recommended that governors be given the discretion to award additional salary points to those teachers who make a special commitment to school sport (Spencer, 1995c).

The promotion of the ideology of competition through sport is most closely aligned to team games. The previous Sports Minister, Iain Sproat, set the tone in an ardent speech delivered early in 1994:

> The best way to lay the foundation for national victories (in sport) in the future is to start again teaching games widely and well in our schools. In that way we shall improve not only national morale, but also our children's health and instil in them values and understanding they can acquire so well in no other way. (Sproat, 1994a)

He is referring here to the idea that team games (and he means the five that he has proposed be given priority in schools — soccer, rugby, cricket, hockey and netball) instil character, moral excellence, discipline, commitment, team spirit and good sportsmanship (Wood 1995: p. 1) — an idea which David Kirk (1992: pp. 221-2) reminds us was originally associated with a distinctive culture emanating from upper class males in the public schools during the eighteenth and nineteenth centuries. It was, and still is, unrepresentative of the majority of the British population, especially women. Tod Crosset (1990: p. 46) views "the promotion of manliness in the 19th century as the primary ideological function and catalyst for the organization and growth of early modern sport". Not surprisingly, it has been competitive team sports for men that have been so important in keeping alive until today the gender distinctions in sport that were established nearly two centuries ago.

In its modern form, what I am calling 'sports-education-ideology', sanctions the idea that competitive sports, and especially team games, are more important than any other element of the National Physical Education Curriculum. Intrinsic to the ideology is an assumption about the special character-building potential of team games which has been markedly resistant to critical analysis and has so recently been publicly and rather dramatically consolidated and politicized. The ideology seems now to be entrenched at the very heart of the National Physical Education Curriculum; in some schools, it may very well soon be, as Mr Major has decreed, at the very 'heart of school life' itself.

These events have escalated a process that started with the inauguration of the National Physical Education Curriculum (Department for Education, 1992). The 1988 Education Reform Act (ERA) included in its rubric the intention to promote equal opportunity programmes through the establishment of a national curriculum for all children in maintained schools. But the ERA has not made the implementation of equal opportunities obligatory, and in the case of PE there was a failure, from the start, to take affirmative action with respect to gender equality. Although the National Curriculum Physical Education Working Group (appointed by the government to make recommendations for the PE Curriculum) made some radical proposals, the National Curriculum Council (convened to advise the Minister for Education about those proposals) chose to disregard them. In its Final Report the working group laid down that all children, regardless of sex, should be provided with a broad and balanced experience of movement, including athletic activities, dance, games, gymnastics, outdoor activities and swimming at some time during *Key Stages* 1 to 3 (ages 5-14) (Department of Education and Science, 1991a). Their most radical recommendation was that dance should be compulsory for all children up to the age of 14 years in order to help to extend boys' "restricted perceptions of masculinity and masculine behaviour" (*ibid*: p. 58). Importantly, the report also acknowledged that to equate access with opportunity is mistaken and clearly placed responsibility on teachers to "question the stereotypes which limit children's behaviour and achievements; and to challenge, whenever necessary, instances of racism and sexism". It also articulates that working for equal opportunities in PE requires "an understanding and appreciation of the range of pupils" responses to femininity, masculinity, and sexuality', and that 'both in initial and in-service training, a critical review of prevailing practices, rigorous and continuous appraisal and often a willingness to question long-held beliefs and prejudices' were needed (*ibid*: p. 15). The report's recommendations are unequivocal — that children of both sexes, regardless of their different rates of development and experience, should be offered the same PE curriculum to 'avoid future undesirable sex stereotyping activities' (ibid: p. 57).

But these recommendations were disregarded, and when the Physical Education National Curriculum was finally published, games had priority over all other areas of the curriculum — they were the only aspect of PE to be made compulsory at *Key Stage* 3 (12-14 years). The result is that at a very impressionable age, when boys are consolidating a sense of the masculine, in most schools their curriculum will focus on games and will exclude dance. In this way, traditional gender divisions and identities in PE will be institutionalized and inevitably reproduced (see Hargreaves, 1994: Chapter 7). Significantly, there are no observations or recommendations about the problems of equalizing gender or dealing with sexism in either the Physical Education National Curriculum itself, or in the pack containing non-statutory guidance for teaching and assessing the programme.

Subsequent changes have further emphasised games and reduced still more the significance of other areas of the curriculum.

Following the Dearing Report (1993), draft proposals for the new National Curriculum Orders were published in May 1994, making games compulsory for children of all ages. In spite of the opposition of the majority of *Key Stage* 4 teachers (14-16 years) (Spencer 1995a: p. 9; 1995b: p. viii), the revised PE curriculum (Department for Education, 1995) came into effect last month (August 1995). Opposition has also been voiced from universities and institutes of higher education. It is argued that the slimming down of dance and outdoor activities at *Key Stage* 3 will impoverish boys' aesthetic appreciation and the development of their sensitivity to other people (Spencer 1994b: p. viii), and that the emphasis on games at *Key Stage* 4 will alienate girls (Spencer 1995a: p. 9). Since these reactions were voiced, the publication of *Sport: Raising the Game* (Department of National Heritage, 1995) has taken the sports-education-ideology to a yet new extreme.

The available evidence strongly supports the argument that key decisions about the development and working philosophy of a vital aspect of children's education have been made arbitrarily by people without experience either of philosophies of education, in general, or those of physical education, specifically. The composition of the working party was mixed, and although the majority of the members were male, the group as a whole was representative of different interest groups — those involved in different capacities in schools, higher education, the advisory sector and the inspectorate, a dance officer from the Arts Council, a member of the Sports Council who is also sensitive to the needs of the disabled, two sportsmen, and two businessmen. Although several of the group had little or no experience of physical education or of equality issues or special needs, and some had been immersed for years in competitive sports traditions, they all had the opportunity to see good practice in schools and to consider arguments about the effects of gendered practices and behaviour (as well as other equity issues in PE). The result was that the Working Party's Final Report, described above, was an informed and radical document, incorporating fundamental principles of equality to do with gender (Department of Education and Science, 1991a). Those responsible for dismissing its proposals and prioritizing games appear to have done so arrogantly and without knowledge and consideration of the limiting effects and, for some, harmful consequences, of their decision. John Evans characterizes them bluntly as 'male politicians who thought that cold showers and cricket were the foundations for morality and fitness' (Spencer, 1994a: p. 9). Ironically, ex-public school members of parliament who during their youth were steeped in the male games tradition, hardly provide a good recommendation that such regimes produce either morality or fitness!, and yet the myth continues. There is no doubt that those who have had the greatest power to influence the Physical Education Curriculum and all its developments are men who have a particular and narrow experience and vision of the relationship between physical education and gender. Iain Sproat, for example, is an ex-Wykhamist, and John Major is renowned for his obsession with football and cricket. Those who have been mentioned in the media for giving the policy paper unhesitating support surrounding the time of its launch are all elite sportsmen or dignitaries — namely, Kris Akabusi, Rob Andrew, Roger Black, Sir Colin Cowdrey, Bobby Charlton, Linford Christie, the Duke of Edinburgh, Devon Malcolm and Rory Underwood. And the Prime Minister chose Millwall Football Club as the venue for the press launch. The hidden message is easily understood and confirmed in public consciousness — physical education is really sport, sport is fundamentally worthwhile and fundamentally a male affair, and sport is most clearly understood by men who are the ones who will ensure its future.

In the main, the media have also been supportive of the campaign for games and for the campaign's underpinning ideology. It has been front page news in many newspapers and the debate has been on the political pages of others. The slogan in the Sun, "We'll Make Kids World-Beaters", embodies the popularity of nation-building dogmas, and the *Mirror* headline, The 'renaissance of sport in our schools' will "give every kid in Britain the chance to be a Beefy" (referring to Ian Botham), epitomises the unrepentantly gendered orientation of the popular sports media and reinforces the connection between sport and maleness in everyday consciousness.

The popular press have also presented bigoted and ignorant views of serious issues and oppositional ideas surrounding the school-sports-debate. "Trendy educational theorists" have been derided for undermining competitive games (Spencer, 1995c: p. 9; Shields, 1994) — a repeat of media opposition to the teachers' withdrawal from extra-curricular sport about a decade ago when they were blamed for the lowering of moral standards and for national sporting failures (Evans 1990a, 199b; Pollard 1988). Andrew Sparkes (1992: p. 3) gives the example of 11 July 1986 when on the front page of the *Today* newspaper was the headline 'Barmy Britain', portraying PE teachers as 'a bunch of radicals intent on damaging the place and position of competition in the PE curriculum'. Even the investigative documentary BBC Panorama programme, screened in March 1987, characterized PE teachers as anti-competition trendies, implicating them in the declining standards of national sport, the poor health of students, and the lack of discipline throughout society. Such fervent and distinctively male responses view the present state of sport quite uncritically and fail totally to examine equity issues. The more entrenched and widespread attitudes of this sort become, the more and more difficult it is to engage in a rational debate about them. The nature of ideology is such that it presents biased ideas as rational, masks alternatives, and through the popularity of the subject — in this case, sport — is able to engender support through the use of drama, but without logic.

The combined effect of the media and the politicians taking the moral high ground in relation to aspects of education and culture that the public feel they know and understand (I am talking here about sport itself; the relationship between sport and discipline; and the link between sport and international success), is that their arguments have legitimacy, not only in popular consciousness, but also in the lives and minds of physical education professionals themselves. So the 'goal posts' of the debate have changed — the focus now is on whether or not 'we' have the resources to implement the proposals, and no longer about whether competitive team games are the business of schools in the first place. Not surprisingly, the gendered nature of the debate is hardly ever touched upon by anyone who has a public voice. The imperatives of associating with the government's latest pronouncements about the revitalisation of school sport are powerful. In recent months, the movement has been broadly welcomed by the teachers unions, whose concerns in the climate of monetarist education are more to do to do with cost than philosophy (*Guardian*, 1995: p. 5). And since the publication of *Sport: Raising the Game*, physical education teachers seem to have capitulated. A decade ago it was reported that fewer than one teacher in ten wanted to see pupils playing more sports or having extra time for team games; after the Dearing Report (1993), the majority of teachers expressed concern about the proposed increase in time for games; but following the latest policy paper, the only publicised reaction from teachers has been a reservation that the endorsement of team games should not be at the expense of other sports. To my knowledge, there has not been a thorough, well-articulated debate in the profession about the immediate and long-term effects of government intervention — in terms of the philosophical underpinnings of the suggested changes, concerning the likely effects on different groups of children, or with reference to the potential for changing the professional status of the subject. Neither has there been a co-ordinated campaign to oppose the government's directives.

The sports lobby, led by men, reflects the 'New Right's' influences on education and on sport. There is nothing original about the view that sport is a palliative for moral decline, particularly in relation to young males who are characterised as the main perpetrators of crime and violence. Iain Sproat has declared that 'the decrease in team games and sports within schools has links with the increase in youthful boredom and ensuing anti-social behaviour'. He claims that: "If we had more organised team games in schools we would have fewer little thugs like those who killed James

Bulger" (quoted in Spencer, 1994c: p. 11). There is, of course, no evidence of this connection, but rather, as Evans (quoted in Spencer, 1994c) claims, that "sport has a great capacity for producing bullies and thugs as it has good citizens". Those who are opposing the government's stance are not denying that competitive team games can be beneficial and enriching, but that obsessive and unthinking promotion of them "can also promote selfish individualism, ruthless competitivism, a lasting sense of failure and alien-ation, and a desire to stay clear of physical activities" (Evans, quoted in Spencer 1994c: p. 11). It is also relevant to point to the pernicious nature of the wider sports system outside schools, which is implicitly condoned by the uncritical support and practice of aggressive competition as a part of the school life and education of impressionable children. George Leonard's (1979) well-known paper 'Winning isn't Everything. It's Nothing', exposed the poverty, problems and destructive nature of the competitive ethic. Since that time, match-fixing, dodgy transfer deals, drug abuse, violence, racism, hyped-up nationalism, xenophobia and so on have spread through sport unremittingly.

In the debate about team games, the fact that many boys, *in common with* the majority of adolescent girls, hate the conventions of masculine-style sports and find compulsory games a brutalizing and demoralizing experience, is usually ignored (Messner and Sabo, 1990; Hargreaves, 1994). It has also been argued that those boys who become consumed by the passions of competitive sports are also damaged young people. In fact, it is those who have been immersed in, and successful at, competitive sports at school, who oppose them as adults (Messner and Sabo, 1990). Sean French (1995: pp. 4/5) makes a personal comment:

> I have sometimes felt that organised school sport is an ideal tool for fostering brutality and cruelty ... I write as someone who adored school sport but who looks back on it with mixed feelings. When I played First XV rugby, in one memorable triumph I fought my way to the line, shouldering off an opponent with such force that he had to be helped from the field with a suspected cracked rib. The only problem this raised in our 17-year-old minds was how best to make use of the opportunity provided by the other team's missing man. At a similar age, I read a review in the *New Statesman* of a book of erotic poetry. The reviewer complained that one long poem — about an engineer who constructed a sex machine of such ferocity that it split his wife in half — was a work of such misogyn-istic obscenity that it should not be reprinted even in a work of reference. I was puzzled. Why should anyone object to a ballad that we sang on the coach to and from every away match? My retro-spective alarm is tempered only by a conviction that if groups of men are not doing each other damage on the rugby field, then they are likely to be doing it in more informal venues to non-consenting citizens.

In direct contrast to John Major's and Iain Sproat's claims about the benefits of competitive team games, they are perceived by others as the fuel of violence and neuroses, and contrary to gentleness, intimacy, closeness and co-operation. And when boys become engrossed overmuch in competitive sport (and we know that games [especially football] dominate the social structure for most boys over seven years of age [Phillips, 1993]), they are denied opportunities to develop a wide vocabulary of motor skills and to move creatively and expressively. Dance, in particular, can facilitate the construction of new movement identities for boys, broadening the flawed and limiting mainstream sporting images of physicality and masculinity (Burkhardt, 1995: p. 83-84). It is in fact exactly the unthinking and ignorant support of competitive sport of those men associated with the government's campaign that feeds the notion that to be good at sport is to be a 'real' man and which excites pejorative remarks about boys who choose to participate in 'feminine-appropriate' activities (dance, gymnastics, aerobics, for example). In spite of the increase in the popularity of dance among boys, recent research shows that those who dance are often mocked by their peers and labelled with sexually derogatory terms such as "fags", "fairies" or "wankers". The notion of the feminine-appropriateness and masculine-inappropriateness of dance in schools, especially among male teachers, was most starkly expressed by the headteacher of a high school in Leeds when he said, "Between you and me I think dance is for poofters" (Burkhardt, 1995: p. 82). Griffen (1995: p. 104) argues that, "It takes a young man of rare courage and self-assurance to stand up to such peer or teacher condemnation". Brutality and domination over effeminate boys are commonplace and heterosexual male hegemony is absolutely dominant in boys' competitive sport. There is less of a stigma attached to girls who express a preference for traditional male sports (although girls who play soccer and rugby also stand the risk of being labelled 'lesbian') than to boys who want to dance. But girls who dislike games and are poor at them are portrayed as 'typical girls' and thus fulfil a limiting stereotype. Team games also encourage expressions of machismo, negative attitudes to females and anti-female rituals, as well as homophobia. The 'hidden curriculum' of competitive team games, more than any other aspect of the physical education curriculum, replicates conventional notions of gender differences — male bonding is encouraged, aggression and sexism are endemic, and boys quickly learn that the sporting man is a symbol of masculine character; those who are poor sportsmen are despised and ridiculed as 'less than male'. There has been a strong tendency in PE to apply equal opportunities to girls, and not to boys: the privileging of games allows girls to legitimize alternative forms of femininity, but the lack of an equally-valued aspect of the physical education curriculum (such as dance) limits the chances of legitimizing alternative forms of masculinity and physical awareness for boys.

The observations made above, are not proposed as a rationale for outlawing team games. Opposition to harsh competition and training practices are usually *incorrectly* construed as opposition to games themselves. The argument for equal consideration of different types of activities, is also often incorrectly understood to mean that games should be removed from the curriculum altogether. The common *obsession* with competitive team games, particularly among men, and the false claim that they are of greater value than any other physical activity in building character and inculcating discipline, leads to a blindness about what is actually being proposed. The justification for physical education should not be to ensure that we win test matches, get a Brit in the Wimbledon final, reduce assaults and criminality, or even improve the health of our young people — its main aim should be to introduce all children to a wide range of physical activities in order to develop skills, co-ordination and an extensive movement vocabulary. If equal treatment is given to different forms of movement, children stand a greater chance of becoming fully literate physically. They should be able to use their bodies knowledgeably and creatively in order to experience the sensuous nature of movement in ways which fully develop their potential and enrich their lives. This would include games playing, but would not emphasise aggressive competition, or concentrate on the major games at the expense of others. Part of the process should be a concern for equity and an understanding and appreciation of different types of physical abilities. And although in this paper dance has been used to illustrate particular gender problems, it is not argued that it should be given priority any more than games, but that athletic activities, dance, games, gymnastics, outdoor pursuits and swimming be given equal status.

An increasing amount of research is being done in the field of the sociology of the body about the ways in which our psyches and social behaviour are linked to our physical bodies (Featherstone, Hepworth and Turner 1991; Frank, 1991; Scott and Morgan, 1993; Schilling, 1993; Turner, 1984). It has been argued that there is a correlation between the gendered nature of sporting activities and gendered ideas about masculinity, femininity, sexuality, and the use and representations of the physical body (Hargreaves ,1994; Messner and Sabo, 1990, 1994). I would like to hypothesise that if we had a system of physical education which respected and nurtured the wide-ranging physical capabilities and potential of all children, regardless of their sex, the probable outcome would be better balanced individuals who would most likely value healthy living and be sensitive about the ways they use their bodies and less inclined to be thugs and misogynists. There is more logic in such a hypothesis than arguing for a system which results in a narrow and gendered movement experience.

But such a vision appears illusory. There are additional obstacles to change which are linked to gender relations of power — those which emanate from the logistics of implementing the new directives, and those associated more directly with educationalists and other individuals implicated in the running and philosophy of schools, such as governors, local dignitaries, churchmen and businessmen. The National Curriculum has led in general to a reduction in time for basic PE lessons and a demand for more extra-curricular activities. This, in turn, has resulted in a narrower movement experience for children even in those schools where there is a history and desire for a broadly-based programme. The powers of school governors have been extended as a result of the ERA and, many of whom, like the politicians, make decisions about the subject, but know nothing about its history and philosophy. I was speaking to a female Head of Department of a mixed secondary school whose Headmaster has told her to put her efforts into competitive games and sports, to gear curriculum physical education in that direction as much as possible, and to keep all extra-curricular clubs for school teams and training. "My hands", he told her, "are tied ... the governors want more school teams, more competitions and better results". A similar case is described by Andrew Sparkes in which a school governor, with special responsibility for physical education, demanded "matches, matches and more matche". Anything creative, aesthetic, or which would not attract public attention he dismissed as irrelevant, and he suggested that the popular trampolining and dance clubs be abandoned in favour of running more inter-school fixtures (Sparkes, 1992: p. 9-10). Over a number of years, the female head of department had changed an elitist, skills-dominated, and very competitive (and male oriented regime) into one more compatible, as she put it, "with contemporary educational thinking". She was providing equality of educational opportunity and a balanced curriculum with relevant experiences for all students, but was overruled by one very powerful male governor. In increasing numbers of schools, teachers are losing autonomy and, as Andrew Sparkes has pointed out, in those with falling roles, physical education curricula are increasingly being geared to winning matches in order to attract pupils and increase revenue (Sparkes, 1992; Sports Council, 1990).

More and more, the form and content of schooling are being influenced by parties from outside the educational context whose ideas about physical education are based on their own experiences at school and on traditional gender stereotypes. Sparkes (1992: p. 17) argues that it is possible that 'future appointments in PE departments could be made predominantly according to the candidate's ability to contribute to competitive sport rather than to the general education of children', and team results may become the main component of the appraisal of physical education teachers.

The problem of autonomy for teachers also relates to gender divisions of power and gendered practices in departments of physical education. Sheila Scraton (1992) has argued that 'separate' and 'different' development for girls and boys was a central concept in the planning of PE programmes from the nineteenth century right up until the time of the inception of the National Curriculum, and Ann Flintoff has signposted the difficulties of changing such a long-established tradition. Her research in

Leeds schools shows that men are over-represented in Head of Department positions (Flintoff, 1995a: p. 32), a pattern which is typical for mixed schools throughout the country (75% have male heads of PE). Not surprisingly, many male heads of department favour the competitive ethos and are antagonistic to change. Ann Flintoff's research (1995a: p. 48) has also uncovered the ways in which sexism is inherent in teacher/teacher, teacher/pupil, and pupil/pupil relationships, and she writes about the limited extent to which teachers implement anti-sexist strategies in their work. Gendered practices apply also to initial teacher education. Male and female students are given different and distinctly gendered timetables during their school-based training, especially with respect to games (Flintoff,1995b: p. 65); there is little evidence that "students are being sensitized to the impact of gender in PE" (Flintoff , 1995b: p. 66); the majority of PE mentors are men; and, in general, unequal gender relations are embodied in the structure, organisation and philosophy of specific departments (Flintoff, 1994/5). Ann Flintoff (1994/5: p. 6) has also revealed that "the balance and range of practical PE activities included in undergraduate courses reflect the gendered histories of the institutions" and "deep-seated ...gender ideologies". In brief, she shows how "gender and sexuality [are] a central part of the *experience* and *process* of teacher education" (Flintoff, 1994/5: p. 8). She provides specific examples:

- a number of students only taught children of their own sex
- women students were more likely to have had opportunity to teach across the full range of national curriculum PE activities
- students' opportunities to teach games were heavily limited by stereotypical notions of "girls' games" and "boys' games"; men students largely taught rugby and soccer; women students [largely taught], netball and hockey (although extra curricular opportunities were more relaxed in some schools)

It would seem that both in schools and colleges, gender issues in physical education are seldom dealt with intentionally or rigorously. The overall effect is that many of the advances initiated in the sixties and seventies to break down gendered practices are being eroded, and there has been a serious reduction of discourses about equal opportunities. Although under the terms of the Education Reform Act (1988), it is established in law, and emphasised by the term 'entitlement', that schools provide equal opportunities for all students and staff, there are reasons why this is impossible to implement. The concept of equal opportunities is intangible — it is interpreted and put into action in different ways by different people, made possible by the blurring of the distinctions between physical education on the school curriculum and extra-curricular competitive sport which is under the aegis of the governing bodies (Talbot, 1990). It is also the case that by equal is not meant 'the same', so that it is legitimate for a school to offer boys football, for example, whilst offering girls hockey (Milosevic, 1995: p. 11) explains that:

If the school supports both these activities with equal opportunities to play for school or county, equal time allocation and standard of coaching, both these sports can be described as outdoor team games, fast, tough, and played on grass with a ball. If, however, the girls were not offered any PE activity which resembled the above (perhaps girls did dance while boys did football) then there would be a stronger case for sex discrimination.

But as Margaret Talbot (1995: p. 17) points out,

> ...equal opportunity in physical education is not merely a matter of 'girls measuring up to boys', or boys being able to dance: it is genuinely valuing the different and individual contributions of all children, being willing to challenge sex and gender stereotypes, and teachers being able to recognise the influences of their own behaviour and attitudes, and being able to change them when necessary to ensure that children's choices are kept free and open.

Although some teachers are making positive efforts to break with stereotyped gender images and practices, all schools are faced by concrete constraints and negative directives. The position articulated by Margaret Talbot above has been ignored by male politicians who had the power to influence change. But it is highly likely that these men have themselves been deprived of a full movement experience and for that reason find it impossible to understand that there is no educational justification for games to be given priority over other forms of physical activity, or to appreciate that there are likely to be serious limitations for both boys and girls resulting from the implementation of the new curriculum Orders and the directives in *Sport: Raising the Game*.

John Major's claim that sport is 'part of the British instinct, part of our character' implies a homogeneously gendered nation. In fact, from the nineteenth century, sport has reflected male domination and the building of a particularly male instinct and character. But the chance to change this tradition appears to have been lost. To encourage games playing for all schoolchildren can have beneficial results, but to unthinkingly celebrate games playing to the disadvantage of other types of activities is a predominantly male orientation to physical capital (Bourdieu, 1980). But the real implications of these moves are political. The government's sports and games incentive is a clever attempt to gain popularity for a flagging government by appealing to an aspect of popular culture that most people see as innocent and beneficial. "We want gold medals round the necks of our Olympic athletes, a Brit in the Wimbledon finals and the Ashes back at the MCC", exhorted John Major (*Sun*, 1995: p. 7), appealing to some spurious notion of homogenous nationhood. In his Radio 4 'Letter from America', Alistair Cooke understood the common-sense ideology of this sporting message when he suggested that Mr Major had got it right in emulating the Romans: when the populace is restive, double the bread ration and bring on the circuses (Spencer, 1995c: p. 9). But his desperate concern to "put Britain back on the top of the world" in sport masks the real and insidious effects on equal opportunities in physical education and the perpetuation and possible widening of unequal gender relations.

References

Bailey, C. (1990) 'Games, winning and education', in J. Evans (ed) *Sport in schools*. Reading: Deakin University Press: pp. 141-7.

Beaumont, P. (1993) 'Fury erupts as thousands of play schemes axed', *Observer*, 7 March.

Bloot. R. and Browne, J. (1994) 'Factors contributing to the lack of female leadership in school physical education', *Journal of Teaching and Physical Education*, No. 14: pp. 34-59.

Bourdieu, P. (1980) *Distinction: A social critique of the judgement of taste.* London: Routledge and Kegan Paul.

Burkhardt, J. (1995) '"Between you and me I think dance is for poofters": Balancing the genders in dance', Leeds Education, *Fairplay: Gender and Physical Education*. Leeds: Leeds City Council Department of Education: pp. 82-87.

Carvel, J. and Duncan, J. (1995) 'Major seeks gold in sporting prowess', *Guardian*, July 15: p. 5.

Crosset, T. (1990) 'Masculinity, sexuality and early modern sport', in M. Messner and D. Sabo (eds) S*port, men and the gender order: Critical feminist perspectives*. Champaign, Il: Human Kinetics.

Dearing, Sir Ron (1993) *Final report: The National Curriculum and its assessment*. London: S.C.A.A.

Department of Education and Science (1991a) *Physical Education for ages 5 to 16*. London: HMSO.

Department of Education and Science (1991b) *Sport and active recreation*. London: HMSO.

Department for Education (1992) *Physical Education in the National Curriculum*. London: HMSO.

——— (1995) *Physical Education in the National Curriculum: New Orders*. London: HMSO.

Department of National Heritage (1995) *Sport: Raising the game*. London: Department of National Heritage.

Drysdale, N. (1995) *Inside Track*, 23 April : pp. 8-9.

Equal Opportunities Commission (1989) *Gender issues: the implications for schools of the Education reform Act 1988*. Manchester: EOC.

Evans, J. (1990a) 'Defining a subject: The rise and rise of the new PE', *British Journal of Sociology of Education*, Vol. 11: pp. 155-169.

———— (1990b) 'Ability, position and privilege in school physical education', in D. Kirk and R. Tinning (eds) *Physical education, curriculum and culture: Critical issues in the contemporary crisis.* Lewes: Falmer Press: pp. 139-167.

Featherstone, M., Hepworth, M. and Turner, B. (eds) (1991) *The body.* London: Sage Publications.

Flintoff, A. (1995a) 'Anti sexist practice in secondary Physical Education', Leeds Education, *Fairplay: Gender and Physical Education.* Leeds: Leeds City Council Department of Education: pp. 32-51.

———— (1994/5) 'Keeping gender on the agenda: PE teacher education in the 1990s', *Working Papers in Sport and Society*, Vol. 3. Coventry: University of Warwick.

———— (1995b) '"We have no problems with Equal Opportunities here... We've got mixed changing rooms": Gender, Initial Teacher Education and Physical Education', Leeds Education, *Fairplay: Gender and Physical Education.* Leeds: Leeds City Council Department of Education: pp. 62-69.

Frank, A. (1991) 'For a sociology of the body: An analytical review', in M. Featherstone, M. Hepworth and B. Turner (eds) *The body.* London: Sage Publications.

French, S. (1995) 'The couch trip', *Guardian 2*, 12 July: 4/5.

Griffen, P. (1995) 'Homophobia in Physical Education', Leeds Education, *Fairplay: Gender and Physical Education.* Leeds: Leeds City Council Department of Education: pp. 102-105.

Hargreaves, J. A. (1994) *Sporting females: Critical issues in the history and sociology of sport.* London: Routledge.

Kirk, D. (1992) 'Curriculum history in Physical Education', in A. Sparkes (ed) *Research in Physical Education and sport.* Lewes: Falmer Press: 210-230.

Leeds Education (1995) *Fairplay: Gender and Physical Education.* Leeds: Leeds City Council Department of Education.

Leonard, G. (1979) 'Winning isn't everything. It's nothing', in A. Yiannakis (ed) *Sports sociology.* Dubuque, Iowa: Kendall Hunt.

Messner, M. and Sabo, D. (1994) *Sex, violence and power in sports*, Freedom, CA: The Crossing Press.

Messner, M. and Sabo, D. (eds) (1990) *Sport, men and the gender order.* Champaign, Il: Human Kinetics.

Milosevic, L. (1995) 'Gender issues in Physical Education', *Fairplay: Gender and Physical Education*. Leeds: Leeds City Council Department of Education: pp. 8-13.

Miles, S. and Middleton, C. (1990) 'Girls' education in the balance: The ERA and inequality', in M. Flude and M. Hammer (eds) *The Education Reform Act, 1988: its origins and implications*. Lewes: Falmer.

Phillips, A. (1993) 'Football crazy, football sad', *Times Educational Supplement*, Sept. 24: pp. 1-2.

Pollard, A. (1988) 'Physical education, competition and control in the primary school, in J. Evans (ed) *Teachers, teaching and control in physical education*. Lewes: Falmer Press: pp. 109-123.

Preston, B. (1995) 'State schools struggle to play the game', *Times*, 14 July: p. 4.

Ryrie, J. (1995) 'Matthew Murray High School Case Study Research', Leeds Education, *Fairplay: Gender and Physical Education*. Leeds: Leeds City Council Department of Education: pp. 18-23.

Schilling, C. (1993) *The body and social theory*. London: Sage Publications.

Scott, S. and Morgan, D. (eds) (1993) *Body matters*. London: Falmer Press.

Scraton, S. (1986) 'Images of femininity and the teaching of girls' Physical Education', in J. Evans (ed) *Physical Education, sport and schooling*. Lewes: Falmer Press.

—— (1992) *Shaping up to womanhood: Gender and girls' Physical Education*. Milton Keynes: Open University Press.

—— (1993) 'Equality, co-education and Physical Education', in J. Evans, (ed) *Equality, education and Physical Education*. London: Falmer Press: 139-153.

Shields, A. (1988) 'Competing interests', *Sport and Leisure*, March/ April: pp. 26-7.

Sparkes, A. (1992) 'The changing nature of teachers' work: School governors and curriculum control in Physical Education', in N. Armstrong (ed) *New directions in Physical Education*. Champaign, Il: Human Kinetics: pp. 1-31.

Spencer, D. (1994a) 'No winners in PE Order', *Times Educational Supplement*, Nov. 18: p. 9.

—— (1994b) 'Competition set to become compulsory', *Times Educational Supplement*, Nov.: p. viii.

—— (1994c) 'Staff say no to more sport hours', *Times Educational Supplement*, 25 February: p. 11.

——— (1995) 'Unions refuse to cheer Mr Major's side', *Times Educational Supplement*, July 21: p. 9.

Sports Council (1990) *Education Reform fact sheet for Governing Bodies of Sport and Local Sports Organisations*. London: Sports Council.

——— (1993) *Women and sport: Policy and frameworks for Action*. London: Sports Council.

Sproat, I. (1994a) reported in the *Daily Telegraph*, 9 February.

——— (1994b) reported in *Times Educational Supplement*, 21 October.

——— (1994c) reported in *Daily Telegraph*, 28 February.

Sun, (1995) 14 July: p. 7.

Stewart, A. (1995) 'Sportsmark and gold star awards for high standards in school sporting provision', letter enclosed with *Sport: Raising the game*, (Department of National Heritage).

Talbot, M. (1993) 'A gendered Physical Education: Equality and sexism', in J. Evans (ed) *Equality, education and Physical Education*. London: Falmer Press:

——— (1995) 'Gender and National Curriculum Physical Education', Leeds Education (1995) *Fairplay: Gender and Physical Education*. Leeds: Leeds City Council Department of Education: pp. 14-17.

Thorne, B. (1993) *Gender play: Girls and boys in school*. Buckingham: Open University Press.

Turner, B. (1984) *The body and society*. Oxford: Basil Blackwell.

Vines, G. (1988) 'Is sport good for children?', *New Scientist*, 21 July.

Wood, N. (1995) 'Major's game plan to revive nation's sport', *Times*, 14 July: p. 1.

Woods, P. and Hammersley, M. (eds) (1993) *Gender and ethnicity in schools: ethnographic accounts*. London: Routledge.

Outlaws in Sport and Education? Exploring the Sporting and Education Experiences of Lesbian Physical Education Teachers

Gill Clarke

University of Southampton

Another brick to add to the wall — the longer I live, the more people I get involved with, the more complicated and painful it gets. I hate lying, deceiving, misleading, but I'm so damn good at it, I do it to myself all the time. (Harriet, 28 February, 1995)

Introduction

Living a lesbian existence in a heterosexist and homophobic world as Harriet reveals can be both complicated and painful. This paper illustrates the complexities of the teaching and sporting lives of lesbian physical education teachers in secondary schools in England. In so doing, it reveals how they manage their lesbian identity in order to appear to comply with dominant discourses of hegemonic heterosexuality and femininity.

The social and political context

Before illustrating some of these identity management strategies, it is necessary to locate these women's lives within their social, cultural and political context since this impacts on the way that they live their lives and how they should be understood. The current political climate for lesbians continues to be a chilly one, although on the surface there may appear to have been some advances for homosexuals, for example: the lowering of the age of consent for gay men from 21 to 18 — as opposed to a hetero-sexual age of consent of 16; lesbian heroines in soaps, Dyke TV and so on. I would argue that these are but superficial changes which, in many ways, mask the rise and power of the New Right and the pursuit of traditional

45

family values and the desire to return to some mythical golden age of the family. Anne Marie Smith (1995) makes a powerful case for a recognition of the Right's evisceration of liberal democracy. She traces the emergence of a new type of homophobia which masquerades as a type of liberal democratic 'tolerance'; this pseudo-tolerance she argues is reserved for the 'good homosexual', not the dangerous queer. This is the homosexual that knows their place, that can assimilate (cf. to the discourses of racism) and return to the closet. Section 28 of the Local Government Act 1987-8 has done much to keep teachers in the 'good homosexual's' closet. This legislation — passed in the Thatcher years when there was an attempt to gain political mileage by linking the left wing of the Labour party with pro-gay policies (see Miller, 1995: p. 503) — stated that:

> A local authority shall not — (a) intentionally promote homosexuality or publish material with the intention of promoting homosexuality; (b) promote the teaching in any maintained school of the acceptability of homosexuality as a pretended family relationship. (Smith, 1994: p. 183)

It is clear how this repressive legislation portrays lesbians and gays in a negative light and serves to legitimate hegemonic discourses of heterosexuality and to fuel prejudice and hatred.

Though it has been argued that Section 28 is vaguely worded and "Imprecisely drafted and dangerously open to misinterpretation, its implications are far-reaching. Already operating to encourage damaging self censorship, Section 28 strikes at the civil liberties of us all" (Colvin with Hawksley, 1989, Back cover). The impact of this legislation has been to make many teachers afraid of disclosing their (homo)sexuality for fear of reprisal and job loss — hence, as is later illustrated, the compulsion many feel to employ heterosexual passing strategies so as to conceal their real identity. Despite the fact that Section 28 may be only of symbolic power as "The scope of ... (its) provision has yet to be interpreted by the courts ..." (OutRage and Stonewall, 1994: p. 33), it continues to impact negatively on the identities of lesbians and gay men.

Nevertheless, in the conservative and politically sensitive world of education it should be noted that these fears appear to have some grounding. Take for instance the case of Hackney headteacher Jane Brown who turned down the offer of subsidised tickets to her school to see Romeo and Juliet at the Royal Opera House for a number of reasons, including her much-quoted reason that the ballet was "entirely about heterosexual love". Despite the fact that there were other very good educational and economic reasons put forward for not taking up the offer, the press got hold of the story. When they:

> ... discovered where — and with whom — Jane Brown lived. Her defence was detonated. The woman was dyke. That explained everything! (Campbell, 1995: p. 18)

The *Sun* referred to her as a "hatchet faced dyke" and announced the story on their front page with the heading "ROMEO, ROMEO, where art thou homo?". Such was the witch hunt of the tabloid press that Jane Brown was forced to leave her home and go into hiding in order to escape — not only this media persecution, but also from the death threats that she had received. After nearly eighteen months the investigation was concluded, and Jane Brown was exonerated. It is perhaps no wonder that many lesbian and gay teachers feel threatened by what happened to Jane Brown. This then is the backdrop against which these lesbian lives must be interpreted: this is their lived reality.

Lesbian teachers

The stories and scenarios that are portrayed in this paper emanate from research into the lives and lifestyles of lesbian physical education teachers. The vignettes are derived from questionnaires and in-depth interviews/conversations with 14 white able bodied women. The questionnaire was distributed in the summer of 1995 and focused on their sporting pastimes, and the interviews were conducted between 1993 and 1995, focusing on: lesbian identity, activities of teaching, interaction with pupils and relationships with colleagues. These areas for discussion grew out of my experiences as a 'good' lesbian teacher [that is, I think I passed fairly convincingly as (pseudo) heterosexual] and out of my reading of Pat Griffin's (1992) and Madiha Didi Khayatt's (1992) research into the lives of lesbian teachers in North America. The women in this research are aged between 23 and 47 and their teaching experience varies from just over one year to over 25 years. At the time of the interviews they taught in a variety of schools from: mixed Comprehensives, Roman Catholic, Church of England to Independent schools. In order to preserve their anonymity, all the women were from the outset given a pseudonym; they were also informed in writing of the procedures that would be adopted to maintain this confidentiality and how the information was to be subsequently used. This was essential as none of the teachers were totally out about their sexuality in school. I make no claim here that these women are necessarily representative, indeed I believe there is no generic lesbian women, nor am I arguing for any false universalism of their experiences.

Covering our tracks: strategies for concealing a lesbian identity

The following section illustrates some of the strategies employed by these teachers to conceal their identities from both colleagues and pupils. None of the teachers were totally open about their sexuality at school; for most, their lesbianism was carefully concealed from all but a very small number of 'trusted' colleagues. Indeed for some of the teachers, their true identity was known to no-one within the school. All the teachers feared that should their lesbianism be revealed then they would be likely to be viewed differently and in a non-positive light by both colleagues and pupils, and that ultimately they would lose their job. To avoid this, they constructed sometimes quite complex boundaries around themselves in order to deflect any suspicion about their sexuality. This meant that they had to be constantly vigilant about the public persona they presented: hence they felt the need to 'live two lives' and to endure the stress and strain that this entailed. These two lives were the school life and the home life — the former required that a pseudo-heterosexual lifestyle was portrayed, and the latter for some of the women also required at times the adoption of similar strategies. Fay, for instance, commented on the need to 'cover her tracks' and the resultant stress that this created. She described how:

> When you go into school you know it is different .... I find it very difficult to cope with because you know my sexuality to me is a very important part of me and then all of a sudden you are faced with here we go, back again to the conservatism of it all and we are covering our tracks by not saying who we live with, who we go out with, what we do at weekends. You are only choosing to tell the bits that aren't going to tell a story.

We can see from this statement how "covering our tracks" involves a number of different ploys, including strict self censorship. This self censorship necessitates a monitoring of what is said about the self and others and a holding back of significant parts of the self. Thus certain situations within school become the possible sites for exposure and unwelcome attention. Hence these social situations might be avoided for fear of revealing too much about the self — thus for example conversations in staffrooms were often consciously avoided when heterosexual staff were talking about their families, children and so on. Gabby described how she distanced herself:

> ... by not talking about my personal life (and by) ... not getting involved in anything socially at school where staff would be taking their partners. ... So in that kind of way I look after myself.

'Looking after myself' also involved the ability to deflect questions about boyfriends from both colleagues and pupils. This heterosexual presumption was dealt with in a variety of ways: for example, Harriet revealed how she would sometimes lie, even though she didn't like to do so because in a way she felt that this was a 'putting down' of herself. She also described how she was asked directly by some of the lower school pupils if she had a boyfriend and how she felt so much on the spot that she told them that she did have a boyfriend. Another strategy that she sometimes felt compelled to employ in order to deflect suspicion was to "be overtly flirtatious with young male staff". Others also described how their 'street cred' was improved if they were seen by staff or pupils in the company of men. For some, the invention of mythical men did much to preserve their pseudo straight identity. It is clear from these brief scenarios how compulsory heterosexuality remains the order of the day in the public world of the school, and how not only must tracks be covered but in some instances false trails laid.

The staffroom, as previously mentioned, provided another site for possible exposure when conversation on occasions turned to issues to do with homosexuality. Many of the women believed that if they were to join in such conversations then their identity was further at risk due to attention being directed at them. Thus not only did such conversations have to be side-stepped but also homophobic jokes had to be endured and openly tolerated, for few felt able to challenge such abuse. One of the women, Ivy, felt safer to do so because she was the Equal Opportunities officer for the school so this enabled her to challenge under the "Equal Opps. umbrella". For most, this keeping silent was both frustrating and upsetting. Harriet commented on how she had had an argument with somebody at work who knew about her sexuality:

> ... it does get me down when they start sort of gay bashing in the staffroom or in the pub and she says, "well why don't you say something?" — but I can't, you know, you've got a family, you've got a husband and two boys to hide behind almost but I haven't so I can't. I really feel that I can't.

For two of the teachers who had been married it was possible to hide behind their married title. Maud admitted that she had kept the title 'Mrs', albeit probably subconsciously, to hide behind, though most of her colleagues knew that she was divorced. Ivy felt that the 'Mrs' title was a buffer for women, and as a lesbian it was an even greater buffer. It was a title that she said she wouldn't lose at all, although she conceded that on her own private letters to businesses she always referred to herself as Ms. She posited the view that:

> If you are a Miss there are certain connotations drawn, either spinster or the lesbian/feminist type, but if you are a Mrs you have conformed to the rules of society, and if you haven't got a husband then it doesn't really matter. You actually have been at one point ... you are accepted.

Caroline, although single, also commented on how she too thought that the title 'Mrs' provided a cover from the gaining of a lesbian reputation that she felt 'Miss' in physical education often suffer from.

Teachers at risk?

The very physicality of the subject and the centrality of the body to physical education pose particular threats to lesbian teachers. In a homophobic and heterosexist world where New Right discourses about the family hold hegemonic power over other lifestyles, to be a lesbian teacher working with children is to be seen by some as Lucy remarked as "a paedophile or per-vert". All the teachers feared such accusations and went to great lengths to avoid getting 'too close' to pupils. Fay remarked that:

> ... it is different for PE teachers because you are involved with the physical side of things. It has got to be worse, it's not like you teach English or you teach Humanities or whatever, you teach PE. There has got to be a different stigma attached to it and everything else that goes with it, and I think this is what people are afraid of. ... I think it frightens a lot of people that if that was found out, they would think you were molesting or you were some kind of pervert. You know the only reason you are teaching PE is because you can see all the kids undress.

All the teachers who had to supervise pupils changing and showering after lessons were extremely anxious about how their presence in these situations would be perceived. Thus they sought to distance themselves from these locations and in particular the showering ritual by remaining in their offices or in the background. For one of the teachers — Gabby — These fears became a nightmare when she was called into the Headmaster's office after a pupil had complained:

> ... that I watched her in the showers ... I'd always thought that when I was in that situation, which was my worst nightmare, that I would go bright red because I am rubbish at lying, and I didn't. I just felt the colour drain from my face and I looked absolutely shell-shocked ... and the Head said "we're only asking about this because we want to disprove it". They (the parents) complained to the Local Authority, ... I was absolutely gobsmacked and they (the Head and Deputy) said they were meeting with the parents in a weeks time about it and there were other things they were meeting about as well, and the parents didn't bring it up. The Head wrote a letter to the Authority saying that as far as he was concerned any claim made about me was completely unsubstantiated and the school was prepared to support me to the last ... but that was a very nervous moment.

Other "nervous moments" were sometimes caused when the teachers had to support female pupils, Ethel described how she felt vulnerable when she had to support pupils in gymnastics or help pupils to hold a racket or a piece of athletics equipment correctly, generally any situation where she came into physical contact with a pupil caused her anxiety.

As regards the vulnerability of heterosexual teachers in these situations, it was acknowledged that they too could be at risk, but it was generally felt that it was not to the same extent as lesbian teachers. Kay remarked "no teacher likes to be faced by this situation — but the problem is very sensitive and a threatening one to a lesbian teacher". For as Annie commented:

[It's] Not to the same degree because any false allegation would be less believed if the governors found they had a lovely boyfriend but if the governors found you had a lovely girlfriend I'm sure it would open some homophobic doors.

The homophobia and heterosexism that these teachers experience in their daily lives was — as we shall see for some of them — not dissimilar to that found on the sports field. Ivy observed, "Why should sport be any different to anything else?!"

Sporting a difference

Most of the women were involved in some form of sport outside of their working lives; they participated in a wide variety of activities, some played just for fun, whilst others competed at various levels from club to international. Their motivations for involvement varied slightly, but almost all said that they participated because they enjoyed being active and the social contacts that they made whilst engaged in sport or physical activity.

Some of the women were out about their sexuality to some extent in their chosen activities, (only two were totally out) and in these cases it was only to a small group of people. Kay, for instance, revealed that her sexuality was not admitted to all, but that she had disclosed it to a small few. Those who were not out gave a variety of reasons including:

My sexuality has never been something that I wished to discuss with my team mates. (Ethel)

I would find it job threatening to be out to anyone on an ad hoc basis. My status as a PE teacher would soon come out. I fear for my job if it got back to school. (Ivy)

Within the activity or the club that they were involved with most believed or knew that there were other lesbians also involved. For the vast majority of the women this had not been a factor when they were choosing their activity. Kay commented: "I became involved in this sport long before I knew the meaning of sex!!"; and Ethel said: "I play my sport for the sake of the sport, not because it will introduce me to other lesbians. Hockey was important in my life *before* I became aware of my sexuality".

Like their lives in school, compulsory heterosexuality also impacted upon their sporting experiences in that most of the women still feel the need to conceal their lesbianism, through conforming with dominant discourses of hegemonic heterosexuality and femininity.

Harassment and anti-lesbian comments

This research has provided considerable evidence of anti-lesbianism within sporting activities; many of the women had had direct experience of verbal abuse. For example, Barbara recalled how a supporter had shouted "lezz" when she'd scored a goal, Caroline described how other netballers had mocked the county coach who was a closet lesbian. Deb remembered how she had umpired a mixed tournament and drunken men had made anti-lesbian comments along the side line. Ethel recounted how on several occasions when training or preparing for a game when people had walked past the pitch they had made comments such as: "look at the lezzies, there must be a few lesbians out there". However, she also said that she had never experienced anti-lesbian comments on the pitch. Harriet revealed that the captain of the men's hockey 1st. XI said that the majority of the men's teams didn't attend social functions because of the high proportion of lesbians in the women's teams who attend the social functions and are not discrete in displaying their sexual preferences. Lucy recollected that homophobic comments had been made when she was younger, but nothing had been directed at her personally, but she remembered being made aware that lesbian activity was not approved of by her peers at that time. Naomi had also heard homophobic comments, though again they had not been directed at her personally; at social events she had been aware of negative comments and jokes being made about lesbians.

What do these scenarios tell us about lesbian women in sport? I would contend that although these are the experiences of only a small group of lesbian women. they are not necessarily atypical. The sporting arena has historically been the prerogative of men and the training ground for the development of hegemonic masculinity, it was an arena women entered at their peril. For the Victorians, a woman was a frail character, whose femininity and reproductive role was to be protected; sport was seen as potentially deleterious to her health and child bearing functions. This legacy has been a long time passing — as the history, for instance, of the Modern Olympics bears witness: women continue to compete in lesser numbers and in fewer events than men. For those women who dared to enter this male domain, their performances were subject to the scrutiny of the male gaze, which in many cases trivialised their performances and also suggested that where they performed well then they must be some sort of freak of nature, indeed possibly a man! What I am trying to do in this historical snapshot is to illustrate that women in sport have not had an easy time, and this has been particularly so in those sports that have traditionally not been seen as stereotypically feminine. Thus whilst it may be socially acceptable for a woman to be a successful gymnast/ice skater. it may be less acceptable for her to be a successful rugby/football player. The former carry an acceptable (heterosexual) feminine image whereas the latter do not: that is, the image is not feminine, therefore it must be masculine, and hence women engaged in such sport must be masculine and therefore lesbian. As Messner and Sabo (1994, p: 110) comment:

> Lesbianism is thus recast by heterosexist culture as an emulation
> of masculinity. In contrast male homosexuality is considered a
> negation of masculinity.

It is perhaps no wonder that many women would feel uncomfortable playing in sports in an environment where their sexuality is likely to be questioned. Therefore, it is not surprising that many women within sport seek to distance themselves from any possible suggestion of or association with lesbianism through the making and confirming of their femininity and their (hetero)sexuality overtly visible. Thus we often see evidence of what has been described as hyperfemininity (see Felshin, 1974 and Lenskyj, 1994) — that is, the wearing of make-up, jewellery and other adornments to proclaim a so called 'normal sexuality'. This is not confined to the way that the athlete presents herself: it is also replicated by the way that the media portray women in sport; very often it is not their performance that is commented on but the fact that they are a mother, wife and so on. Reference is also frequently made to what they are wearing and to their appearance. As sport is now big global business, the media moguls and sponsors are increasingly all powerful in determining what constitutes an acceptable, marketable image and product. It is clear from the female sporting superstars who have made it that heterosexuality and hyper-femininity are the order of the day. When Martina Navratilova came out as a lesbian she lost millions of dollars in sponsorship and endorsements. By this stage of her career arguably she could afford to, but how many others could? Most then choose to keep their lesbianism carefully hidden for fear of their careers being destroyed.

The world of sport as has been illustrated in this paper is not a welcoming one for lesbian participants. What is also disturbing is that within this sporting world we have largely failed to discuss and address the difficulties that lesbian women face within this arena. There have been some notable exceptions to this claim (see for example the work of Griffin and Lenskyj). But whilst we remain silent, I would argue that we continue to perpetuate and reinforce myths, stereotypes and fears about lesbian women in sport. Through these practices we deny them the right to participate openly and fully in sport. This right to participate should be a basic human right and not something reserved for the heterosexual majority.

It is apparent that at all levels of sporting participation, lesbian women feel the need to remain invisible if they are to survive. This has also meant that when they were aware of homophobia or anti-lesbianism they did not always feel able to challenge it. Harriet indicated how she was:

> ... resigned to being put down, and am not always surprised or deeply hurt by it when I hear it now — if you hear it often enough you begin to believe it and accept it.

It's OK as long as we don't draw attention to ourselves

This final section seeks to analyse the lesbian sporting experience. What is evident from the vignettes portrayed here is that sport for these lesbian women seems in general to be another arena where they still cannot be themselves. Or perhaps they can be, but at a price — so as long as they don't draw attention to themselves, and know how to be a 'good' lesbian in sport they are 'tolerated'. But as we saw previously, the moment they reveal their sexual preferences they are not welcome. Harriet described how "a member of our women's first eleven wished to transfer to the other major club in [the town] but they have discussed her transfer and have denied it, on the grounds of her sexuality". Clearly, this woman would seem not to be a 'good' lesbian. Others too have found their sporting progress curtailed when they failed to display heterosexual credentials. As Lenskyj (1992, p: 28) states:

> ... there is ample evidence that the women in sport and physical education who are lesbian have to survive in a most inhospitable climate because of the pervasiveness of homophobia, which often takes the form of discriminatory hiring and firing practices.

Indeed, Gert Hekma's (1994) research into the discrimination that Dutch lesbian women and gay men experience in organised sports in Holland was pointedly titled: 'Als ze maar niet provoceren' ('If they don't provoke'), a comment that was made by two sports clubs who said that they had no problems with gays and lesbians as long as they did not provoke. This would appear to mean that it's OK to be a lesbian or gay man in sport, but don't make it obvious, don't do anything that will give your (homo) sexuality away. It is clear from this small scale research that these women make every attempt not to make their sexuality obvious; for instance, only two of the 14 women interviewed were totally out in their sports; the remainder were either out to only a small group of friends or to none of their team mates. For those who were out to a certain extent, this was not necessarily a positive experience. Harriet revealed that her team mates at hockey found out more by mistake than design and that she wished they didn't know. She made it clear that she has no intention of telling those with whom she plays other sports. Further to this, she commented:

> When some of my married, heterosexual friends at hockey found out about me, they quickly changed their way of relating to me and talking to me. I felt let down obviously and, but I also felt "dirty", like I really was doing something wrong.

This feeling "dirty" reveals still further the power of the lesbian label to intimidate women regardless of their sexuality. However, it should not be thought from these examples that lesbian women are powerless — rather, by virtue of living a lesbian existence they are challenging compulsory heterosexuality. And for some women, the lesbian label is a powerful source of unity and pride. Lenskyj (1994, p: 365) reveals how:

> Lesbian sporting leagues organized on feminist principles provide one example of the potential for sport to be reclaimed ... (and) to include the celebration of female physicality and sexuality.

Though Lenskyj is referring to sporting leagues in North America, it should be noted that there are a number of lesbian sporting teams, for example: 'Dynamo dykes' (volleyball), 'South London Studs' (football), 'The London Amazons' (softball) and 'London Hiking Dykes' (a lesbian walking group). What is indicated, though, by Harriet is that lesbianism is something to be feared and avoided in case of contamination. Again in the light of such views, it is no wonder that many women may fear even entry to the sports field. I find these fears and phobias in some ways paradoxical, and in many ways confusing. If LeVay's (see Vines, 1992: p. 2) claims are accepted — that homosexuals are *born*, not *made*, since sexual orientation is established in the womb as a result of the action of hormones on the brain of the developing foetus — how then can anybody become 'contaminated'? They've either already 'got' it (that is lesbianism), or they haven't! What I also find interesting, yet troubling, is the scrutiny with which we interrogate lesbianism, yet in the main heterosexuality has largely escaped this. (A notable exception is the work by Sue Wilkinson and Celia Kitzinger.) In reflecting on Harriet's words, what is perhaps most disturbing is how she is led to feel, that it is something wrong and dirty that she is engaged in. In the light of her feelings and the actions of homophobic heterosexuals it is no wonder that the suicide rate for young lesbians and gays is higher than for other groups. Are lesbian women really so dangerous? Certainly there seems to be a belief that we are, that we threaten the cultural norms of heterosexuality and patriarchal power, and that other women need to be protected from us. Where, might we ask, is the evidence that supports these views?

The impact of the events described above is abundantly clear; to be out is a personal risk, the costs of which many understandably are not prepared to face. These concerns, I would argue, serve to keep most sporting lesbians invisible and silent and preserves the privileging of the hegemonic heterosexual order.

It should be noted, though, that this is not the case for all lesbian women: some have found the space within sport to occupy the ground that they wish — as Yvonne Zipter (1988) clearly describes in 'Diamond's are a dyke's best friend'. And more latterly this is illustrated by Susan Fox Rogers (1994) in 'Sportsdykes: stories from on and off the field'. Both books celebrate and explore the lesbian sports experience. Zipter writes about dykes in softball, "... assessing its [softball] place and function in our community nation-wide, why most of us love it (but some of us don't), its origins, foibles, and pitfalls" (Zipter, 1988: p. 14). Rogers, on the other hand, has edited a rather eclectic collection of articles which range "From serious investigative journalism to works of lyrical fiction, the life of the 'girl jock' is vividly revealed..." (Rogers, 1994: Front book jacket).

Before closing, I want to return to some of the findings of Hekma's (1994) research since they are relevant to my own findings. Perhaps most telling was his conclusion that discrimination against lesbians and gay men occurs regularly in organised sport. Though the women interviewed for this research had not all been subject to homophobic comments and so on, the majority thought that it was common in sport. Hekma found that the most common form of abuse took that of verbal comments. This too was evidenced by the women in this study, and took the form of remarks made by spectators or passers by. Some of the women were also subjected to anti-lesbian comments from their team-mates rather than the opposition. By way of contrast, some of the women had had no experience of homophobia — but I would suggest that this may be associated with the fact that they are so deeply hidden in the closet, that nobody knows they are there.

In conclusion, it can be seen how — for this group of women — a lesbian existence is perceived as somewhat perilous. The conservative world of education and in particular physical education makes for a precarious existence for lesbian teachers. To survive requires that these teachers are able to at least 'pass' as heterosexual and to cover their lesbian tracks. The sporting world for these women is not so dissimilar to that of education. The homophobia and heterosexism faced by these women has led them in the main to continue to conceal their lesbian identity. What is manifest from both these worlds is the power of the lesbian label to force women into narrowly prescribed gender roles; it is a power that few feel able to confront and challenge. Until we remove the power and stigma of the lesbian label, little is likely to change.

References

Clarke, G. (1994) 'The research that dare not speak its name: doing controversial research in physical education', Conference Proceedings of the 10th Commonwealth & Scientific Congress University of Victoria, Canada.

Cahn, S. K. (1994) *Coming on strong: Gender and sexuality in twentieth-century women's sport*. New York: The Free Press.

Campbell, B. (1995) 'Hard lessons', *Diva* (Aug/Sept): pp. 18-21.

Colvin, M. with Hawksley, J. (1989) *Section 28: A practical guide to the law and its implications*. London: National Council for Civil Liberties.

Dewar, A. (1993) 'Would all the generic women in sport please stand up? Challenges facing feminist sport sociology', *Quest*, Vol. 45, No. 2: pp. 211-229.

Epstein, D. (ed) (1994) *Challenging lesbian and gay inequalities in education*. Buckingham: Open University Press.

Felshin, J. (1974) 'The dialectic of woman and sport', in E. W. Gerber, J. Felshin, P. Berlin and W. Wyrick (eds) *The American woman in sport*. USA: Addison-Wesley Publishing Company, pp. 179-279.

Gerber, E. W., Felshin, J., Berlin, P. and Wyrick, W. (1974) *The American woman in sport.* USA: Addison-Wesley Publishing Company.

Griffin, P. (1991) 'Identity management strategies among lesbian and gay educators', *Qualitative Studies in Education,* Vol. 4, No. 3: pp. 189-202.

—— (1992) 'From hiding out to coming out: Empowering lesbian and gay educators', in K. M. Harbeck (ed) *Coming out of the classroom closet: gay and lesbian students, teachers, and curricula.* New York: Harrington Park Press.

Hargreaves, J. (1994) *Sporting females: Critical issues in the history and sociology of women's sports.* London: Routledge.

Hekma, G. (1994) *Als ze maar niet provoceren. Discriminatie van homoseksuele mannen en lesbische vrouwen in de georganiseerde sport.* Amsterdam: Het Spinhuis.

Khayatt, M. D. (1992) *Lesbian teachers: An invisible presence.* USA: State University of New York Press.

Kitzinger, C. (1987) *The social construction of lesbianism.* London: Sage Publications.

Kolnes, L. (19950 'Heterosexuality as an organising principle in women's sport', *International Review for Sociology of Sport,* Vol. 30, No.1: pp. 61-77.

Lather, P. (1986) 'Issues of validity in openly ideological research: between a rock and a hard place', *Interchange,* Vol. 17, No. 4, Winter: pp. 63-84.

Lenskyj, H. (1990) 'Combating homophobia in sports', *Off Our Backs,* Vol. 20, No. 6: pp. 2-3.

—— (1992) 'Unsafe at home base: Women's experiences of sexual harassment in university sport and physical education', *Women in Sport and Physical Activity Journal,* Vol. 1, No. 1, Spring: pp. 19-33.

—— (1994) 'Sexuality and femininity in sport contexts: Issues and alternatives', *Journal of Sport and Social Issues,* November, Vol. 18, No. 4: pp. 357-376.

Messner, M. and Sabo, D. (1994) *Sex, violence and power in sports: rethinking masculinity.* USA: The Crossing Press.

Miller, N. (1995) *Out of the past: Gay and lesbian history from 1869 to the present.* UK: Vintage.

Moses, A. E. (1978) *Identity management in lesbian women.* USA: Praeger Publishers.

Pharr, S. (1988) *Homophobia: A weapon of sexism.* USA: Chardon Press.

Rich, A. (1980) 'Compulsory heterosexuality and lesbian existence', *Signs: Journal of Women in Culture and Society*, Vol. 5, No. 4: pp. 631-660.

Rogers, S. F. (ed) (1994) *Sportsdykes: Stories from on and off the field.* New York: St Martin's Press.

Sears, J. T. (1992) 'Researching the other/searching for self: Qualitative research on (homo)sexuality in education', *Theory into Practice*, Vol. XXX1, No. 2, Spring: pp. 147-156.

Smith, A. M. (1994) *New Right discourse on race and sexuality: Britain, 1968-1990.* Great Britain: Cambridge University Press.

———— (1995) 'Resisting the "New Homophobia" and the Right's evisceration of liberal democracy', paper presented at the New Sexual Agendas Conference, Middlesex University, 14-15 July.

Smith, D. E. (1987) *The everyday world as problematic: A feminist sociology.* Milton Keynes: Open University Press.

Sparkes, A. C. (ed) (1992) *Research in physical education and sport: Exploring alternative visions.* London: Falmer Press.

———— (1994) 'Self, silence and invisibility as a beginning teacher: A life history of lesbian experience', *British Journal of Sociology of Education*, Vol. 15, No. 1: pp. 93-118.

Squirrell, G. (1989a) 'In passing...teachers and sexual orientation', in S. Acker (ed) *Teachers, gender and careers.* London: Falmer Press.

———— (1989b) 'Teachers and issues of sexual orientation', *Gender and Education*, Vol. 1, No. 1: pp. 17-34.

Troiden, R. R. (1988) *Gay and lesbian identity: A sociological analysis.* New York: General Hall, Inc.

Vallee, M., Redwood, H. and Evenden, M. (1992) *Out, proud and militant: The fight for lesbian and gay rights and the fight for socialism.* London: Militant.

Vines, G. (1992) 'Obscure origins of desire', *New Scientist*, 28 November, No. 3: pp. 2-8.

Wilkinson. S. and Kitzinger, C. (eds) (1993) *Heterosexuality: A feminism and psychology reader.* London: Sage Publications Ltd.

Woods, S. (1992) 'Describing the experience of lesbian physical educators: A phenomenological study', in A. Sparkes (ed) *Research in physical education and sport: Exploring alternative visions.* London: Falmer Press.

Zipter, Y. (1988) *Diamonds are a dyke's best friend.* USA: Firebrand Books.

Examinations in Physical Education and Sport: Gender Differences and Influences on Subject Choice

Bob Carroll

University of Manchester

Introduction

The introduction and development of examinations in Physical Education (PE) and sport at school and further education (FE) level over the last twenty five years has been discussed by Carroll (1982, 1994). This development has included the following; the introduction of the first examinations at the Certificate of Secondary Education (CSE) level at mode 3 (school syllabus and assessment with external moderation) in the 1970s; the introduction of PE in 1986 in the General Certificate of Secondary Education (GCSE), which was a new examination at 16+, an amalgamation of the former General Certificate of Education (GCE) and the CSE; and the establishment of syllabuses (PE and Sport Studies) at GCE 'A' level. These have been paralleled by the development of vocational examinations in recreation and leisure in the FE sector (Carroll 1994). These have included the following; the introduction of City and Guilds (C&G) in the 1970s and the later development of syllabus 781; the entry of the Business and Technology Council's (BTEC) college based courses in the mid 1980s, and more recently the advent of General National Vocational Qualifications (GNVQ). Most of the early C&G courses were initiated by PE teachers in FE colleges and had a sport bias, whilst many of the BTEC courses had a sport focus.

Carroll (1994) identified four phases and their characteristics in the development of examinations. These were:

1. Early 1970s Introduction of CSE in PE in specific regions. Getting established and accepted, ironing out difficulties

2. Mid/late 1970s Extension of CSE to all regions. Expansion of number of centres and pupils.

3. Early 1980s   Introduction of CSE mode 1's (examining board's syllabus and assessment) in PE in certain regions. Change from mode 3 to 1. Slower expansion.

4. Mid/late 1980s   Introduction of GCSE in PE, and pilot 'A'level in PE and Sport Studies. Rapid expansion of GCSE. Refinement of syllabuses and assessment.

Now, it can be suggested that we are in phase five of development. This phase can be said to have started in the early 1990s with the general acceptance of GCSE, whilst the A levels came out of their successful pilot stage and increased the number of centres and candidates in both syllabuses. On the vocational front, the early 1990s have seen the piloting of the new GNVQs in Leisure and Tourism. Many students interested in sport and jobs within sports facilities and provision take this route.

Current situation in examinations in PE and sport

The current situation is that there are two general types of courses and qualifications in PE and Sport in schools and colleges, the academic and the vocational. The academic route includes GCSE PE offered by all four English examining groups, The Midland Examining Group (MEG), the Northern Examinations and Assessment Board (NEAB), the Southern Examining Group (SEG), the University of London Examinations and Asessment Council (ULEAC), and also by the Welsh Joint Education Committee (WJEC) and the Northern Ireland Schools Curriculum and Assessment Council (NISEAC). The academic route also includes the two A level syllabuses in PE and Sport Studies offered by the Associated Examining Board (AEB). There are also GCSE's in Dance (NEAB) and Outdoor Education (NEAB, ULEAC) and an A level in Dance offered by ULEAC. In Scotland where there is a different system, the Scottish Examination Board (SEB) offers an examination in PE at both Standard Grade (SG) and Higher Grade (HG), the equivalent of GCSE and A level respectively. The vocational route offers more general courses in recreation and leisure at four levels. There has been an emphasis on developing GNVQ levels 2 and 3, the equivalent of National Diploma (ND) and Higher National Diploma (HND). GNVQ level 1, approximately equivalent to the GCSE, is now being developed at present. The standardisation of syllabuses through GNVQ means that both C&G and BTEC offer the same, but there is still the option to offer college based courses with BTEC, and some colleges do continue to offer sport science and their own leisure courses at ND and HND levels.

One thing which stands out across all the phases is the increase in interest in qualifications in PE, sport, recreation and leisure. This is reflected in the numbers of candidates for all the examinations. For example, the figures for GCSE PE increased from 18,831 in 1988 (the first year of GCSE) to 56,449 in 1994 for the five examining groups in England and Wales, which is approximately three times as many candidates in six years, and makes it one of the fastest growing subjects. The provisional figures for 1995 are around 68,000. In Scotland, the figures increased from 6060 (1990) to 13,317 by 1994 in SG, and there were 1889 candidates for the first HG examination in 1994. It has not been possible to get precise figures of registrations for vocational courses for each year, but in 1991/2 there were 7864 registrations for BTEC and 7468 registrations for C&G across all levels in recreation and leisure studies. In 1993/4 there were 2578 candidates for GNVQs, now out of its pilot period (Young 1994). According to a press release from the Joint Council of National Vocational Awarding Bodies there have been 9753 GNVQ awards in Leisure and Tourism over the three levels of foundation, intermediate and advanced with the majority being at the intermediate stage.

The explanation for the introduction and expansion of examinations has been discussed by Carroll (1994). What is remarkable about the development of PE as an examination subject at school level in the first phases in the 1970s is the establishment against very strong institutional opposition, such as the examination boards and their advisers. Carroll (1994) has shown the need to change the ideological base of PE from recreational to educational in both schools and colleges at that time. The development was tied up with status of the subject, and this is also relevant to developments in phase five. What is particularly different about the current phase is the political ideological climate of the 1990s. This is one of market forces philosophy applied to education, so schools and colleges are in competition with each other. This is effected through parental choice and a per capita funding system. One of the yardsticks of school and college performance has always been examination results, but the Government has intensified the use of this measure by publishing examination results league tables which contain both academic and vocational qualifications. Not surprisingly, what this has done is to value examination subjects and their results more highly, and has put a premium on those subjects which can contribute to league table success. These subjects will gain the most resources within the school or college. Therefore we are likely to see an increasing number of schools and colleges entering the examination field in areas such as PE and Sport Studies and vocational qualifications such as Leisure and Tourism. The recommendations of the Dearing Review, which suggested that schools be allowed to develop a wider range of courses including vocational at key stage 4 will probably mean the expansion of vocational courses in schools (Dearing, 1993). Also, we are going to see an increasing emphasis on selection of pupils for examination subjects, and discouragement for those not likely to do well. This will apply equally to PE as other subjects, and it has a direct and very strong bearing on subject choice, which I will come to later in this paper.

Gender differential

A breakdown of examination statistics for academic examinations by gender in PE and related areas (dance, outdoor education) over several years reveals a consistent pattern of a discrepancy between the number of

male and female entries. Separate statistics for males and females have not
always been available, particularly through the CSE years. However, data
gathered by Carroll (1982) directly from the schools shows this discrepancy
has existed since the early days. A perusal of the GCSE years shows that
there is little difference in the level of this discrepancy in any year. Table 1
shows the number of entries for 1992 and 1994 for GCSE in PE, Dance
and Outdoor Education, the three subjects which come under the umbrella
of PE in the National Curriculum, and A levels in PE, Sport Studies and
Dance, and for SG and HG in Scotland.

**Table 1   Number of candidates for academic qualifications
in PE areas by gender 1994 and 1992 (in brackets)**

Exam group	Exam title	Total	Males	%	Females	%
MEG	GCSE PE	10,648 (7252)	7258 (5003)	68 (69)	3390 (2249)	32 (31)
NEAB	GCSE PE	13,401 (10,130)	8822 (6565)	69 (65)	4579 (3565)	31 (35)
	GCSE Dance	3,639 (1268)	223 (72)	06 (06)	3411 (1196)	94 (94)
	GCSE OE	118 (119)	83 (99)	70 (83)	35 (20)	30 (17)
SEG	GCSE PE 1	13,634 (10,629)	9083 (6947)	67 (65)	4551 (3673)	33 (35)
	GCSE PE 2/3	626 (598)	395 (429)	63 (72)	231 (169)	37 (28)
ULEAC	GCSE PE 1*	14,215 (8799)	9736 (5908)	68 (67)	4474 (2891)	32 (33)
	GCSE PE 3	54	35	65	19	35
	'A' l. Dance	518	49	09	470	91
WJEC	GCSE PE	3871 (3305)	2466 (2094)	64 (63)	1405 (1211)	36 (32)
SEB	PE SG	13,317 (11,520)	9340 (7793)	70 (67)	3397 (3577)	30 (33)
	PE HG	1889	1295	69	594	31
AEB	"A' l. PE	3621 (1361)	2357 (795)	65 (58)	1264 (566)	35 (42)
	'A' l. SS	2015 (1113)	1281 (696)	64 (63)	734 (407)	36 (37)

* 1991 figures in brackets

These figures reveal that there were always approximately twice as many males as females entered for the PE examination, yet 1994 was a year when there were more females than males entered for GCSE and more female subject entries across all the subjects. There is a remarkable consistency across all the examining groups, for example, the percentage of males entered for GCSE PE mode 1 for each group in 1994 was 68, 69, 67, 68 and 64, and 70 in SG in Scotland. The four English groups increased their entries between 32% and 45% from 1992 to 1994, but the biggest change in the gender differential was 4% increase in favour of males (NEAB). All this shows that the variety in the syllabuses makes no difference to the gender discrepancy and not one syllabus favours the girls. Also, the massive increase in interest is attracting males and females in the same proportion as before.

The A level statistics reveal a similar picture. The syllabuses show a 65% and 64% entry for males in 1994. Sport Studies showed an increase in entries of 90% from 1992 to 1994 but the ratio of males to females remained almost identical, whilst in PE the increase in entries was in the order of a phenomenal 180% and this resulted in an increase of 7% males. In Scotland, HG produced a 69%–31% split in favour of males.

The figures for Dance are equally revealing. The NEAB GCSE is now the only one offered at this level, and the dropping of MEG's and ULEAC's syllabuses possibly accounts in part for the huge increase of 187% in entries on the 1992 figure. However, this has made no difference to the gender discrepancy, which in this case is 94%–6% in favour of the females. ULEAC's A level in Dance shows a female to male ratio of 91%–9%.

It has not been possible to obtain the equivalent figures for all the years for vocational qualifications, but a perusal of statistics for the years obtained reveals a similar differential, for example, in 1991/2 the number of registrations across all levels shows BTEC registrations as 63% to 37% ratio and C&G as 69% to 31% ratio in favour of males. This differential is narrowed slightly at the higher levels where there are considerably less entries and also after awards have been given, which may mean there is a higher drop out or failure rate with males. However, the GNVQ awards in Leisure and Tourism reveals an equal balance between the sexes (Fitzgibbon, 1995). This may be a result of different syllabuses combining tourism with leisure rather than a real change in the gender differential in leisure studies. In my analysis of the gender differential below, I will not deal with vocational qualifications because of the different nature of the syllabuses and it requires a separate investigation. However, some of the explanations and issues raised will have some applicability to vocational qualifications, particularly where there is a sport focus.

All these figures show that in a period of rapid expansion when, perhaps, under-represented groups might be expected to increase their proportion of entries, the male to female ratio remained almost the same.

It is not clear why this gender differential exists and is so persistent. It does not appear to have been investigated before, although gender issues in PE have been discussed frequently, for example, Evans (1984, 1989, 1993), Leaman (1984), Scraton(1986,1992), Talbot(1990), and in relation to dance by Flintoff (1991). Research has shown that girls have a less favourable attitude to PE at this age (Van Wersch, Trew and Turner, 1992), and participate less in physical activity and sport (Cale and Almond, 1992. Sports Council 1994). Therefore it can be assumed that the differential is a function of these factors. However, I wanted to treat it as more problematic than that because there may be other factors at work. For example, it is not apparent whether the differential is due to individual preferences and aspirations, or to institutional constraints and barriers, or any other pressures such as parents, peers or more general societal ones. The figures suggest that there is an equal opportunity and equity issue, but whether this is an institutional access problem is not clear. This issue is one of increasing importance as PE examinations can provide career opportunities in a way that PE did not do previously. It is not only a question of access to a qualification as such, but also access to the different zones of knowledge contained in the examination syllabuses. This is because the GCSE PE course is entirely different to non examination PE (see Carroll, 1994). GCSE PE alters what Bernstein (1972) called the "classification" and "framing" of the subject. That is, it extended the boundaries of the subject and the way it was taught. The two routes provide different educational experiences which can influence leisure and career choices. The research on examination subject choice, for example Stables (1990, 1995), at both GCSE and A level neglects PE, but this perhaps is not surprising when one considers the relative newness of PE as an examination subject. It is however included in some research on subject preference, for example, Harvey (1984), and Stables (1990).

In an attempt to examine this issue, it has been incorporated into a research project on influences and advice on subject choice. Phase one of this project has included samples of year 10 pupils and first year A level students, a total of around 400 from two schools and two colleges. Data has been collected through questionnaires and group discussions and interviews. The sample includes respondents who have chosen PE as an examination subject and those who have not. Year 10 pupils were asked why they did or did not choose PE as an examination course, and A level students were asked why they selected their subjects. Both groups were asked about the advice they had received. At this stage of the research I am more interested in the range of explanations for choice and influences upon those choices in the selection process. I am conscious too that the sample size is small and not representative enough to answer the question more generally. However, the responses may well be indicators of the type of explanations more generally. Therefore I am incorporating these findings and ideas into the following discussion without giving detailed statistics.

Subject choice

Subject choice is a complex social process. It is a combination of personal perceptions and mediating influences.

Personal perceptions

Research shows that the most important reasons for choosing a subject for both girls and boys is liking it and being good at it, and in addition for examination subjects, career requirements (Harvey, 1984, Stables, 1990). For this study too, these are the most prominent reasons at both GCSE and 'A' level with career featuring more strongly with 'A' level students as one would expect. For those pupils in year 10 not taking PE as a GCSE subject, 'not liking PE', 'not liking some of the activities' in GCSE featured strongly for both boys and girls as reasons for not taking it, whilst 'not good at PE' was given much more often by girls than boys. "Not liking PE" may reflect gender biased syllabuses. The syllabuses were drawn up by panels of men and women specialist PE teachers so this is unlikely, and an analysis of the syllabuses reveals that the practical activities offered reflect activities normally available to both boys and girls PE in the curriculum. However, it may be the activities offered in GCSE in any one school, who teaches them or the way they are presented which reflect a gender bias. It is the area of theoretical knowledge which is not usually offered in the non examination curriculum, and it is possible that sports science does not appeal to the girls as much as the boys. However, it is not clear how much detail the pupils know of the actual content or teaching of the examination course or how this affects subject choice. It is likely to be based on their experiences of PE prior to the choice.

Perceived competence is clearly an important factor in subject choice. 'Not being good at PE' may partly reflect a lack of confidence in some cases rather than a true lack of ability to take the subject at this level. Research has shown that lack of confidence in other subjects is stronger for girls in mixed schools rather than single sex schools (Stables, 1990). Therefore this may also apply to PE, and lack of confidence may be stronger in mixed PE contexts than in single sex, where girls may make unfair comparisons in relation to physical attributes or in relation to specific contexts of activities. The context in which pupils most often have to show their ability in PE is within direct intensive competition, for example, in games or athletics, and this is different to other subjects and may not favour some girls. The physical activities offered by the school before year 10 and in GCSE PE will be crucial in their perceptions of the subject, and their decision to take it as an examination subject. However, the range of contexts in GCSE PE in which pupils have to show their ability is greater than in National Curriculum PE, and includes knowledge and understanding in a written form in which girls could do better. However one of the areas of knowledge and understanding is sport science, which may not appeal to girls as much as boys, but I have no evidence that this is so. It would be interesting to see whether there were any differences in the performances of boys and girls on different aspects of the syllabus, such as, the practical performance, sport science knowledge, social science knowledge, activity knowledge or project, but there is no breakdown available. The nearest information available is from SEB, which shows that girls did better in knowledge and understanding but worse in evaluating and in practical performances (SEB 1995). It should be noted that those girls who did take GCSE PE in 1994 did better than the boys at higher grades, for example, in all English examining groups the percentage of girls gaining A's and B's was higher by 1%, 2.4%, 3.4%, 0.6%, and they did better at A-C grades in all except one. The difference at 'A' level was 7.7% (PE) and 2.7% (SS) at the two highest grades in favour of the girls. The exception to this was in Scotland where boys did better than girls. The better performance of girls is probably a function of a greater selectivity process, a combination of school and personal processes discussed in this paper.

Individual decisions of liking or not liking a subject such as PE may relate to the subject itself, for example, the nature and content, or the way it is presented or taught. This is reflected in such answers as 'don't like some activities' (frequently given) and 'don't like the way it is taught' given by a minority of those not taking GCSE PE. However, their experiences over many years build up to general perceptions of their liking or disliking, the origins of which cannot often be specified. However, these are tied to the general nature of the physical activity and sport context and mask perceptions of the suitability of PE and dance for boys and girls in general and as individuals more specifically. Thus the very nature of the subject, the masculine image of many sports, media images of sport, and compatibility with images of femininity and masculinity have been identified as influencing factors in boys' greater participation and interest in PE and sport (see Scraton 1986, 1992, Evans 1993). The same argument in reverse in respect of the sexes may be made for dance and its compatibility and acceptability with males (see Flintoff 1991). The numbers taking dance as an examination subject certainly bears this out. These factors, plus the greater numbers of males taking part in extra curricular activities in the schools and in GCSE PE, may well influence the perceptions of the subject as predominately male. However, very few of either the GCSE or 'A' level samples thought that the subject was more suitable for males, and where they did, there was a tendency for males to state this rather than females. This was an unexpected finding. Stables (1990) has suggested that girls may conform to gender stereotypes in their subject choices in relation to science. Therefore, this finding may mean that some girls in their subject choices are conforming to a gender stereotype in not selecting PE, but are not perceiving the subject in gender specific terms. Perhaps perceptions and images of PE and sport as a male preserve are changing.

Boys and girls perceptions of PE as an examination subject were sought to see whether they accounted for a difference in uptake. Most thought that examinations in PE were a good idea, that they did not spoil the enjoyment, that they would improve skills and knowledge, though it would not necessarily help them to work harder in PE. There was little differences between boys and girls, so this is unlikely to affect the gender differential.

Mediators and influences

Whilst there are a number of personal perceptions to be considered, such as ability, and career aspirations, individual pupil decisions are influenced in varying degrees by parents, teachers, friends, other relations and career advisors in each case. There is no simple equation. In any individual decision, any of the above people could be an important 'choice mediator' (Wood 1976). All of the above were mentioned frequently in the present study not only as people to ask and receive advice, but also as having influence on the decision. In Wood's (1976) research, sometimes the influence of these mediators was so strong as in the cases of parental compulsion and strong guidance, and in the case of institutional 'channelling', that he refers to the process as 'the myth of subject choice'. There were examples, particularly of the latter, in this study.

The influence of parents in this study appeared to be strong. The majority of both GCSE and 'A' level samples had received advice from at least one of their parents, and a large number admitted to having been influenced by it. Advice tended to be, 'take subjects good at', 'take subjects like', ' relate to a job', but there appears to have been little direct career advice. There appeared to be no difference between the sexes. There was evidence of some encouragement by parents, and very few instances of discouragement and no sex differences here also. There were a few however who appeared to have received no advice at GCSE level. This relates to the research of Wood (1976), who identified two groups of pupils with different perspectives, basically two polarised sub cultures, pro school and anti school, but these two were also related to social class of parents. The middle class group of parents gave the most advice and were a much stronger and more powerful influence. Therefore it can be expected that middle class parents take a more active role in subject choice, regardless of the sex of their children. In the present study there is no data on social class. However, some children received none or very little advice. In the present climate of the intensification of examination results with league tables, Wood's (1976) research suggests that the middle class group would benefit. However, other aspects have changed since 1976 such as the lack of jobs on leaving school, and the greater numbers staying on in education after age 16, so there is a need to look at this issue again.

One of the mediators which Wood did not mention is friends. Friends did give advice and sometimes influenced decisions, and 'friends not doing it' was given as a reason for not taking GCSE PE in some instances and more often by girls than boys. At 'A' level and GCSE level it was mentioned occasionally as a reason for taking PE and more often by males.

Schools and teachers play a strong mediating role in three ways: the presentation of option blocks, the selection process on pupil options, and encouragement/discouragement of choices. The option block in which PE appears will play a crucial part in pupil selection because of subject preferences and perception of status of a subject. There are a number of subjects which tend to always have more entries from either males or females, so, putting it into a block with other subjects which girls favour, such as, expressive arts, music, home economics, art and design, history, and languages may reduce the entries for PE. This could partly be an answer to the differential in some schools. In the present study, both boys and girls of the non GCSE PE candidates preferred other subjects in the option block, but this answer was given by many more girls. Also, many more females than males saw other subjects in the option block as more important than PE. This may relate to the status of PE more generally and girls perception of it, or, to the particular subjects at each school. Although PE comes very high up in subject preference with both boys and girls in some research, it comes low down in subject importance in the same research. Stables (1990) reported that only drama , music, religious education were lower in importance with the boys, and music, drama, craft and religious education lower for girls in mixed schools, and only the first two of these were lower in importance for girls in single sex schools. Status is clearly an important variable in subject choice, and particularly for those who may not have high ability in the subject, and for those who do not need it for career aspirations. This may relate to perceived competence in the subject.

Whilst there was evidence in some instances of teacher encouragement and discouragement, there was also evidence of a more direct influence through the subject selection process. A number of pupils stated that PE was not open to them and only certain pupils were allowed to take it, and there were more instances of girls stating this than boys. There is no doubt that this is partly related to the ability of the pupils and the teachers perceptions of how well they will do. Are girls at a disadvantage here, particularly in mixed PE settings, where their performances could be seen in a less favourable light in relation to boys? For some pupils clearly, in some subjects, it is only an illusion of choice, which supports Wood's findings (Wood, 1976). This selection process is now becoming stricter as the need to show good examination results for the league tables. In the days of CSE, pupils in low ability groups were often encouraged to take PE in the hope that they would achieve something even if it was a low grade, and even 'sink' groups were not unknown in PE (Carroll 1982). It is now clear that only the better pupils will be encouraged to take the subject. Perhaps girls are not getting the encouragement they need, particularly if they lack confidence as has already been suggested.

Some children choose subjects because they are an easy option (Wood, 1976), and even if non examination PE is seen as easy, GCSE and A level PE are not easy options. They demand a wide range of abilities, both intellectual and physical, and many pupils in this study at both GCSE and A level mention the commitment required and the heavy workload. It does not suit the non committed or those lacking in confidence, and this message may well be spread by friends, if not by teachers.

In the early days of CSE there was a gender bias in favour of boys, and this appeared to be due to the higher interest of male PE teachers. There were more single sex schools and separate departments for boys and girls in mixed schools. Often only boys would be offered CSE PE. Although the situation has changed and there are now more mixed schools and PE departments, it may be that there are still more male PE teachers favouring examination courses than female, and so are more inclined to become involved. If this is the case, then it may well influence pupil choice, with less girls choosing PE as an examination subject. However, it is not known from this research whether this is the case or a reason for it. Perhaps the combined factors of the number of male and female teachers involved in examination work and the teacher selection process result in the school unwittingly colluding in the gender stereotyping of PE and Dance.

Conclusion

The gender differential in PE examinations is very clear and consistent over the years. In view of the attention given to equal opportunity issues in education generally (see Weiner, 1985), and the attack on the gender differential in certain subjects (see Stables, 1990), and the issues raised in PE by such writers as Evans (1993), Leaman (1984), and Talbot (1990), it might be expected that the differential would have been eroded, at least to a degree, by 1994. This is clearly not the case at either GCSE or A level. or in any particular syllabus. An examination of the syllabuses does not reveal any particular gender biases. Clearly there is an equal opportunity and equity issue here with an access problem to qualifications. These qualifications, and particularly A levels, are increasingly used as a general qualification for entry into higher education, and more specifically for careers in PE, sport and leisure. This has established a growing link between school and college PE and sport and careers in teaching and leisure. These qualifications open up different zones of knowledge than non examination PE. Therefore, this gender differential and access problem needs to be explained. However, the explanation is certain to be complex and multifaceted.

A review of this study reveals that the explanation lies in a combination of personal preferences and perceptions which give rise to personal constraints, for example, perceptions of ability and status of the subject, and mediating influences, which result in institutional constraints and barriers, such as presentation of the option block and the teachers' selection process. Some expected findings such as girls' perceptions of PE as a male subject, and examinations in PE not being a good idea were not confirmed. This may mean that some girls in their subject choices are conforming to a gender stereotype in not selecting PE, but are not perceiving the subject in gender specific terms. It is also suggested that the school is colluding, though unwittingly, in this process. It is clear that this research has not fully clarified the reasons for the differential, and has left many questions to be answered in a later phase.

References

Bernstein, B. (1972) 'On the classification and framing of educational knowledge', in M. F. D. Young (ed) *Knowledge and control.* London: Collier-MacMillan.

Cale, L. A. & Almond, L. (1992) 'Children's activity levels: A review of studies conducted on British Children', *Physical Education Review*, Vol. 15, No. 2: pp. 111-117.

Carroll, B. (1982) 'Examinations and curriculum change', *Physical Education Review*, Vol. 5, No. 1: pp. 26-36.

———— (1994) *Assessment in Physical Education.* London: Falmer.

Dearing, R. (1993) *The National Curriculum and its assessment.* (Final report). London: SCAA.

Evans, J. (1984) 'Muscle, sweat and showers. Girls' conception of the PE curriculum. A challenge for research and curriculum reform', *Physical Education Review* Vol. 7, No. 1: pp. 12-18.

———— (1989) 'Swinging from the crossbar. Equality and opportunity in the PE curriculum', *British Journal of Physical Education*, Vol. 20, No. 2: pp. 86-87.

Evans, J. (ed) (1993) *Equality, education and physical education.* London: Falmer.

Fitzgibbon, C. (1995) 'Teaching and learning in A level and Vocational courses'. Paper given at ECER 95 conference, University of Bath.

Flintoff, A. (1991) 'Dance, masculinity and teacher education', *British Journal of Physical Education*, Vol. 22, No. 4: pp. 31-35.

Harvey, T. J. (1984) 'Gender differences in subject preference and perceptions of subject importance among third year secondary school pupils in single sex and mixed comprehensive schools', *Educational Studies*, Vol. 10, No. 3: pp. 243-253.

Joint Council of National Vocational Awarding Bodies. (1995) Press release. August 21.

Leaman, O. (1984) *Sit on the sidelines and watch the boys play. Sex differentiation in physical education.* London: Longman.

Scraton, S. (1986) 'Images of femininity in the teaching of girls' PE', in J. Evans (ed) *Physical education, sport and schooling.* London: Falmer.

—— (1992) Shaping *up to womanhood; Gender and girls' physical education*. Milton Keynes: Open University Press.

Scottish Examination Board (1995) *Gender and SCE examinations*. (Research 3). Dalkeith: SEB.

Sports Council. (1994) *OPCS National survey of young people and sport*. London: Sports Council.

Stables, A. (1990) 'Differences between pupils from mixed and single sex schools in their enjoyment of school subjects and their attitude to science and to school', *Educational Review*, Vol. 42, No. 3: pp. 221-230.

—— (1995) 'Gender differences in students' approach to A level subject choices and perceptions of A level subjects: a study of first year A level students in a tertiary college', *Educational Research*, Vol. 37, No. 1: pp. 39-51.

Talbot, M. (1990) 'Equal opportunities and physical education', in N. Armstrong (ed) *New directions in physical education* (Vol. 1). Leeds: Human Kinetics.

Van Wersch, A. , Trew, K. & Turner, I. (1992) 'Post-primary school pupils' interest in physical education: age and gender differences', *British Journal of Educational Psychology*, Vol. 62, No. 2: pp. 56-72.

Weiner, G. (1985) *Just a bunch of girls*. Milton Keynes: Open University Press.

Wood, P. (1976) 'The myth of subject choice', *British Journal of Sociology*, Vol. 27, No. 2: pp. 130-149.

Young, S. (1994) 'GNVQs beat path to degrees', *Times Educational Supplement*. 26 August.

Gender and Adolescent Sexual Cultures: The View from Some Boys

Lynda Measor, Coralie Tiffin, and Katrina Fry

University of Brighton

Introduction

This paper is based on a piece of research concerned with adolescents' informal cultures which affect and structure their leisure patterns. It focuses specifically on adolescent sexuality and draws attention to the gendered nature of these cultures and indicates the extent to which boys and girls bring different values and perspectives to the subject. The data indicate the importance of gendered informal cultures for understanding leisure patterns amongst adolescents, and shows that interventions which seek to inform or alter those cultures need to take account of them.

We know very little about adolescent sexuality and it is difficult to research. This study looked at sex education seeing it as an arena where patterns of adolescent sexuality might be accessible to study. It concentrates on gender issues and suggests that girls and boys respond differently to sex education schemes and that boys react more negatively than girls. While we document the reactions of all pupils in this paper, the focus is on understanding the reactions of the boys and patterns of male sexuality and masculinity.

Methodology

The data in this article are drawn from a qualitative study conducted in 1994 which looked at the sex education programmes in several co-educational secondary comprehensive schools and youth work settings in the south of England. Most of the adolescents we researched were between the ages of fourteen and fifteen.

Sexual socialisation

Our theoretical starting point in studying adolescent sexuality and sex education was that sexuality is socially constructed, and that sexual behaviour and sexuality is at least in part made and shaped by social learning (Weeks, 1985; Giddens, 1992; Seidman, 1992). Learning is involved whatever part of the sexual self is considered "natural."

Schools are one of the agencies involved in providing information about sexuality and school sex education is one of the places where formal socialisation is attempted. They are also involved in the regulation of sexual behaviour and its social control. Schools also have informal spaces where alternative social constructions about sexuality and what counts as appropriate sexual behaviour are communicated.

Gender and sexuality

> I set out to write about sexuality, I found myself writing about gender. (Giddens, 1992: p. 1).

As the research developed, we started to sense that it was very difficult to understand the adolescent reactions we witnessed without a consideration of gender: "Gender is a pivotal category for analysis of sexuality" (Seidman, 1992: p. 132). Feminist analysis argues that sexuality like other aspects of life, work, culture or science is gendered. Sexuality is an integral element in learning about gender, it forms a central plank in our notions of gender identity. Our gender identity will in turn affect the characteristics and practices of our sexuality. The inequalities which are associated with gender will affect behaviour and attitudes in fundamental ways. However, it is worth emphasising that research into this area in still developing and the linkages are complex and not perhaps fully understood.

> Somehow in a way that has to be investigated, sexuality functions as a malleable feature of self, a prime connection point between body, self identity and social norms. (Giddens, 1992: p. 15)

If we return to this paper we are left with a number of questions about specifying how this theoretical material relates to the sex education programmes in schools that we want to discuss. Adolescents are at a crucial stage in their life cycle development in terms of both gender identity and sexual development, receiving gender and sexual socialisation at the same time. There is a dynamic relationship between the two processes which can make it difficult to disentangle and make sense of the reactions.

If Giddens is right that sexuality is 'a prime connection point' between body, identity and the social world, then adolescents can be expected to react strongly to the socialisation messages that they are offered since they relate to core aspects of identity. The blueprint laid down touches very significant areas of the self. The blueprint for sexuality which is offered in schools is only one of many which exist in our society. Pupils bring with them into sex education lessons their own perspectives, drawn from a range of "localities " — home, community and peer group.

The data

We use an excerpt from our data in order to focus our discussion. It originated from a school where the same lesson on the topic of contraception was delivered to two separate groups, one girls and one boys. We present material from both lessons in order to demonstrate the contrast in responses from boys and girls. In this paper, however, our main interest is to analyse the boys' reactions. The girls' reactions have been dealt with in a separate paper which also looked at the policy implications of the data in relation to single-sex provision of sex education (Measor, Tiffin and Fry, forthcoming).

We need to emphasise that the lesson was distinctive because it was given by a visitor to the school. A team of health professionals, funded by the Health Authority provided a sex education programme for the school (see Measor and Tiffin, 1995 for a fuller account of the programme). The lesson on contraception was given by one of that team, a family planning nurse, who showed pupils the currently-used contraception techniques. The class was split into small groups of four to five pupils, which were allowed and encouraged to handle the devices, fill in a worksheet and discuss any questions the session had raised.

It is important to set the context of the sessions we describe. The lesson on contraceptives was set in a broader sex education programme and fitted into it at an appropriate time. Each of the classes had conducted preparatory work on the topic before the lessons we describe and all had feedback sessions afterwards.

We present an account of the girls' lesson first; the group consisted of about twenty girls aged between thirteen and fourteen. We refer to the family planning nurse as "Sue" in the field notes which follow.

A single-sex lesson — the case of the girls

The lesson was a picture of conformity, there was no giggling and the girls did not seem embarrassed.

The family planning nurse handed out devices to each small group and then circulated the groups giving information. The girls indicated their interest by frequently interrupting and asking for more information. Sue encouraged this:

"Feel free to ask questions at any time, just shout them out."

Later in the session the nurse drew the whole group back together and discussed the contraceptives using the worksheets.

She added information as she talked, for example which kinds of devices are appropriate for younger girls and advice on their effectiveness. The girls repeatedly asked for more information. They wanted to know, for example, exactly how the contraceptive pill worked — and how many days it takes from beginning the pill until it becomes effective.

Towards the end of the session Sue dealt with condoms as a method of contraception. She held several up and then handed them around. All the girls looked at and felt the condoms. Sue described how to open condoms and advised caution to any girl with long nails when opening the packets, and then showed the girls how to put on a condom using the plastic penis supplied by the condom company for this purpose. She finished with the line:

> "So if you get some guy who can't put one on you can do it for them."

The pupils remained attentive throughout the hour long session and continued to ask detailed careful questions, pupils seated in corners of the room craned their necks to see diagrams when they did not have a perfect view. The girls reacted with "Ugh" and "Urr" sounds of distaste when they got spermicide on their hands and objected mildly to the rubber smells of the condoms, but at no point did Sue have to issue any discipline message, nor did she have to strive to get any girl's attention or interest. The researchers did not have the opportunity to interview the girls after this lesson, therefore had only field notes and a questionnaire-type evaluation done by the school to define the girl's reactions. Pupil interest was clear:

> "You need to know about it, it is important to know these things."

Adolescents stated these matters were identified as significant in their lives, welcoming the opportunity to learn things that were new to them.

> "It answered a lot of questions about contraception and family planning."

The field notes suggest a lesson in which the girls were quiet and purposeful. It appeared to be the case that they were interested and engaged with the material that was presented to them. There was no resistance to the lesson and the girls worked in small co-operative groups discussing the work with each other without much apparent embarrassment. The nature of the girls' reaction is thrown into sharper silhouette by an account of the boys' reaction to their single sex lesson.

A single-sex lesson — the case of the boys

The second extract describes the same lesson at the same school, delivered to a group of boys of the same age, but the contrast in atmosphere was absolute. There were about the same number of boys in the group as there had been girls, but the room seemed to be filled to overflowing with people, noise, chaos and disruption, pushing and shoving. Bags were thrown and so were some half-serious punches; chairs squeaked and scraped, boys squirmed and desks rattled.

> In the combined teaching, teaching practice supervision and research experience of the two researchers, we had rarely seen such high levels of disruption in a class and we have struggled to find language to provide an evocative picture of the situation. Sue tried constantly to create order and discipline in the class, demanding silence and asking for attentive behaviour. She was unable to secure it.
>
> Each small group of boys was given contraceptive devices and worksheets. Sue stood at the front of the room and held up a Femidom to give to a particular group. The boys exploded at the sight of the Femidom. Voices were loud and laughter was raucous, jokes were shouted out. A group of boys bounced the flexible ring from the Femidom around their desk.
>
> Boy 1: "It looks like a windsock."
>
> Boy 2: "What do you use that with — submarine?"
>
> Boy 3: "That"s about big enough for my dick."

There was, it occurred to us as observers, an atmosphere almost of panic in the room. Boys continued to react strongly to the sight, smell and feel of the devices throughout the lesson. The horseplay and the throwing of contraceptive devices around also persisted. Sue showed diaphragms to the group, there was again a loud reaction, one boy bent the cap into two and flipped it around the classroom, it ended up in a dusty corner. The pattern that emerged is one in which boys object to the activities provided and in which they make their objections very clear.

Sue displayed IUDs and discussed the way they work, provoking the reaction:

"It looks like a fish hook."

When Sue passed an example of an IUD around the room for the boys to handle they felt the short ends of wire that emerged from the end of the IUD and made jokes about it,

> Boy 1: "It looks like fishing line."
>
> Boy 2: "Fourteen gauge to be exact."
>
> Boy 3: "Yes to reel it in."

The boys drew on things that were familiar, like fishing tackle, to interpret the unfamiliar. They also drew on things that were male to deal with things that were female. The boys did not see these contraceptive devices as being relevant to them in the same ways as the girls. Above the general noise individual boys engaged in loud, joking behaviour which could be heard by the whole class.

Sue handed out the pill for pupils to see. A couple of boys pretended to eat the pill, leading to others shouting out, "Look at Joey and that lot."

When Sue dealt with condoms the reaction was stronger than it had been to other types of contraceptives. A group of boys virtually rioted when condoms were handed to them. There was loud shouting and shrill screams, none of the boys were still — arms waved, legs jerked, heads circled and eyes ogled. Boys picked up condoms and snapped them, like long elastic bands, threw them at each other, or blew them up and allowed them to float off like balloons. One boy put a condom onto his head, stretching it around his scalp. He removed it and complained, " It smells of inner tubes". Another pushed a condom into his friend's face: the friend responded, "Aghhhh!! It stinks, it smells all pooey." A boy secreted a condom in his pocket; another boy told Sue what he had done and she retrieved it. During the laughter that resulted, boys shouted jokes to each other, some related to oral sex:

"Mr Brown be sensible please and tell me what flavour you think this condom is? "

However most centred on the subject of penises and specifically on competition between boys about penis size. Some of the joking was a in a kind of boastful celebratory mode. "Which is the longest?" one boy shouted as he grabbed a condom across the table. "That one will be for me then", is one typical example.

We are aware of the value laden nature of the language used — 'a virtual riot' is a very strong term. We are seeking, however, to communicate a picture of exceptional circumstances and pupil behaviour, outside of what we have 'normally' seen in classrooms. What happened in this school was repeated in the six other schools we researched. Whenever we saw condoms demonstrated to groups of boys in school sex education, we observed this pattern of reaction. All the activities offered to the boys in the sex education lesson seemed to provoke opposition, however the reaction was particularly strong to condoms and later on in this paper we speculate about why this might have been the case. By the loud joking that could be heard, the boys ensured everyone knew they were objecting to this activity.

The boys did not display attentive interest in the subject material in the way the girls had. There were two exceptions.

> When Sue began to talk about the pill and deliver information, the majority of the class quietened down, listened and were attentive. Later she produced charts of the reproductive system and began to talk to the whole class and at this point the boys listened and were attentively interested. Like the girls, they craned their necks to be able to see the chart properly.

This data seemed interesting to us, showing boys responded selectively to different styles of teaching. When Sue offered a formal teaching strategy which offered scientific information then the boys responded by becoming more conformist pupils and "paying attention." Their difficulties were pronounced in relation to handling contraceptives, but not when they were asked to handle information.

The other key point, as the following extract shows, is that different boys responded in different ways.

> The group had a small pile of condoms on the table in front of them, many of the boys giggled uncontrollably, several had their hands over their faces. One sat on the back two legs of his chair, leaning far away from the condoms his hands raised in front of him, saying, 'keep them away from me.' In the middle of one of the loudest groups a boy who was particularly small and slow in physical maturation sat sucking his thumb. His neighbour kept smelling his hands after he handled condoms saying "pooh" very loudly. Other boys smelt the spermicidal jelly and pronounced it disgusting — the discussion of what the smell most resembled ended up in a fight with boys hitting each other to enforce their points of view.

We thought it was important to note the behaviour of the one boy who sucked his thumb. It is impossible to know why he did so, but it is fair to say that he had a reaction that was distinctively different from the majority of his peers. Not all boys responded in the same way to the lesson, and this is an issue we return to later in this paper.

The data show the boys displaying squeamish distaste for the activities. The girls had some reaction but there was more pronounced reaction from the boys.

> Toward the end of the lesson Sue demonstrated putting on a condom, she took out the plastic penis and warned the class "Watch then." Sue held up the condom and said, "Remember you can only put a condom on an erect penis." The boys collapsed in hysterical giggles, the noise level was higher than ever. The smallest boy started to suck his thumb once more. The jokes began again:

"Can I put it over my head, I've done it before."

"Can you use Vaseline on them?"

Sue told him that this is inadvisable another boy suggested:

"Use WB 40 oil then."

The pattern of the boys reacting particularly strongly to condoms was again in evidence here. The general reaction throughout the class was negative, and the boys did not display attentive interest in the subject material in the way the girls had. There was one exception.

> While Sue was talking she received no supplementary questions of the sort that the girls had asked. There was one exception, a boy who looked more physically mature than average asked a question about the location of the young people's clinic where underage adolescents are able to get advice and supplies. He then asked for accurate directions of how to find the clinic and listened carefully to Sue's reply. The remainder of the class was not interested in listening.
>
> The boys reacted negatively to this sex education lesson and material from the school evaluation backed-up the impression gained from participant observation. We have presented the boys' reactions with the spelling and grammatical errors uncorrected. A number of boys made the point that they were bored by the material; unlike the girls they did not consider it helpful or useful:
>
> "The talks were boring."
> "The talks were long."

They insisted that a contributory factor was that they knew all of the information already:

> "I knew most of it already."
> "Not a lot was tort."
> "The activities were childish."

Evaluation sheets revealed a lack of seriousness:

> "I'm staying selabot and becoming a monk."
> "My mummy said not to have sex till I'm married."

Explanations of the boys' behaviour

What are we to make of this data? It establishes our claim that there were clear differences in the reactions of boys and girls to the sex education they received. It is also clear that the boys objected more strongly and more openly than the girls did to the sex education material. A full explanation of the boys' behaviour is difficult in our view, and we can only begin to make tentative suggestions about some of the processes involved. We deal firstly with methodological issues and what might be called 'common sense explanations' and then go on to look at how more theoretical insights can be applied.

We appreciate that there may be methodological problems in erecting an analysis on this data. We cannot know for certain how these boys behave in the other lessons. We may not be witnessing behaviour specific to sex education, but rather routine behaviour of a difficult group of boys in a poorly disciplined school. However, this school is a successful one in league table terms in an affluent small town in the south of England, and it is unlikely that the boys typically behave as badly as this across all areas of the curriculum. We have not the space to present all of the data we collected in this paper. We observed lessons which followed this format and demonstrated contraceptives in different schools. In all of them, the teacher or medical practitioner giving the session had difficulty in maintaining discipline.

It may be that the situation we have described here is simply the product of pupils reacting to a stranger visiting their school and attempting to run their classes. The class recognises that they are being taught by someone inexperienced and that they can push against the everyday rules and boundaries. We suspect that this did play an important role — the family planning nurse was not teacher-trained. This explanation does not, however, account for the gender differences we have documented.

Immaturity is another explanation for the boys' reactions; a teacher in the school said that it would make sense for the family planning nurse to offer the same session to the boys two years later than to the girls. However we are concerned about this common sense explanation because it leaves the definition of 'maturity' very unclear, and fails to acknowledge the extent to which it is a socially constructed notion.

We do not know why the boys objected to the input from the health professionals. The boys felt the material offered to them in this sex education programme was wholly inappropriate. The boys said they found it embarrassing and boring. The programme was devised and presented by a female team and we have to consider that material was selected which appealed to the girls and met their needs while failing the those of the boys. The boys on their evaluation sheets stated they felt aggrieved that:

> "The session dealt more with girls than with boys."

> "I felt embarrassed because most of the contraception is for women."

> "I diden like it when it was only about wimmin."

Other boys complained about the provision of sex education by a female:

> "They was all women."

> "No Men."

> "There were no men to talk to us man to man."

There are obviously policy and training implications here about getting more men into this field of work.

A second set of explanations starts from the critique made by some health education professionals of sex education programmes. They suggest that sex education fails because the adolescents' own concerns are not taken into enough consideration by those who plan the programmes. In this scheme there was no consultation with pupils about what they considered they most wanted to know, or account taken of the informal culture of these adolescents. Adults decided what ought to go into the curriculum. We discussed earlier the potential for conflict if sex education contravenes the values of pupils. It touches key aspects of the self and therefore opposition will be strong.

There is a growing body of research which suggests that girls' levels of knowledge about the key issues in the sex education fields are higher than boys (Winn, Roker and Coleman, 1995). We know from other research, notably Allen (1987), that boys are the most likely to miss out on sex education at home. This may partially explain the disparity in knowledge, but it may also affect their values and attitudes. If the majority of boys are not offered the opportunity of gaining sexual information from trusted adults, their knowledge base develops from different "locations", and the cultures which operate there may be different from school or home. The peer group was the main source of information for most boys we encountered. Whilst we cannot go into detail here, boys said they also used pornographic films, the satellite television channels, videos and the Internet. They explained that they valued pornography because it provided *specific and explicit* information about sex in contrast with school sex education. This may explain part of the boys' resistance to hearing information from a health professional.

Gender theory

The other sets of explanation require a focus on gender theory and specifically on recent research into masculinity. The social construction argument claims that gender is not biologically given and immutable. Masculinity is defined as a set of positions and cultural choices which are chosen:

> Rather than something which is unassailably and existentially rooted in an ontologically secure understanding of the world.
> (Morgan, 1992: p. 12)

Without doubt, work on masculinity can be of use here with the micro data we have documented. Research suggests that in order to be seen by others as properly masculine boys have to behave in particular ways. Morgan commented that specific behaviours, "elaborate particularly masculine themes". We can make sense of the boys' behaviour in the sex education lessons if we see it as elaborating these gender themes.

A number of these behaviours have been identified. Proving masculinity "may require frequent rehearsals of toughness, the exploitation of
women and quick aggressive responses" (Arnot, 1984: p. 46). The rapid,
loud joking behaviour we documented in the lesson is an example of boys'
behaving in ways which fit this blueprint.

Corrigan, Connell and Lee (1985: p. 52) claim:

> Playing football, drinking, marauding around town and so on
> constituted as it were almost a quantitative index of manhood,
> prowess in those culturally exalted forms of masculinity made you
> more of a man.

Morgan identified related behaviours which apply more directly to this
data: being part of a group of males may also, "provide the opportunity for
the elaboration of particular masculine themes through horse play, trading
insults, sexual references and mock homosexual attacks" (Morgan, 1992:
p. 92, citing Roy, 1960, Collinson and Collinson, 1989). There was clear
evidence of this kind of activity in the lesson. When boys are presented
with material which has a sexual connotation the question of how to
behave is highlighted. They need to show they recognise it as something
sexually provocative to avoid any suggestion of lesser masculinity. This
may help explain the exaggerated responses boys made to contraceptive
devices and why they responded differently when faced with charts and
scientific material that did not carry the sexually symbolic load which
demanded a response.

Men may need women to act as a contrast to themselves; they stand
defined as masculine in a sharper silhouette against women. The
differences underline the meaning of masculinity for men and of course
femininity for women.

> A sense of being a man or less than a man come to the fore in
> relation to women. What it feels like to be a man can only be fully
> answered in the context of gender encounters where sexual or
> gender difference is accented. (Morgan, 1992: p. 202)

This may enable us to understand why the boys were so affronted by a
woman presenting this material to them, and it may help explain some of
the strength of their resistance to the session. We know from other feminist
work that boys may resist the control of women teachers as early as three
or four years old, in nursery schools (Walkerdine, 1981).

Connell's notion of hegemonic masculinity is also relevant. He suggests boys continually compete to outperform each other for masculine
status. There are hierarchies between women and men but there are also
hierarchies between men and men, one of the most significant ways
of establishing those hierarchies is through sexual and other types of
harassment (Connell, 1987). The horseplay might have represented
competition for status within groups of boys, and between groups of boys.
The most outrageous displays — throwing contraceptive devices around,

making loud jokes that could be heard publicly and showing oneself unresponsive to the control of a woman, could all win status in an informal culture (see Measor, 1984: p. 182 for a longer account of how these processes might work).

Work on masculinities alerts us to the power dimensions involved in signalling masculinity and we have emphasised this aspect in relation to this data. There is, however, evidence in this data of another, distinct theme of male anxiety about sex and sexuality. Behaviour we observed throughout the sex education lessons could be a response to this anxiety, although this is not a topic that can be explored in any detail here. We collected evidence that status can be won or lost by having or lacking knowledge about sex and contraception in adolescent male culture: a lesson which threatened to expose ignorance was therefore a threat.

In the sex education lesson the boys responded in culturally prescribed ways in order to 'elaborate particularly masculine themes'. We argue that the boys reacted negatively to this provision of sex education because it affronted their sense of their sexuality or gender identity in some way. Resistance to the lessons indicated an assertion of their own adolescent view and values.

References

Allen, I. (1987) Education in sex and personal relationships. London: Policy Studies Institute.

Arnot, M. (1984) 'How shall we educate our sons?', in R. Deem (ed) Co-education reconsidered. Milton Keynes: Open University Press, pp. 37-55.

Connell, R. W. (1987) Gender and power. Cambridge: Polity Press.

Carrigan, T., Connell, R. W., and Lee, J. (1985) 'Hard and heavy phenomena: The sociology of masculinity', Theory, Vol. 14: pp. 551-604.

Collinson, D. L. and Collinson, M. (1989) 'Sexuality in the workplace: The domination of men's sexuality', in J. Hearn, D. L. Sheppard et al. (eds) The sexuality of organization. London: Sage, pp. 91-109.

Giddens, A. (1992) The transformation of intimacy. Oxford: Polity Press.

Measor, L. and Woods, P. (1984) Changing schools. Milton Keynes: Open University Press.

Measor, L. and Tiffin, C. (1995) 'All this and not a Mars Bar in sight: The impact of health professionals involvement in sex education in schools,' Paper presented at the Association for Public Health Annual Conference.

Morgan, D. (1991), Discovering men. London: Routledge.

Roy, D. F. (1960) 'Banana time: Job satisfaction and informal interaction', *Human Organisation*, Vol. 18: pp. 156-68.

Seidman, S. (1992) *Embattled Eros*. London: Routledge.

Walkerdine, V. (1981) 'Sex, power and pedagogy,' *Screen Education*, Vol. 38: pp. 14-24.

Weeks, J. (1985) *Sexuality and its discontents*. London: Methuen.

Winn, S., Roker, D. and Coleman, J. (1995) 'Knowledge about puberty and sexual development in 11-16 year olds: Implications for health and sex education in schools', *Journal of Education Studies*, Vol. 21, No. 2 (June): pp. 187-202.

Part II

Provision for Play

Politically Correct Play

Barbara Hendricks

KOMPAN A/S[1], Denmark

Children play for the fun of it — it is their way to express themselves and interact with their environment. Children play because they are children not because there is some benefit or result produced.

Modern western society, however, has censored children's play behaviours at the same time as the adult built world has eliminated many of the places where children have played. The result is that those few play opportunities available to children in urban areas today are those the adults think are worthwhile — i. e. politically correct play.

The interface between play and education crosses through a lot of conceptual territory. Ideas about play, children's development, ways of learning and the structure of the formal educational system are all caught up in this web. So too are some latent adult prejudices and cultural biases. Often the children's right to play is rejected in favour of some adult society goal. Much of the conflicting ideas and problems of the interface can be observed in the trends in design and furnishing of urban playgrounds.

This paper explores the phenomenon of the Nature Playground — an adult idea of how children should access nature in the city — and contrasts this with how children interact with nature in play. There is no one correct formula for the provision of play opportunities for children, and this paper raises more questions than answers.

Trends and fashions in playground design

> It is becoming more and more popular to take playground equipment out of the playground and design nature playgrounds instead. A cycle path, a climbing wall and a fireplace, along with a great deal of grass and green trees — this is what belongs on a modern playground.... Out with standardised seesaws and swings and in with that which inspires the fantasy. (Reimers in *Fyns Sondagsavisen*, 1995: p. 1)

89

So begins one of many newspaper articles on the move toward a new form of outdoor play yard. It goes on to describe that the play area has been renovated to include a gardening area, woven willow huts, mounds of earth along with two playhouses (one sponsored by a large international brewery). There is a football field and in the future they would like to add on a workshed for various messy construction activities. The suggestion is that play areas are places that are to be organised and landscaped in accordance with a fixed pattern as set by fashion and these news reports are describing the latest trend — the nature playground. It is newsworthy because it is a new trend or fashion.

What is happening here? Have these people who made this play area discovered something new about the way children play? What is the basis for the rejection of swings and seesaws? Do children in 1995 no longer like to rock and swing? Must swings and seesaws inspire fantasy to be successful in their function on the playground? Are places where children play to be set out in accordance with a preordained pattern? Should these be places that are all the same, to be changed like hairstyles when the fashions change? The answers to these and other questions are not to be found in the article quoted above. For the most, such articles provide a description of a group of adults (usually parents) who have put in a great deal of effort and energy to provide their children with a new, trend-setting play area — a modern one — a "natural" one.

Unstated, but important to know, is that the playground described in the newsaper article quoted above is a supervised area attached to an after-school institution for school-age children. Doesn't the playground start to sound like a variation on the building and adventure playgrounds that were written up so much twenty years ago? It does, but there is also a new element here that was not part of the adventure playground package — a new element that is part of the 1990s and a necessary consideration to be "in" in the western world. The key to this new element is the word "natural".

The making of the "natural" playground is well-intentioned and the concept contains all the elements of contemporary 1995 social values. Among the values inherent in this remaking of the places where children play is a good dose of "political correctness" — for the most, we are responsible citizens and have guilty consciences about the conditions of this planet and we think more should be done.

Today it is a 'must' to be seen to be riding on the ecological bandwagon — recycling, buying ecological sourced/organic food and 'green' cotton textiles, using the right cleaning materials, using the bike and public transport rather than cars, and other behaviours that distinguish the responsible citizen from the slob. We feel very righteous when we turn off a light someone else turned on and we feel great when we can remind a colleague to turn off their computer or other electronic device when it is not in use. I will only mention in passing the issue of smoking and non-smoking — most people know the various sides of that argument. We are riding on a wave of righteous busybodyness that is related to the original political correctness and has grown out of the same well intentioned efforts to chart new pathways for living together with greater understanding and in harmony. Unfortunately, like the other political correctness, the good intentions have become replaced with a tyranny of 'do-goodism', conventionalised behaviours that are aimed at publicising the heightened awareness of the doer. This is what has happened with the environmental movement. We are all aware of the need to alter traditional modes of behaviour and to act in a way that is more in harmony with the local and global ecological cycles of the planet. But what to do? No worries — here the media is full of reports on the latest trends in environmental awareness and consumerism. Every day brings a new idea, another trend. It is difficult to distinguish between appropriate behaviours — those things we do because they are the right things to do, and the politically correct behaviours — what we do because those are the behaviours that we hope will win approval and admiration. The politically correct solution is to surround our children with items that are considered environmentally appropriate and fitting with the ecological movement. It is, after all, the next generation who must bear the real burden of this mess we have created — they may as well come to know about it all when they are young. But there is a choice to be made between those places which provide the children with varied and interesting play opportunities that the children find to be fun and those places where the children are offered opportunities that adults find worthwhile. To choose the politically correct "nature playground" is to impose the adult values and fashion trends. The right choice is the place that the children would enjoy. Being introduced to ideas, issues and activities that are important to the adult culture are valid parts of the childhood experience. But my argument is that this should happen in places other than the playground and in time other than free play time. The play place is the place to promote the culture of childhood.

Of course, we need to be aware consumers, and children should understand about where food comes from and where the garbage goes. However, when we redesign the children's play area — the only urban oasis devoted to children and childhood — by bringing in references to the problems we have created on this planet, whose purposes are we serving? What are the results? Children are very quick to understand the unspoken meanings in their surroundings and we need to carefully consider what are the appropriate messages to send children when we make a play place. Children understand environmental problems to be such things as pollution and the disappearance of the forest and animals. They rarely connect such issues with their own activities in nature until they are 8 years or older (Bugge and Hendricks, 1995).

When we make nature playgrounds which are full of references to the adult world environmental issues are we not introducing conflicting and contradictory messages, messages that may serve to worry the children and lead to less playful activities, less fantasy? And of course there are other messages as well — the commercial messages and public-relations-generated material from various corporation and government and volunteer groups that try to gain public approval by appearing to be on the ecological bandwagon. This too is part of the story behind such headlines as "A Natural Playground". The local community is looking for good PR for its very modern consciousness of the ecological movement and of the need to immerse the children into environmental awareness — not for its awareness of children's play needs.

Play places for children

Play places for children should be places where children can play care-free. They should be places where children can experience the joy of living and the wonder of being alive on this planet. Children should have good positive experiences with other living things so they can learn to love and care for nature and this planet. Children come to love nature and care for it, not through knowing how it works and learning about ecological cycles, but through positive, happy, playful experiences in and with nature.

There are other elements in a happy childhood. Among them are the children's drive to playfully explore the characteristics of the surrounding physical world. In doing so, those items the children explore need to be robust enough to withstand use by many children. Natural materials like tree trunks and earth mounds and living things on the play area must be of the kind that will withstand the vigorous activities of many children over and over again. One way to ensure this is to provide large areas of nature relative to the number of children. However, urban playgrounds are usually very small, with the result that the tree trunks and earth mounds are soon worn out and the plants die away. Maintenance of the area is not enough: frequent renewal with new planting and replaced earth, and tree trunks are required. Communities like the city of Odense in Denmark who have been making these types of "nature playgrounds" for some years now also admit that the maintenance of such places is becoming problematic. To give nature a chance to survive requires a higher ratio of land area than is often currently available per playing child. This means devoting more land in urban areas to children's play places. This is a good idea, a necessary idea — but not one that has hit the top of any political agenda I have seen.

Another feature of the play of young children is that they are very physically active and enjoy a whole variety of movements — not only running but also climbing, jumping, swinging, sliding, rocking, rolling, hanging and many more ways of using the body. In modern cities, play areas are one of the few places where children are permitted to move freely, and where there are purpose-made frames that support activities like swinging, sliding and rocking. That these are standardised has to do with our concern for the durability of the construction and for the safety of the children. Is this a bad thing? Children enjoy these kinds of movements. They are fun, particularly when in the company of friends and playmates. They are symbolic of play. They can be part of a good children's play place.

Examining the playground

Let us look more carefully at the new elements on the renovated playground described in that newspaper article. There are two parts to the play area — one section with a mound and fireplace. The other section has a football field, sledding slope, and a gardening area with two playhouses. Dividing the two sections is an alley ending in a cycle path. In the future the children will plant willows and weave the branches into willow huts. There are also plans for an outdoor workshop area. But sledding, playing in playhouses, running and rolling down the slopes of a mound are all part of the ways children have played and expressed their joy for many generations. Building huts and constructing things have also been part of the play of school age children. Football fields are a standard provision in urban areas. So what is so new about this play area? What seems to be new are two things. New (again) is the gardening area and the fire area — features found on the school ground at the beginning of the twentieth century (note: *school* ground not playground). The other new feature is that the traditional support frames for interesting movement activities like seesaws, slides and swings have been banned from the playground. Why? Because they are not 'natural'.

But what is natural? Is gardening natural? Certainly it means working with soil and living plants. The debates around gardening as a natural activity vary from those who advocate total ecological based methods, to those who state that we should do nothing — there should be no intervention by human hand at all. And then there are those who enjoy the everyday gardening activity of producing foodstuff and flower gardens using mixed means which may include non-organic fertiliser to support a favourite plant, and may use chemicals to fight insects and weeds. What has gardening to do with play? Gardening is an ordinary and pleasurable activity that humans have engaged in for thousands of years — and should be part of everyday life. But let us not use up the precious little play space we allow children — let's make more gardens.

One trend to be observed in this nature playground movement is the introduction of centuries-old peasant crafts as organised play activities for children of the late twentieth century — such as weaving of fences and structures out of willow, using plant parts for crafts activities and of course the production of food. There is a strong nostalgic longing for a simpler past in this movement toward the nature playground. That these were work activities of peasants in the middle ages does not make them 'natural' for children's play of the twenty-first century. Participation in such activities can bring a much more vivid understanding of the history of humankind and can be a good teaching tool. But should teaching tools take over the play place? We must not forget that we in the industrialised western world have a long and colourful history. And if we do not know and appreciate our heritage from history we are not fully equipped to go forward. We need to help our current generations to understand what it was like to live in times past — but this is not the goal of children's play .

Our ancestors evolved in nature and all humans have a need for contact with nature. Children have a particularly strong urge to make contact with nature — in forms that the children know as nature. This is a challenge when we live in such high concentrations as we do in western cities. We need to give much more careful consideration to children's access to nature and we shouldn't confuse that need with the children's need for free play outdoors. Nor should we organise the children's play to include forms of adult-interpreted nature that are not really meaningful to the children.

Play and education — the interface

This paper is part of a larger series of discussions around the issue of leisure, sport and education. This issue fits in well in my opinion because there is so much adult energy devoted toward turning play into an educational experience or justifying play as a learning experience. There is also a concern that sport is replacing children's free play to the detriment of children's learning (Evans, 1995). The naturification of children's urban play areas is but one more move to make sure that children learn the right things and become adults with the 'right values'. This interference with children's free play is a negative side of the politically correct play idea. Playgrounds should be devoted to play and not to education in much the same way as adult leisure centres are devoted to leisure activities and not to work.

Adults 'earn' their leisure after a work week of somewhere between 35 and 60 hours of work (at least in the western world). Some time between the ages of 60 to 70 most of us also can enter into the life of leisure, of retirement, or the "golden years", in perhaps more politically correct terminology. The working hours and years of adults are seen to be their contribution to society, and society has a responsibility to offer, in return, opportunities for amusement and relaxation. There are of course the benefits to the labour force to have workers who have taken advantage of the offers for leisure activities to maintain a sound physical condition and who have taken the time to develop many interests, hobbies and continue to be curious and explorative of the world around them — all elements of a well used leisure time.

It is the same with childhood and children's play. Childhood, before the age of school, is seen to be the first golden years when children are free from the responsibility to make a contribution to the society. School attendance is the young child's contribution — it is not a direct contribution but it is their way of fulfilling their duty to learn how meet the future needs of the adult society. It is a good thing and a very practical thing that adults responsible for children's education have discovered that children learn best when the educational activity takes on playful forms. It is, however, a misuse of adult authority to try to take away children's free play time and space and turn them into a learning experiences and places.

Children have done their duty to society in the 18 to 32 hours in school each week plus their participation in after school cultural lessons — music, dance and so forth.

That children learn through play is also well known, as is the fact that play is necessary for a healthy happy childhood. It is the manipulation of play and play places to serve the future adult needs that does not belong on a children's outdoor play place. The way in which educators interact with children during school time may be playful — but this is not to be equated with playtime. While education is an essential part of children's preparation for future duties it is also true that if children only learned what adults can teach them, the human race would have died out long ago — perhaps after the first generation. We need to leave play alone — to stop trying to turn it into an education opportunity or to convert it into an organized sport, for that matter. Play is far too essential for the survival and well being of the future human being for us to interfere with it when we know so little about the phenomenon of human development.

Experts and children

Children, childhood and children's play have become the subject of expert adult work in the twentieth century — and today we have more theorists, theories and knowledge about young children than ever before in the history of our civilisation. Children in the western world have access to adequate medical care, good parenting and protection by the state should the parents be unable to provide adequate care. This could lead one to expect that children today have it better today that ever before — but do they? I would suggest that in many areas such as legal protection and health care children in the western world have good conditions. In terms of access to consumer products children in the industrialised west have a great deal.

Another characteristic of the industrialised western world is that approximately 80% of the population lives in urban area, and these urban areas are for the most planned by adults for adult purposes. Children's places are small, unprofitable pieces of land, furnished with a minimum of funding and according to a simple formula without regard to the full range of children's needs for outdoor play opportunities. In the area of access to interesting outdoor places where the children can play freely, children in western industrialised societies are not doing so well. It seems that as we end the twentieth century, children are not as well off in terms of access to interesting, playful outdoor spaces as they were at the beginning of the century.

Is there any relationship between all the experts and the acquired expertise on children and play and the loss of space for children to play? I think there is — but it was never the intention of any of the experts. The influence of experts and the professionalism of children's subjects has meant that the ordinary person has not felt the necessity to consider children: architects, planners, landscape architects, even leisure specialists have left the children's issues to the 'experts'. Unfortunately, the experts have been talking only to themselves and have difficulty influencing the architects, planners, landscape architects and leisure specialists whose work affects children and childhood. For example, I have for many years been presenting papers on children's play at professional leisure and town planning conferences — and the only persons who attend the sessions are those who have some prior knowledge of children's play and an interest in it. For the most they already are aware of the things I talk about. Professional papers, research, books and the like have a limited audience — they are well known in the small world of play professionals but few are known outside of the small circle of experts.

This condition has been a factor in the vulnerability of the design of children's play and playthings to the whims of political correctness, as the non-expert has no basis for evaluating the claims of appropriateness for the children. Another weakness is the connection we make between educators and childhood experts. We have accepted that teachers of young children are the experts in young children, and have then gone further to accept that those factors in the children's environment that support the work of the educators of young children are the best for the children. This is true when it relates to the formal educational curriculum, but there is another part of childhood that has been stolen by this acceptance — that of free play. Few childhood educators are experts on children's play and playspaces. Children have a right to play time just as adults have a right to leisure time. Let us give free play back to the children and give them rich and interesting places in which they are free to play.

What makes a good play place

What should be in a good quality children's play place? The essential element of children's play areas is variety, variety and variety. There is no one set pattern, no matter how good, which should be applied to all play areas. Those three or four places for play that the children in a specific neighbourhood may have access to should all be very different from each other and offer different kinds of play possibilities. The 'natural playground' first described in this paper is a valid and acceptable way to organise a schoolyard to be used for several hours each day by schoolage children who will use the space accompanied by adults. This is not a playground where free play takes place — but it is an interesting schoolyard. It is NOT a formula that should be applied to every play place these children have access to. Every play area should be unique. In my terminology, a school yard and a play ground are two different places — and there should be a playground as part of a school yard. A playground is exactly what missing in the place described in the newspaper article.

There is a whole range of forms, materials and objects to choose from when creating children's play places. The resulting features of the play area should offer a rich variety of opportunities for children to enjoy, and there should be things to do that have components of all kinds of social interactions, many kinds of creative activities as well as opportunities to explore a huge array of ways for children to move, to use their bodies and senses and to explore different kinds of spaces. Elements sourced in nature belong in play places, so do living plants, birds, insects and other living things. Global elements such as sand, earth, water, rocks, air and fire — these too belong in some play spaces. So do contemporary features of childhood culture — making music, pretend play which may be based on the latest TV and movie shows, role play and places for dramatic play. Magical spaces where it can be imagined that trolls and fairies live or places that are visited by space people, belong on play areas as well. Wheeled toys, tractors, space buggies and cycles belong here, as do roller skates and whatever else is an "in" playful activity. Ways to swing, slide and rock, to climb and to move about through space in other ways belong also on the playground — but the support structure need not be exactly the same every time. In fact it should be different in every play place within the same neighbourhood.

Children enjoy beautiful things and gain a great deal of self esteem when their places are beautiful, when they have beautiful things. They know this means that children are important people. Every play area should have some elements of beauty — flowers, sculptures, an attractive entry and other art and ornamentation.

This listing is intended to suggest the wide range of playful possibilities that should be present in good play spaces, it is not a recipe for another version of a modern play place. Rather than a pattern or recipe I see this listing to be much like an artists palette of colours — where different artists use the same basic colours to bring to life on the canvas very different works of art in very different styles. It is not a matter of choosing between trees and swings — both belong on the same palette — each play area is brought to life through using the wide range of choices on the palette in different amounts and ways to make a unique setting.

Conclusion

In the twentieth century we have seen the rise of the childhood expert. Adulthood is, however, the norm against which all other stages of life are measured. Children are still seen however by most adults to be in a position of becoming human — that is, becoming an adult — and children's play is justified because it has or should have an educational content. In this sense we are a very adultist society — a very pervasive form of prejudice. In the future, adult society, if it aims to be a truly free democratic society, should be more aware of the rights of children and the importance of childhood. We need to avoid overwhelming this very wonderful time of life with our adult concerns. We need to move toward an understanding and appreciation of childhood as a valid form of human life — not just a preparatory phase before becoming a real person. We need to value play because it is a part of childhood, because it is important to children, not because it is educational. We need to give time and space to children and childhood and to leave the children free to make their own play.

Within easy access there should be a variety of different kinds of children-friendly places. There should be gardens and gardening areas, there should be nature exploration areas and farms. There should be well designed and maintained school yards and other outdoor educational sites and as well there should be playgrounds reserved for the free play of the children. We need to sort out our thinking about the ways in which we organize childhood experiences — there should be times and places where the children are immersed in the local adult culture and they are learning about the society in which they live. There should be other times and places where children can celebrate the wonders of childhood and enjoy the culture of childhood. The politically correct playground mixes and confuses the activities of childhood and neglects the importance of the culture of childhood.

Note

[1]   KOMPAN A/S is a private company that concerns itself with children's outdoor play and furnishing of public play areas.

References

Bugge, S. and Hendricks, B. (1995) 'Research project: Children and Nature'. Unpublished research paper. Denmark: KOMPAN.

Evans, J. (1995) 'Where have all the players gone?', *International Play Journal*, Vol. 3, No. 1: January.

Reimers, B. (1995) Article in *Fyns Sondagsavisen*, Sunday May 28: p. 1.

Play Strategies: the Vision or the Reality?

Caroline Jackson

Bournemouth University

Play is an essential part of every child's life and vital to the processes of human development. It provides the mechanism for children to explore the world around them and the medium through which skills are developed and practised. It is essential for physical, emotional and spiritual growth, intellectual and educational development, and acquiring social and behavioural skills. (National Voluntary Council for Children's Play, 1992: p. 4)

1. Introduction

Very few people would disagree with such a statement, nor the aims of the National Voluntary Council for Children's Play's (NVCCP) *A charter for children's play*. However, what do 'we' need to do to enable play to happen? Who are 'we' — parents, government, businesses, play workers or carers? What is play? There are so many questions to answer before ideals or even aims can be put into practice. The National Playing Field Association (NPFA), for example, refused to sign the NVCCP children's charter. They agreed with the general thrust of the charter but felt that, "such a broadly based statement of intent, lacking as it does specific objectives and work programmes, can serve to constrain, rather than enable activity" (Torkildsen, 1993a: p. 61). The argument is that mere words cannot ensure action. "Creating opportunities for play demands a serious and planned approach" (Playground Services, 1994: p. 4).

Planning for leisure, as many people have pointed out, seems to be an oxymoron. This seems especially poignant when planning for play. It is difficult to bring together the spontaneous world of children with the organised one of management (Benson, 1993). However, planning is now an accepted part of management and our educational courses. Planning theory takes many forms. One of the current 'fashions' in practice and in leisure theory is that of strategic planning and management. How relevant is strategic management theory to practice and how can practice inform us of the right theories to develop? Can the formality of a strategic approach enhance the future for children's play? The aim of this paper is to begin the process of investigating whether strategic management theories can help in the understanding and management of the future of play provision. It aims to explore whether the play strategies that do exist are mere visions without a realistic plan, or an action plan without vision.

This paper is not going to argue the importance of play for children's development and quality of life, nor that local authorities should be the main provider. Article 31 of the United Nations Convention on the Rights of the Child states that all children have the "right to rest and leisure, to engage in play and recreation appropriate to the age of the child and to participate freely in cultural life and the arts". The case for supporting play has already been well argued by a number of organisations and is well documented, for example in the NVCCP's, (1992), *A charter for children's play* and their more recent *Playing for local government* (1995).

2. Methodology

The next three sections of this report review the literature available on local authority play provision, strategic management theories and the argu-ments about the need for local authorities to take a strategic approach in areas such as play provision. The sixth section covers the current reality of the situation. In an attempt to try and keep the report as brief as possible this main section is structured around the process of strategic develop-ment and the content evaluates both theory and practice (good and bad) together. The concluding section brings together the main findings of both the literature and strategy reviews and identifies what further research is needed in the area of local authority play strategies.

An attempt was made to gather primary data in the form of written play strategies. The only collection of local authority play policies and strategies is that in the National Play Information Centre, London. This was collected in 1992 and has only been added to since by a few local authorities. Most of the information on play was incorporated into wider leisure strategies or policy papers. As the information was not current, and some of the documentation dated back to the 1970s, five other local authorities were interviewed regarding their policies and strategic approach to play and leisure. Of those interviewed, four had new leisure strategies, of which play played a minor role; one had a separate play strategy and one had a new playground strategy. All were local authorities in urban areas in the south, middle and north of England.

3. Local authority play provision

"Play is a generic term for a variety of activities which are satisfying to the child, creative for the child and freely chosen by the child" (NVCCP, 1992: p. 4). Opportunities for play are provided intentionally or not, by a wide variety of people and organisations. This paper is concerned with play services provided by local authorities. This can be defined as a service designed to offer space and adult encouragement to children to enable them to play (Smith, 1993). Local authority involvement in play is varied and sporadic and there are different departments and services being provided within each local authority. Research undertaken by Play Board (1985) found that the most common department involved in play is leisure. This paper concentrates on the development of strategy from the leisure department level and therefore covers district, metropolitan and the London borough councils who are the main providers of leisure opportunities, rather than the county councils.

No national review of play provision, in its widest definition, has been made. The Audit Commission undertook a survey of parks and open spaces in 1994 which covered the provision of equipped play areas and supervised play activities. They found that local authorities in England and Wales spent £64 million, an average of £6.40 per child (Moore, 1994) and £1.27 per head of population (Lubelska, 1994). Their findings were mainly based around the safety and quantity of provision, a similar approach taken by local authorities.

Only a limited amount of published use has been made of the policy and strategy documents available in the National Play Information Centre (London)[1]. Collins (1994) analysed the data and found that the majority concentrated on what they themselves directly provided, playing scant attention to voluntary and commercial sector provision. From a base of 64 local authority documents[2], 53% included play areas; 30%, playschemes and 20% standards of provision (which themselves related to play areas). Provision for children does not just mean play areas and play schemes. Even within leisure strategies, little mention is made of children's play occurring in other built facilities like leisure centres (4%), theatres or museums (0%).

4. Strategic management theory

"Strategy can be defined as the planning that takes you from where you are today, to where you should be tomorrow with maximum benefit and minimum risk" (Mann, 1990: p. 11). Strategic management is one of the 'new comers' in the disciplines of social science. Initiated at the Harvard Business School in 1953 (under business policy), it has developed under a variety of guises in academic courses and in practice. The corporate plans and management by objectives covered in the 1970s are little different to those advocated today as strategic management. Mintzberg (1994b: p. 111) says that his research and that of many others demonstrate that strategy making is an immensely complex process, which involves the most sophisticated, subtle, and, at times, subconscious elements of human thinking.

Most texts state that there are three levels of strategy that could be adapted to suit the local authority structure as below:

- corporate: which is concerned with the overall direction of the local authority and in defining the services it must and wishes to be involved with;
- business unit: which is concerned with how to successfully provide those services, either directly or through others;
- operational: which is concerned with how the operation of the services support the strategy.

In many local authorities the hierarchical nature of its structure means that there may be more than one business unit level. In leisure departments, the business unit, is then broken down, for example, into leisure services, tourism services and arts and museums (Bournemouth). The operational level is then involved in providing sports activities, play grounds, parks etc.

Mann (1990) discusses the need to establish a 'strategic framework' within which to work. It could be argued that the strategic theorists could offer this framework. Strategic management appears very complicated with the variety of tools and techniques that could be used. The basic structure however, is very logical and fits into many situations such as marketing planning. The Chartered Institute of Marketing's text on *Strategic marketing planning* follows this simple format:

- where are we now? strategic analysis
- where do we want to be? strategic direction and strategy formulation
- how might we get there? strategic choice
- which way is best? strategic evaluation
- how can we ensure arrival? strategic implementation and control

Models tend to be descriptive rather than predictive. They are not quantitative models and therefore can only provide guidance to decision making. Attempts are continually being made to make models non-linear and to show the interdependence of the stages. Torkildsen changes his planning process from being a linear (1992) to a circular diagram (1993) but still finds it difficult to illustrate the complexity of the process. An understanding of the process and the content is needed to be able to think and plan strategically. However, this separation into stages underestimates the amorphous development of the content. Whilst appraising the current situation, thoughts are being developed about the possible future outcomes or even the strategic options.

Part of the problem with the discipline is that there has been limited empirical research and a lot of reliance on logic and a flexible approach to application. Little has been done to find out how companies actually approach their strategic management, whether or not it is effective in improving performance and the extent to which strategic management is actually adopted by organisations. Strategic management texts, for example Johnson and Scholes (1989), will give the occasional public sector example but this is invariably very 'internalised', concerned with the organisation and not with the 'community' to which it is responsible. Local authority strategies should involve a plan for all sectors to work in. This is something different from commercial organisations, other than being aware of stakeholders and the external environment. They need to look outside of the organisation not just to how the external environment is affecting them and their customers but who is providing what, why and how and what their customers/citizens may demand in the future. Could a lot of the processes and tools described in the texts be adapted to apply to local authorities or is there a need for different approaches and techniques?

5. The need for a strategic approach

Concern has been shown in recent academic articles about the growing managerialist approach to local authority provision (Coalter, 1990a and b; Nichols, 1993; Ravenscroft, 1993). A lot of this argument is focused around the imposition of competitive tendering which has created what Ravenscroft, Henry and Bramham have termed the:

> bureaucratic managerialist model of local government... [which represents] ... the 'reality' of policy implementation in many local authorities ... [whose] response is likely to be an overriding compliance with the dominant ideology of liberalism and authoritarian centrism. (Ravenscroft and Tolley, 1993: pp. 6-7)

Managerialism is concerned with the depoliticisation of the management of services, as the contracting process supposedly allows managers to manage more efficiently and effectively and to see consumer choice as sovereign. The argument against managerialism is that it undermines the democratic processes of local government and negates the power of citizenship.

A current pressure on local authorities is to adopt some form of strategic management. Corporate planning has been proposed as good management practice for a number of years by organisations such as the Local Government Management Board. Could this be said to part of this managerialist approach, of trying to be more prescriptive and predictive and to emphasise the need to define and measure where the local authority wants to be in a predetermined length of time? Surely it concerns this but also overcomes Coalter's view that "a narrow focus on fiscal and resource efficiency, and an ignoring of the more traditional liberal, humanist concerns with equity and social welfare" (Coalter, 1990). The process of strategic management could enable these values and ideologies to be discussed and brought into the strategic framework.

Leisure managers have complained about the length of time it takes to undertake a strategy. The feeling is that the world of local government is changing so fast that before the process has been completed things will have changed too much; for example, the ruling political party. However, as in all organisations, this is a period of rapid change. The aim of strategic management is that it can help not hinder the process, that it is about, "developing within managers a sensitivity to an increasingly turbulent environment, together with an understanding of the culture of the organisation in which they work and the means whereby they can manage change within that culture" (Johnson and Scholes, 1989: p. xix). The introduction of compulsory competitive tendering (CCT), unitary authorities (AU) and changes in local government finance illustrate the major changes that local authorities are currently going through. When reviewing such change (and there has been a lot since 1988), Benington and White concluded that:

> The challenge of local government, therefore, when faced with commercialisation, privatisation or compulsory competitive tendering, is not to retreat passively into acting as a residuary body...but to take on an even more pro-active leadership role, generating a strategic vision and framework for the whole sphere of leisure, public and private. (1988: p. 246)

At the September 1994 Kids Clubs Network conference, Denise Platt, president of the Association of Directors of Social Services, said that even central government, through the Childrens Act, expected local authorities to take a strategic planning role for their local communities. This meant that everyone needed to think, and then work, across services. Future assessments of need would require a shift in culture from service orientation to outcomes for children and families. This would highlight the need for local authorities to make choices about targeting resources or providing universal services and crisis intervention or prevention (Lubelska, 1994). A number of other organisations are also pushing for written strategic documents. The Audit Commission in all their publications (none specifically on play), insist on the need for written policies and clear, quantifiable and measurable targets. Even financial incentives are being used by grant aiding bodies such as the Sports Council and the new National Lottery Boards. If you have not got a strategy, it is unlikely you will get any money.

Some journal articles discuss the process and content of leisure strategies, such as that of Mann (1990), which is based upon Strategic Leisure's consultancy work for local authorities. Some leisure texts cover leisure strategies, notably Torkildsen (1992, 1993) who discusses the leisure planning process and the more recent Veal (1994) publication which develops in detail the leisure strategy process for local authorities. A current publication by Play Wales (1995) *Developing policies for children's play*, is a very clear, if basic, pamphlet for practitioners. It goes through the process of formulating policies, but also how these could be put into practice. All of this literature demonstrates that a strategic approach to leisure provision is still very new and that the main emphasis is on describing how to do it, with very few examples of good practice or even analysis of the practice or theory.

The National Voluntary Council for Children's Play (NVCCP) have just published a document, *Playing for local government: how local authorities can enhance their corporate strategies and service planning by supporting children's play*. This again puts the case for local government involvement in children's play and argues that because of the very disparate nature of provision:

> ...a strategic and corporate approach needs to be adopted, to ensure that policy and practice are developed in a coherent and reasoned way. (NVCCP, 1995: p. 17)

The strategy needs to be visionary and to provide a shared value base. It needs to clarify the starting point and the goals. Partnerships are essential, involving the voluntary sector and other key agencies, as well as drawing on the views and energy of parents, carers and children themselves. And the strategy needs to work towards clear targets, with proper evaluation and review, if it is to demonstrate its success (NVCCP, 1995: Ch. 5).

The document concludes with 'strategies for play' which offer some realistic starting points, rather than the ideal adoption of the *Children's Charter*. It is about allowing space for informed discussion and the creation of policies and strategies in a broad but realistic framework. It also gives examples of good practice, building on earlier documents about the Children Today Projects (Meichan and Collins, 1992).

6.   The reality

As well as the NCPRU and NVCCP documents mentioned above which try to bring practical examples together, there has been limited research into local authority play policies and strategies. Toner (1994) undertook a study of the situation in Northern Ireland. With a 93% response rate she found a positive interest in children's play. However, out of the third that said they had a council policy on play, only one covered all aspects of direct play provision including outdoor provision, play schemes and summer schemes. Toner found that "in general councils do not have formal policies on play in Northern Ireland" (p. 14). All the councils did however provide outdoor play facilities and all but one provided summer schemes. It isn't that councils are not doing or that they do not have a policy framework but that this is not formalised.

From the information on play policies and strategies at the Play Information Centre, it was found that fifty local authorities had some form of documentation on policy and to some extent strategy as well (Collins had identified sixty four). Eighteen local authorities had only sent information

leaflets, on activities such as summer playschemes. It is assumed that they
were trying to show that they may not have written policies but that they
were doing something for play. The initial methodology approached was to
evaluate each document against a strategic development process developed
from existing frameworks proposed by Torkildsen, Mann and taking the
simplest of the theorist's texts. The process also tried to incorporate some
of the policy issues covered in the NVCCP *Children's Charter.*

Undertaking the task it was found that the documents were so
different and of such differing ages and approaches that it was unfair to
use the information in a quantitative way. What was required was a more
in depth view of the process of strategic thinking and management by
undertaking qualitative interviews with managers having just undertaken
or currently undertaking the production of a strategy document. All of the
leisure managers interviewed discussed the need to evaluate what was
being provided and why, especially in light of actual or threatened budget
cuts. Pip O'Byrne, head of Camden Play Services and chair of the Kids
Clubs Network said that she "was working for an effective local authority
play strategy backed by sufficient resources, but had found that play
was rarely a political priority and frequently fell victim to budget cuts"
(Lubelska, 1994: p. 26). This was found to be true in a number of leisure
strategies, including South Bedfordshire District Council. They stated that
to "operate efficiently and effectively the Council will look towards
more commercial management methods..." (South Bedfordshire District
Council, 1992: p. 3). What this meant for play was not spelt out although
they aimed to develop a play development plan.

In their introduction to their review of Nottingham playgrounds,
Playground Services state that:

> What is required is a co-ordinated strategy — a strategy given the
> same status as that afforded to adult sport and recreation — a
> strategy which embraces the skills of the many departments within
> the authority, which influence and shape the content of the
> physical environment.... . (Playground Services, 1994, p. 4)

However, playgrounds seem to have been the main starting point for review
of local authorities. This is understandable, taking into account the need
for managerial efficiency and effectiveness which is now part of local
authority culture. Playgrounds are foremost in the review as they take up
the majority of the revenue and capital involved in play provision. However,
responses to financial pressures may have resulted in a decline in
provision:

> All of the local authorities involved in this study see play provision
> as a central element in their services.... However economic pres-
> sure have led to a favouring of unstaffed, fixed equipment play-
> grounds rather than professionally staffed play provision of more
> informal kinds, including adventure playgrounds and city farms.
> (Hughes, 1994: p. 2)

Playgrounds need a strategy and management plan, as what was needed when they were built may not be the same now. Even the current refurbishment plans, the introduction of safer surfacing and replacement or removal of unsafe equipment has been done as a reaction to public and litigation demands. Very few playground refurbishment schemes actually take a strategic approach and ask what are we achieving in terms of play opportunities for the children of our district? What are our aims? How best could we achieve these with the resources we have or could have, rather than just doing a playground inspection and having a rolling plan for surfacing, fencing and equipment? An example of what should be done is the play survey undertaken in Leicester in 1987. It not only measured safety, as most playground reviews currently do, but measured play value:

> The measurement was based upon 31 factors of 1-3 on how well the area provided for the active, stimulative, developmental, well being and environmental aspects of play for children. A standard of play values as well as play area provision needs to be established to enable a better planning in the provision and improvement of play areas. (Leicester City Council, 1988: p. 4)

However, most playground reviews are concerned with a programme of refurbishment (Bournemouth, 1995; Hull, 1995; and even Leicester, 1988). Even playgrounds need longer term plans, as one problem with fixed equipment is its limited flexibility. As with other forms of leisure, tastes and fashions are changing quickly. Even managers and designers of the new indoor play facilities are realising that some form of modular construction, or redesign strategy is required within a short space of time (Stephens, 1995). A child's attention span is very short. If the need for regular stimulation, to gender creativity and enjoyment, is to be provided by playgrounds they need to be more flexible or to be changed more regularly.

There are many approaches to undertaking a strategic review and producing a strategy document. The Sports Council advocates the use of issue papers. Torkildsen and Veal use flow diagrams and Mann uses a hierarchical, 'family tree'. Pre-stage one would be a brief, either to consultants or in-house teams. Most current leisure strategies are developed from panels or working-groups. These however have been based on current structures and business units within the local authority (for example, Cardiff City Council). These have limited the scope to what the local authority already provides. Taunton Deane, for example, had three panels, sport (which took the lead), arts and countryside. This was also supported and influenced by national government agencies such as the Sports Council, Arts Council and Countryside Commission officers and documents. What chance was there for play in this? The following sub-sections use the basic strategic structure, as described in section four, to analyse very briefly the theory and practice of existing play policy and strategy documents.

Where are we now? strategic analysis

This section would cover an evaluation of the current position of play provision in the geographical area of the local authority and beyond. In Torkildsen's leisure planning process this would be stage two of the process. However, his stage one is really part of the question of 'where are we now'? It needs not only a revision of the services provided but of the policies and aims of the local authority. This can either be done in-house or by consultants. Playground Services Ltd state in their introduction to their review of Nottingham's playgrounds:

> The review should be seen as a first step, a sound starting point — not as a fully fledged policy document. Equipped playgrounds only form a small part of a play development strategy. A truly comprehensive play policy for Nottingham would need to include ALL supervised play projects, catering for ALL ages and ALL children, including those with special needs: e.g. adventure playgrounds; play areas; etc. It would also include liaison/consultation with local community organisations, and local, regional and national voluntary bodies. The next step in this process would be to develop a corporate approach to the subject, including an analysis of housing, letting policies, admission processes, sport and leisure, education, youth service, voluntary organisations, community organisations, etc. (Playground Services, 1994: p. 3)

Veal (1994: p. 54) has developed a grid to help identify what information needs to be gathered. In strategic management theory terms a strength, weaknesses, opportunities and threats (SWOT) and political, economic, social and technological (PEST) analysis would be advocated.

Most of the strategy and policy documents had some form of position statement, explaining what services were already provided. This mainly referred to the direct provision of the local authority, and in most cases this was just playgrounds. Very few had undertaken a comprehensive audit of facilities and services. The best of the strategies which covered playgrounds had evaluated the current position in the following ways:

- identification of playground location
- ownership
- play equipment against BS5696 Pts I, II, III
- safety surfacing (BS7188)
- fencing
- number of pieces of equipment compared directly against the current NPFA standards (adopted by the Citizen's Charter) of Local Areas for Play (LAP), Locally Equipped Area for Play (LEAP) and Neighbourhood Equipped Areas for Play (NEAP)

The last category, which uses the standards approach advocated by the NPFA (and Audit Commission through the Citizens Charter), was undertaken by the more advanced and current of the documents. In most cases consultants were used to gather and analyse the data because of the technical nature of the evaluation. This highlights the influence that an organisation such as the NPFA has on play provision. Perhaps if there were such standards and guidelines to cover quality and other activities, more comprehensive developments of play provision could be made.

Where do we want to be? Strategic direction and strategy formulation

Another starting point in the strategic process was reviewing existing policies (Torkildsen, 1992, 1993). However, there also needs to be debate about what they should be now and into the period of the document. A local authority needs to assess, in light of its overall corporate role(s), its role in leisure provision. This needs to be done before any mission or vision statement is written. There needs to be fundamental discussion about what approach the local authority is actually going to take. Henry would call this 'service policy orientation'. Henry (1993) describes the ideologies of the 1980s as being: minimalism and cost control; traditional service development; voluntarism; entrepreneurial style; community development; economic development and cultural politics.

Henry develops the view that in reaction to the changes of the 1990s that local authorities have taken one of three approaches: 'left Fordist', 'left post-Fordist and 'right post-Fordist'. He argues that, despite localisation of policy decision, national and even trans-national pressures have resulted in most local authorities adopting 'right post-Fordist' policies. Fordist leisure policy emphasises the social democratic rights of leisure and post-Fordism views leisure as a tool of economic, and in some cases, social, regeneration.

It could be argued that perhaps here, through the managerialist approach of 'post-Fordism', that strategic management could allow more left-wing ideologies to develop. Strategic management is about providing an environment in which managers can be flexible, both reactive and proactive. It accepts and works within the external environment to enable service outcomes to meet agreed policies. It is not that they should always provide and manage but that the customer, or citizens, get what they need. This could mean greater delegation of responsibility and power to the consumer or citizen. Could this be one reason why there has been so little quality consultation with or empowerment of the public? Can politicians and officers 'lose control' of the production? Can social objectives be written so that they are quantifiable and measurable?

Another reason for so few play strategies could be that authorities do not really understand what play is, let alone then have the knowledge to formalise it. What Torkildsen says about recreation can be said for play: "The problem in viewing . . [play] solely as experience is that it is almost impossible to define operationally, and it is difficult to communicate with understanding. We therefore need to find tangible criteria on which to base planning, management and programmes" (1992: p. 113). This has however, in its infancy, been concerned with standards measured in quantity and not quality. The NPFA standards are being questioned by both local authorities and the current Comedia/Demos study of urban parks. The study found that sometimes there is:

> ..."too much space and nothing done in the space".... Therefore questions of quality are now the order of the day, and it is important to shift the strategic arguments about parks and open spaces from crude statistical approaches, to more specialist, needs-based approaches. (Greenhalgh and Worpole, 1995: p. 21)

Who decides what the vision of the future for play is?

> Developing a play policy is not just a matter of getting a few officers around a table.... To be fully effective, it requires a consultation process with the community it is being designed to serve, including the children who will be its prime beneficiaries. The process of developing the policy can become a method of involving people in meeting children's play needs. (Rennie, 1991: p. 185)

If play is being provided by and with so many people and organisations, surely they should be part of this process in the strategy development? Public involvement is difficult to achieve. Too many people can make the process unwieldy. However, it can be done through market research and by getting managers to think strategically. It is too easy for managers to be focused on what they are currently doing and what would be feasible or acceptable. Mintzberg argues that "vision is unavailable to those who cannot 'see' with their own eyes. Real strategists get their hands dirty digging for ideas, and real strategies are built from the occasional nuggets they uncover" (Mintzberg, 1994a: p. 111). In his new book, *The rise and fall of strategic planning* (1994), he argues that vision is more important than a detailed plan of who is doing what, when. His main argument is that:

> ...*strategic planning* is not *strategic thinking*. Indeed, strategic planning often spoils strategic thinking, causing managers to confuse real vision with the manipulation of numbers. And this confusion lies at the heart of the issue: the most successful strategies are visions, not plans. (Mintzberg, 1994a: p. 107)

He says that the strategy-making process should be:

> ...capturing what the manager learns from all sources (both the soft insights from his or her personal experiences and the experiences of others throughout the organization and the hard data from market research and the like) and then synthesizing that learning into a vision of the direction that the business should pursue. (Mintzberg, 1994a: p. 107)

Perhaps play itself can help the strategic process by encouraging adults to explore, investigate, manipulate, create and learn. To put the decision making in the hands of the participants to enable freedom of choice. There is a need for more emphasis on the participant rather than the outcome (like the play theorists say is part of play). Would this help local authorities create the right environment for play opportunities to flourish rather than be concerned with how many playgrounds and schemes there are?

It is too easy to become product orientated, concerned with activities and facilities. This is particularly evident with play strategies, where the concern is over safety standards and numbers. Market orientation is very much part of the managerialist language Henry in some ways criticises in his analysis of the post-Fordist state. Perhaps the terminology is now more acceptable and understandable to local authority managers than seeing parents and children as citizens. An analysis of the 'market' is vital to any strategy, whether economically or socially based. Only a few strategies gave any detailed information or undertook any analysis of the market. Again, it seems to be the later documents, that have learnt from others and perhaps the text books, that have.

It has been identified that 20% of the national population is under 16 years of age (Torkildsen, 1993: p. 10) and that children are the main reason for people visiting their local park (Greenhalgh and Worpole, 1995: p. 7). Bournemouth Borough Council's draft *Leisure Strategy* identifies that 11% of their residents were under 12 years of age and that there was a predicted increase of 20,000 by 2001. They discuss the need for the provision of organised play and for a play strategy to be developed. The current provision of equipped play areas is given more space and is discussed in more detail. The underlying proposals here are to take out a number of smaller playgrounds, deemed not to fit the newly proposed standards of provision, and create improved and larger neighbourhood playgrounds. It is felt that the problems associated with equipped small play areas and their lack of play value is outweighed by the benefits gained from larger, yet still accessible, playgrounds and the provision of better landscaped open space left as a result. The main criteria for this has been the imbalance of provision to areas of a lower child population than others. The analysis for the proposed site changes has been based upon:

- child population within the local districts
- major and busy roads and railway lines which act as boundaries to residential areas
- the proximity of urban countryside/beach which provide opportunities for informal and adventure play for children
- the size of residential gardens
- proximity to other outdoor play provision such as adventure playgrounds or school play provision

Bournemouth have attempted to understand the nature of supply and demand and to devise a method of planning provision on the character-istics mentioned above. However, their argument is not substantiated and more in depth research and analysis is required if any lessons can be learnt from their example.

There is no proposed formal proactive consultation with children in Bournemouth's leisure strategy. There are a number of roadshows and workshops organised; otherwise people will have to purchase or refer to the document to fill in their comments form. Most of the proposals that will be adopted will therefore be based on the views of adults. Young people have however been recognised as a group that needs to be consulted with. As part of the market research process, there was an attempt to ascertain where young people 'hang out'. This covered the 12-16 year olds who said that the most popular meeting places, other than the home, in order of popularity were, the beach, the park and the street. As part of the topic paper for leisure opportunities for young people it was stated that "it is especially important to recognise and respect the advice and opinions of young people and allow them to influence the service that is being provided through consultation and involvement" (p. 16). This was certainly stressed as a key issue, with suggestions at the official launch presentation of the strategy, of investigating the establishment of a Youth Council after unitary authority reorganisation.

How might we get there? Strategic choice and evaluation

Greenley (1989) argues that there are three strategic alternatives: growth, stability or defence. Comments about early local authority strategies sug-gest that they were concerned with growth, that they were just 'wish lists' of facilities that the authority wanted to provide. However, growth in such economic and political times is very unlikely and strategies have remained 'on the shelf'. In the current climate the approach has, to some extent, been defensive, proving the value of the services provided at a time when they could be questioned:

> At a time when resources are under increasing pressure the need to manage resources effectively becomes more important. It is only through an understanding of the current provision, demands and the setting of predetermined goals, that resources can be utilised to the maximum effect.... (Hull, 1995: p. 5)

> ...For the current level of resources there are too many playgrounds to support at the required standard. Unless additional resources can be found there will have to be a system of prioritising sites which will result in the down grading of some playgrounds with the removal of equipment. (Hull, 1995: p. 29)

It is about being realistic with the resources available, but also creative to enable services to remain stable (if different) or to improve. The fear is that strategic choices are being made on poor information and that decisions are being influenced by managerial problems. For example, proposals are being made in many strategies to close small play areas on the basis of nuisance caused; lack of play value and changes in lifestyle, especially access to transport and gardens.

One local authority started the process of a playground review which was done in great detail and the draft report submitted in 1994. Since then the document has only been used to identify areas that need more maintenance attention. However, it has not been developed into a playground strategy, the initial intention. This is mainly because the proposals within the document have been based upon reviewing the playgrounds against the NPFA standards in terms of safety and quantity of provision. This latter area has been the one of most concern, especially concerning the LAPs in terms of numbers and locations. In some authorities, this means that they are short of hundreds of play areas. To many managers this requires unjustified resources and could result in a multiplication of the management problems that small play areas cause in terms of noise and complaints. The aims of the NPFA policies may have seemed acceptable but once evaluated in terms of strategic choice and practicality they were discarded.

How can we ensure arrival? Strategic implementation and control

Once decisions on what strategies should be adopted are made, they then need to be implemented. Action is far more important than words. The human aspects of strategic management cannot be overlooked, especially at the implementation stage. Strategies are formulated and implemented for and by people. It relies on managers to be able to understand what and whom they are being influenced by. As following diagram shows (from Greenley, 1989), there are four internal factors influencing a manager's process of planning:

Source: Greenley, 1989: p. 196.

In one authority it was found that there were some assistant directors who were thought of as good managers, operationally, but who did not understand the concept of strategic management. It was not clear whether this was through a lack of capability or the attitude that strategic management was not worth while. As a result they had not undertaken their service strategy as part of the overall plan for the directorate. The chief officer believed in the need for strategic management, but felt that it could not be prescriptive. The process, nor the resulting document would not work if key personnel in the organisation did not understand or believe in it. Attempts would therefore have to be made to change those people's attitudes and capabilities and not just to leave gaps in the process.

One authority was contacted owing to the strength of its strategic document in the National Play Information Centre. It was, however, found to be a document that had been shelved and was not being used. According to the chief officer, the strategy document was "done as a result of a financial opportunity and most probably because the officer concerned thought it was the 'done thing' and would look good on his curriculum vitae". A playground strategy had however just been undertaken, as no audit of existing facilities had ever been done. They did not even know how many playgrounds the authority actually provided, as different departments were responsible for them. It was felt by the chief officer that the earlier document must have been full of unreal expectations that could not be met in the existing political and financial climate. It was believed that a more pragmatic and realistic approach would be to start off from where they actually were and to work from there. The chief officer stated that it was "more important to get your own house in order before trying to tell others what they should be doing".

There is also the need to involve all stakeholders in the process, otherwise they will not own the responsibility for its implementation. It could be argued that:

> ...calculated strategies have no value in and of themselves; to paraphrase the words of sociologist Philip Selznick, strategies take on value only as committed people infuse them with energy. (Mintzberg, 1994a: p. 109)

In the commercial sector it is easier to argue that:

> ...business-unit managers must take full and effective charge of the strategy-making process. The lesson that has still not been accepted is that managers will never be able to take charge through a formalised process. (Mintzberg, 1994a: p. 112)

In local authorities there are many people who could be involved, from politicians and officers to local residents and group organisers. It is easier to have a formalised process if a large number of people are going to be involved and if a more representative view is to be made.

The formalised methods used by most local authorities, if any at all, were either a list of recommendations and action, or an action plan. The early indications, on the more recent documents, are that the action plans are being implemented. However, a lot of them were very generalised and would need to be built into a hierarchy of plans such as marketing, budgets and operations — one officer reported that at least they now had a focus and found it easier to explain to people what they were trying to do and that they now had the ability to say no to people. Certainly more research is required to see whether strategies have collected dust or whether they have actually been used. The present findings show that the process itself is very useful, but whether detailed plans are developed and used from it is another question.

7. Conclusions and recommendations

It appears, from a review of the published literature, a brief investigation of the existing documents in the Play Information Centre and in-depth interviews with five different local authorities that there are a number of approaches to strategic management. These can be simplified into those that concentrate on a vision, through either stating their aims or policies and others that have taken a more pragmatic approach. They feel that it is better to start from what they feel is a more realistic base, to find out what playgrounds the Council provides and to get these improved or changed within existing resources. There really needs to be a mixture of both and only those local authorities that have been developing play policies and provision for a number of years are actually doing this (Leicester, for example). There needs to be a lot more research done in this field to be able to then persuade and show local authorities what could be achieved. The Play Wales and NVCCP documents go some way to doing this but they need to be 'sold' to the local authorities and action taken.

It needs to be proven whether the formalisation, the writing down of policies and plans, add benefit to the practice. The more detailed methods of strategic planning need to be analysed to see whether they are applicable or useful to local authority leisure and play strategies. Initial findings indicate that local authorities are finding it difficult, in these times of change, to think strategically. It is understandable that resources are being concentrated on keeping current services running. The additional time found to prepare for CCT in leisure services is now being used to prepare for unitary status. Most people at senior level acknowledge the importance of strategic planning but are finding it difficult in terms of time and training of staff to undertake it. Theoretically, now is the ideal time for strategic thinking, to have a vision of the future, whether unitary status has been 'won' or not. The next stage would be to plan for that future. A lot of the leisure strategies are actually statements of intent. The action plans are full of doing further strategies such as one for play. These will only be successful if they are part of people's day-to-day work. Another pile of paperwork, unless it is seen as improving the service or its delivery, will not be welcome.

Leisure managers now say that they have developed, or are developing, documents that are used and not just left on the shelf. Only time and research will tell whether this is true or not. Surely now is the time for such documents (if they have to be documents) to be utilised as a means of giving direction to new structures. Many local authorities are not going to be changed under unitary status but they have and should continue to look at their organisation and what they are trying to achieve. The process of preparing for possible unitary status has actually halted or slowed down the process of strategy preparation. Time seems to have been taken up with preserving what already exists rather than viewing what could be achieved. This is reflected in the fight for the recognition of leisure and the need to integrate into unified but independent departments (ILAM, 1994). Surely this should be seen as part of strategic thinking and not a defensive mechanism? But which chief officer would not fight to safeguard the existing structure or look to build the empire in the name of leisure?

What should be the new role for local authorities in these changing times is only being realised to a limited extent. As Benington and White said in 1988:

> Local authorities are in a position to provide the kind of imaginative leadership which would allow them to orchestrate a wide range of leisure facilities and services which are not all under their direct control — creating a lively framework of ideas, values, strategies, plans and programmes which would effectively harness the energies of many different agencies (public, voluntary and private) behind a common vision and sense of direction for leisure services for the whole community. This would involve a very much more outgoing, entrepreneurial, catalytic and interventionist role for local authorities than is traditional; a commitment not just to provide high quality services to those who come to use them but also to reach out into the community to identify unmet need; to develop solutions in dialogue with the potential users of services, and in conjunction with other agencies. This new kind of role for the local authority has implications not just for service-delivery at the field level, but also for strategic planning and resource-management and organisation at the corporate level. It means active and imaginative local government, committed to the highest standards of quality in its service for the public. (Benington and White, 1988: p. 252)

This sounds exciting and gives a positive vision for local authorities. However, the reality is less than visionary and more research and dissemination of information on how local authorities realise this dream is required. It is too easy for local authorities to say that they do not have the finance or the time to provide for new services such as play. Some very difficult facts need to be faced and decisions made in light of current and future changes. Local authorities will not be able to maintain the level of leisure provision that their communities may need. They must develop policies and strategies to work with the community so that they can be jointly realised. Small local authorities with very limited resources need to be shown that it is easy to make a start, that the process of having a vision that includes play does not cost a lot of money or time. A lot is already being done by the voluntary sector and now more by the commercial sector. Redman concludes, in his review of play projects, that each "has amply demonstrated that, in a world where almost all of the activity comes directly through voluntary involvement, the injection of relatively small amounts of cash resources, well placed and managed, can reap great rewards in terms of enhanced play provision to the benefit of our children and our communities" (Redman, 1992: p. 42). This could be done through a process of strategic thinking, planning and management.

Note

1   The National Play Information Centre address is 359-361 Euston Road, London NW1 3AL.

2   Full details/references for data sources can be obtained from the author [Department of Service Industries, Bournemouth University, Poole BH12 5BB).

References

Benington, J. and White, J. (1988) 'The need for a new strategic vision for leisure services', in J. Benington and J. White (eds) *The future of leisure services*. Harlow: Longman, pp. 245-252.

Benson, J. (1993) 'Children's reality', *Leisure Management*, Vol. 13, No. 6: pp. 38-40.

Bolton, N., (1995) 'A leisure strategy for Cardiff', *The Leisure Manager*, Vol. 13, No. 1: pp. 16-18.

Bournemouth Borough Council (1995) *Bournemouth leisure strategy: a vision for the future*.

Coalter, F. (1990a) 'Analysing leisure policy', in I. Henry (ed) *Management and planning in the leisure industries*. Basingstoke: MacMillan.

——— (1990b) 'The politics of professionalism: consumers or citizens?', *Leisure Studies*, Vol. 9, pp. 107-119.

Collins, M. (1993) 'Team play', *Leisure Management*, Vol. 13, No. 3: pp. 53-58.

——— (1994) 'Play grounding', *Leisure Management*, Vol. 14 , No. 3: pp. 32-33.

Greenhalgh, L. and Worpole, K. (1995) *Park life: Urban parks and social renewal.* Stroud: Comedia and Demos.

Greenley, G. E. (1989) *Strategic management.* Hemel Hempstead: Prentice Hall.

Henry, I. and Spink, J. (1990) 'Social theory, planning and management', in I. Henry (ed) *Management and planning in the leisure industries.* London: Macmillan.

Henry, I. (1993) *The politics of leisure policy.* London: Macmillan.

Hughes, B. (1994) *Lost childhoods: The case for children's play.* Comedia and Demos.

Hull City Council (1995) *A playground strategy for Hull.*

ILAM (1994) *Local government reorganisation: The case for leisure services.*

Johnson, G. and Scholes, K. (1989) *Exploring corporate strategy* (2nd ed). Hemel Hempstead: Prentice Hall.

Leicester City Council (1986) *Parks for people.*

Leicester City Council (1988) 'Children's play areas', report of the Director of Recreation and Arts to the Recreation Committee and Policy and Resources (Finance) sub-committee, April.

Lubelska, A. (1994) 'Forward play', *Leisure Opportunities,* No. 128: p. 26.

Mann, P. (1990) 'Planning and management of local authority leisure strategies', *The Planner,* 6 April, pp. 11-14.

Meichan, A. and Collins, M. (1992) *Children today — a national overview.* London: The National Children's Play and Recreation Unit.

Mintzberg, H. (1994a) 'The fall and rise of strategic planning', *Harvard Business Review,* Jan-Feb: pp. 107-114.

———— (1994b) *The rise and fall of strategic planning.* Hemel Hempstead: Prentice Hall International.

Moore, V. (1994) 'Playing with figures', *Leisure Management,* Vol. 14, No. 11: pp. 54-56.

National Playing Fields Association (NPFA) (1992) *The six acre standard: Minimum standards for outdoor playing space.* London: NPFA.

National Voluntary Council for Children's Play (1992) *A charter for children's play.* London: The Children's Society.

———— (1995) *Playing for local government.* London: National Children's Bureau.

Nichols, G. (1993) 'Evidence of encroaching managerialism under the compulsory competitive tendering of leisure facilities'. Draft unpublished paper.

Play Wales (1994) *Developing policies for children's play.* Cardiff: Play Wales.

PlayBoard (1985) *Make way for children's play.* London: Playboard.

Playground Services (1994) 'The City of Nottingham: playgrounds review', NPFA, unpublished draft report.

Ravenscroft, N and Tolley, J. (1993) 'Ideological dominance in recreation provision: The response of local authorities in Britain to compulsory competitive tendering', paper presented at LSA 3rd international conference , 'Leisure in Different Worlds' (July).

Ravenscroft, N. (1993) 'Public leisure provision and the good citizen', *Leisure Studies*, Vol. 12, pp. 33-44.

Redman, W. (1992) 'Organising play: The evaluation of the strategic projects of NCPRU', unpublished, KCA.

Rennie, S. (1991) 'Play and playwork', in N. Borret (ed) *Leisure services UK.* London: Macmillan, pp. 159-189.

Smith, M. (1993) 'The place for play in children's services', in NVCCP/ ILAM, *Securing a future for children's play* (Conference pack).

South Bedfordshire District Council (1992) *Leisure strategy.*

Sports Council (1991) *District sport and recreation strategies.* London: Sports Council.

Stephens, S. (1995) 'Flexible trend', *Leisureweek*, Vol. 6, No. 20: p. 21.

Toner, K. (1994) *Agenda for play: The way forward.* London: Save the Children and PlayBoard.

Torkildsen, G. (1992) *Leisure and recreation management.* London: E and FN Spon.

—— (1993a) *A review of national support for children's plan and recreation.* London: The National Playing Fields Association.

—— (1993b) *Torkildsen's guide to leisure management.* London: Longman.

Veal, A. J. (1994) *Leisure policy and planning.* Harlow: Longman/ILAM.

Wilson, R. M. S. and Gilligan, C. with Pearson, D. J. (1992) *Strategic marketing management: planning, implementation and control.* Oxford: Butterworth-Heinemann Ltd., in association with the Chartered Institute of Marketing.

Urban Playgrounds: Re-thinking the City as an Environment for Children's Play

Stephen Williams

Staffordshire University

Introduction

In this paper I want to argue several inter-related positions. First, I will start by reiterating what is surely not a contentious point, namely that one of the primary interfaces that we should recognise between leisure and education is experiential learning through play. It is therefore a matter of concern that contemporary trends in urban outdoor play signal clear reductions in the play horizons and experiences of our children. Secondly, I want to suggest that several of the key presumptions on which limitations on play activity are based arise from perceptions of risks that over-emphasise the threat of hazards that children at play might encounter. Thirdly, I will argue that if the full educational value of play is to be recovered we need first to develop a coherent and effective play policy, one that recognises the realities both of what children across the age spectrum require for play and what authorities can actually deliver. Secondly, and more fundamentally, we need a revision in basic attitudes towards the urban environment and the position of children within that environment.

Play and learning — the interface

Amongst the many interfaces between leisure and education, one of the most fundamental is the experiential learning that children derive through the varied experiences of play. Play is not just an activity through which entertainment and pleasures are gained but is also a mechanism for the development of children as individuals and a means for assimilation into the adult world. Barnett (1990), in summarising an extensive literature on the developmental psychology of children, shows how play can be central to their cognitive, emotional and social development, whilst Moore (1986: p. 12), in what is one of the most engaging studies of children at play in urban environments, puts the case with simplicity and directness. "Playing is learning", he writes, and "the child's playful interaction with the environment and his or her absorption of worldly experience produces a feeling of competence, a sense of mastery and control over the environment".

The German educator Scherler (cited in Moore, 1986) has suggested that play embraces six functions that advance children's development and learning — learning here being defined in the broadest of senses. These functions may be briefly summarised as follows:

1. the *adaptive* function. Play is a primary mechanism through which the physiological capabilities of children are advanced. Many forms of play are based upon running, jumping, skipping and other forms of movement and help foster in children the development of strength, speed, stamina, agility and balance.

2. the *comparative* function. Play will often possess competitive dimensions that reflect the degree of physiological development that the child has attained. Play thus affords a medium through which children learn to compare themselves with others and become attuned to concepts of winning or losing; success or failure.

3. the *expressive* function. Capacities to cope with failure or losing can be amongst the most difficult for young children to acquire and the expressive function, which Scherler conceives as essentially an emotional dimension, is particularly important. Play helps children learn to experience and cope with basic emotions: fear, excitement, curiosity, pleasure, sadness, annoyance and fulfilment. These skills link directly with

4. the *communicative* function. Play contexts can help children gain experience of how to relate to others: to co-operate, to accept rules and to create and maintain networks of social contacts. They identify others with whom they like to associate, they learn whom they can trust and with whom they emphasise. Conversely they also come to recognise other children with whom they have little in common. Where adults are involved in play, whether in formal play schemes or the informality of play within a family, valuable skills in how to relate to the often confusing world of adults will be developed.

5. the *explorative* function. Many forms of play contain an explorative dimension as children interact with different places, environments or situations. This may advance elements such as tactile appreciation of different materials, development of spatial cognition or simpler acquisition of knowledge concerning their surroundings, including the flora and fauna. Such understanding gained through exploration may assist in

6. the *productive* function. Routine forms of play will help children learn how to make and alter things. Use of constructional toys, for example, helps younger children in the perfection of manipulative skills, whilst

amongst older children, the making of dens and hideouts or the collecting of objects are variations upon the same productive theme.

The balance and emphasis between and within these various functions will alter according to particular play contexts and the developmental stage that the child has attained, but their centrality to personal development and acquisition of life-time skills underscores the educational and learning value of play.

Shrinking worlds of urban play and the perception of risk

In the light of this significance and the almost self-evident values of play, it is not an unreasonable expectation that urban authorities would be pursuing a vigorous policy of development of play opportunity.

Yet this is clearly not the case. Collins (1995), for example, has shown how in Britain play provision is fragmented (with no lead agency at a national level), under-funded, and too often unable to see beyond conventional equipped play areas, the play values of which have been doubted and their capacity to hold the attention of children shown to be severely limited (Brown and Burger, 1984).

More significantly, perhaps, the natural play horizons of urban children — the locations that lie outside the realm of designated, equipped playgrounds and which the children themselves colonise and manage — have probably become more restricted. Children construct environments in a quite different manner to adults, and features and places in urban areas that adults might not accord a second glance can become empowered with a deep significance in the play world of the child. A tree, a street corner, a lamp post, a patch of wasteground, for example, may become key elements in children's play environments — as meeting places, play props, or even as secret places of the child's own making. It is very important that children have access to such 'found places' (as they are sometimes termed), yet the capacity for children to create these places is becoming increasingly limited. In a longitudinal study of patterns of play in New York City spanning 60 years, Gaster (1991) showed that the minimum age at which children were allowed into their neighbourhood unsupervised had risen, whilst the number and quality of the settings that they were able to visit had declined. Obstacles to play (physical development, road traffic, areas controlled by street gangs or other groups perceived as 'anti-social' etc.) had become more widespread and an increased proportion of activity was being concentrated into designated play spaces and supervised play programmes. The study concluded that, overall, the capacity of the urban neighbourhood to support children's play had declined significantly.

Why has this contraction in urban play worlds come about? First, it should be acknowledged that there is an element of choice that is made by the children themselves and which is encouraged by the youth cultures in which they reside. Leisure in general has tended to become more home-centred (Roberts, 1989) and for many children the appeal of television, video, recorded music and computer games is very real and a major deflector of activity from outdoor play.

Secondly, it may be argued that the focusing of play into designated spaces and managed schemes is a classic response to the management of an activity that is essentially problematic. Corralling our children in this way is a convenient solution to managing a group that is easily perceived as a potential nuisance. And it is a policy that is easy for politicians and urban managers to defend (at a superficial level) since it becomes possible to present outwardly convincing cases that issues are being addressed through the establishment of a tangible response in, for instance, playground provision, appointment of play workers and the funding of play schemes.

However it is evident, thirdly, that negative images of urban life that draw attention to personal risk through crime, the hazards of traffic, of 'dangerous' places and increasingly endemic social malaise, have led directly to children experiencing a significant raising in the level of (adult) restrictions, not just upon their play but upon a whole range of routine movements around urban areas. For example, twenty five years ago only around 1 in 10 of primary and junior school children were escorted to school by adults; today only 1 in 10 are unescorted. Revealingly, too, in Moore's (1986) study of children in London, Stoke-on-Trent and Stevenage, he found that whilst many parents reminisced fondly on the way in which they had roamed widely as children, few now felt sufficiently confident to permit their own off-spring the same degree of freedom.

Parental protection of the child is, of course, a normal part of life through which the inexperienced child is shielded from the worst outcomes that their play may generate. But have we gone too far in limiting where children may go and what they may do? There *are* risks attached to play — there have to be, otherwise how does a child learn to recognise hazards and danger? But the greater risk, surely, lies in limiting play itself, simply because children whose actions are closely regulated will fail (or find it harder) to derive the competencies (outlined above) that a rich play experience can afford, and will be rendered less able to cope with the adult life that follows.

It is a truism that most risks are far more imagined than real and, in the context of play, this paper argues that the restrictions we place upon the play of our children to counteract such 'risk' need not be as extensive as they are tending to become. We steer children away from one of their favourite play mediums — water, yet accident statistics (OPCS, 1993) show that deaths from drowning by children aged between five and fourteen are half the rate for the population as a whole. We discourage our children from climbing into high places and spend millions of pounds installing 'safe' surfaces beneath apparatus on equipped playgrounds, the efficacy and value of which has been challenged (Ball and King, 1990). But children are actually the least likely group in the population to suffer death or serious injury from falling. Similarly, the inevitable publicity that cases of child abduction and/or murder attract, makes such crime one of the primary parental fears that causes them to limit their children's activity. However, the rates of such crime in the UK have remained largely unaltered over several decades and children are actually at much greater risk in the home and from the actions of people they know than from malevolent strangers. It may of course be that the statistics tell the story they do *because* parents have become so protective of their children, but the contention here is that the real risks are not generally as serious as many tend now to believe.

The one area in which there is a serious and increasing risk to children at play in the urban environment is that of road traffic. Crude accident statistics from the Department of Transport (1992) show that, as pedestrians, children up to the age of 14 years are twice as likely to suffer death or serious injury from road traffic as people over 14 years (children—494 per million; adults—252 per million per annum) and whilst the aggregate rate for cyclists is lower (children—124 per million killed or seriously injured; adults—74 per million), the rate would be higher if it were expressed as a proportion of those who actually cycle, especially amongst children where play with bicycles is far more commonplace than is cycling amongst adults. Road traffic, therefore, is a real limitation on play and this is an issue that urban play policy — and indeed, planning policy in a wider sense — must address.

Restoring the values of play

So far this paper has suggested that the significant potential educational values of play are being eroded by the manner in which urban play environments are becoming more restricted: through changes in the environment itself, through adoption of managerial attitudes that favour what is effectively only a narrow range of provision, and through the constraining actions of parents whose images of cities tend to promote greater levels of concern over child safety than previously. The net effect of these changes has been a re-centring of play into the home and into a relatively limited range of designated and managed play places — environments, it is argued, that will deliver only a part of the full educational value of play. If we are to restore the breadth of opportunity, a range of actions and changes needs to be set in motion. I want to suggest three general areas for action, each of which contains several possible avenues for development.

a. Filling the Policy Vacuum

First, there is a clear case for development and maintenance of a coherent and viable policy (or set of policies) for play, although there are several dimensions to this problem. The lack of a clear lead from government is one such issue. Government has flirted with policy guidance in, for

Figure 1   **Theoretical hierarchy for play provision**

Level of Provision	Location	Purpose	Area	Landscaping and Equipment
Doorstep play area	within 50 metres of the home	mainly for under 5s; meeting place for adults; separate sites for older children for social play	small; 50 - 100 sq. metres	hard and soft surfacing; protected from wind but receiving plenty of sunlight; planting; on larger sites slopes, mounds, hollows and wild areas to attract birds and butterflies
Local play space	within 400 metres of the home	mainly for children over 5; or adults with small children	at least 1 hectare	favourable micro climate created by walls and/or planting; slopes and hollows; natural areas with climbable trees, bushes, long grass and water; traditional and adventurous play equipment; sand; flat area for ball games; paths for wheeled toys; seats and benches; lighting
Adventure playgrounds	within 400 metres of the home	to provide challenging play experience for children of all ages under adult supervision	between 1,000 and 10,000 sq. metres	Fenced site with play hut with electricity, water, toilets and storage space; child-managed land-scape with playhuts, dens, gardens, sand, hutches for animals and water
Neighbourhood park / playspace	within 500-600 metres of the home	to provide for all age groups from young children to the elderly	about 4 hectares	landscaped area with different levels, slopes and mounds; natural areas with trees, water and wild flowers; pitches for formal games; benches; shelter; play equipment
District park / playspace	within 2-3 kms of the home	to provide for all age groups from young children to the elderly	at least 20 hectares	as above but with the addition of formal areas; lakes (with boats); sports facilities — e.g. tennis, bowls; cafeterias; pavilions

Source : adapted from Coffin and Williams (1989: pp. 27-30)

example, the well-known Circular 79/72 (DoE, 1972) and in more recent pronouncements on playground safety (NCPRU, 1992), but such sporadic and half-hearted interest falls well short of the type of co-ordinated and committed participation for which calls have been made (CPAC, 1988). Any national level policy for play must also address the issue of resourcing, which is critical. A recent report in the *Independent on Sunday* (cited in Hughes, 1994) notes, for example, that for every £100 spent by the Department of Heritage on adult leisure needs in urban parks, spending on children's needs in the same areas amounted to just 3p. The myopia and injustice of such a pattern of expenditure (if reported accurately) beggars belief and represents a serious failure to recognise the value of investing in children's play.

Secondly, at the local policy level, local authority leisure service and land planning units need to adopt a more enabling stance. Heseltine and Holborn (1987) highlight two problems: first the tendency of local land planners to find a designated use for every available patch of land rather than leaving some areas unused but available for colonisation by children at play. Secondly, there is a tendency, born of the convenience to which reference has already been made, to conceive play environments in terms of fixed apparatus at unsupervised, designated sites — a very popular idea with planners but unfortunately less so with children.

Thirdly, policy for play must be realistic and it must reflect the breadth of needs that children (who after all constitute a remarkably diverse group) will profess. There has been no shortage of advice to policymakers as to how children's play should be provided. Figure 1, for example, represents a typical attempt at setting out a pattern for comprehensive provision as proposed by Coffin and Williams (1989). But such schemes, worthy though they be, suffer two distinct deficiencies. First, there is a lack of realism in such recommendations because, whilst the suggested catchment areas accurately reflect the very limited ranges that many children experience when at play (Parkinson, 1987), when it comes to delivering such a system the resources do not exist, nor are they likely to exist. Williams (1995a) calculates, for example, that to install the play hierarchy set out in Figure 1 in a typical small British city such as Exeter (population circa 100,000), would involve creation of over 2000 play areas, mostly of the doorstep type as described by Coffin and Williams. The prospect of securing sufficient land and financial resources to afford basic equipment necessary to provide such a scheme seems remote, at the very least.

The second major difficulty with schemes of this type is that they tend to overstate the value of designated spaces. In reviewing the contemporary literature on provision there is an evident tension between advocacy of a structured, comprehensive and well-resourced approach to provision and the tacit recognition that children often get the better experiences from places that they themselves locate, personalise and manage. The problem for providers is that it is very difficult to take such 'found' places into account, not least because of the practical difficulty for adults in appreciating what type of casual space will interest a child. But it argued here that the attempt should be made. Confining children's play to designated spaces, no matter how diverse and interesting they may be, will not deliver all the benefits in personal development and experience that play can afford. Donnelly (1980: p. 66) talks of "a need for ambiguous places, even slightly dangerous places" — woods, ponds, natural areas, undergrowth, old buildings etc., that support and enable fantasy play — "child-made places where dens can be built, where collectibles such as blackberries, conkers, newts, tadpoles, even items of rubbish may be garnered and put to use in imaginative play, places where secrets may be shared, trees climbed, tin cans stoned and fires lit" (Williams, 1995a: p. 144). The conventional urban playground, even the so-called adventure playground, provides relatively few of these opportunities. But that is not to say that the urban environment at large cannot provide for such activity if we want it to.

b. Changing attitudes to children

To achieve such a transition requires a fundamental change in attitudes — in our expectation of the urban environment as a whole and the experiences it can provide and, critically, in our attitudes towards the place of children within that environment. A number of studies including, conspicuously, that by Moore (1986), emphasise the need to accommodate children on their terms. Yet all too often, officialdom in its various guises treats children at play as an obstacle to be removed from public gaze and confined to designated space — out of sight and most definitely out of earshot! Too many urban parks still prohibit activities that children enjoy — cycling, even ball-games — whilst modern residential neighbourhoods seem to make fewer and fewer concessions to the needs of children. Elson (1989) notes that even where planning permissions for housing developments place obligations upon developers to provide children's play areas, such space often fails to materialise, not least due to objection from residents whose homes lie close to proposed play space. But so long as we view children as being 'associate' rather than 'full' members of society, real advances in provision for play will be difficult to achieve.

c. Re-thinking the urban environment

In a sense, though, I am less concerned about a failure to provide the requisite number of playgrounds according to some arbitrary planning norm since the argument I am advancing here is that such play space should only be one element in a much broader portfolio of play environments that should be found throughout our towns and cities. In particular, play on the street and play within a range of natural or semi-natural urban spaces should also be possible. To achieve this, though, requires fundamental re-thinking of the urban environment.

The street is potentially a very valuable leisure space (Williams, 1995b) and is a particularly important play environment, both historically and, despite the onslaught of motor traffic, within the contemporary world too. Streets are accessible; they offer a surface that well suits a range of popular activities, especially using wheeled toys; and they offer an interesting social environment through the presence of others who are on the street. Play policy ought therefore be seeking to reclaim a significant proportion of residential streets to enable this incidental use by children. Calming of traffic and the physical redesign of street areas to suit a range of recreations should be a priority. Urban authorities in the Netherlands, in Germany and in parts of Scandinavia have shown that street uses can be diversified in this way (especially through the creation of the *woonerf* — the "living street"). Although some local authorities in the UK are beginning belatedly to appreciate the recreational utility of streets, there is clearly still a long way to go. In a recent article in a professional planning journal, Sheldon (1990: p. 22) presents something of a nadir in blinkered thinking in the approach of urban planners, stating quite openly that "street play is totally unacceptable" and that the challenge to planners is "to keep children off the street". Sheldon misses completely the point that making streets and public areas safe and enjoyable for children's play also makes them amenable for other leisurely uses by the urban community at large.

Part of any process of re-thinking urban environments ought also to embrace re-design of suburban residential neighbourhoods. For play (and other recreations) to flourish we don't just need regulation of traffic: the street and housing environments themselves need to be made visually interesting through importation of innovation in civic design. Years of formula-based urban planning, guided by spacing norms and constrained by planners' collective views that all patches of land should have a clear and designated use, have endowed the UK with a suburban environment that is bland, predictable and uninteresting. For children, their limited geographical range ensures that the neighbourhood is their primary play environment, so any policy that aims to re-design spaces to accommodate play ought to look first at the housing areas in which we live. Re-configuration of the roadway can be a part of that process, but we need to find less regimented ways of setting out housing plots and, as a part of that process, to allow residual spaces that will suit various forms of children's play to form a natural part of the neighbourhood land mosaic.

One of the most effective ways in which we can enliven dull suburban streets is through wider incorporation into neighbourhoods of natural and semi-natural spaces; recent increases in attention accorded to greening the city are very much to be welcomed (Nicholson-Lord, 1987). Children value play in natural environments particularly highly. Natural areas — woodlands, ponds and streams, untended grass and undergrowth — are ideal for the private, 'found' places that most children enjoy and which they can utilise in different ways as they grow and their interests and capabilities evolve. It is important, therefore, that not only do we encourage initiatives which bring natural spaces into cities, but also that in declaring preferred uses for such spaces (the rationales for which are often guided and dominated by conservationist thinking), their utility as play spaces should not be overlooked. Children will become, *de facto*, users of natural and semi-natural environments wherever they occur, so managers of such spaces need to recognise the fact and take it into account in devising land management strategies. In this way the play utility of new forms of natural spaces that are beginning to appear within British cities, for example through the work of Groundwork Trusts or the land reclamation policies of some of the more forward-thinking local authorities (see for example Birmingham City Council, 1989; Leicester City Council, 1989), will be properly realised.

Conclusion

This paper is arguing three inter-related themes. First, there is a fundamental link between learning and play in children and the activity of play can often have a seriousness and a significance that, paradoxically, the word 'play' usually tends to deny. The evident contraction in the play horizons of contemporary children is therefore viewed as a matter of concern, although it has been suggested, secondly, that some of the factors that have become powerful limitations upon the independence of children in urban places have been overstated and that a more balanced and realistic perception of risks that children face might permit a valuable broadening of play experience. Thirdly, there is an evident need for a coherent and purposeful play policy; but the paper has also argued that, within any such policy, formally designated playgrounds should be but one element in a much broader range of play spaces which also embrace natural, wild and child-managed urban spaces. This is seen as both a pragmatic response to the impossibility of actually providing adequate play spaces within a framework of formal designation, reinforced by the firm belief (born of personal experience) that the best play spaces are often the ones children find for themselves. To do this requires, above all else, changes in attitudes and expectations — as the sub-title to the paper suggests, that we re-think the urban environment. As Ward (1978: p. 87) remarks, "the failure of the urban environment can be measured in direct proportion to the number of playgrounds".

References

Ball, D. and King, K. (1990) 'Play right', Leisure Management, Vol. 10, No. 3: pp. 54-57.

Barnett, L. A. (1990) 'Developmental benefits of play for children', *Journal of Leisure Research*, Vol. 22, No. 2: pp. 138-153.

Birmingham City Council (1989) *Birmingham — a greener future: a nature conservation strategy for the 1990s*. Birmingham: The Council, Department of Recreation and Community Services.

Brown, J. G. and Burger, C. (1984) 'Playground design and pre-school children's behaviors', *Environment and Behavior*, Vol. 16, No. 5: pp. 599-626.

Coffin, G. and Williams, M. (1989) *Children's outdoor play in the built environment*. London: National Children's Play and Recreation Unit.

Collins, M. F. (1995) 'Children's play — Little Orphan Annie in the British leisure system', in D. Leslie (ed) *Tourism and leisure — perspectives on provision*. LSA Publication No. 52, Eastbourne: Leisure Studies Association, pp. 175-186.

Crime Prevention Advisory Committee (CPAC) (1988) *Growing up on housing estates: a review of the play and recreational needs of young people*. London: National Association for the Care and Resettlement of Offenders.

Department of Environment (1972) *Children's playspace*, Circular 79/72. London: HMSO.

Department of Transport (1992) *Transport statistics Great Britain 1992*. London: HMSO.

Donnelly, D. (1980) 'The child in the environment', *Built Environment, Vol. 6*, No. 1: pp. 62-67.

Elson, M. J. (1989) *Recreation and community provision in areas of new private housing*. London: Housing Research Foundation.

Gaster, S. (1991) 'Urban children's access to their neighbourhood. Change over three generations', *Environment and Behavior*, Vol. 23, No. 1: pp. 70-85.

Heseltine, P. and Holborn, J. (1987) *Playgrounds: the planning, design and construction of play environments*. London: Mitchell.

Hughes, B. (1994) *Lost childhoods: the case for children's play*, Working Paper, No. 3 (The Future of Urban Parks and Open Spaces). Stroud: Comedia/Demos.

Leicester City Council (1989) *Leicester ecology strategy*. Leicester: The Council Planning Department.

Leslie, D. (ed) (1995) *Tourism and leisure — perspectives on provision*. LSA Publication No. 52, Eastbourne: Leisure Studies Association.

Moore, R. C. (1986) *Childhood's domain: play and place in child development*. Beckenham: Croom Helm.

National Children's Play and Recreation Unit (NCPRU) (1992) *Playground safety guidelines*. London: Department of Education and Science.

Nicholson-Lord, D. (1987) *The greening of the cities*. London: Routledge and Kegan Paul.

Office of Population Censuses and Surveys (1993) *Mortality statistics 1991*. London: HMSO.

Olszewska, A. and Roberts, K. (eds) (1989) *Leisure and life style: A comparative analysis of free time*. London: Sage.

Parkinson, C. E. (1987) *Where children play: an analysis of interviews about where children aged 5-14 normally play and their preferences for out-of-school activities*. Birmingham: Association for Children's Play and Recreation.

Roberts, K. (1989) 'Great Britain: socio-economic polarisation and the implications for leisure', in A. Olszewska and K. Roberts (eds) (1989) *Leisure and life style: A comparative analysis of free time*. London: Sage, pp. 47-61.

Sheldon, T. (1990) 'Children's play and recreation', *The Planner*, Vol. 76, No. 13: pp. 20-21.

Ward, C. (1978) *The child in the city*. New York: Pantheon.

Williams, S. (1995a) *Outdoor recreation and the urban environment*. London: Routledge.

—— (1995b) 'On the street — public space for popular leisure', in D. Leslie (ed) *Tourism and leisure — perspectives on provision*. LSA Publication No. 52, Eastbourne: Leisure Studies Association, pp. 23-35.

Part III

Protection and
Safety Issues in
Sport Environments

The Commercialisation of Outdoor Education — Profit and Loss in Adventure!

Barbara Humberstone

Buckinghamshire College, Brunel University

Introduction

This is a discussion paper which attempts to begin an analysis of the changes occurring in outdoor education and to set these changes within broader social and political context. For me the difficulty lies not in describing these changes and how constituent groups within the broad 'field' and those outside have responded, but rather the problem of drawing upon a framework(s) which can allow for comprehensive, sensitive and critical interpretation and explanation. To consider exclusively equity issues and the under-representation of various groups in outdoor education would be a needful project as would analyses of gender identities in various 'hazardous' activities. Focusing merely on the National Curriculum and its consequences for outdoor education provision would provide a convenient focus. But outdoor education tends to be marginalised in the school curriculum (Humberstone, 1995) and yet has a vast network of 'advocates' and providers. Further, not only are there a variety of popular images of adventurous activities in the outdoors, but also scholarly discourse (what little there is) around dimensions of outdoor education is fragmented and often unreflexive and largely uncritical. Outdoor education itself is an amalgam of different ideologies and has diverse representations. 'Jo and Mary public' are presented with outdoor education as epitomised in the 1993 Channel 4 documentary of the experiences of business men and women on a course at John Ridgway's 'Adventure school' and the subsequent newspaper headlines 'Suffering for your firm' and 'Corporate inhospitality'. The image created of outdoor education by the media in this scenario was largely of the provision of somewhat macho and sometimes humiliating experiences. Viewers and readers of these might well consider that the culmination of outdoor and adventurous activities delivered through various bodies provides similar insensitive experiences. Yet there are other media images which portray outdoor education as the very opposite, 'a soft option' in its 'use' as media for 'personal development' for young people considered to be 'at risk'.[1]

Outdoor education at the interface of education, sport and leisure

One could argue that outdoor education has for some time rather uncomfortably straddled the interface of education, sport and leisure. Challenging sports in an outdoor environment, such as climbing, walking and canoeing for example, have for many years been utilised as 'vehicles for personal and social education' by agencies. Although it is not only 'traditional' activities which are utilised for this purpose, nor is it always the able-bodied and those with 'good' health to whom it is made available [see Hopkins and Putnam (1993) which provides many case studies and an extensive historical background located largely from within a liberal perspective].

Perceptions of outdoor education

Any critical inquiry needs to unpick the various ideologies around outdoor education (OE) in its varied forms and locate and analyse these in contemporary social and political contexts. One might first ask, 'what constitutes outdoor education, what does it encompass and what does it stand for'? There have been attempts by advocates to 'define' outdoor education, adventure education, outdoor pursuits. More recently the National Curriculum has legitimated the term outdoor and adventurous activities as that aspect of outdoor education provided for in the physical education (PE) curriculum. Humberstone (1992; 1993) explores these questions in the context largely of schooling. Moreover, the media conveys other expressions and there are a diversity of providers of outdoor education. There appears a range of activities associated with OE, a variety of rationales for its 'use' and a diversity of professional advocates.[2]

Proponents have for many years argued that outdoor education is not a subject but an approach to education which is concerned with the overall development of the pupil (cf. DES 1991: p. 222) and, in industry, it is regarded by its advocates as a significant medium for development training (cf. Everard, 1993). This perception of OE is not new and in education and training was elucidated in 1977 as follows, "It (OE) is not a subject but an approach to education encompassing all age groups and abilities ... crossing curricular boundaries" (HMI, 1977). It has been suggested that we now know what is meant by different aspects of outdoor education and therefore need no longer concern ourselves with interpreting what are the 'meanings' given to it. Bunyan and Boniface (1994: p. 72) suggest that "Whilst there remains some ambiguity over these definitions (outdoor education; adventure education and outdoor pursuits) the debate appears exhausted and laid to rest". I would suggest that such arguments provide for the possibility of easier descriptions but inhibit debate around different perspectives and so foreclose analysis. As long as there are competing images and representations of outdoor education, there is the need to explore the ideologies, and thus the ambiguities surrounding 'definitions' which underpin them, locating them within a broader social, political and economic context.

Commercialisation

Consequently, through this paper, I hope to encourage scholarly interest in and debate around what a variety of a 'advocates' loosely call the outdoor world or more frequently now is called the 'outdoor industry'. Here, in this paper, I want to begin to raise issues around the political expediencies of the 'market place' and outdoor education. Rojek (1985) discusses the organisation of leisure in modern capitalism. There are, he suggests, increasing tendencies toward its commercialisation, "The leisure industry seeks to organize leisure activities on strict market principles, i.e. in pursuit of the accumulation of profit rather than the satisfaction of social need" (Rojek, 1985: p. 21). This paper provides evidence to indicate that this process is occurring in the outdoor industry as a direct consequence of Conservative policies. The 1989 amendment to the 1988 Local Government Act enabled the Thatcher Government to undermine the public sector provision of leisure more generally through the imposition of Compulsory Competitive Tendering (Aitchison, 1993) evidences its detrimental effect upon women).

Political Context

Likewise, a further consequence of the Conservative government's particular market governed ideologies, the Education Reform Act (ERA) (1988) has arguably done much to undermine diversity in provision and the establishment of greater equity in schooling (see Evans, 1993). Evans and Davies (1993) and Thomas (1993) analyse the processes and priorities which have underpinned the ERA and its effects on provision of physical education.

Yet, despite the 'New Right's' emphasis on free market forces and its adherence to Hayekian liberalism which supports the notion of 'rolling back the state' (i.e. reducing state intervention), there has been considerable and remarkable government intervention in the school curriculum through the provisions of the National Curriculum and of what was PE in school and is now PE and SPORT. Prime Minister Major's almost obsessive interest with competitive team games at the expense of any other physical activity and the financial and other support being directed to ensuring that sport (as opposed to a more balanced physical education) is, "put back at the heart of weekly life in *every* school" (DNH, July 1995: p. 2), will continue the disadvantaging of various groups of young people and the privileging of competitive sport over other forms of physical activity. It is pertinent here that there is no mention in '*Sport: Raising the Game* of 'minority' sports such as competitive canoeing, for example, which has provided the UK with many Olympic successes.

The effect of local management of schools (LMS), a result of ERA, has had significant effects upon the ability of Local Education Authorities (LEA) to support facilities and provision which are county controlled and not individual school based. Under LMS, local authorities (LAs) were required to devolve funding to schools (see Thomas 1993 which locates these policy decisions within a critical dimension). This, in many cases, left local authorities with insufficient funding to support many of their outdoor activities centres which had been one of the most frequent provider of outdoor education (cf. House of Commons 1995; p. vi-vii). Further, at present, there seems to be little possibility of support or funding opportunities through any government schemes with the present prominence being given to competitive team games and lottery funding being made available only for facilities and not for funding staff. As a direct consequence of LMS and the policies associated with 'capping' many local authority centres have been closed, downsized or restructured (TES, 19 February, 1993).

Case study of a Local Authority

I want to draw attention now to 'restructuring' in OE by referring briefly to ongoing research in one local authority which I have been investigating for sometime[3].

Like the reported effects on OE centres throughout England and Wales, this 'case study' LA has been obliged to respond to the changing economic and political environment over preceding decades. In the early 1980s, one large residential outdoor centre was threatened with closure as a consequence of decisions made regarding allocation of funding available to the then largely Conservative led County Council (CC). For a number of years that particular centre's future remained uncertain and with it the security of the permanent teaching staff[4]. The centre was admonished to find ways to cover much of its expenditure. Throughout this time the centre and its supporters, under the leadership of the then director, amassed a strong and persistent lobby, managing, through public relations and media effort, to prevent, more than once, a last minute decision by full meetings of the County Council to close the centre.

However, during this period steps were taken to change first the status of the permanent staff working at the centre and then the funding location of all the county's centres. Staff at the large centre changed from educational salaries (the Burnham Scale conditions of work) to Joint National Council (JNC) youth and community salaries. However, at that time, the actual salaries of those staff already under contract were protected. This meant that any new staff would be appointed on the JNC scale which had less favourable conditions and pay than those offered through the educational structure. Prior to this there had been a very low turn-over of permanent staff despite the considerable amount of overtime undertaken as extraneous duties, including working on average one weekend a month and one evening/night a week.

In addition, the responsibly for all outdoor education facility provision and funding was passed from the Education Department to the Recreation (Countryside and Community) Department. In early 1992, the CC employed management consultants from outside the outdoor industry to advise on how best the centre might be managed. After examining the centre and undertaking time and motion studies on staff, the consultants' recommendations were acted upon. Three of the top management, including the director, were made redundant. These staff had worked enthusiastically to keep the centre from closure during the stress of the preceding ten years. A manager was then appointed, who had himself been involved in business rather than the outdoor world, to run the centre on a salary slightly above the maximum of the Main Professional Grade for teachers. The remaining staff were also made redundant but invited to reapply for their posts. Their job descriptions had been redefined and the salaries significantly reduced. The posts were, however, 'ring fenced' ensuring that staff would be re-employed, if they so wished. The job description included reference to 'marketing' for head of department posts. Consequently, some of the more qualified and experienced staff opted not to apply for the senior posts as they felt their expertise lay in teaching and provision of the activities not marketing.

The salary of one such member of staff (Elton)[5] dropped by over a third, whilst other staff salaries were reduced by around £5,000 per annum. The staff did draw in the assistance of a national teaching union but this made little difference to their situation. However, in 1994, on finding that 'marketing' was not actually being undertaken by the new heads of department and feeling aggrieved at the substantial loss in salary whilst continuing to carry out virtually the same duties, Elton asked for help from another national teaching union. Individually he is attempting to gain recompense for this loss in earnings. It seems likely that the action taken by the CC may well have been illegal under European law but it is yet to been seen whether this will be challenged at a Tribunal or in a court of law.

Over the years, the possible closure of the centre had become a local political issue and any County Councillor recommending such action would certainly have incurred the wrath of the local voters. Thus rather than closure the authorities 'adjusted' the employees pay and conditions, possibly contrary to European law. Pay and condition anomalies were thus created between this large residential centre and the other smaller and mainly non-residential County outdoor facilities. Ironically, the CC invested a substantial amount of money into refurbishing the residential centre.

The economic screws were continuing to bite on this now marginally held Conservative Council and, in 1994, the Recreation Department called for tenders from management consultants to examine the remaining outdoor facility provision. On this occasion, the successful consultants were constituted from the outdoor world. Their recommendations are at present being considered by the staff and the Recreation Department[6]. However, what is interesting is the way in which the outdoor world itself, as exemplified by these consultants, is responding to economic and political imperatives. Proposals include recommendations for consistency of pay and conditions across the outdoor provision in the County in line with the poorer conditions now set at the larger centre. The proposals draw this conclusion from a survey of pay and conditions in outdoor residential centres. This survey ranged from LEA through charities to private sector controlled outdoor centres and indicated that LEA controlled centres offer the higher pay and more beneficial conditions of work than do the others. But the report argued that of the LEA centres surveyed, "all but two of them are facing drastic review of their operation and in some cases are threatened with closure". The report suggests that staff pay and conditions in those centres would be affected adversely. Thus their recommendations were to likewise affect adversely the pay and conditions of this County outdoor facility staff. Arguably, there is little else that the consultants could advise if their remit was partly to consider costs of the provision. In a sense, outdoor education providers were shunted from their location within education to a location within recreation/leisure. The latter field has maintained a disadvantageous position in the pay and conditions professional hierarchy. Like outdoor education professionals, the leisure field has no worker/professional union with any real strength to support employees' interests. Despite these detrimental effects on OE personnel in this particular county, provision there is much less effected than LA provision across England and Wales which has seen a significant demise (cf. House of Commons 1995: p. vi-vii).

Increased commercialisation

With the reduction in the number of local authority centres more widely and the restructuring and downsizing of those remaining, more privately funded and commercially focused centres have emerged or expanded to cater for the demands of schools and the interests of young people. As a direct consequence of government led market forces policies, then, we see the gradual demise of public educational provision for OE and the erosion of the pay and conditions of many of those lucky enough to be employed on permanent contracts, together with the steady expansion of commercialisation of the OE industry. There are, of course, many private and charitable outdoor activity centres and providers with extremely high reputations and extensive experience which have good safety and professional teaching records. However, evidence suggests that some providers may not have the expertise and knowledge gained from long term experience and of course financial considerations and the pursuit of profit are paramount in private enterprise.

Monetary profit and personal loss

The 1993 Lyme Bay tragedy (in which four pupils died in a sea canoeing accident undertaken under the auspices of St Alban's privately owned outdoor centre) does, if we examine the evidence, highlight the apparent importance for commercial providers, as exemplified in this case, of profit over the needs and well being of young people for whom they cater and the possible disastrous consequences. Prior to the tragedy, in July 1992, two instructors who had gained their experience and qualifications previously from the Local Authority residential outdoor centre referred to earlier resigned from St Alban's outdoor centre after working there for five weeks, because of what they saw as inadequate safety provision and procedures[7]. They claimed: "...there were no flares, tow-ropes, waterproofs or first aid kits provided and there were too many children per instructor" (TES, 6 December, 1994). The costs to the business to redress these omissions would have been monetary, the benefits the well being of the young people. It seems that the management considered that any threat of a possible accident resulting possibly in the loss of life, of which they had been warned, was insufficient to warrant spending money to ensure safety. In the first successful case of corporate manslaughter in England, the business which ran the centre was fined £60,000 and the managing director of the firm was convicted of manslaughter through negligence and sentenced to three years in prison. In his summing up at the end of the trial, the Judge said that Kite (the managing director) had put 'sales before safety'. He added that "the matters revealed in this trial demand an immediate and thorough reappraisal by the government...the potential for injuries and death are too obvious to be left to the inadequate vagaries of self-regulation" (Jamieson, 1994: p. 1).

Commercialisation and quality loss?

It is also argued by advocates of OE that not only is safety compromised in the advance of commercialisation but also the quality of the experience provided[8]. For Nick, much involved, largely voluntarily, in the process of developing recognised competencies (National Vocational Qualifications) in the outdoor industry, the commercial sector has captured the outdoor market by less than honest means:

> The recreational aspect (of outdoor education) is problematic. Private enterprise have creamed off clientele (in management development). In relation to young people provision they have called themselves educators but are providing fun not development. (One particular commercial organisation) now provides for more schools /young people than all the statutory centres put together.

Dore (1994) reported a case of a commercial outdoor activities business whose pursuit of profit seemed to be at the expense of good practice and concern for quality. It was reported that the firm, taking advantage of the public's concern about safety generated by the Lyme Bay tragedy, advertised for sixth formers to spend seven days on a course. The advertising material for the course suggested that it would provide students with the possibility of gaining up to twenty outdoor activity qualifications — providing "a great career opportunity" (Dore, 1994). The advertising material appeared to be endorsed by the various Governing Bodies. The Governing Body representatives, however, were adamant that they had not given permission for their names to be used nor had they authorised any link between themselves and the scheme. The scheme was considered to be totally inadequate in providing participants with the appropriate competencies to teach/instruct the activities. This then was an attempt by a private enterprise to profit from previous tragic events. It also highlights the commodification of qualifications for teaching outdoor activities and a private organisation's disregard for the procedures for gaining appropriate qualifications developed over time by Governing Bodies of the various hazardous activities.

Legislation and outdoor provision

As a direct consequence of the Lyme Bay disaster and a general concern about standards in the outdoor industry, an outdoor adventure activity providers' Code of Practice was drawn up by the UK Activity Centre Advisory Committee (ACAC) (a group constituted by individuals representing voluntary, charity and commercial interest groups) in April 1994. The Code and associated activity guidelines formed a framework within which providers could develop their own operating procedures to ensure that the principles and expectations expressed in the Code of practice are realised. It recommended that, along with guidelines established by ACAC, guidelines issued by National Governing Bodies of the sport should be followed. Concern was expressed by some of the general public and a number of providers that the Code did not go far enough. Its guidelines were not legal requirements and so, it was argued, could not be enforceable and would therefore be largely ineffective. As a consequence of intensive government lobbying, the Activity Centres (Young Persons' Safety) Act became law on June 28th 1995. It "makes provision for the regulation of centres and providers of facilities where children and young people under the age of 18 engage in adventurous activities, including provision for the imposition of requirements relating to safety" [Activity Centres (Young Persons' Safety) Act 1995]. It does not affect sports clubs, youth clubs or organisations such as the Scouts or Girl Guides on an individual basis. A consultation document was made available to organisations and others for comment within two months. Regulations are expected to be effected in April 1996 and the system to become fully operational in 1997. It is expected that the regulations will identify which providers and hazardous activities the legislation will apply to and that there will be clear proposals as to the required competencies and qualifications of leaders and instructors.

There is to be a single Licensing Authority established accountable to the Health and Safety Council, which would be appointed by the Health and Safety Executive after invitation to tender for the work. Although many in the Outdoor Industry support the idea that the Licensing Authority "should be non-profit making, independent and having the confidence of the industry" (NAOE, 1995), it will be interesting to see whether a commercial enterprise or a non-profit group will be awarded the authority to inspect and licence outdoor provision and what structure it will adopt. Will the inspection be licensed out to commercial groups or will the members of the Licensing Authority undertake its own inspections, and what percentage of the authority will be drawn from the outdoor industry?

Concluding remarks

The Hayekian Liberal imperative on which the present Conservative Government's policy is based of 'rolling back the state' and thus compelling the discipline of the market to operate has, it would seem in OE, brought greater state intervention in legislative terms both in relation to safety and in relation to the school curriculum. Depending upon one's particular standpoint or theoretical framework, this intervention might be differently interpreted as greater surveillance of or accountability in the OE industry.

In this paper, I have drawn attention to popular images and representations of outdoor education and to the perceptions of proponents within the outdoor field. The demise of public sector OE provision in the light of 'New Right' ideologies and policies has been depicted and exemplified by one LA case study. The tendency to commercialisation in the outdoor industry has been discussed together with the recent safety legislation which has been applied to it. I set out to stimulate critical interest in and scholarly debate and discussion into the outdoor industry and around its constituted ideologies. I hope this paper has gone some way to facilitate this and to raise social and political questions around adventurous activities and their provision in the outdoors.

Notes

[1] We have seen the media portrayals of the young women on probation sent on a so-called 'holiday' aboard a sail training vessel and the youths whose 'punishment' has been 'holidays' on adventure courses.

[2] A number of professionals in nursing and mental health care argue that outdoor education can have therapeutic effects on their clients (see Rose (1990); Card (1991); Mills (1992).

[3] I have been researching outdoor education within this particular County for over twelve years. The main research methods which I have utilised over the last few years have been informal interviews and collection of documentary evidence. Research of outdoor education more widely and its advocacy bodies has been undertaken as a participant observer and through documentary evidence.

4   Outdoor education providers generally tend to employ both permanent
    staff and instructors on short term contract. The latter for board and
    lodging and a nominal payment teach various adventurous and /or
    environmental activities. Most local authority centres and reputable
    charity and commercial organisations have traditionally trained these
    temporary staff to appropriate Governing Body technical qualifications.
    They then work alongside a core of permanent usually well qualified
    staff. The Governing Bodies qualifications include those available
    through such bodies as British Canoe Union, Royal Yachting Asso-
    ciation and Mountain Leader Training Board etc.

5   Any names presented are pseudonyms.

6   Consequently I am unable to identify the report fully.

7   On their resignation, the two staff wrote to the managing director indi-
    cating they were leaving because of poor safety conditions and warned
    the centre that they could well be confronted with an accident. This
    letter enabled the subsequent action to be taken in court.

8   I have argued elsewhere that the quality of the experience in terms of
    forms of communication and teaching process is interlinked with
    technical competence in providing safe experiences (cf. Humberstone
    1993).

References

Activity Centres (Young Persons' Safety) Act (1995) *Preamble*. London:
    HMSO.

Aitchison, C. (1993) *Gender, leisure and the contract culture*. London: North
    London Polytechnic.

Bunyan, p. and Boniface, M. (1994) 'The process of enlightenment', in
    S. Thomas (ed) *Outdoor education, perspectives*. University of Exeter,
    pp. 72-79.

Card, J. (1991) 'The great Russian adventure', *MENCAP News*, October: pp.
    16-17.

Department of Education (1991) *Physical education for ages 5-16*. London:
    HMSO.

Department of National Heritage (1995) *Sport: Raising the game*. London:
    Her Majesty's Stationary office.

Dore, A. (1994) 'A good company afloat?', *Times Educational Supplement*,
    15 April, 1994.

Evans, J. and Davies, B. (1993) 'Equality, equity and physical education', in J. Evans (ed) *Equality, education and physical education*. London: Falmer Press.

Everard, B. (1993) *The history of development training*. London: Development Training Advisory Group (privately published).

Her Majesty's Inspectorate (1977) *The curriculum 11-16*. London: HMSO.

Hopkins, D. and Putnam, R. (1993) *Personal growth through adventure*. London: David Fulton Publishers.

Humberstone, B. (1992) 'Outdoor education in the National Curriculum', in N. Armstrong (ed) *New directions in physical education. Vol. 2 Towards a National Curriculum*. Champaign, Il: Human Kinetics.

———— (1993) 'Equality, physical education and outdoor education — ideological struggles and transformative structures?', in J. Evans (ed) *Equality, education and physical education*. London: Falmer Press.

———— (1995) 'Bringing Outdoor Education into the physical education agenda: Gender identities and social change', *Quest* Vol. 47, No 2: pp. 144-157.

Jamieson, D. (1994) 'The Lyme Bay canoe tragedy', 22nd March. Unpublished notes from trial, December.

NAOE (1995) *Newsletter National Association for Outdoor Education Editorial*. No. 16, July.

Rojek, C. (1985) *Capitalism and leisure theory*. London: Tavistock.

Rose, S. (1990) 'The value of outdoor activities', *Nursing*, Vol. 4, No. 21: pp. 12-16.

Mills, A. (1992) 'The great outdoors' *Nursing Times*, Vol. 88, No. 33: pp. 48-49.

Times Educational Supplement (1993) 'Gates to the outdoors slam shut', 19 April: p. 3.

Thomas, S. (1993) 'Education reform: Juggling the concepts of equality and elitism', in J. Evans (ed) *Equality, education and physical education*. London: Falmer Press.

Safety at their Leisure — A Study of Youth Sport Courses[1]

Jennifer Anderson

Southampton Institute of Higher Education

The March 1993 Lyme Bay incident, in which four school children died in acanoing accident,has focused attention on the safety of young people on outdoor adventure courses. The Activity Centres (Young Persons' Safety) Act 1995 is currently the latest initiative in the process of regulation and licensing of young people's leisure. Although the spotlight is now on safety provision in outdoor adventure courses there is emerging interest about safety on youth sport courses which take place in the community on a non residential basis during holiday periods. These may be one off events, taster sessions, daily or weekly courses in a range of indoor and outdoor sports. Some youth safety issues are similar for both adventure and community sport courses, but other issues reflect the contrasting environments in which they take place.

This paper explores attitudes towards the safety of young people on non residential sports courses. Safety in sport is discussed from the perspective of child, parent, and coach. It is a case study based on a community sports programme in Southampton where safety guidelines for youth sport courses have been developed to meet local needs in consultation with young people, parents and coaches. As a result of this research, safety guidelines were incorporated in the 1995 summer youth sport programme. Research was initiated and organised jointly between the Sports Development Officer at Southampton City Council and a lecturer at Southampton Institute.

There are many reasons for the recent expansion of non residential community sports courses. On the one hand the benefits of sport, in the mid 1990s have gained a higher media profile, on the other hand recent studies reveal that not only do young people have fewer opportunities for physical education in schools (Sports Council, 1994) but there is evidence of increasingly sedentary youth lifestyles (Armstrong and Balding, 1990; Sleap and Warburton, 1994; Wallace, 1995). Physical activity has become *an issue for* politicians (Munn, 1995) resulting in a higher profile for youth sport with the initiation of organisations such as Youth Sports Trust. Sport is being used to combat other juvenile problems such as youth crime, drugs and drinking. Mounting evidence indicates adult activity patterns may be established in childhood (Welshman, 1995) therefore emphasizing the significance of early childhood experiences in sport and physical education. Other evidence pointing to the rising awareness of the role of youth sport comes from public and voluntary sector involvement. At local level just under a thousand Sports Development Officers were estimated in 1995 within local authorities in England (Collins, 1995). Of these about fifty are estimated to be targeted primarily at youth. Governing bodies of sport are developing strategies specifically orientated at youth.

Many sports have become accessible to young people. Technological innovation in the design and manufacture of youth equipment has transformed some equipment-based youth sports such as short boards for windsurfing, junior safety life jackets for rowing and youth equipment for athletics. New youth versions of sports have been developed such as short tennis and mini rugby. With the growth of single parent families and as the geographical dispersion of families becomes more prevalent, parents are looking for worthwhile non family related activities for their offspring during school holidays. Many school children have thirteen weeks holiday, while for parents four to six is the norm. Increasing full and part time female employment has affected previous family holiday behaviour in that some form of child care has to be organised for more children.

As school sport provision declines so the parent has a more significant role in determining leisure choices especially if transport is required. Understanding the parents' role is becoming increasingly important (Hultsman, 1993). There is a lack of research about parents' role in children's sport, especially about beliefs, attitudes, values and expectations. "Everybody talks about the role of parents in children sport but nobody does any research on them" (Brustad, 1992). The mother has been identified as the primary decision maker in sending a child on a sports course (Howard and Madrigal, 1990). However in terms of holiday making decisions, children subtly and sometimes strongly influence parents' decisions (Cullingford, 1995). Other studies indicate that the older the child the more influence the child has on both consumer decisions (Ward and Wackman, 1972), and on family vacation decision making (Jenkins, 1979). Further studies indicate that children from families with higher economic status have more influence on decisions (Roberts *et al.*, 1981).

A bewildering range of sporting opportunities for young people is available during the school holidays to parents with sufficient disposable income. Although many of these opportunities have been available for over a decade, others are recent innovations. Provision for non residential sports courses through public, voluntary and commercial sectors is fragmented, complex and rapidly expanding. These include work based holiday schemes (e.g. Civil Service), local authority sport centre courses, commercial activity centres, charitable trust schemes, voluntary community play schemes, commercial indoor play centres (e.g. Action Station), commercial holiday playschemes, uniformed groups and local authority schemes. As youth sport course provision proliferates often crossing the traditional school / local authority / commercial and voluntary framework, public perception and understanding of who is actually providing courses becomes vague. A course may be provided by a local voluntary sports club, in commercial premises and advertised through the local authority, or it may be a commercial organisation running a course in an educational venue. With increasing partnerships, new sporting cultures are evolving that are neither completely school, local authority nor club based.

The safety of young people on sports courses is a fundamental responsibility of the provider under the common law Duty of Care (tort of negligence). This may be modified by statute, in some cases made more strict. The Health and Safety Act 1974 places a statutory obligation on the local authority to not put the health and safety of third parties at risk. Failure to do so can result in criminal prosecution. If anyone suffers an injury which that person can prove was the result of any other person's or organisation's negligence they can sue in civil courts for compensation. Hence the importance of carrying proper insurance although insurance cannot be obtained to cover penalties under affirmative action (Health and Safety at Work Act 1974). Many organisations have become involved in specifying safety standards by a variety of methods. They may include guidelines, sets of rules, instructions, codes of conduct and codes of practice. Much uncertainty exists amongst grassroots practitioners within the industry about the differences in terminology and the interpretation of legal aspects.

Confusion also lies in the number of agencies involved in setting youth safety guidelines. There are local authority, local education authority, county councils, local scheme and local sports centre guidelines. Numerous organisations are or have been involved in safety. Some operate at a national level, these include Welsh and English Tourist Boards (Activity Centre Advisory Committee), Sport and Recreation Lead Body with its occupational standards of competence, the Health and Safety Executive, the Development Training Advisory Group, and large commercial companies specialising in outdoor sports. The last mentioned have very detailed rules for staff working with young people. Some governing bodies of sport provide specific advice on safety practice e.g. Amateur Athletics Association, British Canoe Union. For many parents the norm is handing a child over to the school with the teacher acting *in loco parentis*. Schools have safety rules which have grown through years of experience. Within outdoor recreation the Jameson Bill is providing a focal point of attention but within community sport there is, as yet, no such focus.

Case study — background to 'Stay with Sport'

Southampton City Council runs a 'Stay with Sport' scheme that encourages young people to take part in sports courses in the holidays, and promotes links between school and voluntary clubs. Initiated in 1987, Stay with Sport was one of the first of its kind in the country. It caters for young people between the ages of eight to eighteen, with the early teens being the largest age group. Over forty different sports are included in the programme at Foundation and Introductory level including football, tennis, riding, watersports, basketball, bowling and athletics. A part time Stay with Sport officer is employed with a grant in 1995 of £14,000 in addition to a Sports Development Officer with a broader remit. The scheme is directed at certain groups in the community including girls, young black and ethnic minority people and young disabled people. Currently there are one thousand children on the database with over four thousand young people attending over the last eight years. Provision is concentrated in summer holidays with some provision at Easter and the half terms.

The City Council have mainly taken an enabling role in providing youth sport courses filling the gaps left by other providers. Within the sports development continuum the scheme has a strong community focus as opposed to income, sports development or niche market (McDonald and Taylor, 1995). Key tasks include advertising courses, contacting young people, giving grants and advice, booking coaches and venues. Over the past three years as the programme has expanded, the council has taken a more proactive role because some voluntary coaches were unable to meet the growth in holiday period day time demand. Coaches have been employed, with only three of the courses in summer 1995 being completely run by the voluntary sector clubs (rowing, athletics and bowls).

The research schedule

Four research steps are outlined and discussed in this section. The research process took place between April 1994 and September 1995 — firstly, a postal survey of Stay with Sport families in June 1994; secondly focus groups with 200 young people in July 1994; thirdly, a parent focus group in September 1994; and fourthly coach consultation in November 1994. Presentations about the research process were also made to senior leisure council officers in October 1994, and the voluntary Southampton Sports Council in April 1995. In addition, video observation was carried out on summer sports courses.

Briefly, the postal survey provided the foundation of this research/ consultation process. Results from this survey lead to separate focus groups for young people and parents. Results of all three initiatives were discussed and evaluated by a group of Stay with Sport coaches and providers. City Council officers developed the safety guidelines as a result of this consultation and they were introduced for the summer programme 1995.

Postal survey — parent and child

The first step was a postal survey. Four hundred young people on the Southampton City Council Stay with Sport database were sent a postal questionnaire with an incentive of a £30 gift voucher to increase the return rate (Gitelson, 1993). It was printed on coloured A3 paper with sporting animations in an attempt to be user friendly. One side was intended for the child, the other for the parent/guardian. The first mailing received 65 responses; responses increased to 208 (just over 50%) with the second mailing four weeks later (after the start of the 1994 summer holidays). Data was processed on SPSS. At this stage in the research process, safety in sport was a secondary issue. The primary aim was to explore parent and child values in non residential sports courses, the decision to attend the course, and marketing communication information (Anderson and Banning, 1995).

In the postal questionnaire, young people and their parents were asked what they most liked about sport courses outside school, it was a closed question. There was a remarkable similarity between the order of priority from parent and child. Both young people and their parents were attracted primarily by fun. This is confirmed in other studies (Fox, 1994; Whitehead, 1994; Griffen, 1993). The second most important aspect of sports course provision for both child and parent was 'good coaches'. Inherent in the term 'good coach' is the provision of a safe environment. The children rated 'I was really good at this' and 'friends went as well' as more important than the parents did, but the remaining list of eight possible factors was in a similar order of priority. These were 'friendly environment', 'feel good through sport', 'get fitter' and lastly 'something to do'. The fact that parent and child did have a similar perspective on sports courses has important marketing implications, but may also lead to ways of best tackling safety issues in youth sport.

The postal questionnaire included an open question on safety concerns for parents. Sixty percent stated they had no concerns over safety. It is worth noting that the Stay with Sport programme is advertised through the City Council, and many parents had a positive image of the Council which encompassed the sport courses. Of the forty percent of parents who did have concerns, these appeared as follows:

Parental Safety Concerns

Supervision	18	(adequate, careful, ratios)
Qualified staff	12	(enough experienced qualified staff, teachers, coaches)
First aid	9	(expectation that staff are qualified)
Safety education	9	(safety explained and taught to children)
Other children	6	(bullying, not getting on, left out, positive atmosphere)
Spare time	6	(lunch, toilets, off court, leave area)
Fear of injury	6	
Equipment	5	(dangerous equipment maintained)
Others	4	(stranger danger, gangs, weirdos)
Environment	2	(dirty water if it rains)
Health	3	(child has leukaemia, asthma, wheelchair)

Sport and safety parent focus group 1994

To further evaluate these safety concerns a focus group for parents was conducted in the evening in a centrally located Squash and Cricket Club. At the end of the postal questionnaire there was section to complete if parents were interested in attending a discussion on safety. Fifty parents (25% of all replies) originally indicated an interest, but by October only a small group actually attended the session. Discussion was focused on the results of the postal questionnaire. It was jointly led by both researchers and lasted two hours. The session was taped, transcribed and evaluated by qualitative methods.

In the parent focus group these concerns were discussed. 'Adequate supervision' was recognized as a key feature of safety provision in the postal questionnaire. Group size appeared to be the critical issue. Differences between safe sports such as badminton and riskier sports such as watersports were acknowledged. Specific sports coaches would be appreciative of the dangers of their own sports. Initially, age appeared as the critical factor in determining group size but, after discussion, it emerged that the specific site and location of a sports course may be even more important. Critical factors were whether the venue is inside or outside, whether the whole site is open/visible and, more importantly, whether the venue is self-contained — i.e. is there a barrier to keep young people in and other people out? In Southampton many sports take place in a large outdoor sports centre open to the public, so there is a high awareness of the problems of open access on urban sports venues.

Some parents assumed courses would be safe because they were advertised through the council even though publicity clearly stated that they were run by voluntary clubs. Other parents made their own checks by observing courses and listening to their children. There were anecdotes of unacceptable standards. One mother commented that at another sport scheme she had actually withdrawn her children because coach attitudes were too lax on the first day. Another commented on a scheme outside the Council area where children were delivered and picked up by car an activity centre. In departing, parents "drove onto a large field, stopped the car, the child ran up jumped in and that was that — no checks, no nothing". Arrivals and departures were recognised as important: "It's a handing-over — the responsibility for my child is now yours".

Regarding staff, the terms 'instructor' and 'coach' had similar connotations to parents. They recognised that coaches had different training to teachers 'but they expected the coach to have 'teacher qualities'. In an American study comparing coach and teacher behaviour, significant differences were found in that coaches were expected to give more pre-instruction, to praise more, and to be silent more often; while teachers were expected to spend more time managing classes (Rupert and Buschner, 1989). The role of helpers was not discussed by parents, possibly because they were unaware of their presence. There is a growing number of helpers supporting teachers and coaches in sport in schools and clubs, and legal aspects of helpers in school have been documented elsewhere (Eve, 1994). Parents assumed that coaches would have been specifically trained to coach young people and that discipline would be established early in the course. They also assumed coaches would be experienced at handling groups. One mother said her son had been bullied at school, but "on these courses coaches seem to know what is going on". First aid, break-supervision and visits to public toilets were further concerns: "I'm happy if my child goes with another child but not if he goes alone".

Towards the end of the session more sensitive issues were raised such as police checks on coaches, vetting of adults volunteering to work with children, and contagious diseases such as AIDS. It appeared that many parents had not given these topics serious thought before. There was a feeling that these were one-off unusual events, and of not such concern compared to other issues discussed above: "It's a question of the odds of it ever happening to your child".

Because courses were advertised under the Council banner there was an interesting expectation that safety education was part of the course. This should be provided "at the right level for the age of the child every day". One parent saw this process as an 'education' which the young people would pass on to their own children. A parent's responsibility to educate their own children in safety was discussed — the balance between not wanting to worry young children, yet making them prepared to cope. One mother had taught her three children that strangers were not necessarily the main threat "but there might be times they would need to draw back from adults they know. I don't go over board about it". Another father commented ,"If you labour it too much you can be too alarmist and spoil their childhood". Parents knew safety education was important but lacked confidence in knowing the most effective way to approach it. There was a sense that they wanted to pass responsibility on to the coaches, who they perceived as experts.

The parents in this group felt strongly that it should be a case of 'safety at all costs'. If they pay for their child to go on a course, they expect a high quality of safety. Safety procedures should be adjusted to the specific needs of young participants. Because of increased risks in sport, the coach *in loco parentis* would be expected to have a higher level care. Parents have become accustomed to handing children over school teachers where there are very clear legal rules and regulations to govern sporting activities. Parents appreciated that some of the increased safety costs would be passed on to the consumer. Parents are increasing their level of skilled consumption in this area. One of the issues raised by these discussions was the number of incorrect assumptions made by parents about the role of provider.

Sport and safety child focus groups

The third research step was a series of focus groups for young people which took place in the last week of the summer term 1994. Two hundred 10 to 12 year old young people were interviewed in groups of four to eight. There were forty group interviews in total each lasting from 20 to 30 minutes. These were all single sex groups and where possible groups were interviewed by an interviewer of the same sex. Interviewers were selected for their 'streetwise' empathy with young people. They were casually dressed to clearly distinguish them from teachers in the schools visited. All focus groups were tape recorded and transcribed. Four schools were selected to represent the range of children across the city. One was in the inner city with people from different ethic groups in the catchment area, the second school from an area with rented and owner occupied housing, the third school one mile from the city centre and the fourth in a large council estate with high rise flats five miles from city centre.

The semi structured questionnaire was based on issues arising from the postal survey (June 1994). The quality of resultant discussion was dependent on the ability and articulateness of the young people, and the technique of the interviewer. There was considerable variation in response quality between groups. Interviews took place in the school environment. The teacher, if present, was in the background.

A preliminary step in the qualitative analysis of data was discussion with the six researchers who led the interviews which was recorded and transcribed. Each of the topics was discussed and evaluated. The young people's focus interviews generated 200 pages of A4 that were analysed qualitatively. The entire text was read quickly through. A form of inductive analysis was chosen for analysis allowing patterns, themes and categories to emerge from the data as a form of grounded theory. Indigenous concepts were applied i.e. categories developed and articulated by people in the study.

Young people's perception of safety and leisure

In the youth focus groups the safety questions came at the end of a session covering broader sporting issues once rapport and confidence had been established with young people. The intention was to gain a deeper understanding into child perception of safety in their leisure time, the role of danger in sport and the significance of taking risks in sport. There is a growing awareness of the need for young people to be consulted (De Knop, 1995) which has been observed in community holiday playschemes (Turner, 1993).

Young people were asked about safety in the streets they lived in. There was an overwhelming feeling that streets were not safe for children to play on their own. Two principal dangers being traffic and stranger danger. Many had stories of friends who had been knocked over. Young children are also well versed in 'stranger danger' with a wealth of language to illustrate their fears. Many reiterated their rules for the street, normally limitations in terms of time, distance, and who accompanies them. This was not prompted. Mothers were most likely to be referred to as the rule maker, "Not allowed out if dark", "only to the end of our road," " they let me out with my friends but not on my own" and " I'm not allowed to the park it's not safe, I've got to play on the street". Girls were more likely to comment about being allowed to go to the shops.

Young people were questioned about which sports they felt were dangerous. A total of thirty five different sports were mentioned. The range spread across the sports they participated in, sports accessible in their local community, recognisably dangerous sports such as bungee jumping and boxing, and sports which have been glamorised by television such as ice hockey and surfing. Both girls and boys pointed to rugby and football as the most dangerous sports with boys in particular highlighting the dangers of rugby. Children perceived danger as injury and death through the activity itself, but were aware that all sports have the potential to be dangerous: "Most sports are dangerous, you just don't notice it".

Overall there was a rational approach to the dangers of sport. Young people seemed to be well aware of the risks and protective measures that should be taken in choosing to play different sports. An understanding of the importance of about making sporting choices came from boys and girls. "if they want to play them then they should play them". Some commented on the restriction of choices available to them:

"Depends on what age they are."

"Depends if you know the sport and if you have the right equipment."

"As long as it's under control."

"As long as you trained properly."

Girls were stronger on the need for good supervision and to follow rules:

> "If you do not play by the rules anything can be dangerous."

In addition to seeing coaches as experts, as motivators and communicators young people saw coaches as being in control with strong discipline and a remit for fair play:

> "Most adults say, Oh, no, it's like they think kids are really weak and can't.... my mum doesn't think like that because she knows I'm strong."

> "Its like people say, Oh kids can't drive this. You're too young. Most kids 'round here can drive."

> "My mum hasn't let me grow up yet."

In response to a question about whether people should take risks in sport there was little difference between boys and girls. A minority view was put forward by four or five children that children should not be allowed to take big risks, but the majority view was that you have to take risks to learn how to do things: "They don't want to be scared all their lives, they should have a go". Many boys linked risks with excitement: "Some sports are dangerous, it's exciting because its dangerous", and "Taking risks is important — they play chicken up the railway, don't they".

A minority took the discussion to a different level, linking the risks taken in sport with the risks in life: "Life's a risk, isn't it"; and "Important to take risks because you only have one life".

Young people in this study appear to have a high awareness of safety and risk in sport. They see compelling reasons for risk and excitement to be included in their sport. Their interpretation of safety and danger is much narrower than the adult interpretation: i.e. they did not think about safety in the broader terms but specifically in terms of physical injury.

Legitimate opportunities for young people to take risks have declined. Playgrounds have been sanitised, and playschemes, for example, have become less adventurous through concerns for safety (Turner, 1993). The value of risk-taking is recognized as the difference between perceived and real risk, and objective and subjective risk (Mortlock, 1984). Over-caution can inhibit development, and 'personal growth' implied going beyond the comfort zone of everyday life (Jeffers, 1989). The effective coach will make activities and risks appear more perceived than real. Risk-taking is encouraged "within safety limits, often defined in terms of rules and regulations. Little research exists on young peoples' perception of risk" (Kleiber *et al.*, 1986: p. 169) and even less on the parental role and perception,

The focus groups highlighted the essential difference between the risk and safety intrinsically within in the sporting activity itself and the broader safety issues about young people being outside the home environment and away from direct parental control. Young people were far more concerned with the former; within the sporting context none mentioned broader safety issues. Overall there was a sensible, rational view towards the dangers inherent in sport, with young people revealing a strong awareness of rules and regulations.

Coach consultation

The fourth research step was with coaches and organisers already acquainted with Stay with Sport. A meeting was organised November 1994 for coaches and course organisers. Three discussion groups were formed — centre organisers, professional sports coaches and voluntary club coaches. Those coaches unable to make the session were contacted by post. Overall there was a 64% return in this consultation with coaches. Groups were asked to give responses to specific issues that had been generated by the previous research. Groups wrote their own record of decisions and main comments. Some issues discussed were broad general principals for example, are safety guidelines necessary on Stay with Sport courses? Should they be produced by the City Council, ? Other issues were specific day to day administrative points such as registers being taken at every session and coaches wearing name badges. Discussion explored the 'grey' areas of coaching provision in a non threatening environment. The researchers, in the main, stood back from this process.

There was strong consensus on both general and specific issues. General safety recommendations should be developed on all courses. The City Council should set general guidelines but the was recognition of the role of governing body of sport in sport specific guidelines. A rugby coach felt both parents and children would feel happier if the City Council were closely associated with safety standards. Several coaches felt guidelines must be realistic and manageable otherwise clubs would just drop out of Stay with Sport or they might deter potential coaches and new clubs joining in. Coaches recognised that there was a difficulty in pitching the guidelines at the right level and that coaches should therefore be involved in the development of guidelines. Many coaches mentioned the importance and the need for experience in group management — i.e. pastoral care.

Coaches employed by the council would obviously be police-checked, but coaches and volunteers working for the voluntary club may not be. Most coaches felt uncertainly here with one respondent unsure about how to go about it. Insurance was also discussed. Qualified club coaches are insured through the governing body but what about helpers. On first aid, coaches agreed someone should be qualified but felt many injuries were sport specific and that the coach has a valuable role here because of his or her expertise. There was also discussion on the level of first aid qualification needed for courses,

There was considerable variation of response as to who should check facilities before a coaching session ranging from the hirer of facilities, to the club, to the coach on the day. All but one coach felt they should supervise at breaks. Overall there was a strong consensus from coaches. The question of how much you could and should put into safety did arise. One coach concluded 'remember that coaches can only do their best'.

Additional consultation

Further presentations were made to senior leisure Council policy makers and the voluntary Southampton Sports Council which lead to discussions on safety and provided an opportunity to reflect on the research process. A subsidiary step was videoing a range of sports courses in the last week in July 1994. Over one hundred hours of sport was videoed including tennis, skiing, sailing, football, golf and mixed indoor sports. Camera operators were instructed to film at prescribed intervals and also at arrivals, departures and breaks. They filmed activity off the centre stage — i.e. away from the instructor. The intention was to observe informal, sideline, peripheral activity. The tapes have been informally analysed.

Development and implementation of guidelines for Stay with Sport

Safety guidelines subsequently developed by the Sports Development Officer were checked by the council Health and Safety Officer, Insurance Officer and Senior Leisure Development Officer. For any club or coach wanting to join the 1995 Stay with Sport summer programme a detailed set of guidelines had to be signed, known as the Seal of Approval. (In youth publicity material a 'Sammy the Seal' logo was included.) A brief version of the seal of approval was included in the Stay with Sport publicity. Council, child, coach and parent guidelines were developed as part of the Seal of Approval. Pre course publicity now clearly states that the Council can only take responsibility for courses it directly organises, but is committed to raising standards elsewhere.

A brief version of the Stay with Sport safety guidelines is as follows (Benning, 1995):

- Prior to the session chief coach must carry out a risk assessment to check that:

   a. Facilities are sound.

   b. Sufficient qualified coaches are available.

   c. Ratios comply with National Governing Body, County Council / City Council guidelines. (The latter is currently one qualified coach per 12 — 16 children unless deemed hazardous by County Council guidelines). The role of sport leader is also defined.

   d. Equipment checked and appropriate for age of child.

   e. Access to a working telephone and first aid box.

- Each course must have one staff member qualified in Basic First aid who is introduced to course members as the first aider.

- All coaches and leaders must hold a recognised qualification for the level of coaching taking place. (Checked by Sports Development Unit.

- Coaches paid by invoice method must carry their own public liability insurance of £2m. (Checked by Sports Development Unit.

- Clubs working in partnership must carry their own public liability insurance.

- All Coaches, Sports Leaders and designated helpers must introduce themselves and wear a name badge.

- A register should be taken every day.

- All names, telephone numbers, doctor's name and medical details should be held by the Course Coordinator.

- Safety points to be explained daily at the appropriate level for young people.

- Safe and suitable warm up for every session.

- Lunch breaks should not be too long (20-30 minutes recommended).

- Coaches/helpers arrange rota to cover the break.

- Coaches should not carry out their own training during a course.

- On large outdoor courses a helper should monitor toilet visits. Children under 13 should always go in pairs.

- Name badges should not be used for children.

- Bullying should always be stopped by coaches.

- Coaches must never make arrangements to meet children on their own. All future coaching arrangements should be made with the parents and child.

- In the case of an accident appropriate procedures should be followed and paperwork completed.

In pre course publicity the responsibility of the parent and child were also clearly outlined in the Seal of Approval — i.e. the parent should deliver the child at the correct time, venue and collect at the end of the session, ensure children have correct clothing and equipment and ensure registration form, disclaimer and correct contact number has been given. Child responsibilities include listening to coach instructions, arriving on time, asking permission before going to the toilets and having fun! Publicity established that safety is a four-way process involving young people, parent, coach and council.

At the end of the summer over 200 evaluation forms were received from participants. There was 87 % awareness of the Seal of Approval and appreciation that new safety procedures had been in force. Informal feedback from coaches to the to date has been positive. Further discussion with coaches is planned, as is more consultation with a sample of young people about the nature of guidelines. It is likely, at this stage, that further research will focus on empowerment of coaches and young people in exploring safety awareness and training.

Like the effect of the Children Act on holiday play schemes for the under-8s (Turner, 1993), there was some resistance to the increased paperwork and bureaucracy. For the officers involved, the workload increase was substantial as there is more monitoring and checking detail: for example, copies of coach qualifications. The safety initiative was seen as part of a quality process as the whole scheme and coaching young people matures.

In Southampton only one coach dropped out as a result of the new safety regime: "I've been coaching for thirty years — why should I change now?". The low drop out rate could be due to the fact that Stay with Sport has been running for eight years. It has been built up gradually on the respect and good relations between club and council officers. The delicate balance between voluntary and public sectors in this instance has been strengthened, but nevertheless it is a fragile, tenuous relationship based on the individual people involved.

Discussion

Safety in youth sport has gained a higher profile nationally through the Jamieson Bill. As skilled consumers, parents are more aware of safety practices and issues. Safety expectations are rising. After the Cairngorm 1970, Landsend 1985, Austrian Alps 1988, and Lyme Bay 1993 incidents, the public is less prepared to accept that incidents and accidents involving young people are unavoidable. The legal climate is changing, and the pursuit of compensation is likely to increase as parents and children are constantly being made aware of their legal rights (Raymond, 1994). Many courses are run in public venues so parents may observe activity enabling them to make their own minds up about standards of safety. Consumers are more prepared to complain. One viewpoint from the parent focus group was that most parents did not think about safety but that they probably should.

In discussing safety in youth sports there is a need to distinguish between danger and safety within the sporting activity itself and broader safety issues that affect all organised youth activities outside the family control and home environment. Both are closely related and of concern to providers and coaches. The former is easier to identify and define and the latter more nebulous.

Parents today feel they were brought up in a safer environment (Bernardo's, 1995). There were fewer distractions in terms of drugs, glue and drink (HMSO, 1995). There is a growing belief that a child's ability to cope and sociability is being damaged by too much supervision and over protection. This view is voiced by Kidscape — an organisation which campaigns for young people to be taught independence. There is an argument that society has become too safety conscious with young people at leisure. Too much safety works against risk-taking. Over caution inhibits development.

For many it is easy not too take risks as we have been conditioned to look for security. It may be that children's bedrooms have become the new electronic adventure playground, with children spending increasing amounts of time there using "skilfully marketed electronics for entertainment, diversion and solace" (Neustatter, 1995). Childhood today is constrained by parents' fears of letting children out of the home environment or by direct parental control. As a result children internalise parental anxieties because they are not out exploring and making sense of their own world. It is the difference between long- and short-term approaches to safety. Many of the things that have to be learnt (by experience) cannot be taught (Ogilvie, 1990). Parents and young people had greater concerns about 'stranger danger' than about other safety issues, reflecting the findings of national studies (Barnardo's, 1995). As courses take place in the community, often in urban environments, there is often unrestricted access to sports venues. Although the focus group parents knew that 'stranger danger' might be statistically unlikely, the possibility nevertheless prompted their protective behaviour.

For the parent too there is the risk of sending a child on a new venture. Parents today have little experience of assessing the risk of different schemes. They have become accustomed to standards set by education, and may soon become accustomed to standards introduced by a commercial sector. Some new commercial indoor centres have capitalised on parents' fears with developments such as using elaborate safety measures as a key selling point to parents. In one scheme young people will be electronically tagged, heavily supervised and monitored by surveillance cameras once in the centre. In another scheme parent and child will receive barcoded tickets so that one cannot leave without the other (Gilling, 1995).

One of the more enlightening results of the parent focus group was the level of confusion and number of assumptions surrounding safety in non-residential, community youth sport. Some assume that if a course is advertised through the council that "someone else has made sure everything is as it should be". Parents have become accustomed to the standards of care at school and sometimes appear to have the same expectations of provision of other sports courses. Parents in the study indicated they were prepared to pay for safety, a finding which possibly supporting those of a Scottish Sports Council study that the cost of entrance had a relatively low relevance in the decision to participate or not (Coalter, 1993).

Parents' confusion about who the provider is in many local sporting contexts not surprising — fragmentation of out-of-school sport is well recognised (Munn, 1990), as is the desire to do something about it (Campbell, 1995). Differences in safety standards between individual sports exist and, even within the same sport, coaches will have different interpretations of the rules. With this fragmentation, perhaps the case should be made for national guidelines that 'bolt-on' to specific governing body guidelines — not just for hazardous sport but for all youth sports courses, events and on-off taster sessions.

In the development of this case study, guidelines were produced to reduce the uncertainty and ambiguity surrounding provision but also to disseminate ideas about good practice. The existence of such guidelines may not solve all the problems but they are a starting-point in developing a quality safety culture. Local clubs not involved in Stay with Sport will also have access to current ideas about good practice through the dissemination of information. It is the starting point in a debate — what is exactly going on in local grassroots clubs dealing with young people. There are problems inherent in this process. Perhaps the range of sports, locations, venues and age groups in community sports programme mitigates against the effectiveness of a single set of guidelines. What are the implications for coaches and providers if guidelines are not met? Should they be referred to as 'guidelines', 'rules', 'codes of practice', 'codes of conduct' or indeed a 'seal of approval'? With any guidelines there are loopholes. For example, an independent coach could book school facilities and advertise Hi/her own session on a school notice board but that coach would not need to be police-checked.

Some of the good practice outlined in the Seal of Approval requires additional adults either for administration or pastoral care at lunch breaks and toilet visits. In Southampton these roles are increasingly being carried out by volunteer parents whose children are involved in courses. The case has been made for appropriately qualified teaching assistants in schools to support physical education teachers within the national curriculum: perhaps the same case could be made in clubs (Campbell, 1995).

For all those involved, whether coaches, parents or local authority officers, the question is how far could and should you take measures to ensure reasonable safety and to avoid foreseeable accidents. For example, the idea of police-checks on coaches was acceptable to all coaches in the study, but as more volunteers are required to support coaches, will it be possible to police-check all volunteers, often at short notice? This is irrespective of the effectiveness of police checks (Brackenridge, 1995).

To what extent can and should the local authority 'control' the voluntary sector in provision of youth sport? The voluntary sector has been frequently described as the backbone of British sport. The intention is obviously not to stifle the voluntary sector with rules, regulations and additional expense. The strength of this local research initiative is that the guidelines have grown as a response to local needs reflecting local conditions and involving local parents, coaches and young people. The research and consultative process has been almost as important as the production of the Seal of Approval. Because of the confusion about safety issues and because of the proliferation of providers, we feel that national guidelines should be developed for young people on sports courses that would complement governing body regulations. In addition to this, research into empowering young people (and their coaches) to take control of their own safety should be undertaken in the very near future.

Note

[1] Christine Benning, Sports Development Officer and Joint Researcher, acted as technical adviser in the production of this paper.

References

Anderson, J. and Henning, C. (1995) 'Research into young people and parents' views on sports courses', Presentation at 4th National Sports Development Conference. Nottingham. (Unpublished).

Armstrong, N., Baling, J., Gentle, P., Williams. J., and Kirby, B. (1990) 'Patterns of physical activity among 11 to 16 year old British children', *British Medical Journal*, Vol. 30, No. 1, pp. 349-358.

Assel (1987) *Consumer behaviour and marketing action* (3rd edition). Boston MA: Kent Publishing Company.

Barnardo's (1995) *The facts of life*. London: Barnardos Publications.

Beedle, P. (1993) 'Risk-taking: The consensus view', *Journal of Adventure Education and Leadership*, Vol. 11, No. 2: p 13-17.

Benning, C. (1995) *Stay with Sport. Guidelines for the conduct of sports courses, events and taster sessions*. Southampton City Council. Internal Document.

Brackenridge, C., Summers, D. and Woodward, D. (1995) 'Educating for child protection in sport', this volume, pp. 167-190.

Brustad, A. (1992) 'Integrating socialization influences into the study of children's motivation in sport', *Journal of Sport Exercise Physiology*, Vol. 14: pp. 59-77.

Buschner, R. (1989) 'Teaching and coaching. A comparison of behaviours', *Journal of Teaching Physical Education*, Vol. 9: pp. 49-57.

Campbell, S. (1995) 'Coordination of effective partnerships for the benefit of school age pupils', *British Journal of Physical Education*, Summer Vol. 26, No. 2: pp. 10-12.

Collins, M. (1995) *Sports development locally and Regionally*. London: Sports Council/ILAM.

Coalter, F. (1993) 'Sports participation: Price or priorities', *Leisure Studies*,, Vol. 12, No. 3: pp 171-182.

De Knop, P., Theeboom, M. and De Marteaer, K. (1995) 'Towards a sound youth sports policy in the club', *Physical Education Review*, Vol. 1, No. 1: pp. 6-14.

Eve, N. (1994) 'Safety implications for partnerships — in loco parentis', *The Bulletin of Physical Education*, Vol. 30, No. 3: p 6-8.

Everard, B. (1994) 'Safety principles, codes of practice and value statements', *Journal of Adventure Education and Outdoor Leadership*, Vol. 11, No. 1: pp. 23-24.

Cullingford, C. (1995) 'Children's attitudes towards their holidays', *Tourism*, Vol. 16, No. 2: pp. 121-127.

Gilling, J. (1995) 'Inside looking out', *Leisure Management*, Vol. 15, No. 8: pp. 23 (August).

—— (1995) 'Interview with Mark Grenside', *Leisure Management*, Vol. 15, No. 8: p 23 August.

Gitelson, R., Kerstatter, D. and Guadagnoto, F. (1993) 'Research note: The impact of incentives and three forms of postage on mail survey response rates', *Leisure Sciences*, Vol. 15, No. 4: p. 321-327.

Griffin, L. Chandler, T. and Satiscany, M. (1993) 'What does fun mean in physical education?' *Journal of Physical Education Research Sulppement* Nov/Dec, Vol. 24, No.4, p. 10.

Harrison, P. (1995) 'Partnerships between physical education and sport', *The British Journal of Physical Education*, Summer, Vol. 26, No. 2: p. 4.

HMSO (1995) *Self reported drug misuse in England and Wales*. Home Office RPU Paper 89. London: HMSO.

Howard, D. and Madrigal, R. (1990) 'Who makes the decision, parent or child? The perceived influence of parents and children on the purchase of recreational services', *Journal of Leisure Research*, Vol. 22, No. 3, pp. 244-258.

Hultsman, W. (1993) 'The influence of others as a barrier to recreation participation among early adolescents', *Journal of Leisure Research*, Vol. 25, No. 2: pp. 150-161.

Kleiber, D. Larson, R. and Csikszentimihali, M. (1986) 'The experience of leisure in adolescence', *Journal of Leisure Research*, Vol. 18, No. 3: pp. 169.

Jeffers, S. (1989) *Feel the fear and do it anyway*. London: Century.

Jenkins, R. L. (1979) 'The influence of children in family decision making: parents' perceptions', in W. L. Wilkie (ed) *Advances in consumer research*, New York: Association in Consumer Research, pp. 413-419.

Larner, C. (1995) *Rosemary Conley Health Club Management*. Hitchin (UK): Fitness Industry Association: p. 7.

Mintel (1995) *Youth lifestyles 1995*. London: Mintel.

McDonald, I. (1995) 'Sport for All R.I.P,? A political critique of local authority sports development', in S. Fleming, M. Talbot and A. Tomlinson (eds) *Policy and politics in sport, physical education and leisure.* LSA Publication No. 55. Eastbourne: Leisure Studies Association, pp. 71-94.

Mortlock, C. (1987) *The adventure alternative.* Milnethorpe: Cierone Press.

Munn, J. (1995) Sports partnerships for young people', *British Journal of Physical Education*, Summer, Vol. 6, No. 4: pp. 30-34.

Neustatter, A, (1995) 'Girls and boys come in to stay', *The Observer*, 18 June. Supplement, *Childhood: An innocence betrayed*, p. 12.

Ogilvie, K. (1990) 'The management of risk', *Journal of Adventure and Outdoor Education.*

Roberts, M. L., Wartzel, L. H and Berkeley, R. L. (1980) 'Mothers' attitudes and perceptions of children's influence and their effect on family consumption', in K. B Monroe (ed) *Advances on consumer research.* Ann Arbor, MI: Association for Consumer Research, pp. 424-426.

Sleap, M. and Warburton, P. (1994) 'Physical activity levels of pre-adolescent children in England', *British Journal of Physical Education Research Supplement*, No. 14, Summer: pp. 2-6.

Sports Council (1994) *National survey of young people and sport.* London: OPCS.

Turner, R. (1993) 'The holiday factor', *The Leisure Manager* (Report on Shifting Sands supported by National Children Play and Recreation Unit) April, Vol. 11, No. 4: pp. 29.

Ward, S. and Wackman, D. B. (1972) 'Children's purchase influence attempts and parents' yielding', *Journal of Marketing Research*, Vol. 1: pp. 316-319.

Welshman, J. (1994) 'Children's fitness and activity levels', *British Journal of Physical Education*, July, Vol. 6, No. 4, pp. 13.

Wallace, J. (1995) 'The health of a nation', *The Leisure Manager*, Aug/Sept Vol. 13, No. 3, p. 27.

Whitehead, J. (1994) 'Why children choose to do sport — or stop', in M. Lee (ed) *Coaching children in sport.* London: E & FN Spon, pp. 107-120.

Educating for Child Protection in Sport

Celia Brackenridge, Diana Summers and Diana Woodward

Cheltenham and Gloucester College of Higher Education

This paper presents a case for the implementation of an educational agenda for child protection in sport. It begins with an exploration of the current state of theoretical and empirical knowledge about child sexual abuse and then moves on to a consideration of how childhood itself is socially constructed and perceived within sport in ways which serve to deny or limit the autonomy of the child. The coach education system in Britain is described in relation to the debate about accountability in public institutions. The paper ends with a discussion of an educational agenda for child protection.

Before commencing, it is important to set out the parameters of the paper. We are concerned with children not adults: that is, those persons covered by the terms of the Children Act 1989 — although we recognise that, in terms of non-legal definitions, the boundary between 'child' and 'adult' is unclear (for a discussion of the term 'child' in relation to sexual abuse see Doyle, 1994). Although girls suffer the vast majority of incidents of child sexual abuse (Dempster in Waterhouse, 1993), our concern here is with potential victims of either sex. Conversely, since males represent the majority of perpetrators of child sexual abuse — Doyle (1994: p. 43) reports a consistent ratio of about 1:30 of female to male abusers and Dobash, Carnie and Waterhouse (1993) found 99% of abusers to be male — the coach is referred to throughout as 'he'. Whereas the public and private sector are engaged fairly extensively in programmes of sports provision for children, we limit our attention here to children's sport in the voluntary sector which, we assert, is less closely regulated and therefore more vulnerable to exploitation by those seeking access to children for clandestine activities.

167

This work has an unashamedly political agenda which is to bring about change in the way sport is structured and managed. The moral framework for the work rests on two basic assumptions: first, that sexual contact with a child is *always* wrong and secondly, that the coach is *always* responsible for his actions.

Child sexual abuse — theory and practice

Empirical knowledge about the prevalence and incidence of child abuse is drawn mainly from social work (such as Waterhouse, 1993), clinical sources (such as Riley, 1991) and the National Society for the Prevention of Cruelty to Children (NSPCC) (such as Wattam, Hughes and Blagg, 1991; or Creighton, 1992) and focuses on intra-familial abuse. Data about sexual abuse are both difficult to collect and extremely unreliable because of a host of problems to do with revelation, confidentiality and fear of reprisal. Regardless of the definition of sexual abuse adopted, which in itself is an enormous area for debate (see, for example, Brindle, 1995; or Doyle, 1994: pp. 20-28), the available evidence suggests that a significant minority of young people, perhaps including twenty-five percent or more of girls, can expect to experience sexual abuse of one kind or another before reaching adulthood (Fisher, 1994).

The major theoretical explanations of child abuse derive from sociological (such as Finkelhor, 1986; Bart and Moran, 1993) and feminist analyses (such as Wise, 1991). The latter, in particular, have been driven by a strong desire to intervene in the social process in order to prevent abusive behaviour towards females (see, for example, Kelly and Regan, 1993). Feminists have construed sexual abuse as a sub-set of a continuum of sexual violence which ranges from mild to extreme (Stanko, 1990). In our work, we have used a working model of sexual violence in which institutional sex discrimination and personal sexual abuse are the two ends of the sexual violence continuum, with sexual harassment in the middle (see Figure 1).

We recognise that this construct is susceptible to the criticism that it simplifies what is, in fact, a highly complex, dynamic combination of power and sexuality. Nevertheless, it has proved a useful model thus far for the analysis of female athletes' experiences of sexual violence by their coaches (see for example Brackenridge, forthcoming; and Brackenridge and Summers, forthcoming) and will continue to be used until a more effective set of definitions can be found.

The most widely used theoretical explanation of child sexual abuse comes from Finkelhor (1986) who suggests a sequential, four stage model (Figure 2).

SEX DISCRIMINTATION	SEXUAL HARASSMENT	SEXUAL ABUSE
INSTITUTIONAL ◄────────────► PERSONAL		
"the chilly climate	*"unwanted attention"*	*"groomed or coerced"*
• vertical and horizontal job segregation	• written or verbal abuse or threats	• exchange of reward or privilege for sexual favours
• lack of harassment policy and/or officer or reporting channels	• sexually oriented comments	• rape
	• jokes, lewd comments or sexual innuendos, taunts about body, dress, marital status or sexuality	• anal or vaginal penetration by penis, fingers or objects
• differential pay or rewards or promotion prospects on the basis of sex	• ridiculing of performance	• forced sexual activity
	• sexual or homophobic graffiti	• physical sexual violence
• poorly/unsafely designed or lit venues	• practical jokes based on sex	• groping
	• intimidating sexual remarks, propositions, invitations or familiarity	• indecent exposure
• lack of counselling or mentoring systems	• absence of security	• incest
	• domination of meetings, play space or equipment	
	• condescending or patronising behaviour undermining self-respect or work performance	
	• physical contact, fondling, pinching or kissing	
	• vandalism on the basis of sex	
	• offensive telephone calls or photos	
	• bullying based on sex	

Figure 1   The sexual harassment/sexual abuse continuum

Source: Brackenridge (forthcoming, in Clarke and Humberstone)

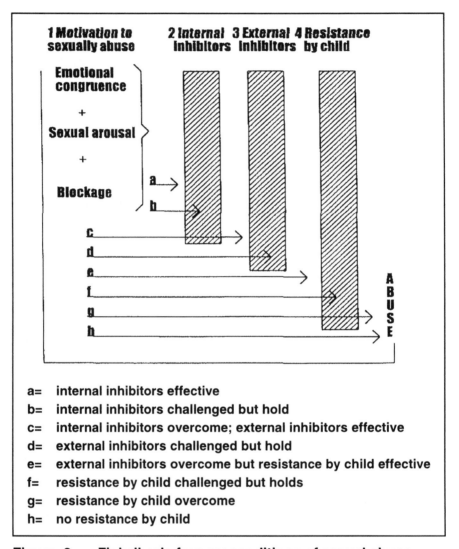

1 Motivation to sexually abuse   **2 Internal inhibitors** **3 External inhibitors** **4 Resistance by child**

Emotional congruence

+

Sexual arousal

+

Blockage

a= **internal inhibitors effective**
b= **internal inhibitors challenged but hold**
c= **internal inhibitors overcome; external inhibitors effective**
d= **external inhibitors challenged but hold**
e= **external inhibitors overcome but resistance by child effective**
f= **resistance by child challenged but holds**
g= **resistance by child overcome**
h= **no resistance by child**

Figure 2   Finkelhor's four preconditions of sexual abuse (adapted)

First, there must be motivation to abuse together with sexual arousal to children; next, internal inhibitors must break down, then external inhibitors must fail and, finally, the resistance of the child must be overcome. Abuse occurs only when inhibitions or resistances have been weakened and overcome at each stage. Thus, a highly motivated sexually aroused potential abuser may fail to reach a target if either his own internal inhibitions or external inhibitions put in his way by other agents successfully block his path.

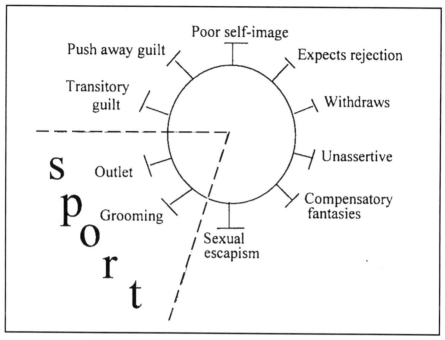

Figure 3   Wolf's Cycle of Offending — adapted to show the area of responsibility of sport.
Source: Fisher (1994)

Wolf's Cycle of Abuse (1984) (see Figure 3) is also frequently used to illustrate the sequential nature of paedophile withdrawal into sexual fantasy, the use of grooming to prepare victims for abuse, subsequent feelings of guilt and low self-esteem which then reinforce withdrawal and begin the cycle again. Whilst this model of behaviour may fit certain types of paedophile it does not, according to our findings, help to explain many of the examples of sexually abusive behaviour in sport which we have studied, where the abusing coaches reported to us appear to have good social skills, high visibility and a high level of sexual confidence and assertiveness.

One approach to enhancing child protection has been to generate perpetrator profiles in order to assist with the prediction of potential abusers. Profiling in this way is very controversial, as with criminal profiling by psychologists, but has been found to be effective in helping those who treat and rehabilitate offenders. The Federal Bureau of Investigation in the United States has developed perpetrator profiles which they call 'preferential', i.e. sexually oriented to children by preference, and 'situational', i.e. sexually oriented to children if the situation arises (Armstrong, 1995), and David Finkelhor (1993) has produced five profiles of incestuous offenders. However, the emphasis of such profiling work has been on *intra-familial* cases and, whilst Wolf's model offers a useful approach to predicting some *extra-familial* paedophile behaviour, our critique of the model leads us to posit that more than one profile applies in sport.

It is probably fair to say that most research on sexual abuse has focused on the psycho-dynamics of the behaviour involved rather than the situational contingencies, a point also made by Martin and Hummer (1993). (See, for example, a review of research on sexual violence by Muehlenhard and Linton, 1987.) Yet, if Finkelhor's model has any efficacy, it demands that we look at both situational *and* personal risk factors. In other words, we need to understand not only individual susceptibilities either to perpetrate or to suffer abuse, but also what constitutes an abuse-prone context. Research into the organisational context of sport and the social construction of sub-cultural life in sport is therefore an essential component of our search for understanding about sexual abuse of athletes. Indeed, in an earlier paper (Brackenridge, 1994a), it was suggested that theories of sexual abuse might follow the same path as theories of leadership which moved from a *trait*, through a *state*, to a *situational/contingency approach*. Subsequent work (Brackenridge, forthcoming) has mapped a table of emerging risk factors under the headings 'coach', 'athlete' and the 'sport' itself.

Sexually abusive behaviour is notoriously resistant to rehabilitation and, in the case of certain types of paedophile, extreme persistence is demonstrated in seeking out potential victims. Clearly, attempts to prevent abuse, in whatever setting, will be most effective if the internal inhibitors themselves remain strong. However, given the apparent widespread failure of internal inhibitors, the focus of preventative work must be on improving external inhibition in the situational and organisational context and increasing the resistance of the child through education.

Helen Armstrong (1995) uses a triangular model depicting the 'abuser', the 'victim' and the 'onlooker' (Figure 4). The term 'victim' is problematic in that it implies a continuous negative status, whereas many who have come through experiences of sexual violence positively prefer to define themselves as 'survivors'. Doyle (1994: p. 12-13) also suggests that the term implies weakness, whereas it could be argued that it is the perpetrator who exhibits weakness, not the recipient of abuse. Armstrong accepts that, because of the extreme persistence amongst abusers of the motivation to become sexually aroused to children, trying to effect change with abusers is like "trying to change the world". She also suggests that trying to help victims is almost impossible as they feel so powerless. This means that the only effective point of pressure or intervention lies with the onlooker(s), who may be individuals, organisations or institutions. Onlookers must be encouraged to develop allegiance with the victim rather than the abuser: in sport, this may mean asking those with a vested interest in supporting the coach, such as parents, governing bodies, administrators, other coaches or even peer athletes, to accept the word of children and to act on their

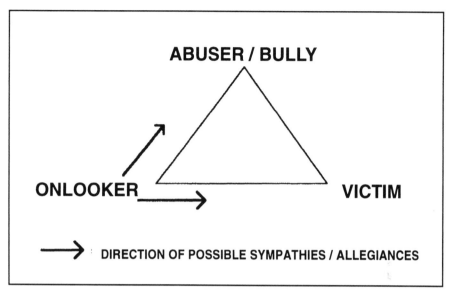

ABUSER / BULLY

ONLOOKER **VICTIM**

DIRECTION OF POSSIBLE SYMPATHIES / ALLEGIANCES

Figure 4 **Competing interests in abusive situation (after Armstrong, 1995)**

behalf. However, if incentives for reporting an abuser are lacking, then onlookers may prefer to keep quiet. Welch and Wearmouth (1994: p. 7) give a list of reasons why individuals might refrain from becoming involved in disciplinary actions and they set out informal grievance procedures and disciplinary guidelines for sport organisations. Certainly, both personal and organisational support is needed for those who wish to 'blow the whistle' but who lack the courage, or who fear sanction, for doing so.

We need to ask ourselves who are the onlookers in voluntary sport and where are their habitual allegiances? Cuts in public spending have caused more people to be dependent upon the voluntary sector, yet the laissez faire, non-interventionist approach of Government to this relatively unregulated sector has rendered it open to infiltration by individuals with personal agendas. Our enquiries suggest that onlookers like clubs and National Governing Bodies of Sport (NGBs), and even national agencies like the National Coaching Foundation (NCF) and Sports Council, find it easier to align with the coach since alignment with the victim would, by definition, draw them into accepting that there are flaws in the very institution which established them: that is, organised sport. Child athletes or former athletes can easily be disbelieved simply because they are disempowered in our society (see discussion below), and because they can be dismissed as disgruntled failures. The stakes are so high for an NGB that, even where it is widely known that an abuser is at work, it is safer for officials to keep quiet, to safeguard the possibility of medal successes. Our research shows that peer coaches find it hard to believe that one of their number, perhaps a trusted and respected colleague, is guilty of sexual abuse and that, even where sexual misdemeanours are known about, they are often rationalised as one-off incidents, part of the rough and tumble of sport or even as an extension of the rights of the coach! A child's peers are also onlookers for whom the safest course of action is to keep quiet, to side with the coach and to spurn the victim. There may be elements of hero-worship, infatuation and even love involved, where children will react strongly against anyone amongst their peer group who reports the coach. Also, a young female's sexuality, not yet fully identified or developed, may well be reinforced by the sexual advances of a coach who is able to affirm her femininity in a context where femininity is frequently denied or about which there is ambivalence. In this scenario it is common for the abused girl to become ever more isolated, or even expendable. Some of our interviewees have found themselves ostracised by their peer group for reporting abusive coaches to the authorities. Some have subsequently been dropped from teams or squads or victimised in other ways because they have dared to challenge the authority of the coach (see Brackenridge 1994b; Brackenridge and Summers, forthcoming).

Children and sport

The complexities of children's rights are only a sub-set of the issue of rights *per se*, and children's rights in sport comprise a smaller sub-set again. Rights exist in three broad forms: civil, political and social rights (Marshall and Bottomore, 1992). They are conveyed by custom or by law, and as such are historically and culturally located (Thompson, 1991). Philosophically, the foundation of rights is located in the debate between what is a citizen and what is a society and the nature of the inter-relationship between the two. There is a tension between expectations, or *rights*, and responsibilities, or *duties*. The creation of a right for one person always creates a duty for someone else; the two are connected. When rights are at issue, so are definitions and the power to create definitions. Power is intimately linked to the debates for rights, whose rights are dominant and valid and whose are not.

Children's rights hinge upon the definitions of adult and adult responsibility and on the delineation between adult and child. Contemporary perceptions of children's rights can be located on a continuum from *in need of care* to *self-determining*. In the last fifteen years debates about the status of children have been located more towards the right hand end of the continuum, emphasising autonomy and self-determination (Franklin, 1995; Lyon and Parton, 1995) but this has been contested by those who argue against children having full participant rights in decision-making relating to them (see discussion below).

When looking at children in sport — either as participants or, in the terms of this paper, as those who are abused by more powerful individuals — it is important to understand that the terms 'child' and 'childhood ' are culturally-constructed concepts. Some would also argue that the notions of child and childhood are peculiar to the modern Western world (Pinchbeck and Hewitt, 1973; Franklin, 1995; Ennew, 1995), but even here no clear universally accepted delineation exists between adulthood and childhood, with anomalies and disparities between rights and responsibilities. For example, in Britain, criminal liability is taken as ten years old, an age when one is deemed responsible for one's actions, yet sexual and political rights are not conferred until sixteen or eighteen. The idea of 'child' is a fragmented one even intra-culturally; for example, upper class children may be sent to board at preparatory school from the age of eight, whereas cultural traditions in some working class districts proscribe children being left in the care of anyone other than female kin. With such difficulties besetting the definitions of such apparently simple concepts as 'child' and 'childhood', inevitably this creates problems in defining child abuse.

In Britain, changing perceptions of the term childhood can be identified through analysing legal representations of children over the last three hundred years (Parton, 1985; Pinchbeck and Hewitt, 1969). Before this time, children were not sufficiently demarcated from adults for childhood to be an identifiable separate status; they were seen as working members of the community as soon as they were physically independent of their mother (Pinchbeck and Hewitt, 1969). In the sixteenth century the Tudor Poor Law included the care of abandoned children, looking after them for their first six years then sending them to public schools if they showed intellectual promise, or to places of work to train in a trade. Marshall and Bottomore (1992: p. 15) saw the Poor Law as the 'aggressive champion of social rights' through legislation that attempted to replace the genuine social rights of community that had gone before. The 1834 Poor Law legislation meant that those who required welfare had forfeited any right to be considered citizens; 'those who accepted relief must cross the road that separated the community of citizens from the outcast company of the destitute'. Society was to be protected from the attacker within. This concern with protecting society from delinquents affected legislation for children right up until the 1970s (Parton, 1985).

In the three hundred years after the Tudor Poor Law children were, in legal terms, primarily seen as the property of their parents who could do with "their unhappy offspring as they chose" (Pinchbeck and Hewitt, 1973: p. 350). It was only from 1800 onwards that legislation pertaining to children's welfare began to emerge with the 1802 Health and Morals of Apprentices Act, which restricted cotton apprentices to working twelve hour days. Legislation over the next century was based in a paternalistic view concerned with children as objects of welfare, promoted by such reformers as Lord Shaftsbury who supported the welfare of children as long as it did not conflict with the rights of adults (Pinchbeck and Hewitt, 1973; Parton, 1986; Franklin, 1995).

In the 1980s, when according to Franklin (1995) children's rights 'came of age', legislation (both nationally in Britain and internationally) began to create the child as subject rather than object, who should have some say in their lives. The United Nations (UN) Children's Charter (1989) was an international expression of the rights of the child which, although representing a major move forward, was qualified in its achievements. It only advocates that children's welfare be '*a* primary consideration' rather than *the* primary consideration (Franklin, 1995). Other criticisms of the Charter include a monocultural bias deriving from a Western view of children (Ennew, 1995). It has, however, been the most widely and the fastest-ratified UN convention. In Britain the Children Act (1989) was 'intended to acknowledge and concede children's abilities as autonomous decision-makers' (Franklin, 1995: p. 3). But Britain's record on children's rights is not good: Britain agreed to ratify the UN Children's Charter without agreeing to the protection of sixteen year olds in the labour market, to change immigration laws concerning children and to cease the incarceration of young offenders in adult custody. The Children Act, too, is not without its critics. According to Lyon and Parton (1995), whilst it appears to forward children's rights and provide more and new opportunities for advancing the autonomy of children and young people, this is 'very qualified'. They go on to say:

> The articulation of children's rights, rather than constituting children and young persons as subjects, has provided a new set of strategies and mechanisms for using the voices of children as elements in the newly constituted government of families. Rather than subjects in their own right, children have become reconstituted as legal — as opposed to welfare — objects for the purpose of governing families at a distance. (Lyon and Parton, 1995: p. 53)

This new 'legal child' is another discursive creation used to give children meaning within society. To identify all discourses relating to children is impossible: they are, by their nature, nebulous and self-mutating. However, we can identify some broadly similar groups of myths about children that may differ in degree but are based around a similar premise. Early Calvinistic doctrines and the concept of original sin create the 'devil incarnate' image (Pinchbeck and Hewitt, 1973), still found in Christian fundamentalism today and also in much media coverage of children (Franklin, 1995).

Apparently contradictory but mutually supporting discourses about children can sit side by side, such as the notions of 'innocence betrayed ' and 'devils incarnate' in the tabloid newspaper coverage of the James Bulger trial (Franklin, 1995). Another source of myths is the sexual child of Freudian psychoanalysis that links personal identity with sexual identity, which is recognisable in the 'Lolita' image that lures men into sex (Campbell, 1988). The incremental moral learning theories of developmental psychologists such as Piaget (1965) support a common view of the child as a *tabula rasa*. This view was shared by writers on citizenship and political legitimacy such as John Stuart Mill (1972), Locke (1924) and Habermas (1988).

Sport has not been free from this process of discursive creation and reinforcement. Foucault (1977) maintained that its inclusion in many of the early 'disciplinary' institutions was a crucial part of the discourse of 'correction' and 'normalisation'. Sport was used both in both public school and corrective institutional work on children to perform "a pedagogical and spiritual transformation of individuals, brought about by continuous exercise" (Foucault, 1977: p. 121). He sees the disciplinary nature of exercise as part of the rising industrialisation of Europe, "the body becomes a useful force only if it is both a productive body and a subjected one" (p. 26). Sport is the discipline of the body that ultimately disciplines the mind and heart.

According to Shier (1995), Article 31 of the UN Children's Charter (1989) is concerned with the rights of the child to have "rest and leisure to engage in play and recreational activity". He points out "it is a right to *participate fully and equally as individuals*" (p.14) (*emphasis added*).

> The human body was entering a machinery of power that explores it, breaks it down and rearranges it; a 'political anatomy', which was also a 'mechanics of power', was being born; it defined how one may have a hold over others' bodies, not only so that they may do what one wishes, but so they may operate as one wishes, with the techniques, the speed and the efficiency that one determines. Thus discipline produces subjected and practised bodies, 'docile' bodies. (Foucault, 1977: p. 138)

Books on coaching represent the child as fragmented into the physiological child, the psychological child, or the sociological child but never the whole child. In the positivistic tradition of the sport sciences, the child is represented as raw material for performance enhancement (Weiss and Gould, 1984; Magill, Ash and Smoll, 1982; Grisogono, 1991). Sports pedagogy has been concerned with the developmental nature of the child, investigating the effects of sport on moral development (Lee, 1986; Bredemeier, 1988) and in the creation of proper citizens (Martens, 1988). However, the child is still constituted as an 'empty vessel', rather than being held capable of rational thought and autonomous participation from a very early age.

Moves in the wider society towards greater autonomy for children and greater choice are in direct conflict to the government's prescriptions for children in state education, such as the treatment of sport in the Education Reform Act (1988) and in the subsequent amendments. Here, increasing central control of the curriculum and tighter regulation of children's choices are apparent. For example, team games were made compulsory at Key Stage Four whereas before they had been optional.

Another argument about children and sport which has emerged over the last fifteen years concerns the effect of competitive sport on children: does competitive sport help to create more moral and rounded adults, or does it rather increase aggression and retard social and moral growth in children? As Roberts and Treasure (1993: p. 4) point out:

> ... the supportive evidence for either position is largely anecdotal ... systematic research which specifically focuses upon the impact of competitive sport on children's psychosocial development needs to be undertaken.

This is paralleled by the lack of research on child protection issues in sport. There is a need for research which explores in some depth the situation and experiences of children in sport, not only, as Gilroy (1993: p. 24) points out, to determine how children's sport is organised, but to see who organises it and who benefits from it; "we need therefore to look critically at what is happening in children's sport".

Part of the problem lies in the social construction of children and the imputation of children's needs by others without reference to the children themselves. With no voice in the decisions that affect them most closely both inside and outside sport, children lack a political force other than through the advocacy of others. Who actively wants to allow children their own advocacy when the power over them and for them is so useful?

Coach education in the UK

Together with school-based physical education, coaching, whether in the voluntary sector club or association or the local authority scheme, has been one of the major avenues through which children have been introduced to playing sport. Whereas the dedicated amateur could, at one time, enter coaching with few or no formal qualifications, coaching has become increasingly centred around those holding recognised qualifications. Coach education in the UK is delivered through: the National Coaching Foundation (NCF), the National Governing Bodies of sport (NGBs), Local Authorities (LAs) and Further and Higher Education institutions (F/HEIs).

The NCF was first established in 1983 by the Sports Council to "enhance performance by providing highly skilled coaches" (NCF, 1995: p. 11). Despite resistances from certain quarters of the sports establishment and the protection of sectional interests from a number of governing bodies which wanted to maintain their sovereignty over their own coaching award schemes, the NCF grew rapidly. In 1986 the National Council for Vocational Qualification (NCVQ) was set up to develop a national framework of qualifications for workers of all occupations and professions (Fennell, 1995). The subsequent development of Sport National Vocational Qualifications (S/NVQs) for sport facilitated further expansion of the NCF network of coach education modules, and by mid 1995 the NCF was working towards the implementation of S/NVQs with 83 NGBs (NCF, 1995). In addition, the NCF works in partnership with LAs through Champion Coaching, a scheme for talent promotion, and local coaching strategies including coaching courses for sport development workers. F/HEIs also liaise with the NCF through its national network of centres to provide introductory coach education and NGB coaching awards, and Certificates and Diplomas in Sports Coaching.

We have not yet completed a comprehensive analysis of the curricula for coach education of all these agencies, but suspect that very few incorporate content on child protection and sexual abuse. The 1995 National Programme of Key Courses offered by the NCF at 15 centres in England, Scotland, Northern Ireland and Wales included only one course out of eleven with a focus on coaching children and only two on coaching methods *per se*, with all other courses focusing on aspects of performance enhancement such as developing endurance, injury prevention, or motivation. This is unsurprising since *performance enhancement* lies at the heart of the coaching process. However, the NCF has, from time to time, also involved itself in a number of broader equity issues including work on women as sports coaches (White, Mayglothling and Carr, 1989), sexual harassment (Tomlinson and Yorganci, 1993) and 'fair play' in children's sport (Lloyd and Campbell, 1990). Interestingly, whilst educational initiatives have flowed from some of these issues, they have *not* been incorporated into the mainstream programme of 'key courses'.

The NCF is also working together with the National Association of Sports Coaches (NASC) (formerly British Institute of Sports Coaches) to improve its Codes of Ethics and Practice for affiliated coaches. However, recent and ongoing institutional struggles over organisational autonomy and control between the NCF and NASC appear to have slowed progress on the development of these codes, effectively deflecting attention away from the introduction of an integrated child protection system in sport.

Accountability and child protection in the voluntary sport system

Little research exists on voluntary sector sport. Indeed the precise definition of the voluntary sector in any area is difficult.

> Voluntary action is notoriously difficult to quantify, definitions of voluntary organizations are contested, and the boundaries of the sector cannot be drawn with confidence. (Justin Smith *et al.*, 1995: p. 2)

Although Justin Smith *et al.* are referring here to the health sector, their comment is echoed in the statement made by the Sports Council representative to the government Environment Committee (1985) that the estimated part of the market held by the voluntary sector was 'incalculable'.

Organisational theory drawn from business and management studies provides some frameworks for the analysis of the voluntary sector in sport. Handy (1988) has written about voluntary organisations *per se*, and while homogeneity, even within similar areas, cannot be assumed, his work offers some useful models. Much of the leading edge work on sport organisations is being done in Canada by people such as Slack and Kikulis (1989), and Thibault, Slack and Hinings (1993), focusing on the structures of National Governing Bodies, their reactions to change and their increasing professionalisation and bureaucratization. Studies which do exist on voluntary sector sport in Britain, such as that of Bishop and Hoggett (1986) on mutual aid in leisure, have lacked hypotheses and, as such, have offered little in terms of theoretical value. Other work exists such as the recent study on National Governing Bodies and Organisational Change by Carnegie National Sports Development Centre for the Sports Council (Abrams *et al.*, 1995), but its findings were considered by the Sports Council to be so sensitive that the report is not at present available for public consumption.

There is little or no work on accountability in voluntary sector sport organisations so the models described below are drawn from health sector work where, with changes in funding and increasing emphasis on voluntary sector provision, the accountability of voluntary providers is of growing concern. Rochester (1995) identifies three levels of responsibility in voluntary organizations: accountability with sanctions, explanatory accountability and responsive accountability. The first two work on the basis of external watchdogs who can either use sanctions, if behaviour does not match requirements, or demand an explanation but who have no power to impose sanctions. The last level of accountability is based on the willingness of organizations to be answerable for their actions. In voluntary groups any overall executives are often members of the group itself. Although classifications are never discrete, the last type identified by Rochester more closely resembles the 'self-help' organizations described by Bishop and Hoggett (1986).

Sport organizations rarely have external watchdogs to demand accountability, except perhaps the Sports Council which has a 'negative' right to withhold grants on the basis of non-compliance with set criteria. However, monitoring of organizations requires human and financial resources which are in scarce supply. Organizations which do not require grant aid need not comply with any of the Sports Council's stipulations. An example might be the Football Association which is vehemently resisting attempts to be regulated by others and insists instead on self-regulation (Hoey in Hansard, 1995: pp. 827-831).

Crucial to the issue of accountability in the voluntary sector is the willingness of the organisation to submit to scrutiny. Britain's largest federal body for voluntary sport, the Central Council For Physical Recreation (CCPR), has an historically strong tradition for independence and resistance against statutory control:

> ...this country is probably one of the very few in the world where sports enthusiasts can determine for themselves policies and strategies without the interference or domination of a national government. (CCPR Annual Report 1985/6: Foreword)

The CCPR have stood against governmental policy on, for example, the boycott of the Moscow Olympics. This resistance to external involvement in the affairs of the Council's members indicates that efforts to control through government legislation would be difficult either to bring about or to impose. This stance is, however, quite congruent with the present government's minimalist approach to the state.

There is no reason to suppose that sport should be exempt from the general pressure for accountability currently being experienced in other public institutions (Nolan Committee Report, 1995). However, Iain Sproat MP (Conservative), Parliamentary Under-Secretary of State for National Heritage, with responsibility for sport, when questioned by Ms Kate Hoey MP (Labour) in the House of Commons on 30 January 1995 about the "back-handers, bungs and fixes" (in Hansard, 1995: p. 828) being exposed in the Football Association, made the government's position in relation to sport organizations and governing bodies clear:

> It is right that private clubs and governing bodies should be allowed to operate freely without government interference — as long, of course, as they are seen to be acting in a responsible manner. (Sproat in Hansard, 1995: p. 834)

Ironically, publications calling for fair play have burgeoned during this time of so-called political sleaze. Examples include: the United Nations Educational, Scientific and Cultural Organisation International Charter of Physical Education and Sport [Article 2] (1992); the International Committee For Fair Play Manifesto (1992); the European Code of Sports Ethics (1992); the Central Council for Physical Recreation Fair Play Charter (1990); and the Playboard/NCF booklet 'Play The Game' (1986) concerned with children's sport. Most recently, the Sports Council has collaborated with the British Olympic Association, the British Institute of Sports Administration, the NCF, the National Sports development Centres, the Sports Council for Wales and the Scottish Sports Council to produce a booklet 'Getting it Right' to offer guidance for both individuals and organisations in sport, whether working in a voluntary or professional capacity (Welch and Wearmouth, 1994).

With regard to children and voluntary sector sport, the Children Act (1989) has placed a range of new requirements on organisers such as the amount of space provided per child or the registration of activities lasting longer than two hours. However, the requirements may be circumvented if organisers do not wish, or do not feel able, to comply.

As with the health service, decreasing funding in the statutory sector inevitably increases the workload of the voluntary sector. Local authorities are moving from being direct providers of services to being enablers (Leach *et al.*, 1994), and the voluntary sector is being used to supplement provision. Employees in the statutory sector who work with children must be police vetted (for previous criminal convictions to do with children): this is not the case in voluntary sector provision although some major children's charities have taken part in pilot scheme for police vetting (Unell, 1992), and a small number of voluntary organisations have subscribed to a privately-run vetting service (Armstrong, 1995). There is therefore an indeterminate, but sizeable, unscrutinised workforce in voluntary sport. Compulsory Competitive Tendering (CCT) also creates a new form of accountability, that of contractual accountability (Leat, 1995) which introduces a form of consumer rights. If local authorities care to insist, they could use their contractual obligations as a lever to insist on the checking of children's workers.

There is a conflict, therefore, between adult's rights to conduct what-ever leisure they choose in whatever manner they choose and children's right to be protected. Since it appears unlikely that the present government will intervene specifically for child protection in voluntary sport (beyond the parameters of the 1989 Children Act), any such initiatives will have to come from within voluntary sport itself. However, the ideology that British sport organisations should be self-policing has been called into question by the increasing number of prosecutions for assault and grievous bodily harm brought by athletes against their opponents (Wearmouth, 1995). Whereas at one time such disputes might have been dealt with by internal enquiry and internally-determined penalties, today recourse to law is not unusual for those who feel wronged or who have been physically damaged (Young, 1992). Indeed, the Sports Council's booklet 'Getting it Right' makes it very clear that organisations *are* responsible for the "control of conditions under which participants compete and train so as to ensure their safety and well-being" (Welch and Wearmouth, 1994: p. 3). It is therefore reasonable to raise the question of how long it might be before an NGB is brought to law by, or on behalf of, an athlete for failing to acknowledge and to deal with criminally abusive behaviour by one of its coaches? Already there have been a number prosecutions for sexual abuse of former coaches, some of whom work or have worked at Olympic level (BBC, 1993), but there have been none, to our knowledge, which have resulted in a counter claim by the defendant against those who trained him and/or accredited his coaching qualifications, such as his NGB or the NCF. It is not inconceivable, however, that an athlete or parent might claim against a club or NGB for failing in their duty of care to protect a child against reasonable risks, including exposure to molestation.

An agenda for education

If we accept Finkelhor's Four Stage Model of the preconditions for sexual abuse (Figure 2) then we must also accept that there is nothing we can do to prevent certain individuals from becoming sexually aroused by children and seeking out opportunities to gain access to them through activities in the voluntary sector. Sport is perhaps one of the most obvious outlets for such behaviour because it depends on a vast pool of voluntary labour, because it focuses on physicality and because large numbers of aspiring young children are involved. It therefore behoves those responsible for children's sport to recognise the potential risks in the system and to address them as systematically as possible in order to strengthen external inhibitors on child sexual abuse and to increase the child's capacity to resist. A number of mechanisms might be adopted to enhance the effectiveness of external inhibitors, including:

a) the introduction of **codes of ethics and codes of conduct** for sports leaders and coaches;

b) the adoption and regular updating of comprehensive **registers of coaches** to monitor who moves where between clubs, sports or regions;

c) the introduction of **criminal record checks** for all those placed in a leadership role, whether it is paid or not

d) the introduction of **compulsory child protection modules** in all coach education syllabi and governing body awards

e) the development and dissemination of **training materials for parents, athletes and coaches,** including simple codes of practice, checklists or contracts for all concerned to guide them to follow simple, basic rules of conduct

f) the collection and dissemination of **examples of good practice** in child protection in the voluntary sector of sport.

At the same time there is a need to add proper **grievance systems** for those coaches who might feel victimised by athletes or who, on occasion, might face false accusation of a sexual misdemeanour. Indeed, there is also further work to be done in examining the rights of the coach in respect of defence against false accusation.

Any one of these mechanisms taken in isolation will be inadequate to bring about effective child protection. **Codes of conduct** are helpful where coaches subscribe to them and where coaches must first register membership in order to practise. The British sport coaching system is based on a long tradition of voluntarism: governing bodies and clubs are usually only too pleased to welcome volunteer labour, especially from those holding recognised NGB qualifications, yet relatively few sports are governed by a specific code of conduct. **Registers of coaches** do not yet exist in a form which would facilitate monitoring and, as far as we can ascertain, are based on sport-specific or regional rather than national populations. **Criminal record checks** are both expensive to carry out and susceptible to falsification: police records are not all computerised and, where they are, the systems are not yet compatible for networking. Also, official records indicate only where a successful prosecution for a sexual offences against a child has been secured: given the tiny proportion of offences which get reported, let alone taken through the courts successfully, this information is far from complete. Record checks also fail to spot first offenders or those who have successfully evaded identification by using false names. Some organisations hold 'lists' of offenders, for example List 99 held by the

Department for Education: informal lists of offenders may also be held by sport organisations as is the case with Gymnastics in the USA (Hudson, 1995), but it seems possible that lists could also give rise to complaints from coaches about restraint of trade.

The last three listed mechanisms listed above — **compulsory child protection coach education modules, training materials for parents, athletes and coaches** and the **collection and dissemination of examples of good practice** — provide an educational agenda for child protection in sport.

Compulsory child protection coach education modules are needed to raise the level of awareness of child sexual abuse in general and of abuses in sport in particular. Such modules should be taken by all coaches, teachers, managers and instructors. No survivor of sexual abuse by a coach interviewed for this research to date has reported that they knew about sexual abuse *per se* outside their sport or felt that they had any real avenue inside their club or NGB through which to report problems with a coach. On the contrary, the system appeared to conspire against them in that they felt vulnerable and isolated and, in the few cases where reports were made, met either inertia or active blocks from peers, other coaches, administrators or even the police. Child protection modules need to be geared towards both recognition of signs of abuse *outside* sport and towards establishing good practice in the treatment of children *within* sport settings. They should help coaches and organisations to establish clear role specifications and channels of communication through which child protection concerns can be reported and addressed. Moreover, it is also essential that child protection in sport be located within the wider legal and social services system of child protection if sustainable improvements are to be made. At present, child protection vocational standards are built into a limited number of S/NVQs, thanks to initial work by the Royal Yachting Association and the National Society for the Prevention of Cruelty to Children (NSPCC), and subsequent liaison between the NSPCC and NCF (1995). However, child protection from abuse and neglect is not just the responsibility of individuals seeking S/NVQ accreditation, such as teachers and coaches, but of all individuals and organisations engaged in delivering sport to children.

Training materials for parents, athletes and coaches might incorporate advisory checklists for each party including, amongst other things, items about where and with whom to coach/train, how to arrange practice and meetings times, what travel and accommodation arrangements to observe, how and where to report any uncomfortable feelings or complaints and who might be used as an independent listener (David Smith, 1993). As Gerrilyn Smith (1995) points out, simply exhorting children to say 'No' puts the responsibility upon them and fails as a protection mechanism because it assumes that abuse is a one-off, impulsive behaviour rather than a carefully planned and executed strategy. Whilst education without regulation is unlikely to offer complete protection, it is perhaps one of the most effective mechanisms by which to improve child protection in sport. However, even the introduction of S/NVQ standards for child protection will go only part-way towards closing existing loopholes since paedophiles are extremely persistent and highly skilled at grooming both onlookers and children. Indeed, qualifications offer a coach a useful screen behind which to gain access to children. Whilst our investigations do not yet indicate any link between the level of a coach's qualifications and the likelihood that sexual abuse will occur, it is clear that the possession of formal qualifications does contribute to the alibi of an abusive coach. Coach education is therefore only one of several interlocking parts of the education system needed in sport if we are successfully to protect against sexual abuse.

The collection and dissemination of examples of good practice is an important vehicle for maintaining an optimistic mood amongst coaches and administrators. Our work has been criticised as a witch-hunt against coaches, but we are just as much concerned to publicise good practice as to expose bad and to assist those in the coaching community to raise their own standards. Sadly, we have very few examples of good practice available at present. However, the next phase of our work will include case studies of NGBs which are tackling the issue of child protection and, we hope that this will reveal further examples of successful child protection systems.

Conclusions

Child sexual abuse occurs in sport and will continue to present a threat to children until and unless steps are taken to intervene in risk situations. It occurs because of a general systems failure in which 'collective blindness' (Gerrilyn Smith, 1995) is compounded by lack of knowledge and lack of political will.

Sexual abuse of children is a product of a particular cultural system in which adults have power over children. Sexual abuse of children in sport is a product of a particular sub-culture in which the structural imbalances between adults and children are exaggerated and justified in the pursuit of competitive success. Indeed, we aver that sport is more susceptible to incidents of sexual abuse than other areas of the voluntary sector because of its hierarchical status, its requirement for total obedience and commitment to the word of the coach, its propensity for isolating children from their families and peers, the centrality of the body and sport's potential for the eroticisation of power relations. A great deal more empirical research is needed to establish any degree of support for such propositions. Our own future work will include: tests of such propositions through both qualitative and quantitative enquiry; a survey of NGBs' policies and practices with regard to child protection; and the development of what we hope will be effective predictive models of risk factors for the coach, the athlete and the sport situation. Research of this type is never completed soon enough for those children who have already suffered and those who are currently being sexually abused. In the meantime, however, implementation of the educational agenda for child protection in sport need not be delayed.

References

Abrams, J., Long, J., Talbot, M. and Welch, M. (1995) *Organisational change in national governing bodies of sport.* Unpublished.

Armstrong, H. (1995) Personal communication.

Bart, P. E. and Moran, E. G. (eds) (1993) *Violence against women: the bloody footprints.* London: Sage.

BBC (1993) Unpublished transcripts from 'On the line', 25 August.

Bishop, J. and Hoggett, P. (1986) *Organising around enthusiasms: mutual aid in leisure.* London: Comedia.

Brackenridge, C. (1994a) 'Fair play or fair game: child sexual abuse in sport organisations', *International Review for the Sociology of Sport,* Vol. 29, No. 3: pp. 287-299.

———(1994b) 'Sexual harassment and abuse in sport. "It couldn't happen here"', *Kvinner — en utfordring for idretten?* Rapport fra en konferanse i anledning OL'94 i Lillehammer. Arbeidsnotat 2: pp. 69-77.

———(forthcoming) '"Monsters don't get near to children, nice men do": ethical issues in researching sexual harassment and sexual abuse in sport', in G. Clarke and B. Humberstone (eds) *Writing in women: Critically researching women, physical activity, sport and physical education.* London: Macmillan.

Brackenridge, C. and Summers, D. (forthcoming) 'Taking the lid off sexual abuse in sport: A discussion of theory and practice', in C. Engelfried (ed) *Sexual abuse in sport.* Germany.

Bredemeier, B. (1988) 'The moral of the youth sport story', in E. Brown and C. Brant (eds) *Competitive sports for children.* Champaign, IL: Human Kinetics

Brindle, D. (1995) 'One in 6' children molested. *The Guardian,* 14 June.

Campbell, B. (1988) *Unofficial secrets. Child sexual abuse: The Cleveland case.* London: Virago.

Central Council for Physical Recreation (1985/86) *Annual report.* London: CCPR.

———(1990) *Fair play charter.* London: CCPR

Children Act (1989) HMSO.

Creighton, S. (1992) *Child abuse trends in England and Wales 1988-1990 and an overview from 1973-1990.* London: National Society for the Prevention of Cruelty to Children.

Dempster, H. (1993) 'The aftermath of child sexual abuse: women's perspectives', in L. Waterhouse (ed) *Child abuse and child abusers: protection and prevention*. Research Highlights in Social Work 24. London: Jessica Kingsley Publishers.

Dobash, R., Carnie, J., and Waterhouse, L. (1993) 'Child sexual abusers: recognition and response', in L. Waterhouse (ed) *Child abuse and child abusers: protection and prevention*. Research Highlights in Social Work 24. London: Jessica Kingsley Publishers. pp. 113-135.

Doyle, C. (1994) *Child sexual abuse: a guide for professionals*. London: Chapman Hall.

Education Reform Act (1988) HMSO.

Ennew, J. (1995) 'Outside childhood: street children's rights.' in B. Franklin (ed) *The handbook of children's rights: Comparative policy and practice*. London: Routledge.

Environment Select Committee (1985) *Second report from the Environment Committee session 1985-1986*. Commons paper 241. London: HMSO

European Sports Council (1992) *European code of sports ethics*. European Sports Council.

Fennell, E. (1995) 'Lighting the way for higher standards', *The Times* , NCVQ special supplement.

Finkelhor, D. (1993) 'Incestuous offenders', Paper to a National Conference "Sex offenders and their victims: how we learn together to protect children", National Society for the Prevention of Cruelty to Children, Manchester University, 4-5 November.

Finkelhor, D. (ed) (1986) A sourcebook on child sexual abuse. London: Sage.

Fisher, D. (1994) 'Adult sex offenders. Who are they? Why and how do they do it?', in T. Morrison, M. Erooga and R. C. Beckett (eds) *Sexual offending against children*. London: Routledge, pp. 1-24.

Foucault, M. (1977) *Discipline and punish: The birth of the prison*. London: Penguin.

Franklin, B. (ed) (1995) *The handbook of children's rights: Comparative policy and practice*. London: Routledge.

Gilroy, S. (1993) 'Whose sport is it anyway; adults and children's sport' in M. Lee (ed) *Coaching children in sport*. London: E and FN Spon.

Grisogono, V. (1991) *Children and sport: Fitness injuries and diet*. London: Murray.

Habermas, J. (1988) *Legitimation crisis*. Cambridge: Polity Press.

Handy, C. (1988) *Understanding voluntary organisations*. London: Penguin.

Hansard (1995) January 30. London: HMSO.

Hudson, M. A. (1995) 'When a coach crosses the line', *Los Angeles Times,* 20 May.

International Committee For Fair Play (1992) *Fair play for all.* Munich and Paris: ICFP.

Kelly, L. and Regan, L. (1993) *Abuse of women and children: A feminist response.* London: Child Abuse Studies Unit, University of North London.

Leach, S., Stewart, J. and Walsh, K. (1994) The changing organisation and the management of local government. Basingstoke: Macmillan.

Leat, D. (1995) 'Funding matters' in J. Smith, C. Rochester, and R. Hedley (eds) *An introduction to the voluntary sector.* London: Routledge.

Lee, M. (1986) 'Moral and social growth through sport: The coach's role' in G. Gleeson (ed) *The growing child in competitive sport.* London: Hodder and Stoughton.

Lloyd, W and Campbell, S. (1990) *The play sport guide.* Leeds. NCF.

Locke, J. (1924) *Two treatises of government.* London: Dent.

Lyon, C. and Parton, N. (1995) 'Children's rights and the Children Act 1989' in B. Franklin (ed) *The handbook of children's rights: Comparative policy and practice.* London: Routledge.

Magill, R. A., Ash, M. J. and Smoll, F. L. (eds) (1982) *Children in sport.* Champaign: Human Kinetics.

Marshall, T. H. and Bottomore, T. (1992) *Citizenship and social class.* London: Pluto.

Martens, R. (1988) 'Helping children become independent, responsible adults through sport' in E. Brown and C. Branter (eds) *Competitive sport for children and youth.* Champaign: Human Kinetics.

Mill, J. S. (1972) *Utilitarianism: On liberty and consideration of representative government* (editor H. B. Acton) London: Dent.

Muehlenhard, C. L. and Linton, M. A. (1987) 'Date rape and sexual aggression in dating situations: Incidence and risk factors', *Journal of Counselling Psychology,* Vol. 34: pp. 186-196. Cited in: p. Y. Martin, and R. A. Hummer (1993) 'Fraternities and date rape on campus', in P. E. Bart and E. Geil Moran (eds) *Violence against women: The bloody footprints.* London: Sage, pp. 114-131.

National Coaching Foundation (1995) 'The power of partnership', in *Super-coach* Leeds: National Coaching Foundation, Summer, p. 11.

NSPCC (National Society for the Prevention of Cruelty to Children) / National Coaching Foundation (1995) *Protecting children: A guide for sportspeople.* Leeds: NCF.

Nolan Committee Report (1995) HMSO.

Parton, N. (1985) *The politics of child abuse.* Basingstoke: Macmillan.

Piaget, J. (1965) *The moral judgement of the child.* New York: Free Press.

Pinchbeck, I. and Hewitt, M. (1969) *Children in English society. Volume I. From Tudor times to the eighteenth century.* London: Routledge and Kegan Paul.

Pinchbeck, I. and Hewitt, M. (1973) *Children in English society. Volume II. From the eighteenth century to the Children Act 1948.* London: Routledge and Kegan Paul.

Playboard/National Coaching Foundation (1986) *Play the game.* Leeds: NCF

Riley, D. (ed) (1991) *Sexual abuse of children: Understanding, intervention and prevention.* Oxford: Radcliffe Medical Press.

Roberts, G. C. and Treasure, D. C. (1992) 'Children in sport', *Sport Science Review*, Vol. 1, No. 2: pp. 46-64.

Rochester, C. (1995) 'Voluntary agencies and accountability' in J. D. Smith, C. Rochester, and R. Hedley, R. (eds) *An introduction to the voluntary sector.* London: Routledge.

Shier, H. (1995) 'The UN Charter for Children and what it means for play' in *The Leisure Manager*, Vol. 13, No. 2: pp. 14-16.

Slack, T. and Kikulis, L. (1989) 'The sociological study of sport organisations: some observations on the situation in Canada' in *International Review for the Sociology of Sport*, Vol. 24, No. 3: pp. 179-198.

Smith, D. (1993) *Safe from harm: A code of practice for safeguarding the welfare of children in voluntary organisations in England and Wales.* London: HMSO.

Smith, G. (1995) 'Child abuse: A feeling of failure. *The Guardian* 'Society' section, 9 August, pp. 6-7.

Smith, J. D., Rochester, C. and Hedley, R. (eds) (1995) *An introduction to the voluntary sector.* London: Routledge.

Stanko, E. (1990) *Everyday violence.* London: Pandora.

Thibault, L. Slack, T. and Hinings, B. (1993) 'A framework for the analysis of strategy in non-profit sport organisations', *Journal of Sport Management*, Vol. 7, No. 1: pp. 25-43.

Thompson, E. P. (1991) *Customs in common.* London: Penguin.

Tomlinson, A. and Yorganci, I. (1993) *Male coach/female athlete relations: Gender and power relations in competitive sport.* Unpublished report to the National Coaching Foundation.

Unell, J. (1992) *Criminal record checks within the voluntary sector: An evaluation of the pilot schemes.* Second Series Paper No. 2. London: The Volunteer Centre UK.

United Nations (1989) *Children's charter.* UN.

United Nations Educational, Scientific and Cultural Organisation (1992) *International charter of physical education and sport.* UNESCO.

Waterhouse, L. (ed) (1993) *Child abuse and child abusers: Protection and prevention.* Research Highlights in Social Work 24. London: Jessica Kingsley Publishers

Wattam, C., Hughes, J. and Blagg, H . (eds) (1991) *Child sexual abuse: Listening, hearing and validating the experiences of children.* London: NSPCC/Longman.

Wearmouth, H. (1995) Personal communication.

Weiss, M and Gould, D. (eds) (1984) *The 1984 Olympic Scientific Congress Proceedings.* Volume 10. Champaign: Human Kinetics.

Welch, M. and Wearmouth, H. (1994) *Getting it right: A guide to sports ethics, disciplinary procedures and appeals.* London: Sports Council.

White, A., Mayglothling, R., and Carr, C. (1989) *The dedicated few: The social world of women coaches in Britain in the 1980s.* Chichester: West Sussex Institute of HE.

Wise, S. (1991) Child abuse: the NSPCC version. *Feminist Praxis* Monograph. Manchester: Manchester University.

Wolf, S. C. (1984) 'A multifactor model of deviant sexuality', paper presented to the Third International Conference on Victimology, Lisbon cited by D. Fisher (1994) in T. Morrison, M. Erooga and R. C. Beckett (eds) *Sexual offending against children.* London: Routledge, pp. 1-24.

Young, K. (1992) 'Tort and criminal liability in sport: the conundrums of workplace hazards vs. masculinist consent', Paper to the Olympic Scientific Congress, Malaga, Spain, 15-20 July.

Anabolic Steroids in Education — the Role of the Physical Education Professional

D. F. Christmas, P. S. Holmes, G. B. Nutt and D. M. Woodward

Cheltenham and Gloucester College of Higher Education

Letting the genie out of the bottle: the spread of illicit anabolic steroid use in Britain

In 1889 a French physiologist, Brown-Sequard, possibly became the first anabolic steroid user after he managed to isolate and self-administer a crude concoction made from the distilled sex glands of dogs and guinea pigs, brewed in brine. As a result of this experiment, he noted 'marked' increases in his own virility and strength. Unknown to him, these effects were caused by the male hormone testosterone which was present in the concoction he had been injecting into himself (Goldman and Klatz, 1992). These primitive experiments were refined by other scientists, who began to experiment with distilling and fractionating extracts from male animal sex glands and, by 1930, Kotch had successfully identified and isolated testosterone. By 1935 Ruzicka had developed the first synthetic testosterone for use within legitimate medical practice (Wright and Cowart, 1990; Goldman and Klatz, op. cit.). Soon after testosterone had been isolated and synthesised, there was a rapid growth in the development of synthetic anabolic steroids for use in medicine. The underlying physiological basis for their clinical use lay in their ability to stimulate protein synthesis, which led to the revelation that anabolic steroids could be used to promote wound healing and recovery (Wright and Cowart, op. cit.).

Despite this intended use for anabolic steroids within the clinical setting, Boje suggested that anabolic steroids could serve a more sinister purpose, proposing in 1939 "that the administration of the male hormone testosterone or its synthetic derivatives might, theoretically, be able to enhance athletic performance" (Boje, 1939). In 1953, Boje's vision was

191

realised when the chemical structure of testosterone was modified by the removal of its 19th carbon atom. In this new form, the modified testosterone was able to induce substantial tissue building at a minimal dose with only minimal androgenic activity. The resulting substance, norethandrone, became the first commercially available anabolic steroid (Wright and Cowart, *op. cit.*). Towards the end of 1954, academics in the United States and Britain agreed that anabolic steroids were being abused by top level amateur and professional athletes (Goldman and Klatz, *op. cit.*). This marked the first diffusion of anabolic steroid use from the clinical setting to the elite level of organised, competitive sport (Eady, 1993). Nowhere was this diffusion more marked than in East Germany, where anabolic steroid use was sanctioned and controlled by the government under State-Plan 14.25 (Hildreth, 1993). This diffusion increased access to anabolic steroids for sports men and women, through gyms and clubs, and for the first time presented adolescents with images of steroid-enhanced sporting role models through the media (Goldman and Klatz, 1993; Strasburger, 1989).

Since these initial observations, research conducted in Britain (Sports Council, 1995; Korkia and Stimson, 1993; McKillop, 1987) and the United States (Goldman and Klatz, 1993; Yesalis *et al.*, 1988; Buckley *et al.*, 1988) has suggested that the use of anabolic steroids has diffused into the performance and participation levels of sport. Despite these observations, researchers have tended to conclude that the diffusion is isolated to specific sports such as weight lifting and that, in most sports, anabolic steroid use is still confined to athletes participating at the elite and performance level of sport (Korkia and Stimson, 1988; Sports Council, 1995).

However in the United States it has been hypothesised that:

> ...the elite athletic population may be the smallest but most visible user group and that a much larger group exists comprised of lower level amateur and recreational individuals with perhaps other reasons for use. (Wright and Cowart, 1990: pp. 9).

This appears to contradict the argument that anabolic steroid use is confined to specific sports. This hypothesis has gained credence over the last ten years as the results of anabolic steroid user surveys have been published. A survey conducted in the United States (Anderson and McKeag, 1985) identified that anabolic steroids were being used at all levels of sports involvement, in a wide variety of college sports. This suggests that the diffusion of anabolic steroid use from the elite to performance and participation levels of sport is not confined to just a select few sports, as believed by the researchers cited above (see Table 1).

The selection of college athletes for the population surveyed in Anderson and McKeag's 1985 and 1989 studies not only highlights the extent of the diffusion of anabolic steroid use within American college sports, demonstrating that the use of anabolic steroids is not confined to a few select sports; their work also indicates that anabolic steroids were being

Table 1   **Anabolic steroid use by 2,230 male and female varsity athletes at 11 National Collegiate Athletic Association schools in 1989**

% **Males** reporting anabolic steroid use in the previous 12 months				
Basketball n=128	Baseball n = 269	Football n=895	Tennis n=47	Track/Field n=222
2	2	4	2	2

% **Females** reporting anabolic steroid use in the previous 12 months				
Basketball n= 128	Softball n=142	Swimming n=190	Tennis n=53	Tack/Field n=156
1	<1	1	<1	1

Source: Anderson *et al.*, 1991: pp. 96-97

used in an educational environment (Anderson et al., 1991; Anderson and McKeag 1985, 1989). Clearly, without adequate research it would be naive to suggest that the diffusion of the illicit use of anabolic steroids in the United States has been mirrored within British educational institutions, as the nature of both professional sports and high school education as social institutions within American society are very different from their British counterparts. University sports scholarship programmes in the United States arguably treat college athletes as professional athletes, rather than as students, rendering them subject to similarly powerful pressures to achieve good results. However, the use of anabolic steroids within the American college sports community appears to have opened up a third and an important diffusion, to the wider college population as a whole, and thence to schools. Buckley and colleagues conducted a survey of anabolic steroid use among over 3, 000 male high-school seniors drawn randomly from the general school population across the United States, the results of which suggested that there could be as many as 250, 000 male high-school users (Buckley *et al.*, 1988). This research provides strong evidence of a diffusion from sporting to educational settings, possibly via the college sports community (although this does not negate the possibility of diffusion via different routes such as other family members). It also suggests that the diffusion of anabolic steroid use is taking place within education, from higher education to high schools (i.e. secondary education).

Recent research into anabolic steroid misuse presents conflicting findings. On the one hand, research from the United States has suggests that this is no longer purely a sports problem but has become a societal problem, as these drugs are now being taken by both sporting and non-sporting populations for a number of different reasons. These range from the traditionally reported desire to enhance athletic performance to other diverse motives for anabolic steroid use such as the desire to develop a muscular body in order to attract a partner. Recent British research has tended to examine anabolic steroid use within the well-known user groups of weight lifters and gym users (Korkia and Stimson, 1993). This narrow focus is supported by the staff of the coach education unit of the Sports Council's Doping Control Unit, who have recently stated that drug control policy in Britain is based on the premise that the misuse of drugs such as anabolic steroids is only a problem at the elite levels of sport or affecting those striving to compete at this level (Sports Council, 1995).

On the other hand, other research in Britain has suggested that anabolic steroid use may be following the American pattern, in being used in an increasingly diverse range of social settings by groups such as 'ravers' and night-club goers. Their use has also been observed to take place for work-related reasons by bouncers and male prostitutes (Sharp and Collins, work in progress). In addition, pilot work conducted by Christmas and Holmes (1994a) suggested that 25% of a sample of male and female sixth-form students in the south-east of England (n=40) had been offered or had used anabolic steroids during their time in the sixth-form centre. When this research was repeated on a larger scale with a sample of 240 sixth-form students, the results supported the earlier findings that anabolic steroids were being used by a significant minority of sixth-form students, often for non-sporting reasons such as those cited above (Christmas and Holmes, 1994b).

Further support for the argument that the use of anabolic steroids has become diffused beyond sport has emerged from work being conducted by researchers at Manchester Metropolitan University, who have identified a new user group, young Asian males, who are taking anabolic steroids to increase their physical build, in order to discourage or pre-empt bullying by others (Sharp and Collins, work in progress). Despite this mounting evidence of anabolic steroid misuse in settings far removed from sport, this issue appears to be largely ignored within Britain by the relevant authorities (Korkia and Stimson, 1993; Sports Council, 1995).

The case for steroid-specific health promotion work in education

These observations suggest that there is an immediate need to assess the extent and nature of anabolic steroid use by adolescents in Britain. Research of this kind would either confirm that use is confined to elite athletes and their aspirants, or support the emerging evidence that adolescent usage now extends to contexts outside sport. Whatever the findings, the case for steroid-specific health education initiatives are compelling, for as long as these drugs are available in gyms through dealers, the 'germs' will spread to infect others unless they have acquired the knowledge, skills and attitudes that will enable them make informed decisions about rejecting their use (Evans, 1978).

Health educators concerned with the general health and well-being of young people should be concerned with the potential risks associated with any growth in anabolic steroid use among adolescents. This concern should relate to both the general 'drug use problems' such as injecting with infected needles and the transmission of Human Immunodeficiency Virus (HIV), Acquired Immunodeficiency Syndrome (AIDS) and other blood-borne diseases, and to the more specific anti-social behavioural problems that can occur as a result of anabolic steroid misuse, such as episodes of aggression and mania (Pope and Katz, 1988; Johnson *et al.*, 1992). However, because anabolic steroids and other performance-enhancing drugs such as Human Growth Hormone have a number of unique properties associated with their usage, traditional drug-related health promotion strategies such as 'just say no' and the American 'Drug Resistance Education Programme' are unlikely to be effective (Ray and Ksir, 1993; Newcombe, 1992). Any anabolic steroid-specific drug education programme would need to accommodate the following points:

1. These drugs are used instrumentally with weight training and are not immediately euphoriogenic; instead, users derive gratification from the effects of a complex combination of psychological, pharmacologic and societal interactions, delayed until weeks after administration.

2. Anabolic steroid users often engage in polypharmacy in order to mask the visible side-effects of their usage.

3. Anabolic steroid users perceive themselves to be extremely healthy due to the inherent nature of the exercise required while taking anabolic steroids and thus do not typically use other socially accepted drugs such as alcohol and cigarettes, nor do they perceive themselves as drug takers.

4. Recent research has indicated that there is unlikely to be a 'typical steroid user profile' as anabolic steroids are being used by a diverse number of subcultural groups for many different reasons, ranging from club bouncers whose primary motive for anabolic steroid use is to keep their jobs (by developing a physique which is perceived as a prerequisite for the job) or to earn money, to young Asian males, whose primary motive for their anabolic steroid use is to acquire a physical build which will make them less likely to be bullied (Sharp and Collins, work in progress).

5. It is not illegal to use anabolic steroids. It is only illegal to supply anabolic steroids.

As a result of these factors, the traditional 'Stop Taking It' campaigns and those utilising scare tactics have been seen to be highly ineffective (Goldberg *et al.*, 1990). As anabolic steroid users will often utilise a variety of substances in order to minimise the visible side effects of their use, health educators will need to provide education on a whole range of substances. Additionally, research (Sharp and Collins, work in progress) has suggested that strategies which label steroid users as drug users by, for example, utilising needle exchange clinics used by heroin addicts, tend to be unsuccessful. Alternatively, health educators should consider operating harm reduction schemes of this nature in health clubs or at gyms. Finally, as there is unlikely to be a typical steroid user profile, any potential steroid-specific health promotion strategy will need to incorporate a thorough assessment phase and probably a multi-dimensional approach capable of addressing the diverse nature of anabolic steroid users' motives.

In advocating educational initiatives that redress the systematic neglect accorded to the use of anabolic steroids beyond the confines of elite sport, it is essential that educators do more than merely 'medicalise' the problem and 'pathologise' the users. We must recognise the significance of the socio-cultural context in which these shifting patterns of use are emerging, and utilise the educative process to expose the values and attitudes that underpin the choice behaviours of those who, for whatever motive, have been socialised into and within a burgeoning drug culture. In short, we need to recognise that any radical educational initiative cannot be conducted in a value-free vacuum .

A cursory examination of the popular media will confirm that, in this country, issues of health, fitness and exercise have assumed cultural significance during the last twenty years. Certainly, there is evidence that features such as the running boom and the fitness revolution have endured longer than the typical lifespan of fads and now appear to have become well established features on our cultural landscape. As a nation we seem to have developed a pre-occupation with the interrelated themes of fitness, strength, longevity, body shape, youth, beauty and sex-appeal. In fact, it could be argued that, as institutionalised features of contemporary life, they have saturated the public's 'consciousness'; or, at the very least, that of particular and privileged sections of our society. Moreover, many of these issues appear, at some time or other, to have been appropriated and articulated in a variety of social, political and economic contexts by agencies which have been complicit in reinforcing a process by which an ideology of 'vitalism' has been 'commodified', with many of the attendant images functioning as simple metaphors for 'the good life'. At the heart of this emergence of 'vitalism', as a lifestyle imperative, lies the symbiotic relationship that exists between the corporate world and the media.

We need to recognise that as a social institution, the mass media has the power to confer and legitimate social status by bestowing prestige and enhancing the authority of individuals, groups and behaviours. For instance, just as the use of language acts as a powerful arbiter of standards, so visibility enables the media effectively to manage and create images by 'socially (re)constructing reality' in ways that can inform and shape our thoughts, beliefs, values and attitudes about all facets of human life. Not surprisingly, images have come to be viewed as essential tools by the corporate world with youth culture, in particular, identified as a lucrative, yet vulnerable, target population. The pervasive influence of consumer culture is illustrated by Featherstone's assertion that it:

> ... latches onto the self-preservationist conception of the body, which encourages the individual to adopt instrumental strategies to combat deterioration and decay....and combines it with the notion that the body is a vehicle of pleasure and self-expression. Images of the body beautiful, openly sexual and associated with hedonism, leisure and display, emphasise the importance of 'the look'. (Featherstone, 1982: p. 18)

Thus, one of the principal concerns of this paper is to address the ways by which drug education initiatives can problematise those representations of the body that convey messages which reinforce the ideological basis of 'vitalism'. At the outset of any critique, we must come to terms with the socio-cultural and psychological significance accorded the body. As Colquhoun explains:

> ... It (the body) is in itself a socially and culturally constructed and defined entity. We ascribe meanings to our bodies in an attempt to give order to our day to day experiences. The body, which is more than a physical object, is in an interface between the constant interactions in our social world and our beliefs, values, interpretations and explanations of that social world. (Colquhoun, 1991: p. 9)

Similarly, Crawford (1980) reminds us that we use our bodies to display beliefs and practices which reveal core assumptions and valuations derived from structured systems of meaning. Therefore, we must recognise that health and fitness and the attendant imagery are products of our social, cultural and economic environment and be prepared to confront the distorted pictures, messages and values that might otherwise emerge unchallenged and which could have profound social and behavioural consequences for many people in our society; not least the young. As Brett-schneider and Rees (1995) suggest, adolescence is a period of heightened anxiety and vulnerability during which youngsters wrestle with socially constructed notions of masculinity, femininity and sexuality. For instance, masculinity is regularly conveyed by creating images relative to physical power, speed, strength and success, while femininity is represented through the images of grace, beauty, health and sexuality. The consequence is that just as people are intellectually boxed as 'smart, average or dumb', we have a tendency to attach physical, psychological and social competences to body type (Tinning, 1990). Hargreaves has claimed that:

> ... the mesomorphic image resonates strongly with ideologically conservative notions concerning achievement, drive and dynamism, discipline, conformity, cleanliness, efficiency, good adjustment, manliness and femininity. (Hargreaves, 1986: p. 170)

On the other hand, it is also suggested that the endomorph is construed as self-indulgent, lazy, inefficient, unattractive and unhealthy, while the ectomorphic image connotes weakness, lack of adjustment, neurosis and anti-social tendencies.

These traits are consistent with social stratification in wider society and, as such, should invite critical commentary. But this is no easy task since many dysfunctional behavioural consequences are the product of complex and shifting factors that cannot easily be explained by drawing simplistic cause and effect relationships between 'unproblematic' variables. Nowhere is this more evident than in our attempts to understand the underlying causes of compulsive eating disorders amongst young people. But, whilst accepting that conditions such as anorexia nervosa and anorexia bulimia are the product of complex psychological determinants, we must also be prepared to acknowledge that the powerful messages that underpin the 'cult of slenderness' (Tinning, 1986) can have a considerable impact on a vast constituency of vulnerable youngsters. Neither should we be surprised that, for some, this vulnerability may also express itself in the form of exercise obsessions as they seek to conform to a culture that increasingly accords social status and prestige to bodies displaying slim muscularity and resonating with powerful messages of athleticism and sex appeal. The pressures are immense as traits are portrayed in a multitude of settings which continue to reinforce the 'desired' qualities of youth, health, beauty and of living the dynamic life.

Contemporary advertising confirms the ways in which the corporate world has used these inferences to commodify and objectify the female body but, more recently, the male torso has also been used as part of a 'text' to define the profile and characteristics of an ever increasing range of products. The inherent danger of these representations of the body in advertising and other forms of the media is that they appear to go beyond rational descriptions of desirable weight, body shape and lifestyle to become moral imperatives. It could be argued that messages contained within this imagery encourage individualistic perceptions and behaviours towards health, exercise and the body and have been complicit in exposing our vanity, attacking our sense of vulnerability and reinforcing our inadequacies by setting illusory and unattainable goals. The 'moral panic' induced by this 'agenda' has fostered a 'quick fix' mentality in which the consumer is viewed as a passive, uncritical recipient of 'expert' knowledge from the plethora of icons and role models populating the industry and impacting on youth culture. The number of agencies engaged in this process is staggering and, given the competing commercial and vested interests of so many of them, it seems quite clear that they have collectively failed to articulate a clear unambiguous message. Perhaps we have been naive in failing to recognise that a social conscience and commercialism make uncomfortable bedfellows; because there are such conflicting perspectives and motives, we may have been complicit in allowing a culture of distortion and 'misinformation' to evolve. Thus, a new dimension to the cultural politics of the young appears to be emerging; a culture that may have contributed to an attraction and increased incidence of anabolic steroid use. So what needs to be done and who should be charged with the responsibility of helping young people bring clarity to their lives?

It would appear that a case for a co-ordinated multi-agency strategy that would accommodate contrasting and complementary research perspectives is gathering momentum, and since sport and physical activity is perceived by adolescents as the principal mode of experiencing the body (Brettschneider and Rees, op. *cit.*) recognising and utilising the centrality of the physical education professional within this context will be an essential ingredient in any educational initiatives. It will be a challenging task, as our contribution must act as a catalyst in enabling young people to distinguish between authority and influence, as they attempt to gain some measure of control over their bodies and their lives. But to adopt a position of benign resignation would be a failure to accept the moral and professional responsibilities that go with our roles as educators. However, in advancing this view, some consideration must also be given to the prevailing circumstances that are currently impacting upon physical education teachers' lives and careers, as this will influence the nature and extent of their possible future involvement and indicate the constraints that will have to be confronted if they are to have an effective voice with the young.

The role of the physical educator in steroid-specific health promotion work: opportunities and constraints

The position of physical education (PE) at the interface between the formality of schooling and the informality of community and youth culture ensures that PE professionals are strategically placed to make a substantive contribution to the educative process. Yet for too long the role of the physical education teacher has been ignored, understated and prone to caricature, so a redress to the systematic marginalisation of PE as a subject would represent a timely recognition of the contribution it can make in helping young people come to terms with the complexities that confront them. As Tinning concludes:

> ... in one way or another, physical education, concerned as it is with the body, can play a big part in how we develop our sense of selves. (Tinning, 1990: p. 22)

An appreciation of the subject's potential to make a positive contribution to the educative process can be addressed if we examine the challenges and complexity in terms of context and form. Although inextricably bound together, analytical clarity demands that these issues are dealt with separately.

Context

For some time now, teachers have had to contend with a succession of government-sponsored reforms which have threatened a radical redefinition of the nature of their work. The consequence has been an intensification of workload within a context increasingly structured by notions of accountability. Much of the legislation has functioned to increase educational bureaucracy, to emphasise market imperatives and to reinforce an ideological agenda set by the 'cultural restorationists' of the 'new right' (Ball, 1994). Teaching is being defined as a labour process, and articulated more and more in technicist terms in which efficiency, delivery and the perpetuation of an instrumental rationality are constantly being advanced as performance indicators. Thus, it could be argued that there has been a pre-occupation with the measurable, objective, productive and instrumental dimensions of schooling at the expense of the subjective, intrinsic and moral agenda that is central to any critical pedagogy. It goes without saying that, despite its imputed curricular marginality, physical education has not been immune from these forces of change. On the contrary, one could argue that because of its marginal status, physical education is particularly prone to the pressures that have attended this period of intensification. Indeed, Kirk *et al.*'s (1986) critique of the technology of curriculum design and the subject's quest for academic credibility suggests that physical education's attempts to become more 'work-like' are in danger of marginalising, neglecting and squeezing the qualitative and experiential properties out of the curriculum entirely.

For instance, consider the manner in which the micro-political actions of teachers seeking access to a share of finite resources are increasingly being shaped by the market principles and economic expediency that pervades contemporary schooling today. For those members of marginal occupational groups, the allocation of resources has come to represent a key 'site of contestation'. The concern has to be the extent to which physical education's capacity to acquire a shared depth of knowledge, sensitivity and consensus of the subject's contribution to the development of the whole child is being compromised by forces that seem to have little to do with meeting the real needs of the youngsters we teach. But, coming to terms with prevailing conditions will not only require physical educators to engage the institutional micro-politics of schools, but also demands the resolution of tensions generated from within a subject that has not always been at ease with itself. Illustrative of this point are the tensions being generated by, amongst others, the hegemonic reinforcement of competitive (team) games and the centrality of school sport initiatives, the implementation of the revised orders for physical education in the National Curriculum, and the continued expansion of examinations and accredited courses within PE curricula in schools. This, in turn, invites the question as to how physical educators will accommodate the 'permeation' of the essential knowledge, skills and understanding of Health Related Exercise (HRE), within the structures defined by the revised orders of the National Curriculum. The profession needs to recognise that HRE represents a crucial site in moving beyond the instrumental, individualistic and utilitarian concerns with maximising functional capacity that is a feature of much existing work within this area. It is a venue in which we can attend to a range of social, moral and ethical issues by engaging the cultural politics of schooling and the body. This in itself constitutes a major challenge to the physical education profession. Many aspects of the development of health related issues within the curriculum can be described as innovatory but, as Sparkes warns us, although trends and developments in HRE have extended teachers' thinking in terms of curriculum content and teaching styles, they have largely failed to:

> ... probe deeper to the ideological roots of the curriculum process and the manner in which this prevents children gaining a more coherent understanding of health in our society. (Sparkes, 1989: p. 61)

Such a process invites a critical analysis of the values and assumptions that underpin decisions impacting on the content, organisation, teaching and assessment of HRE initiatives. Therefore, children's understanding of HRE issues must be set within a socio-political context that will enable them to gain a greater appreciation that choice behaviours, such as exercise, can be limited by the structured inequalities of class, gender, race and disability in wider society:

> Alongside and connected to information on nutrition, stress, exercise adherence etc. there needs to be included some form of education about the environmental and political limits to health. (Sparkes, *op. cit.*: p. 61)

Clearly, a commitment to a critical pedagogy must not be afraid of challenging prevailing orthodoxies and confronting controversial issues, even if this requires teachers to take on that 'burden of incompetence' described by Stenhouse (1975, cited by Colquhoun 1989) that attends the occupationally stressful processes of 'deskilling' and 'reskilling'. Not only is the resolution and accommodation of these issues contributing to increases in teachers' workload but they are also in danger of radically reshaping the nature and purpose of the subject itself, with concomitant consequences for the professional identity of PE teachers themselves. Similarly, in redefining and extending the criteria used to attach value to the work of physical educators in our schools, there are significant consequences for the nature and relevance of pupils' experiences that will demand our attention. These concerns are not intended to imply that these issues will prevent physical educators from embracing a critical pedagogy, but rather to suggest that any cultural reorientation induced by any of them might act as a major constraint to the development of a democratic curriculum. It will be a challenging task for the profession to establish a balance that does not compromise the notion of entitlement that should underpin National Curriculum developments for all our young people. The implications for the form physical education takes in our schools demands serious consideration.

Form

In advancing a rationale for PE within the National Curriculum, the DES (1991a: p. 5) stated that:

> Physical Education is the only subject which, through the use and knowledge of the body and its movement, contributes to all aspects of the education of young people.

Moreover, the document substantiated claims that the subject provides a context in which youngsters are able to establish self esteem through the development of physical confidence. The link between the use and knowledge of the body and its movement and self esteem is described by Ogundari thus:

> The body is the manifestation of the self in the world. One experiences the world through one's body. The total concept of self is thus influenced by the view of one's physical experience, and the realisation of the physical abilities and potentialities of one's body. (Ogundari, 1986: p. 39)

Given that there is no other venue where all young people are required by law to put their bodies and physical competences on public display, we need to remind ourselves that transacting our responsibilities requires considerable knowledge of and sensitivity to the range of personalities and dispositions that young people bring to their work in our subject area. However, if we are to avoid practices that expose a young person's anxieties and lack of self worth, we need critically to re-examine the pedagogical assumptions that underpin much of what we do. In the first instance, we need to endorse Tinning's (1990) view that although education should transmit all that is culturally valued, we also have a responsibility to challenge practices that perpetuate inequality and oppression, and reinforce the unjust consequences of the social worlds we inhabit. His view is shared by Hill and Brackenridge's (1989) conclusion that education has the power to create awareness and to challenge individual attitudes, thereby increasing the possibilities of change and enhancing the prospect of a more equal society.

However, as we are reminded (DES 1991b), working towards equality of opportunity in physical education in which all young people receive their statutory entitlement involves much more than offering equal access to an increasing range of (competitive) activities. It is a complex process that, amongst others, requires:

> ... an understanding and appreciation of the range of pupils' responses to femininity, masculinity and sexuality, to the whole range of ability and disability, to ethnic, social and cultural diversity, and the ways in which these relate for children to physical education. (DES 1991b p. 15)

The portents for positive action are not encouraging for, despite the 'hustle and bustle of curricular activity' that has attended physical education during the last fifteen years, many initiatives advanced on grounds of equity have been characterised as examples of 'innovation without change' (Evans, 1985). The criticism is that physical education has been reluctant to look beneath the surface of the 'literal world' (Tinning, 1990) as the means of understanding and improving practice for all the young people we come to work with. For instance, the powerful advocacy of 'Healthism' (Crawford, 1980) and its prevailing concerns with the relationship between exercise and the body has rarely been subjected to critical social scientific enquiry within physical education's research community. Accordingly, Kirk and Colquhoun (1989) confirm that although the relationship between physical exercise and health is well documented, the relationship between exercise, fitness and health has remained a largely unproblematic social phenomenon; not least among many PE teachers. They argue that there exists an implicit belief that, "exercise through fitness leads to health, that exercise is essential to health, and that being fit and having a slender body is proof of health" (Kirk and Colquhoun, 1989: p. 10). Perhaps this is because too much of our attention to issues of lifestyle have been advanced and legitimated on scientific and medical grounds alone, with little attention given to the socio-cultural context in which these issues emerge and are reinforced. The allure and appeal of physical activity and its relationship to 'desirable' lifestyle and body imagery demands a research agenda that addresses issues such as: What sort of 'desirable lifestyle' is being celebrated? Whose interests are being served? Who participates in exercise, sport and physical activity and who does not? What motives promote adherence and aversion? What images and messages are being transmitted by the media for senior citizens, the disabled, the lower classes and ethnic minorities? .

In beginning to explain and understand the complexities of the social and cultural worlds we occupy and the impact they might have on our work as teachers, it will be necessary to accept Sparkes' invitation to 'slip on' alternative sets of lenses so that "we are able to see the world around us, our relationship to it and each other, in different ways" (Sparkes, 1992:

p. 1). In terms of extending our understanding, Kirk (1988) also urges us to acquire conceptual literacy by looking beyond the obvious. This view is reinforced by Williams' (1993) claims that we need to interrupt the professional reproduction of practitioners who rarely move beyond instrumental questions of method and efficiency and to re-examine the socio-cultural and political dimensions of our practice. For instance, are we aware of the messages that are reinforced during the day to day transaction of our work? It is now accepted that much more is taught and learned than intended by the formal curriculum and that a hidden curriculum acts as a powerful determinant in a young person's development. Jewett and Bain (1985) described it as the unplanned and unrecognised values taught and learned through the process of schooling.

These implicit values, communicated to students through the context of the learning environment, may or may not be consistent with the explicit philosophy of the programme. Wilmore's conviction serves to demonstrate the inherent dangers. His argument — "How can we (physical education professionals) be effective in promoting health and if our bodies are not living testimonies of our commitment?" (Wilmore, 1982: p. 43) — not only seems to confirm that our professional presentation of self might be highly influential, but also reveals the moral tenor of the body shape metaphor. The suggestion is that physical educators may be complicit in reinforcing an 'ideology of mesomorphism' (Tinning, 1990).

If this is the case, we must consider Colquhoun's assertion that there is a need to "constantly promote the body as a socio-cultural construct and not as a neutral object there to be trained, manipulated, disciplined or controlled" (Colquhoun, 1991: p. 10). This will demand that we do not allow ourselves to become merely classroom functionaries delivering 'expertly' designed curricular packages. The argument is that we need enquiry that reveals the forms of consciousness which pervade our common-sense assumptions and everyday practices relating to issues such as the nature of teaching, the purpose of schooling, curriculum content and school organisation. Once revealed, a pedagogical agenda committed to challenging oppressive structures and processes can be established. Physical education teachers need to find ways in which it will be possible to move beyond the narrow utilitarian and functional parameters of curriculum design and delivery to embrace a critical pedagogy. In this way we may develop a deeper appreciation of the strategic position we occupy and the powerful impact our teaching has on the personal identities and lives of the young people we come to work with. Commitment to this agenda, in both initial and in-service education will require:

> ... a critical review of prevailing practice, rigorous and continuous appraisal and often a willingness to question long held beliefs and prejudices. (DES 1991b: p. 15)

The future: putting the genie back in the bottle

The physical educator can play an important role in a steroid-specific health promotion strategy, specifically in seeking to alert young people to the dangers of steroid use, but also more generally, in helping them to develop more positive perceptions of their bodies. However, the development of effective health promotion strategies requires a variety of approaches tailored to the needs and circumstances of the targeted groups. This, in turn, requires detailed study of current and potential user groups, their subcultural norms and values, and their aspirations, in order to establish the circumstances likely to lead to the use of anabolic steroids.

Research, funded by the Standing Conference on Drug Abuse (SCODA), being conducted by Manchester Metropolitan University and evaluated by researchers from Cheltenham and Gloucester College of Higher Education (Collins *et al.*, work in progress), is currently conducting pilot testing of a new steroid-specific utilising a multi-method programme of harm reduction and prevention. This has four elements:

1. Harm reduction. In this component of the project, 150 existing users of anabolic steroids will be contacted through gyms and needle exchange clinics, provided with educational information and offered free health tests to monitor any side effects associated with their anabolic steroid use. As all users of anabolic steroids directly or indirectly interact with a dealer, the project also plans to contact 12 anabolic steroid dealers, to provide them with education material and seminars, with the expectation that they will then be able to pass this information on to anabolic steroid users.

2. Educating physical educators. During this phase of the project, members of the project team will approach PE teachers at local schools to offer them a course on elements of practical strength training and body building, thereby allowing them to teach students a positive alternative to anabolic steroid use. It is hoped that this will demonstrate to adolescents that they can develop their physiques relatively safely, without the use of anabolic steroids.

3. Student education. During this part of the project GCSE students, self selected as at risk of anabolic steroid use through expressing a desire to increase their physical bulk, will complete an education programme conducted in conjunction with the project team and PE teachers.

4. Resource Pack. A steroid-specific health promotion resource pack and in-service training programme will be developed for use by health educators and PE teachers.

The evaluation of this project should be published in 1996.

This project represents the first wave of steroid-specific health promotion work in Britain. However, there is still a clear need to undertake further research on anabolic steroid users, their sub-cultures, and the patterns of diffusion between them, as an essential precursor to effective health promotion work. Anabolic steroids represent a growing area of social concern which clearly requires further investigation. British research has already demonstrated that their illicit consumption is no longer confined to sport, as suggested by the Sports Council (1995) and Korkia and Stimson (1993), and if these observations are credible, they pose a real threat to the health and well-being of British adolescents. Anabolic steroids are being used outside sport, by many different sub-cultural groups, for many different reasons. However, many users are ignorant about the long term physical and psychological side-effects they risk through anabolic steroid use, and the risk which they pose to their associates and companions from steroid-induced psychosis.

Current work is attempting to develop effective steroid-specific health promotion strategies. However, the role of the physical educator, by virtue of their unique position within the school, needs to be explored further, possibly resulting in a new role and education programme for PE teachers. Their influence is vital in seeking to counter the effects of media portrayals of distorted body images, which may increase feelings of inadequacy and vulnerability among adolescents, possibly perpetuating continued anabolic steroid diffusion within the Britain to other sub-groups.

References

Anderson, W. A. and McKeag, D. B. (1985) *The substance use and abuse habits of college student-athletes (Report No. 2)*. Mission, Kansas: The National Collegiate Athletic Association.

Anderson, W. A. and McKeag, D. B. (1989) *Replication of the national study of the substance use and abuse habits of college student athletes*. Mission, Kansas: The National Collegiate Athletic Association.

Anderson, W. A, Albrecht, R. R., McKeag, D. B., Hough, D. O. and McGrew, C. A. (1991) 'A national survey of alcohol and drug use by college athletes', *Physician and Sports Medicine*, Vol. 19, No. 2: pp. 91-104.

Ball, S. (1994) *Education reform: A critical and post-structural approach*. Milton Keynes: Open University Press.

Boje, O. (1939) Presentation to the Health Organisation of the League of Nations.

Brettschneider, W. D. and Rees, R. (1995) 'Youth culture, body and sport in late modernity: implications for physical education'. Paper presented at the 1995 AIESP World Congress. Wingate Institute, Israel.

Buckley, W., Yesalis, C., Friedl, K., Anderson, W., Streit, A., and Wright, J, (1988) 'Estimated prevalence of anabolic steroid use among male high school seniors', *Journal of the American Medical Association,* Vol. 260: pp. 3442-3445.

Chang, H. (1992) *Adolescent life and ethos.* London: Falmer Press.

Christmas, D. F. and Holmes, P. S. (1994a) 'Pilot study of anabolic steroid use among a group of sixth form students in the South East of England', unpublished.

—— (1994b) 'Prevention by scare tactics — Does it work', *Abstracts of the British Association of Sport and Exercise Sciences,* Annual Student Conference, 11th March 1994.

Clinard, M. B. (1974) *Sociology of deviant behaviour* (Fourth Edition). New York: Holt, Rinehart and Winston, Inc.

Collins, D., Sharp, M., Christmas, D. and Woodward, D. (work in progress).

Colquhoun, D. (1989) 'Health related fitness and individualism: Continuing the debate', *British Journal of Physical Education,* Vol. 20, No. 6: pp. 118-122.

—— (1991) 'Health based physical education, the ideology of healthism and victim blaming', *Physical Education Review,* Vol. 14, No. 1: pp. 5-13.

—— (1992) 'Technocratic rationality and the medicalisation of the physical education curriculum', *Physical Education Review,* Vol. 15, No. 1.

Cowart, V. (1987) 'Steroids in sport: After four decades, time to return these genies to the bottle?', *Journal of the American Medical Association,* Vol. 257: pp. 421-427.

Crawford, R. (1980) 'Healthism and the medicalisation of everyday life', *International Journal of Health Services,* Vol. 10, No. 3: pp. 365-389.

Cybergenics (1993) 'Cybernetics — cybertrim', *Muscle and Fitness,* Vol. 54, No. 3: pp. 128-129.

Department of Education and Science (1991a) National Curriculum: Physical Education Working Group, Interim Report.

—— (1991b) Physical Education for Ages 5-16: Proposals of the Secretary of State for Education and Science and the Secretary of State for Wales.

Eady, J. (1993) *Sports development.* London: Longman Publications.

Evans, J. (1985) *Teaching in transition: The challenge of mixed ability grouping.* Milton Keynes: Open University Press.

Evans, R. I., Roselle, R. M., and Mittlemark, M. B. *et al.* (1978) 'Deterring the onset of smoking in children: Knowledge of immediate physiological effects and coping with peer pressure, media pressure, and parent modelling', *Journal of Applied Social Psychology* Vol. 8: pp. 126-135.

Featherstone, M. (1982) 'The body in consumer culture', *Theory, culture and society*, Vol. 1, No. 1.

Goldberg, L., Bosworth, E. E., Bents, R. T., and Trevisan, L. (1990) 'Effects of an anabolic steroid education program on knowledge and attitudes of high school football players', *The Journal of Adolescent Health Care*, Vol. 11: pp. 210-214.

Goldman, B., and Klatz, R. (1992) *Death in the locker room 2 — drugs in sport.* Chicago: Illinois: Elite Sports Medicine Publications Inc.

Hargreaves, J. (1986) *Sport, power and culture.* London: Polity Press.

Harris, M. B. and Greco, D. (1990) 'Weight control and weight concern in competitive female gymnasts', *Journal of Sport and Exercise Psychology*, Vol. 12: pp. 427-433.

Department of Health (1992) *The health of the nation — A strategy for England.* London: HMSO Publications.

Hildreth, p. (1993) ' Chariots of dope', *The Telegraph*, 11th June, p. 18.

Hill, J. and Brackenridge, C. (1989) 'My body's a complete wreck: The contribution of PE to physical confidence', *Physical Education Review*, Vol. 12, No. 2.

Jewett, A. E. and Bain, L. L. (1985) *The curriculum process in physical education.* Dubuque, Iowa: W. C. Brown.

Johnson, A., Wadsworth, J., Wellings, K. Bradshaw, S. and Field, J. (1992) 'Sexual lifestyles and HIV risk', *Nature*, Vol. 360: pp. 410-412.

Kirk, D. (1988) *Physical education and the curriculum study: A critical introduction. London*: Croom Helm.

Kirk, D. and Colquhoun, D. (1989) 'Healthism and physical education', *British Journal of Sociology of Education*, Vol. 10: pp. 417-434.

Kirk, D., McKay, J. George, L. F. (1986) 'All work and no play? Hegemony in the physical education curriculum', in *Trends and developments in physical education, Proceedings of the VIII Commonwealth and International Conference on Sport, Physical Education and Dance.* London: E. and F. N. Spon.

Korkia, P. and Stimson, G. V. (1993) *Anabolic steroid use in Great Britain — an exploratory investigation.* The Centre for Research on Drugs and Health Behaviour, London: HMSO Publications.

Macleod, I. (1993) 'Johnson caught a second time — and pays the full price with a lifetime ban', *The Telegraph*, March 6th, p. 19.

McKillop, G. (1987) 'Drug use in body builders in the West of Scotland', *The Scottish Medical Journal*, Vol. 32, pp. 39-41.

Newcombe, R, (1992) 'The reduction of drug-related harm: A conceptual framework for theory, practice and research', in P. A. O'Hare, R. Newcombe, A. Matthews, E. C. Buning and E. Drucker (eds) *The reduction of drug-related harm*. London: Routledge.

Ogundari, J. T. (1986) 'Movement education to enhance the self-concept of school children', *Physical Education Review*, Vol. 9, No. 1: pp. 38-40.

Pandina, R., Labouvie, E. and Write, H. (1984) 'Potential contributions of the life span development approach to the study of adolescent alcohol and drug use: The Rutgers Health and Human Development Project, a working model', *Journal of Drug Issues*, Vol. 14, No. 2: pp. 253-268.

Pope, H. and Katz, D. (1988) 'Affective and psychotic symptoms associated with anabolic steroid use', *American Journal of Psychiatry*, Vol. 145: pp. 487-490.

Pope, H. G., Katz, D. L. and Hudson, J. I. (1993) 'Anorexia nervosa and "reverse anorexia" among 108 male bodybuilders', *Comprehensive Psychiatry*, Vol. 34, No. 6: pp. 406-409.

Ray, O., and Ksir, C. (1993) *Drugs, society and human behaviour*. London: Mosby.

Sharp, M. and Collins, D. (Work in progress at Manchester Metropolitan University).

Sparkes, A. (1989) 'Health-related fitness: An example of innovation without change', *British Journal of Physical Education*, Vol. 20: pp. 60-63.

Sparkes, A. (ed) (1992) *Research in physical education and sport: Exploring alternative visions*. London: Falmer Press.

Sports Council, (1995) 'Drugs, sport and young people', *Supercoach*, Vol. 7, No. 1, p. 12, Spring Edition.

Strasburger, V. C, (1989) 'Why "JUST SAY NO" just won't work', *The Journal of Paediatrics*, Vol. 114, No. 4: pp. 676-681.

The Cook Report, (1994) 'Dying to look good', *The Cook Report*, Independent Television Documentary, Autumn 1994.

Tinning, R. (1990) *Ideology and physical education: Opening Pandora's Box*. London: Deakin University Press.

———— (1986) 'Physical education and the cult of slenderness: A critique', *ACHPER National Journal*, March.

Williams, A. (1993) 'The reflective physical education teacher: Implications for initial teacher training', *Physical Education Review*, Vol. 16, No. 2.

Wilmore, J. (1982) 'Objectives for the nation: Physical fitness and exercise', *Journal of Physical Education, Recreation and Dance*, Vol. 53, No. 3: pp. 41-43.

Wright, J. E. and Cowart, V. S. (1990) *Anabolic steroids — altered states*. Benchmark Press, Inc.

Yesalis, C. E., Herrick, R. T., Buckley, W. E., Friedl, K. E., Brannon, D. and Wright, J. E. (1988) 'Self-reported use of anabolic–androgenic steroids by elite power lifters', *Physician and Sports Medicine*, Vol. 16, Part 12: pp. 90-100.

Yesalis, C. E., Vicary, J. R. and Buckley, W. E. (1993) 'Anabolic steroid use among adolescents: A study of indications of psychological dependency', in C. E. Yesalis (ed) *Anabolic steroids in sport and exercise*. Champaign, Illinois: Human Kinetics Publications.

Part IV

Leisure Education

The Leisure and Education Interface Explored

Lesley Lawrence

University of Luton

Introductory musings — problems of terminology

In deciding upon a topic for the original version of this paper, I was in-creasingly drawn towards clarifying [for myself] one of the terms in the Conference title itself — 'Leisure , Sport and Education — the Inter-faces'. Disregarding the well-documented complexities inherent in satis-factorily defining 'leisure', 'sport' or 'education', what precisely is an 'inter-face'? On following this line of enquiry, the following definitions seemed ones I could usefully adopt: "the place at which independent systems meet and act on or communicate with each other" (Penguin, 1985: p. 437); or "a point or area of interaction between two systems, organizations, or disci-plines" (Weiner and Delahunty, 1993: p. 143). Weiner and Delahunty point out however, that such a sense of the word is "deplored by many people, since it is often debased into a high-sounding synonym for *boundary, meeting-point, interaction, liaison, link,* etc." My friendly computer's gram-mar check also considered 'interface' rather uncomplimentarily as "Jargon. Avoid this term in non-technical contexts" (Microsoft, 1992)!

Regardless of such advice, and taking upon board the assertions that leisure and education are "inextricably related" (Kelly, 1982: p. 205) and are "uneasy bedfellows" (Veal, 1987: p. 79), the intention of this paper is first to identify at which 'places' or 'points' leisure and education 'meet and act on or communicate with each other', and then to go on to discuss in greater detail some specific examples. Where does this leave 'sport', if we recall the Conference title? To avoid becoming bogged down in complex debate over the exact nature and differences between the terms 'sport' and 'leisure', the intention is to consider sport as part of the generic term — leisure, thus utilising Alderson's (1993: p. 76) contention that sport can be a major 'leisure product'.

A natural and unavoidable focus when examining any leisure and education interface is the concept 'education for leisure' or 'leisure education'. Unsurprisingly, the concept is open to differing interpretations — I've always been taken by one educationist's rather perceptive description when I interviewed him a number of years ago — education for leisure was "a lovely term, a cliché: most people understand it; they know what it means without being able to define it". It can be easy to be drawn into the many complex debates on definition, justification and implementation of a supposedly straightforward concept. The intention here is not to become so ensnared, but to acknowledge the existence of complexities; the reader is directed toward some of the debates and issues that have been raised (see for example, Simpson, 1973; Paddick, 1982; and Lawrence, 1993). The sort of meaning we are concerned with in this paper resembles the description of education for leisure as proposed by the American Charles Brightbill whose views figured prominently in the debates in the 1960s:

> When we say education for leisure, we have in mind persons developing appreciations, interests, skills, and *opportunities* that will enable them to use their leisure in personally rewarding ways, plus understanding why this way of life is essential to their well-being and to the survival of society (Brightbill, 1960: p. 93).

So, moving on from definitional concerns, where do the activities mentioned by Brightbill happen? At which 'places' do leisure and education meet and 'act on or communicate with each other'?

Leisure and education interfaces

A number of possible places exist. It has been suggested that a wide variety of educational approaches and organisations are involved where education for leisure is concerned, including "formal and informal education, in institutions and in the community, for children and adults", with all having a part to play (Martin and Mason, 1987: p. 261). In this paper, rather than choose to examine the more informal network of family, friends, local community, or the media, I decided to direct attention upon an educational institution, namely, the secondary school as 'the place'. I was mindful though of the oft-quoted Newsom Report extract from the early sixties which considered that "the responsibility for ensuring that this new leisure *is the source of enjoyment and benefit it ought to be, and not of demoralising boredom,* is not the schools' alone" (Newsom, 1963: p. 28). Whilst such a decision could be criticised given that it is some of these other places such as the home, peer group and local communities which are seen as more influential for the learning of recreational skills (Roberts, 1978: p.165), the school is unique in a sense in that it *does* have an explicit responsibility for education. Indeed, going back to the "simplistic cries of the 1960s for education for leisure" (Hendry, 1993: p. 151) and into the 1970s when debates about the value and role of education for leisure in schools were topical in educational circles — some considered that where educating for leisure was concerned the school was the most important institution (e.g. Corbin and Tait, 1973). Retaining such a historical angle, this paper will principally investigate perceived leisure and education interfaces within the secondary school in England over the last 20 years, focusing in particular on the subject of Physical Education [PE], but also reflecting on the notion of a leisure role in other subjects.

Leisure and education 'places' within the school — prominence of Physical Education

Echoing some of the earlier debates of the 1960s, 1970s and 1980s, Alderson (1993: pp. 75/6) asks that if we accepted a need for "*explicit leisure education*" whose responsibility should it be?:

> Should leisure education be a cross-curricular theme, should it be part of PSD [Personal and Social Development] programme or should it be the responsibility of good old PE?

Back in the mid 1970s, the general opinion appeared to reflect the view of Corbin and Tait, who believed it "obvious that physical education can contribute a great deal toward education for leisure" (Corbin and Tait, 1976: p. 66). Two forms of involvement by physical education teachers have generally been recognised. First, when physical education teachers contribute to school-based courses in leisure education. There may be a specific physical education component within a school leisure education programme with curricular and extra-curricular physical education recognised as main areas for leisure education in the school (Sherlock 1979; Hendry, 1983; Murdoch, 1987; and Sleap 1987).

The second form of involvement comes with the existence of some form of leisure aim (sometimes referred to as education for leisure) within physical education teachers' overall aims/objectives in the subject (Kane, 1974; Williamson, 1987; PEA, 1987a; and Lawrence, 1991). Indeed, back in 1976, Margaret Talbot considered that education for leisure was "fast becoming the only stated reason for the existence of p.e." (Talbot, 1976: p. 147). The Physical Education Association[1] in the late eighties considered that "the contribution of Physical Education to the purposeful use of leisure time was catered for in curriculum time and through the provision of " (PEA, 1987b: p. 203). In reviewing the physical education literature in the late 1980s however, a leisure role in the subject did not seem to be a priority and received insignificant coverage; I suggested then that rather than being considered as an unimportant role, such a role could be being taken-for-granted in the profession and seen as 'taking care of itself' (Lawrence, 1991).

Remaining with this second form of involvement, findings from an in-depth study I carried out in the late 1980s[2] which relied largely on the view of physical education teachers themselves, clearly confirmed the view of the existence of some form of leisure aim in the teaching of Physical Education. Teachers hoped that pupils would participate or continue to participate in sport/physical 'leisure' activity after leaving school (Lawrence, 1991). One teacher described his aim, for example, as being "to enable pupils to experience a range of activities thus allowing them to carry on such activities outside of school both now and when they leave school" (f,a,35)[3]. This leisure aim was viewed as a very important aim by many of the teachers; for 73% (n=165), it had become more important since they had started to teach. For some teachers it was the most important aspect of their teaching. As one such teacher explained, "If we do not gear our aims towards future leisure pursuits and the pupils cease sport altogether on leaving school — as nationally most do — then we are completely wasting out time" (m, bh, 44). These findings correspond with a more recent view by Ken Green when examining the topical issue of partnership between Physical Education and other agencies. He states:

> ...the subject community of physical education and potential partnership agencies (particularly sport) seem reasonably united in the belief that at, or at least near, the top of their aims and purposes should come the encouragement in young people of a commitment to lifelong participation. (Green, 1995: p. 27)

Evidence from my study indicated that whilst there was notable variance in the way that an apparently commonly held leisure aim was being translated into practice, the leisure aim was achieved largely through three general areas of leisure practice with both the curriculum and extra-curriculum perceived as playing a part. First, the structure of the physical education programme itself: for example, with as wide a range of sports and physical activities as possible. This was particularly expressed in the form of some options scheme in the senior years with the choice element playing a prominent role. Second, the facilities and opportunities to participate: for example, community links with clubs and facilities, school extra-curricular clubs. And third, the nature of the physical education experience itself: for example, as being enjoyable, and satisfying and thus promoting future activity or just acting as a leisure experience allowing a break from the more academic subjects in the curriculum. Another area of leisure practice identified stressed the health benefits of participation and coincided with the growing influence of the health-related fitness movement in Physical Education in the mid-to-late 1980s.

It is noteworthy that the majority of the physical education teachers in the study indicated a part to be played both in curriculum time and through extra-curricular activity. More specifically, just over 60% of the teachers (n=164) in the survey phase of the research, considered that their leisure aim played a part equally in curricular and extra-curricular time. (For 23% of the teachers, it was mainly in curricular time, but also in extra-curricular time; for 13% it was mainly in extra-curricular time, but also in curricular time). The data being collected in 1988/9 is significant, however, given that the mid-to-late eighties has been regarded as a period of unprecedented change and pressure for change for teachers (Evans and Davies, 1988; Brown, 1989; and McNab, 1989), including an effect on extra-curricular team sport (Mahoney, 1995: p. 364). In the light of this, it is conceivable that where physical education teachers are concerned, the curriculum/ extra-curriculum balance may have differed had data been collected a few years earlier or later. Before moving to look at other possible interfaces in the school, how likely is this contention?

Curricular and extra-curricular roles

Running extra-curricular activities for pupils has been a traditional role of physical education teachers for countless years. From a conference attended by physical education specialists in 1983, a perceived pressure to run extra-curricular activities was reported; doing so was seen to be a traditional and expected role of teachers (Glew and Gilliver, 1987). The diminishing of such opportunity however, was being drawn to attention in popular and academic debate in the mid-late eighties, continuing into the nineties. It was being reported for example, that there had been a decrease in school sports fixtures at weekends and after school (SHA, 1987); and some areas of after-school sport had disappeared (McNab, 1989). Meek (1990: p. 292) contrasted the situation of a few years ago where "clubs flourished" with the present one where, with the exception of a few exceptional schools, extra-curricular work is "in disarray". At the time, this largely pessimistic picture was not surprising given the number of possible contributing factors, including for example: government proposals for rate reform; the massive selling off of school playing fields (McNab, 1989); cost of fixtures; the management of finances in schools [LMS]; the teachers' industrial action from 1984-1986 (provoked by a derisory offer, Lodge, 1989b); and legislation on teachers' contracts of employment, especially the 1,265 'directed' hours innovation. This last piece of Central Government legislation — directed time — made a big impact on the traditional practice of extra-curricular commitments causing a "realignment of teachers responsibilities" (Almond, 1989: p. 9), and was seen as a major reason for the decline in commitment (School Sport Forum, 1988). One of the rejected recommendations by Central Government to the Sport and Young People report (School Sport Forum, 1988) was that teachers' hours should be revised in relation to the number of directed hours in order to cater for extra-curricular activities (Lodge, 1989a). It was "the final indignity for many teachers who had previously been prepared to help regardless of the hands on the clock" (Lodge, 1989b: p. 4).

Five years on from the 1988/9 data-collection period, views appear mixed as to the extent of changes in commitment by teachers as regards their extra-curricular involvement. Penney and Evans (1994) agree that sport as an extra-curricular activity has been hit due to the selling-off of playing fields and by:

> ...teachers who have traditionally lent a hand with after school
> coaching have either redirected their time to meet the burgeoning
> bureaucratic demands of the NC [National Curriculum] or simply
> refused to act outsider their contracted teaching time. (Penney and
> Evans, 1994: p. 10)

Yet, in comparing data collected in 1991 and 1993, they contend that
physical education teachers continue to "devote considerable time to extra-
curricular activities, and invariably on a goodwill basis" (Penney and
Evans, 1994: p. 10). Provision of extra-curricular PE, they determined, had
remained common practice. This contrasts with some of the views
portrayed in the media of reduced extra-curricular involvement by teachers
(not just physical education teachers). For example, Pilkington and Moss
(1994) reported that a recent survey had shown that over the past 10 years
seventy percent of state schools had seen a reduction in extra-curricular
sports activities, and that:

> after the strikes of the 1980s and the ill-feeling generated among
> teachers towards the Government, it is now rare for non-PE staff to
> devote their Saturday mornings to sport.

With no comparative data available over the later 1980s however, we can
only speculate. In the case-study phase of the research I conducted in
the autumn of 1989 though, I found examples both of teachers who had
personally reduced their involvement in extra-curriculum activity for
various reasons, and some who were continuing their involvement at the
same level. Becker's (1971:129) process of situational adjustment ("individuals tak[ing] on the characteristics required by the situations they
participate in") was seen as a useful concept applied to all six case-study
teachers in the study. The teachers, in what was quite a turbulent time
in physical education teaching, were all adjusting to varying degrees of
satisfaction to the particular requirements of the situation they worked in.
For some, this resulted in a change not only in their extra-curricular
involvement, but also in their leisure practice. Jean's[5] case which follows is
an example of this, providing interesting insight as to a teacher's reasoning
behind changes in leisure practice; her leisure practice had changed from
an emphasis being placed upon extra-curricular activity to focusing to a
greater extent on curricular practice. It also supports the contention that
had the data collection in my study taken place ten years earlier or five
years later (rather than in 1988/9), the findings may well have been
different. Namely, a higher percentage of teachers would have laid greater
stress on extra-curricular involvement in an earlier data-collection period,
and that if replicated five years later, involvement would be even lower,
replaced where leisure practice was concerned by greater reliance on other
avenues such as outside clubs, community schemes, and by partnerships
in general. In relating Jean's story, it would be easy to be overly critical of
some of her views and actions; what counts here however, is the practising
teacher's own perceptions.

Jean

A joint Head of Department and Head of Year, Jean had been teaching for 18 years in the same 13-18 comprehensive in the north east of England. Jean believed that "in the past, the extra-curricular time was as important as the curriculum time" in terms of the leisure aim. Previously:

> "I wouldn't have been able to talk to you now [late afternoon] ... because I'd be on a bus going to a match etc. etc. Sometimes two to three matches a week plus practice."

She was of the opinion that "the whole school team element will go altogether", especially with LMS [Local Management of Schools] making it difficult:

> "...and having to go to meetings and so on. For me, the extra-curricular activities are very much reduced to what they used to be."

Her priority at the time lay in concentration on the PE curriculum and improving it and the Department's status in the school. "Winning cups used to be a sign of success in the school, but now others seem to be appreciating the value of what we're actually doing in PE". She and her fellow head of department were working overtime to ensure that PE survived as a department and received its fair share of timetable allocation, having experienced a 50% cut over the last three years.

Jean admitted to not knowing whether present leisure practice "came as a result of aiming for leisure, or whether the aiming for leisure came out of the planning that was forced upon us". With diminishing outdoor facilities — in particular netball and tennis courts cracking up — the PE Department had been forced to approach the local Sports Centre and ask for the use of an area. What began as fairly 'haphazard' usage consequently turned into very strong links with the Sports Centre and heavy usage. Curriculum practice began to swing from the idea that concentration on particular activities such as seven years of hockey would mean "they'd enjoy and be so confident with it that they'd go bounding on and keep playing it". A varied programme that gave an increasing element of choice as the pupils progressed up the school had developed. She believed that, "if you expose them, if you want to use that word, to a variety of activities, then they've got more from which to choose". Jean considered the drop out rate when offering only one activity must be far greater. The one problem she did face with the greater number of activities aggravated by the recent loss of PE curricular time was being unable to give adequate grounding in the basics of the major games in 3rd year. One of her aims during curriculum time was to teach pupils how to use the nearby Sports Centre "properly and to be able to use the facilities confidently, this is the thing". She encouraged her pupils to go in whether this was to participate or spectate. She believed that all this "prepares them for the Sports Centre and leisure activities and a leisure atmosphere as being a way of life".

Jean's leisure aim was:

> ... preparing the pupils for a leisure activity, based on physical activity out of school, and that might be aged 15 out of school, aged 25 out of school, aged 35 out of school ... .

Perceived adequate provision and opportunities for sport elsewhere was one reason given by Jean for the reduction in her extra-curricular commitment: a well-furbished leisure facility lay on the door step; the school, in the past three years, had become a community school 'in the true sense of the word'; and there was expansion in junior sections of clubs in the area catering for pupils wanting representative club sport. It seemed that Jean was perceiving a lessening of responsibility with other avenues open to pupils, though at the same time admitting that the actual time in which she could devote herself to such involvement had diminished. Such a view was supported by a number of other teachers in the study who raised the issue of the increasing role of the community in providing opportunities for participation — for example, the comments of one of the other case-study teachers — Jack — who reluctantly believed that increasingly "less things" will be going on within the school. It was going to become far more important that people were pushed out to do things in other places with the structure of PE changing, the demands on teachers and many being less prepared to give up their time to run clubs and teams. He foresaw less people taking part in activities in five to ten years time as a consequence.

It could be argued that the growing emphasis on providing effective partnerships — one of which is between school and community — which began to feature in the physical education literature in the UK in the late 1980s, has in part been due to concerns over a perceived reduction in the traditional and accepted role of teachers, namely that of extra-curricular involvement. In the late 1980s in particular, there were increasing calls for effective partnerships between school Physical Education/sport and the 'leisure' services provided in the community (e.g. Talbot, 1987; School Sport Forum, 1988; Sports Council, 1990, and SWCSR, 1990). The Coventry Active Life Styles project was the most prominent amongst those examining the potential of such links (e.g. Laventure, 1987; and Sports Council, 1989). The project workers believed that many of the initiatives relating to "education for active leisure" which underpinned much of the project's work, were:

> ...fundamental to the development of the PE Curriculum and should not be seen as peripheral, but part of the 'core' of PE teaching into the 1990s. (Sports Council, 1989: p. 47)

Also receiving prominence at this time were a number of "Link Badge" projects whose aims were "to create tangible links between school and community, in order to encourage the provision of new opportunities for young people to play sport" (Ploszajski, 1988: p. 71). The partnerships theme has continued into the mid-nineties to achieve real prominence today within the physical education literature in the UK. For example, witness Talbot's (1994) pleas for the creation of effective partnership between the various agencies and organisations (physical education, sport, local authorities and the youth agencies), and the fact that the PEA UK devoted a special edition of their journal [The British Journal of Physical Education] to the partnership theme this summer. In this, they featured plans for partnerships in addition to citing examples which were seen as 'good practice'. The editor considered that the articles represented only "a fraction of the good work that is going on in this country" (Harrison, 1995: p.4).

Returning to the 'extra curricular reduction' issue, it must be recognised that despite a diminishing responsibility to extra-curricular involvement, Jean, nevertheless saw herself — as many physical education teachers do — with a leisure role; namely, with a responsibility to encourage pupils to take part in sport/ physical activity throughout their lives. The evidence suggests that the majority of physical education teachers see themselves as having an important leisure role. Yet, what about other subjects in the secondary school curriculum? Is such a leisure role as prominent in say, Mathematics or Biology?

Other sites

One of the problems in determining whether this may be the case or not is a paucity of empirical evidence. This was certainly the case in the 1970s and 1980s when it seemed that little was known about what exactly was going on where education for leisure was concerned, especially in schools in England. The little available data tended to come from Scottish studies, for example, Sherlock's (1979) evaluation of school leisure programmes; Hendry and Marr's (1985) examination of the provision made for leisure education and schools' leisure programmes and further contributions by Leo Hendry and his colleagues over this period.

In the late 1980s, Mike Sleap thus was only able to conjecture that leisure education occurred in the majority of schools:

> ...in the sense of:
> (a) lessons which are not primarily concerned with academic or vocational goals (e.g. physical education, art, music);
> (b) extra-curricular clubs where a variety of activities are on offer (e.g. photography, chess, basketball);
> (c) incidental learning within academic subjects (e.g. studying birds and plants within biology). (Sleap, 1987: pp. 168-9)

Whilst Physical Education is naturally to the forefront when the 'whose responsibility' issue is raised, many have also believed in the past that other subjects in the school curriculum such as Physics, Chemistry and Mathematics have potential where leisure is concerned (e.g. Brightbill and Mobley, 1977; Spedding, 1977; and Fisher 1982). Corbin and Tait (1973: p.

141) contended that in addition to Physical Education, "the fields of music, language arts, drama, and art should include education for leisure" and suggested that all subject teachers have such responsibilities. They cite the views of Milton Gabrielsen who back in 1955 was critical of teachers of subject areas who failed "to recognize the potentials of their subjects as leisure-time activities" (Gabrielsen, cited in Corbin and Tait, 1973: p. 141).

In an attempt to test the validity of such a view over thirty years later, we can examine some of the data I collected but did not utilise to any real degree in the research I conducted at the end of the 1980s (Lawrence, 1991). Although primarily interested in a leisure-related aim in physical education teaching, to place any such findings in perspective, I had asked my sample of physical education teachers whether a leisure-related aim existed in their main other subject [if they taught one]. Whilst obviously the ideal research framework would include data collected from non-physical education specialists and a complete range of curriculum subjects, such data will at least allow some insight. There is potential for further research here. Fifty four percent of the teachers (n=165) were also teaching one or more 'other subjects'. On retrieving and re-examining these data now, the findings are mixed as Table 1 shows; the number of teachers having a leisure aim in their main 'other' subject (42%) just about equalled those with none (43%), though 11% admitted to having 'not really thought about it before/not sure'. Such findings clearly contrast with the physical education findings where for all bar one teacher, a leisure aim existed.

On comparing findings across the various subjects, certain differences can be identified. History, Mathematics and Science for example, were the three subjects with the least number of teachers considering they had a leisure aim in the subject. Indeed, the explanation for many of these teachers was the examination syllabus taking priority, for example, for one teacher of History — "the emphasis is more on exam work, than 'educating for leisure" (*f,gh,35*). Likewise, two other teachers contended that: "The school is geared to an academic syllabus and as I teach the GCSE class in history there is not time" (*m,oh,47*), and "Biology is taught from an academic viewpoint — not from a leisure angle" (*m,a,24*). Whilst the typical response of teachers who taught Mathematics were: "I don't see Mathematics as a leisure activity" (*m,a,30*); "I teach to get students through exams" (*m,a,60*); or "I do not think anybody would want to do Mathematics in their leisure time" (*f,gh,27*), one teacher considered that he did have a leisure aim and saw it as important — the aim was:

> For the children to enjoy mathematical type problems in their own time — be it numerical x-words, rigging sailing boats, planning gardens etc., etc. (*m,a,25*)

He wanted children to view "maths as a help and not a closed subject at school". One teacher who said she didn't have a leisure aim in history did admit that "interest in buildings etc., hobby e.g. archaeology may evolve from history" (*f,gh,29*).

Table 1: Existence of a leisure aim in secondary school subjects

Curriculum subjects being taught (no of teachers=88)	EXISTENCE OF A LEISURE AIM			
	Yes % (n)	Never really thought about it/ not sure % (n)	No % (n)	No response % (n)
PHYSICAL EDUCATION	**99** (164)	—	**1** (1)	—
Mathematics (n=8)	**12.5** (1)	—	**75** (6)	**12.5** (1)
English (n=9)	**55** (5)	**22** (2)	**22** (2)	—
Geography (n=11)	**45** (5)	**18** (2)	**36** (4)	—
History (n=5)	—	**20** (1)	**80** (4)	—
Science (n=10)	**10** (1)	**10** (1)	**80** (8)	—
General Studies (n=4)	**25** (1)	**25** (1)	**50** (2)	—
Religious Studies (n=10)	**50** (5)	**10** (1)	**40** (4)	—
Art/Drama (n=4)	**50** (2)	—	**50** (2)	—
CPVE/Social, Personal Education/Pastoral (n=11)	**73** (8)	**18** (2)	**9** (1)	—
Information Technology/ Computer Studies/commerce (n=6)	**33** (2)	**17** (1)	**50** (3)	—
Health Education (n=3)	**100** (3)	—	—	—
Others eg. Home Economics/ Sociology (n=7)	**71** (5)	**14** (1)	**14** (1)	—
Total [other subject] (n=88)	**42** (37)	**14** (12)	**43** (38)	**1** (1)

As Table 1 indicated, the two subjects with the most mixed reaction (almost equal numbers of teachers with and without a leisure aim in the subject), were Geography, Religious Studies/Education, and the category labelled Information Technology/Computers. So where Geography was concerned, for instance, on the one hand, the aim was that "pupils will develop an interest in travelling — both to foreign countries and other areas of GB" (*m,a,25*), and on the other, the response was "not relevant to exam syllabus" (*m,hb,37*). Another teacher gave it a very low importance rating and considered a leisure aim to be "only a minor part of geography. The leisure influence is probably hidden and may or may not develop in pupils" (*m,a,23*).

The subjects where more teachers considered themselves to have a leisure aim than not, were Health Education where all responses were along the lines of "my leisure aim is to encourage children to lead a healthy way of life" (*m,bh,35*), and unsurprisingly teachers involved in CPVE [Certificate of Post Vocational Education], Social and Personal Education and Life skills. As one teacher said, "an important aspect of CPVE is to develop students' own awareness of opportunities and the need to plan and organise their time [which includes leisure time" (*f,a,36*). Similarly, "Life Skills prepares pupils for their whole life so the leisure aspect is intrinsic in all I teach." (*f,a,29*).

So, how did the non-physical education subjects compare with physical education when respondents were asked to rate the importance of a leisure aim in the subject on a scale marked from 0 (not important), 5 (important) to 10 (very important)? Table 2 below shows some marked differences.

Table 2   Comparative importance of leisure aim across curriculum subjects

Importance rating	Importance of aims in general in PE % (n=165)	Importance of leisure aim in PE % (n=164)	Importance of leisure aim in 'other subject' % (n=88)
0—4 rating	1	9	60
5—6 rating	24	34	15
7—8 rating	34	38	14
9—10 rating	41	20	11
Mean (points on scale)	8	6.9	3.5

As the findings in Table 2 above show, whilst over 90% of the teachers rated the leisure aim in Physical Education at 5 or higher, only 40% did so in their other main subject. To provide some context, the findings when teachers were asked to rate the importance of their 'aims in physical education teaching' in general, are included in the table. On an individual basis, individual teachers in all but a handful of cases, gave a higher rating to a leisure aim in Physical Education than in their other subject. One of those who didn't — she also taught English — for example, considered it "extremely important for them [pupils] to have basic knowledge of English to do anything! To understand written instructions, to read for their own enjoyment i.e. leisure". She rated her leisure aim in English as 10 in contrast with a 7 rating for Physical Education (*f,a,39*).

From a number of issues which could be highlighted from the findings and observations made to date in this paper as regards a leisure role in school subjects, that of inconsistency and the differing opinions of teachers is arguably the most noteworthy. Contrast the views of the teacher of English instanced above — who clearly saw her leisure aim as important — with the view of another teacher of English:

> I don't feel that in English this is a priority. ... There are other things which are far more important; leisure may crop up as an incidental in some lessons (*f, a,40*).

The impression gained from such inconsistency is of much individuality, with teachers clearly having their own views.

Concluding comments

It is interesting to note that such a surprising degree of individuality had also emerged where leisure practice was concerned in Physical Education (Lawrence, 1993: p. 137). Despite a common aim, it seemed that "each teacher works in a different context, doing different things, struggling with different problems, and producing different consequences for their pupils and themselves" (Locke, 1986: p. 33). Lack of guidance from Local Education Authorities was seen as promoting such individuality, as was the fact that Physical Education was not regarded as an examination subject, nor had the National Curriculum been implemented. In the findings just presented, the reason given by many of the teachers for not having a leisure aim in a non-physical education subject was that they had to follow an examination syllabus; this supports Hendry's contention back in the early 1980s, that leisure education in secondary schools existed in non-examinable subjects such as Physical Education (Hendry, 1983).

Perhaps in Physical Education such individuality will have lessened with the advent of greater prescription and standardisation due to the National Curriculum, and the increasing examination profile in the subject? If so, what implications are there for a leisure aim in the subject?

Will education for leisure/a leisure aim be squeezed out as other priorities take precedence? At the same time however, evidence presented above interestingly showed that a leisure aim did exist and was regarded as important for a number of teachers in examination-based subjects.

All this begs a number of fundamental questions; whilst we've considered *what* the teachers' views are and what may happen in practice, the key question seems to be: '*should* there be a leisure role in all school subjects?'. Returning to Gabrielsen's criticism of teachers of subject areas who failed to "recognize the potentials of their subjects as leisure-time activities" (Gabrielsen, cited in Corbin and Tait, 1973: p. 141), should this be part of their remit? Such a question leads us to all sorts of problematic and philosophical issues which strike right at the raison d'etre of contemporary school education. I would suspect that the contention that there is no agreement as to what constitutes sound education (Brightbill and Mobley, 1977) still holds true today, and that many in this country support the view articulated by Spedding as regards the situation in New Zealand. He considers that:

> ...our educational structures have never made anything more than motionless gestures towards an understanding of the significance of leisure in a person's growth. Leisure has been treated as something peripheral that will take care of itself and not worthy of the sort of attention that academic pursuits have attracted. (Spedding, 1977: p. 19)

The belief that schools should be firmly channelled towards preparing pupils for a job, and to obtain the necessary qualifications, will be held by many practising teachers. Others will see education as much more than this, such as preparing children to live a full life throughout their life, of which leisure time will play an important part. To what extent are schools preparing pupils for the future? Perceptions therefore differ depending on an individual's view of the purpose of education. It can be suggested that this, in part, causes inconsistency and individuality such as demonstrated in this paper.

Yet, should there ever be consensus that schools have a part to play where 'leisure preparation' is concerned, we are then faced by other issues which relate directly to the formality of the leisure and education interface. If there is a leisure role, should this be incidental, or as John Alderson asks — reflecting similar debates from the 1960s and 1970s:

> Given the nature of our society and the way in which it is changing, should education for leisure feature formally in the school curriculum? (Alderson, 1993: p. 83).

Should leisure education, as Sleap (1987: p. 168) argues, "be integrated purposefully and not incidentally into the whole curriculum"? Should it be implemented through:

a total approach ... an interdisciplinary curriculum which will sensitize pupils to the overall concept of leisure and its relevance in modern society. (Fisher, 1982: p. 34)

By contrast, Martin and Mason make the legitimate point that if leisure is to remain a time of free choice, "people cannot be taught what to do with this part of their lives" (Martin and Mason, 1987: p. 259).

The questions are seemingly endless; in this paper we have just skimmed the surface. As I have argued elsewhere for the case of Physical Education (Lawrence, 1993), there is a definite need to clarify the leisure role in contemporary school in general and in individual curriculum subjects. Obviously, further research can have a critical part to play in this. Until we have debate and clarification, Kelly's (1982: p. 205) question, 'Can the school be a major contributor to preparation for lifelong satisfying leisure?', will remain one of the many ongoing imponderables in education.

Notes

1   The Physical Education Association [PEA] is the major Association for physical education teachers in the United Kingdom; it changed to PEA UK in 1995.

2   In a two phase study, an extensive questionnaire on aspects of teachers' leisure aims and practices was mailed to teachers in secondary schools in 6 local authorities in England in May 1988 — responses from 165 teachers in 61 schools were analysed. In the subsequent case-study phase in late 1989, there followed greater in-depth investigation of six individual teachers' leisure aims and practices, and influences on practice. Each teacher was shadowed and observed, and interviewed over a period of 2-3 days.

3   To give some indication, albeit brief, of the experience and gender of the teachers making direct comments, quotes are followed (in brackets) by: an *indication of gender* (m/f); *status in the department* (oh=overall head of department; gh=girls head of department; bh=boys head of department, and a=assistant teacher); and *age in years*.

4   Though Mahoney is describing the situation in Northern Ireland, it could be assumed that this was the situation throughout the United Kingdom at the time.

5   Any interviewee names used here are 'fictional' substitutes for the respondents' real names.

References

Alderson, J. (1993) 'Physical Education, sport development and leisure management', in G. McFee and A. Tomlinson (eds) *Education, sport and leisure: Connections and controversies* (CSRC Topic Report 3). Eastbourne: University of Brighton, pp. 73-84.

Almond, L. (1989) 'Introduction', in L. Almond (ed) *The place of Physical Education in the curriculum.* Kogan Pate, pp. 9-36.

Becker, H. S. (1971) 'Personal change in adult life', in B. R. Cosin, I. R. Dale, G. M. Esland and D. F. Swift (eds) *School and society — A sociological reader.* London: Routledge & Kegan Paul in association with The Open University Press, pp. 129-135.

Brightbill, C. K. (1960) *The challenge of leisure.* New Jersey: Prentice-Hall.

Brightbill, C. K. and Mobley, T. A. (1977) *Educating for leisure — centred living,* 2nd edition. New York: Wiley and sons.

Corbin, H. D. and Tait, W. J. (1973) *Education for leisure.* New Jersey: Prentice-Hall.

Evans, J. and Davies (1988) 'Introduction: teachers, teaching and control', in J. Evans (ed) *Teachers, teaching and control in Physical Education.* Lewes: The Falmer Press, pp. 1-19.

Fisher, R. (1982) 'Some cross-cultural consideration of the physical education curriculum and leisure participation', in I. K. Glaister (ed) *Physical Education, sport and leisure: Sociological perspectives.* Report of the NATFHE Annual Conference, London: pp. 33-43.

Glew, P. and Gilliver, K. (1987) '"Time-out" project — an interim report or ... "It will never by the same again!"', *Bulletin of Physical Education,* Vol. 22, No. 3: pp. 13-20.

Green, K. (1995) 'Physical Education, partnership and the challenge of lifelong participation: A shared goal for the 21st century?', *The British Journal of Physical Education,* Vol. 26, No. 2: pp. 26-30.

Harrison, P. (1995) 'Editorial: partnerships between Physical Education and sport', *The British Journal of Physical Education,* Vol. 26, No. 2: p. 4.

Hendry, L. B. (1983) *Growing up and going out.* Aberdeen: Aberdeen University Press.

Hendry, L. B. and Marr, D. (1985) 'Leisure education and young peoples' leisure', *Scottish Educational Review,* Vol. 17, No. 2: pp. 116-127.

Hendry, L. B., Shucksmith, J., Love, J. G. and Glendinning, A. (1993) *Young people's leisure and lifestyles.* London: Routledge.

Kane, J. E. (1974) *Physical Education in secondary schools.* London: Macmillan Education.

Kelly, J. R. (1982) *Leisure.* New Jersey: Prentice-Hall.

Laventure , B. (1987) 'Linking school to community-setting the scene', *The British Journal of Physical Education,* Vol. 18, No. 2: pp. 60-62.

Lawrence, L. (1991) *Understanding teachers' leisure aims and practices in secondary school Physical Education.* Unpublished PhD thesis, Brighton Polytechnic.

────── (1993) 'Leisure in Physical Education', in G. McFee and A. Tomlinson (eds) *Education, sport and leisure: Connections and controversies* (CSRC Topic Report 3). Eastbourne: University of Brighton, pp. 134-148.

Locke, L. (1986) 'What can we do? Profiles of struggle', *Journal of Physical Education, recreation and dance,* Vol. 57, No. 4: pp. 60-63.

Lodge, B. (1989a) 'Ministers pass the team ball to club coaches', *The Times Educational Supplement,* 1st December 1989: p. 4.

────── (1989b) 'MacGregor fails to allay PE fears', *The Times Educational Supplement,* 1st December 1989: p. 4.

Mahoney, C. (1995) 'Sport and the young people of Northern Ireland: An appraisal', *The British Journal of Physical Education,* Vol. 26, No. 1: pp. 35-38.

Martin, B. and Mason, S. (1987) 'Making the most of your life: the goal of education for leisure', *European Journal of Education,* Vol. 22, Nos. 3/4: pp. 255-263.

Meek, C. (1990) 'The government's response to the School Sport Forum Report', *The British Journal of Physical Education,* Vol. 21, No. 2: p. 292.

Microsoft (1992) Microsoft Word Version 5.1. Microsoft Corporation.

Murdoch, E. B. (1987) *Sport in schools.* Desk Study commissioned by the DES and DOE, Brighton Polytechnic.

Newsom, N. (1963) *Half our future.* London: HMSO.

Paddick, R. J. (1982) 'Time on my hands: Hands off my time', *Leisure Studies,* Vol. 1: pp. 355-364.

PEA (1987a) *Physical Education in schools.* Report of a Commission of Enquiry. London: PEA.

────── (1987b) 'Draft statement of philosophy on Physical Education', *The British Journal of Physical Education,* Vol. 18, No. 6: p242.

Penguin (1985) *The Penguin English dictionary.* Harmondsworth: Penguin Books Ltd.

Penney, D. and Evans, J. (1994) 'It's just not (and not just) cricket', *The British Journal of Physical Education*, Vol. 25, No. 3: pp 9-12.

Pilkington, E. and Moss, S. (1994) 'Spoil sport', *The Guardian* March 1: pp2-3.

Ploszajski, T. (1988) 'The link badge: A new Sports Council scheme to bridge the gap between school and adult life', *Sport and Leisure*, Vol. 29, No. 1: p. 71.

School Sport Forum (1988) *Sport and young people — partnership and action*. London: Sports Council.

Sherlock, J. I. (1979) 'The evaluation of leisure programmes in secondary schools', *Journal of Psycho-Social Aspects*, Occasional Papers No. 5, Edinburgh: DCPE.

SHA (1987) *No ball — an enquiry into the provision of Physical Education in secondary schools*. Iles, Bristol: Secondary Heads Association.

Simpson, J. (1973) 'Education for leisure', in M. A. Smith, S. Parker, and C. S. Smith (eds) *Leisure and society in Britain*. London: Allen Lane, pp. 278-287.

Sports Council (1989) *Active lifestyles: An evaluation of the project's work*. London: The Sports Council.

Spedding, A. (1977) 'Education for leisure', NZ JHPER, Vol. 10, No. 1: pp. 19-21.

SWCSR (1990) *From school to community — six years on — a further South-West Study of the relationship of Physical Education to the sporting and recreational needs of young people*. South Western Council for Sport and Recreation/Sports Council, Crewkerne.

Talbot, M. (1976) 'Education for leisure — a critique', *The British Journal of Physical Education*, Vol. 7, No. 3: pp. 147-148.

——— (1987) 'Bridge that gap: Education and sport', *Fellowship Lecture*. London: PEA.

——— (1994) 'The role of Physical Education in a national strategy for young people and sport', *The British Journal of Physical Education*, Vol. 25, No. 1: pp. 27-29.

Veal, A. J. (1987) *Leisure and the future*. London: Allen and Unwin.

Williamson, T. (1987) 'One view of the future', *The Bulletin of Physical Education*, Vol. 23, No. 1: pp. 45-52.

Knowledge or Competence? The Changing Face of Qualifications in the Leisure Industry

John Hunter-Jones, Bob Carroll and Bob Jones
University of Manchester

Introduction — phases of development

The last 25 years have seen massive changes in the leisure industries, notably the rapid increase in the range of available leisure services and public provision, the numbers employed in the leisure industries, the importance to the economy, and the expansion of facilities. Accompanying these developments has been an increasing professionalism and professionalisation of the industry. This is reflected in the establishment of professional bodies such as the Institute of Leisure and Amenity Management (ILAM), career structures, and the development of qualifications specifically for the leisure industries. Of course, the development of qualifications within the leisure industries is not just a phenomenon relating to the development of the industries themselves, it is also a product of prevailing ideologies in society more generally and an effect of this is the expansion of qualifications. Therefore the development is also related to the expansion of further and higher education, the ideologies of vocationalism, professionalism and accountability.

The development of qualifications in recent years can be divided into phases as in Table 1. Looking at these phases, the following general trends can be established.

Firstly, the growth of interest in vocational courses in Leisure. The number of centres and the number of students has shown a rapid increase; for example, Carroll (1994) showed a rise in BTEC registrations for Leisure Studies from 2517 in 1987/8 to 7864 in 1991/2. This number is not likely to decrease, as many traditional areas of employment have declined, the leisure and tourism industries have shown a corresponding expansion and students see this, not only as a pleasant area to work, but one where jobs exist. Furthermore, the independence of colleges and the

Table 1   Phases in the development of vocational qualifications in the leisure industry.

Phase	Educational-vocational	Industrial-professional
1 Pre 1970s	No qualifications.	Individual organisations, e.g. IBRM, NGB of sport coaching awards.
2 Early 1970s	Introduction of C&G Recreation & Leisure, sport based. Establishment phase, ironing out difficulties.	
3 Early 1980s	C&G 481 revised syllabus CPVE units in leisure . Consolidation phase.	
4 Mid 1980s	BTEC R &L college based courses, more academic. Expansion & diversity	Qualifications across sectors of leisure, more professional approach, e.g. ILAM awards, NCF modules in sport coaching
5 Early 1990s	GNVQ Leisure & tourism. Standardisation — content, assessment	NVQ competence based in work place. Standardisation across industries.

BTEC = Business and Tecnology Council

C&G = City and Guilds

CPVE = Certificate of Pre-Vocational Education

IBRM = Institute of Baths and Recreation Management

ILAM = Institute of Leisure and Amenity Management

NCF = National Coaching Foundation

NGB = National Governing Bodies

R & L = Recreation and Leisure

market forces philosophy of the present Conservative government have brought increasing competition between colleges and a premium on college places and on gaining qualifications. Leisure has been seen as an area ripe for development, both demand- and supply-led.

Secondly, the change to assessment led qualifications, and a move to competence-based assessments in the workplace. This has led to a reduction in the knowledge basis, and a drive towards what the Americans call 'authentic' assessment. This 'new vocationalism' has been an attack on the educational orientation of many vocational courses and is particularly reflected in National Vocational Qualifications (NVQs). General National Vocational Qualifications (GNVQs) appear to be a means of placating the educational world within an assessment-outcomes led model as something colleges and schools can cope with away from the workplace (see Table 2).

Thirdly, a change from variety to standardisation. A move to standardise and control competence, and assessment. This is reflected particularly in the demands of and levels of qualifications across different organisations and different sectors of the industry (see Table 3).

Table 2   Vocational Qualification Structure

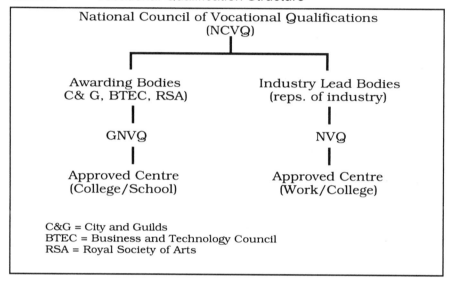

National Council of Vocational Qualifications
(NCVQ)

Awarding Bodies
C& G, BTEC, RSA)

Industry Lead Bodies
(reps. of industry)

GNVQ

NVQ

Approved Centre
(College/School)

Approved Centre
(Work/College)

C&G = City and Guilds
BTEC = Business and Technology Council
RSA = Royal Society of Arts

Table 3   National Qualification Framework (adapted from NCVQ 1991)

Academic route	Vocational route 1	Vocational route 2
Higher degree	GNVQ 5	NVQ 5
First degree	GNVQ 4	NVQ 4
A level	Advanced GNVQ	NVQ 3
	Intermediate GNVQ	NVQ 2
GCSE	Foundation GNVQ	NVQ 1

Variety still does exist in the form of educational courses falling outside GNVQs, for example, Higher National Diploma (HND) in Sport Science, but an emphasis is being placed by the awarding bodies and colleges on GNVQs as this is seen as the route supported by the government and for the immediate future a route into jobs, and one which will also be acceptable in higher education.

Current routes in vocational qualifications

The two routes have arisen since the Government's Review of Qualifications in 1986. It would seem there were two main thrusts to the new developments. Firstly, the need for a coherent structure to the myriad of a growing number of qualifications and awarding bodies, and secondly, a criticism of current vocational qualifications which were too educational based and too divorced from the workplace. To meet the criticisms and needs, the National Council of Vocational Qualifications (NCVQ) was established to set up a system and clear standards for a National System of Vocational Qualifications, which became known as NVQs.

To meet the first thrust, a coherent structure was established involving levels; and to meet the second, Industrial Lead Bodies (ILBs), comprising representatives of the industry, established the criteria and standards of competence. The emphasis was to meet the needs of the industry and individuals in the work situation and this was to be carried out through competence-based assessment in the workplace. The NVQs met this need. However, it was soon realised that the education training system could not realistically meet the demands and therefore it was necessary to establish General National Vocational Qualifications (GNVQs). This allowed the expanding Further Education sector to realistically offer vocational qualifications. The GNVQ had a structure similar to NVQs in terms of outcome demands but inevitably had the educational knowledge-based assessment in the context of the industry rather than competence-based demands. The structure offered a parity across the GNVQ and NVQs and with the traditional academic qualifications of General Certificate of Secondary Education (GCSE), 'A' levels and degrees for the first time (Table 3). It also had the advantage that it attacked the academic-vocational divide and lower status problem of vocational qualifications, again by the government for the first time. However, the parity issue has raised a lot of questions which have not yet been answered, and it remains to be seen whether parity will be achieved in practice.

GNVQ route

Three years ago GNVQs were launched, Leisure and Tourism (L&T) being one of the original five pilot subjects. Since then there has been confusion over their role (Target 1994; Smithers 1995), and criticism of their structure, content, jargon, paperwork, assessment and grading of courses and the constant changes that have taken place. There have been reports from the Office For Standards in Education (OFSTED), the Further Education Funding Council (FEFC), the Association for Colleges (AfC), Channel 4's Dispatches programme, and regular press articles. With the recent formation of the Department for Education and Employment we can expect further change (Nash, 1995). What may seem surprising, in the circumstances, is the united approval for a national vocational alternative to the GCE/A level route, as exemplified by a headteacher:

> In the past, education has been like a train: you get on aged five and stay on as long as you can, and if you are good enough you end up as Professor at your university in your subject. Getting off the train too soon has always been seen as second best. For the average pupil, vocational courses are very exciting. They will be doing something new. They develop an interest and start achieving something. (M. Payne, Head, Kingham Hill School, in Tyler, 1995).

Support for such views has come from many quarters (Smithers, 1993). The GNVQs have been praised by students and teachers (FEFC, 1994), schools (OFSTED, 1994), colleges (AFC, 1994) and funding councils (OFSTED, 1994; FEFC, 1994). Their future also looks assured, according to recent research (THES, June 1995). Not only are GNVQs here to stay, they are likely to expand into higher education (Tysome, May 1995). The Government is also determined that they should succeed and see them as part of their "strategy for securing a well educated, skilled and flexible workforce" (Boswell, 1995). The Labour Party too is committed to GNVQs (Tysome, June 1995) Despite such strong support they have also been much criticised. Examining boards have cast doubt on their worth (O'Leary, 1994), whilst university admission tutors see them as an inadequate preparation for academic life (Blackburne, Jan. 1995) and they are described as "not vocational enough" (Tysome, July 1995; Collins, 1993).

163,000 students started GNVQ courses in September 1994: 35,000 of those students were on Advanced GNVQs. It is expected that there will be over 250,000 students on GNVQ courses for 1995-96, about one in four of all post 16 students. Eight subjects are now widely available (the original five subjects plus Science, Construction & the Built Environment and Hospitality and Catering). By 1996 another seven subjects will be added (including Performing Arts). Numbers, therefore, can only continue to rise. 11,700 students registered for the Advanced BTEC Leisure and Tourism GNVQ in 1994. (BTEC, May 1995)

At present GNVQs are for those in education aged 16+ and are at three levels: Foundation (1yr), Intermediate (1yr), and Advanced (2yrs). The Government's intention is to introduce a new "GNVQ Part One" for 14 year olds (Nash 1995), and these are being piloted in 1995/6. It is the intention here to avoid jargon and discussion of too many boards and levels of GNVQ. Therefore the focus of this paper will be on BTEC Advanced GNVQ, also known as vocational A levels, the level most familiar to those in further and higher education. Table 4 gives a comparison between the GNVQ and the BTEC National. Many of the comments will be applicable to other levels and awarding bodies.

Table 4   Comparison between GNVQ in Leisure and Tourism and BTEC National in Leisure.

	GNVQ	BTEC National
length	usually 2 years (FT)	2 years
equivalent	2 A levels	2 A levels
core subjecs	finance marketing investigating leisure and tourism human resources business systems developing customer service health, safety and security	finance marketing leisure environment people in organisations people in organisations organisation in its environment
skills	application of numbers communication information technology	applying numeracy communication applying technology + 4 others
options	from set list	freedom for college to develop own
unit of work experience	no	yes, college can devise experience
assessment of units	external exams + internal all perf. criteria assess. need not be job centred detached from grading	internal only not standardised should be job related same as grading
grading	pass, merit, distinction course grade separate from unit assessment	pass, merit, distinction each unit graded part of unit assessment

Issues in implementation of GNVQs

In 1991 NCVQ was given the responsibility for GNVQs. It sought to take the NVQ philosophy and apply it within the education system. This ruled out support to established vocational qualifications which could not be equated with NVQs. The closer the mesh between NVQs and GNVQs the more likely that easy "mapping" could be made between the two. That is still true.

> GNVQs have been designed to provide a broad education as a foundation both for training leading to employment, and for further and higher education. This is achieved by ensuring that students develop the general skills, knowledge and understanding that underpin a range of occupations and or professions, and by incorporating a number of additional general skills including application of numbers, communications and Information Technology into every GNVQ. Advanced GNVQs have been designed to be of a standard broadly similar to GCE A level, and provide a suitable preparation for higher education. (NCVQ, 1991)

The NCVQ approach is similar to that of the driving test in that all skills must be tested and achieved, the knowledge and understanding needed only relates to the identified skills. So the approach is to work backward from the skills. In order to achieve this, awarding bodies have had to graft a system on colleges and schools that is alien to them and there have been problems. GNVQs have not only had to accommodate NVQ philosophy but have had to produce grades, and subject students to external tests. The result of such demands is that the GNVQ in Leisure and Tourism has become overloaded with the requirements of the government, NCVQ, awarding bodies, schools and colleges, and expectations of industry, universities and students.

The Advanced GNVQ in Leisure and Tourism is broadly the same in structure as all Advanced GNVQ courses. There are 15 units which have to be completed before an award can be made; 8 units are known as mandatory units (see Table 4); 4 units are "optional" and are drawn up by each award body. BTEC offers a choice of 16 options including, 2 languages. 3 units are core skills at NVQ level 3: application of numbers, communication and information technology. Students can add additional units though these will not affect the award of the GNVQ and its grading. Each of the units is sub divided into sections known as elements. The element states what the student must do to pass (performance criteria); the syllabus (range) underpinning it and what must be produced for the student's portfolio (evidence). Clarification of terms is provided (amplification) and "guidance" given to teachers.

In line with the GNVQ philosophy, students can produce work that they have completed elsewhere in order to exempt them from relevant units, provided it matches the unit specifications and that it can be authenticated, this is known as Accreditation of Prior Learning. Work experience is not part of the GNVQ requirement, though colleges can use it to support the course.

It is left to schools and colleges to decide how to deliver the course. Teaching units need not correspond to the 15 units and there is great flexibility in this area for suiting the local needs of the college. In general the core skills are assessed as part of the assessment of the other units. Assessments for a unit must:

> ...provide students with opportunities to demonstrate competent achievement against the performance criteria; provide opportunities for achievement to be demonstrated across the range; provide opportunities for grading; provide opportunities for assessing core skills. (BTEC, Aug. 1994)

Significantly there is no mention of learning and this is a stark contrast to BTEC's general approach to assessments. Their attitude to assessment is that it is embedded in the course and not separate — "So assessment should be embedded within programmes of study rather than programmes being designed solely with an eye to assessment and consequently emerging as sterile and boring" (BTEC, July 1994). All 8 mandatory units are subject to external tests, of a multiple choice style, in order that national standards can be maintained. Students must pass with at least a 70% mark. Candidates have an average of two minutes per question, and the exam lasts one hour. "External tests confirm that students have learned the essential knowledge which underpins the mandatory units" (BTEC, Feb. 1995). However, many doubt this assertion (Smithers 1993). This approach to assessment is entirely different to most BTEC National courses, though nearer to C& G courses. It is very much a change in the style and techniques of assessment with which colleges have to come to terms.

The assessment system is complex and time consuming. From 1996 all new assessors must pass assessor units. Each GNVQ course has its own assessors, internal and external verifiers. Verification is carried out by way of sampling: the main complaint is that the process is very time consuming although it clearly helps overcome fears of low standards and 'easy' centres/teachers, which has been a criticism levelled at BTEC national courses. Assessment of schools and colleges is also carried out by OFSTED and FEFC. An assessment can cover a number of units and core skills. It can be in written, visual, 3D or oral form. Interestingly there is no requirement to make the assessment a "real life" situation as is encouraged on BTEC National programmes. An example of an assessment for an Advanced GNVQ in Leisure and Tourism is:

The purpose of this task is to investigate the holiday opportunities that exist within the UK and to identify the main destinations. (Owens, 1994)

In no part of the assessment is there an attempt to create a work related scenario — hence the criticism of GNVQ that it is not vocational enough.

One of the more confusing areas of the GNVQ is that the criteria used to obtain a GNVQ are different from the grading scheme. Once all units have been completed and external tests passed, then the portfolio of work that the student has amassed can be graded (Pass; Merit or Distinction) using the following four themes: planning; information seeking and handling; evaluation; quality of outcomes.

The first three themes relate to how the students prepared for their tasks (process) and the last on the work itself. As with assessment, there is a defined approach to how the grades should be calculated. The use of new terms, e.g., synthesis, are explained. There is no individual grading of units, cf. National Diplomas. and so strengths and weaknesses are not revealed in particular subjects. If a student is to obtain a distinction/merit then he/she must reach that level for all four grading themes in at least one third of their work, equivalent to four out of twelve units at Advanced level. So, grading reflects an ability to have reached a sustained level, even though the majority of work might only be at Pass level. There is also no weight given to when the student achieved the level, so that the student may complete final GNVQ assessments at Pass level standard but be awarded a distinction. BTEC Nationals recognise a rising profile in a student. There is a general acceptance that an Advanced GNVQ is the equivalent of two A levels. Distinction is the equivalent of A/B grade, merit: two Cs and a Pass: D/E. This has not formally been accepted by the Government, despite requests from teachers (Preston 1994). By September 1995 2,340 students had completed the Advanced GNVQ in Leisure and Tourism of which 464 (20%) gained a distinction and 1021 (44%) a merit, the remainder, 855 (36%) were left with a Pass.

However, 4,321 students had still to complete all units after at least two years of study (Blackburne, 1995). One of the main purposes of grading was to enable students to progress to higher education, but only a minority of active students will have been able to use their GNVQ results for that purpose, as only 22% of all those who have started the course have obtained a distinction or merit within two years. Last year 700 students with advanced GNVQs entered university, but this number is expected to rise dramatically over the next three years (Young, 1995). Although this route is going to be more acceptable for vocationally orientated degree courses such as Leisure and Tourism, it does appear to be an attack on the academic-vocational divide and the traditional 'A' level gold standard, particularly if it can be shown that students from this route get good results.

It is not surprising that the grading has caused much confusion because of NCVQs unusual approach to the task(OFSTED, 1994). However, if one considers the usual criteria for grading of advanced academic work such themes as research, analysis and communication are common criteria. Other difficulties have been experienced in students not being formally graded until all units have been completed and consequent difficulties in guiding students (and HE institutions) as to their progress. By keeping grading and assessment separate it makes it easier to compare GNVQs with NVQs, which has no grading.

GNVQs have been heralded as the new vocational qualification, equivalent to A levels at Advanced level and offering an alternative route to employment opportunities. It might appear to the lay observer that GNVQs have filled a vacuum. However, BTEC and C&G both offered vocational courses in both Leisure and Tourism, at all levels, before GNVQs and useful comparison can be made (table 4).

One of the main differences between the courses is the combination of leisure and tourism on the GNVQ, so that leisure students must embrace tourism and vice versa. This has forced many students to study areas which they cannot relate to, for instance the study of Sport and the Accommodation sector share few common denominators. Lecturers are also unlikely to have a background in both leisure and tourism. Sampson (1995) and Gilling (1994) are very critical of this combination. If one adds to this the extensive assessment process it is not surprising that many people see the course as being too broad and too shallow (Collins 1993).

It was the original intention of BTEC to phase out its National exams. However, in April 1995, it stated "at Advanced level (GNVQs) do not provide full equivalence in range and flexibility to our National Certificates and Diplomas ...we have decided to continue to make our Nationals available" (BTEC May 1995). The difficulties encountered by everyone in understanding GNVQs, the separation of assessment and grading criteria, the breadth of assessment and the extensive paperwork has made Nationals seem heroic by comparison. However, Nationals are open to far more interpretation by institutions running them and this, although worthy in some respects, has debased their national value as employers/colleges have no clear idea as to the content and standards. The GNVQ, though still in its early stages, does appear to be making it less likely that it will be judged on the basis of the institution rather than the level of qualification. GNVQs adoption of National material has also been a sensible approach. GNVQs have been subjected to much criticism and Leisure and Tourism, in particular, has come in for particular attack with the identification of weak analysis and variable standards by OFSTED (1994) and FEFC (1994). The NCVQ says that the Advanced GNVQ in the Leisure and Tourism offers students the opportunity to develop "in depth knowledge and understanding of the leisure and tourism sector and its component industries" (NCVQ 1995). When one considers the conditions under which the GNVQ was set up it is not surprising that, as the *TES* reported, the "revolution was rushed" (Nash, 1994), and that it has had many faults. However, many of them have been acted upon. There has, though, been little criticism of the need that GNVQs are trying to address. Examination of the criticism suggests that most of the problems are ones of extent, poor communication skills by NCVQ and the awarding bodies, too much breadth, not enough depth, too much paperwork, poor external checks on colleges/schools, not enough contact with employers. These can be dealt with inside the GNVQ framework without losing its strengths.

It is easy to be critical of GNVQs. Its language, style of assessment and grading are alien, and clearly many areas were developed without the benefit of experience and lengthy debate. It is also still subject to poor understanding, witness the lead article by Clare in the *Daily Telegraph* on Aug. 21 1995. "Two thirds of the nearly 200,000 pupils aged 16 to 19 who have taken GNVQs...have failed to complete the course on time". However, GNVQs have no time limit, and many will complete the units at a later date.

It does make sense that GNVQs should run parallel with NVQs, they are, after all, both vocational qualifications, and clearly this allows greater comparison between the two. The difficulty, particularly in an area such as Leisure and Tourism is that it requires a very diluted course to cover all areas and has produced a great variety of performance criteria, with over two hundred in Leisure and Tourism. However, examination of the ranges (syllabi) on the Advanced GNVQ Leisure and Tourism contain what one would expect at this level, but the pressure to keep up with the process of achieving the performance criteria has limited the depth of knowledge and understanding that one would hope to obtain in two years (OFSTED, 1994; FEFC, 1994; AfC, 1994).

Knowledge is gained, academic skills improved, but the thrust of the qualification, that of responding to performance criteria, clearly calls the tune. There is little room for lecturers to dwell on topics in which they may have great experience/knowledge/enthusiasm. The GNVQ lists skills needed but fails to identify those which are essential (Smithers, 1995). So students are denied the opportunity and satisfaction of detailed study. They are also, as already mentioned, less likely to experience work placements and assessments that are work related.

This approach, of parity with NVQs, only makes sense if the course is satisfying to students and improves their chances of employment and academic progression. There is a danger that this qualification will satisfy nobody as it seeks to please everybody. So far, few in the Leisure and Tourism sectors have rushed in to speak up for the GNVQ. In fact the opposite is the case. It has within it the skills and knowledge required by industry and academia but, at present, it is too broad and clearly 'in depth knowledge and understanding' are less likely to be achieved. GNVQs may be here to stay but the Leisure and Tourism GNVQ may well have to undergo further treatment if it is to gain widespread acceptance.

NVQ route

It is not easy to get full information on take up of NVQs as there is no national database of those people starting or completing units. By March 1994, 565,000 full NVQ certificates had been awarded across all industries (NVQ Monitor, 1994), and this had risen to 842,537 by May 1995 (NVQ Monitor, 1995. It would appear that there were another 1.6 million people working towards NVQs according to the NCVQ (Merrick, 1993). The 11 basic categories of commercial and industrial sectors produce about 100 different NVQs offered at various levels. Of those awarded only about 6 percent were level 3 or above (Ringguth, 1993), which even allowing for the fact that there are more areas developed at levels 1 and 2, suggests that there may be a problem in persuading employers and managers that the NVQ model is appropriate at the higher levels.

In spite of this massive and apparently successful take up, there are some areas of concern identified through research. For example, research has shown that both trainees and employers are confused or failed to understand the qualifications or their demands, and those that did thought NVQs too prescriptive and not flexible enough, whilst a shortage of funding hampered progress in some areas (Merrick, 1993; Pyke, 1994). A CBI report showed that a third of employers believed that NVQs were irrelevant (Littlefield, 1994). Another survey revealed that the majority of firms taking part were larger firms with 44% having over 500 employees and only 6% of them having fewer than 50 employees (FEFC, 1994). This raises an equal opportunity issue. There are a number of large firms who do not use the NVQ system but prefer their own in house training such as, in the retail sector, Burtons, Littlewoods, whilst British Home Stores has pulled out of the NVQ system (Merrick, 1994).

The problem with categorising leisure as an industry is that it is not a coherent or readily identifiable unit and its boundaries are not clear. Many industries are related to leisure: shopping, for example, is a very important leisure activity, but retailing may not be thought of as a leisure industry by its employees or the wider public. Probably the most common sectors which are thought of as leisure industries are the following, all of which have lead bodies which are responsible for setting the criteria and standards of NVQs: Sport and recreation, Amenity Horticulture, Environmental Conservation, Hotel and Catering, Arts and Entertainment, Museums, Travel and Tourism. All of these are at different stages of development of NVQs. For example, the Arts and Entertainment Council has only recently developed the units for cultural venue operations (level 2) and cultural venue administration, but further units covering stage management are to be submitted in 1995. Hotel and Catering and Sport and Recreation have well developed areas at 4 levels. Sport and Recreation is one of the most developed NVQs with units in coaching, sports development, sports administration, facility management, sports therapy, outdoor education, spectator control, and playwork. It is worth noting that the three generic units for both levels in Arts and Entertainment covering working relationships and customer care are those developed for people working in administration and in the sport and recreation sector, implying that these are transferable skills.

According to the NVQ Monitor (summer 1995), 672 certificates have been awarded in sport and recreation by May 1995, the bulk of these being at levels one and two in facility operations. In the coaching sector, the Governing Bodies of Sport have had to come to terms with external demands and structure for the first time to bring their own well established and recognised schemes and awards in line with NVQ requirements, but this is being achieved, and some 30 Governing Bodies have made progress. The first NVQs in coaching were awarded by the Football Association earlier in 1995.

The developments in NVQ contrast with previous training and qualifications in the various sectors of the leisure industry, for example, in the arts and entertainment sector due to the nature of the work and short contracts. The introduction of a recognised and transferable qualification is likely to have a positive effect within the industry.

Issues in implementation of NVQs

As already indicated NVQs have not been introduced without controversy and criticism (see e.g. Smithers, 1993; Wolf, 1995). They have been seen as revolutionary and an attack on the education industry in its approach to vocational training (Jessup 1991). The traditional approach in education has been knowledge based, sometimes supplemented by work experience, and assessment has been based on what students know and how to apply that knowledge in what is usually termed theoretical situations and not practically in the workplace. The approach of NVQs is competence based, assessment of skills in the workplace situation, though some can be and others have to be simulated. The traditional workplace training and assessment in the job situation (such as apprentice schemes in craft and manufacturing industries) had been in decline since the demise of these industries in this country, and many service industries such as the leisure industry did not have such schemes. In most industries college courses could not cope with the demands of work placed assessment — not suitable for the full time education students, hence the need to devise GNVQs and continue with existing vocational courses. However, now many colleges are working closely with industry to devise suitable courses for NVQs, and these include sport and recreation.

The arguments for a competence-based assessment in the workplace appear, on the surface, strong — and at least stronger than traditional educational assessments based on academic knowledge within a vocational context. Wolf (1995) has reviewed the evidence on the relationship between educational academic performance and later work performance and the relationship between work-based assessment (work samples) and occupational performance. The overwhelming evidence is that educational performance is an inappropriate assessment for occupational performance and a poor predictor of it, and that work-based assessments are more appropriate and better predictors. However, it should be noted that most of the evidence reviewed in relation to work-based assessments relates to more specific skills (such as craft) and not managerial competences. In the leisure industries it would appear that there is no specific evidence — but, in the absence of other qualifications, it is likely that the people who have done well on the educational courses would get the opportunity for jobs and for promotion, for example, in local authority leisure departments. These courses and qualifications have been used as a yardstick for people's interest, knowledge and willingness to learn, and wider understanding of the industry. What the emphasis on competence-based assessment does is to put a premium on how to do the skills, and the assessment of those skills in the actual workplace, rather than the knowledge about and knowing how to do something in a theoretical situation. It is a technicist approach, and it remains to be seen whether this approach can be successful at all levels. The advantage of this approach can clearly be seen in specific posts such as life guard/swimming pool attendant, and receptionist, but not so clearly in positions such as manager of a large multi complex sports centre, or sports development officer. However, clearly, the idea of valuing work place efforts and competences in the form of qualifications should be of use to everyone at all levels, and especially to those with little or no formal educational qualifications.

This technicist approach has been severely criticised by Smithers (1993) for neglecting fundamental knowledge and principles which can jeopardise performance. Smithers also suggests that it does not compare well with European qualifications. Although this criticism was not being levelled at the leisure industries, in particular the criticism of the principles of narrowness of knowledge and specificity of skills does apply to NVQs more generally. In the NVQ system knowledge required is only seen as that underpinning the job in a functional analysis of the roles of the job. A functional analysis alone may miss wider aspects of the role, for example, box office work covers the sale of tickets, financial control and monitoring, but does not appear to address the wider role acting as interface in marketing, and the need for knowledge about the production or event and policy of the venue. Its relation to other aspects of the organisation and service sector, and issues such as competing demands on individuals and organisations and equal opportunities may be neglected. It is in the service area such as leisure where such knowledge and understanding of the functions of the organisation, its role in the community and wider policy issues may enhance performance in the job (above minimum competence level). However, an examination of the requirements of the criteria, range statements and evidence specifications for NVQs in Sport and Recreation would suggest that they are comprehensive in their demands on both performance and knowledge required. Smither's criticisms may well be unfair in relation to this sector of industry.

One of the immediate effects and issues is the volume of assessment. Each job is divided into units related to a particular part of the job, each unit has a number of elements which make up competences/tasks for that unit. There are range statements to show the range of context and finally knowledge underpinning on which the person is also assessed during or after the task assessment. Thus, for example, Sport and Recreation Coaching Children has 14 units and an average of 5 elements to a unit and 5 performance criteria to an element. This is a total of 70 assessments with 350 performance criteria identified, although many of these can be assessed at the same time. The 2 or 3 range statements identified for each element and the evidence specifications (knowledge underpinning) increase the demands. All this is clearly a very time consuming job and therefore expensive to operate. A system which puts a premium on so many assessments and time by candidates, assessors and employers can be unwieldy and impractical to carry out in many contexts. It should not be surprising, then, to hear that many employers and trainees underestimated the demands and the time required for assessment, had difficulty meeting those demands, and that there was a high drop out rate in small and medium sized firms (Crowley-Bainton and Wolf, 1994; McHugh, 1993. Sport and Recreation ILB, 1994). People in small and medium firms are unlikely to get the opportunities to be assessed in NVQs, and if the system does catch on amongst larger employers, this lack of opportunity to take qualifications may prevent them getting jobs with these firms. However, many large organisations do not take part in NVQ and prefer their own in-house training, for example in retailing, as indicated earlier.

The philosophy of NVQs suggests that it is candidate led. However, it is clear that the candidate needs the support of the employing organisation. This requirement is identified as an important factor in a South West project in the Sport and Recreation fields (Sport and Recreation ILB, 1994). As Wolf (1995) suggests a system which neglects and ignores people's values, judgements in favour of an external quality control system, is likely to break down or in the case of National Curriculum assessments in primary schools.

Although there are very detailed criteria laid down for each occupation as already indicated, NVQs still beg questions and make assumptions about competence and standards. It tends to assume that everyone understands what competence is and what standards should be applied. Whilst this may be true of relatively straightforward tasks at lower levels, it may not be so in some contexts and at higher levels, for example, there may not be complete agreement over what is a good coaching lesson to a group of youngsters. This reliability of assessors has been questioned by Wolf (1995) who shows variable reliability amongst assessors on the 'Blue Badge Guide' scheme awards for tourist guides. This should be taken care of by the training and moderation of assessors. The system tends to support a minimum competence level rather than striving for best performance or excellence.

The emphasis on the functional analysis and the competence criteria neglects completely the consumer view. In the final analysis, in some jobs this may be the only effective measure which really counts — for example in sales, teaching and coaching, and in arts and entertainment.

At the present time, the only report available evaluating implementation of NVQs in Sport and Recreation appears to be the one in the South West already mentioned. This project covered approximately 100 people involved in all levels one to four across facility management, sports development outdoor education and playwork. It identified five main problems, and five lessons learnt, and how problems were overcome (Sport and Recreation ILB, 1994). Some of those mentioned included:

1. Training for work-based assessors more understandable and acceptable in the context of sport and recreation.

2. The need for the organisation to adopt the culture of work-based assessment.

3. Time and demands of assessment underestimated.

4. Difficulties in 'outreach', rural and outdoor adventure situations.

5. Funding of the NVQ process.

6. Educational institutions concern over their role in the assessment process.

The success of this project and the lessons learnt should be an incentive for the successful implementation elsewhere.

Conclusion — knowledge or competence?

We think it can safely stated that much has changed and been achieved in the area of qualifications in the last few years. However, the establishment of work-based competence awards has created an additional structure and route, and resulted in three routes, the traditional academic, and two vocational. The new structure has attacked the traditional conceptions of assessment and qualifications and the academic–vocational divide and the status problem of vocational awards. However, far from solving these issues it has created a divide within vocational qualifications itself. Although this divide has always existed, it has been strengthened by creating a formal structure across all industries. Therefore, we are still left with the problem of some people going down the educational pathway to GNVQs and receiving their knowledge-based qualification, whilst others take the work-based pathway to NVQs and gain a competence-based award. It might seem unfair to suggest that there will be those who 'know,' and those who 'can do', but this has been the gist of the argument for competence assessment in the workplace. Its recognition has only emphasised the divide within vocational qualifications. Can the two routes co-exist? Which route is going to be the most acceptable within the industry? At the present the GNVQ does not appear to be the answer to vocational qualifications in the leisure and tourism industries, though no doubt there will be revisions and improvements which will make it more acceptable.

However, equally, when the NVQ system becomes more established and the implementation problems overcome or at least coped with, then NVQs will become more acceptable and valued awards. The proof will be the value in the industry, and to individuals this means getting jobs or promotion. If the employers see it as a means of gaining a more useful, efficient. cost effective workforce, then it will be used in this way and people will get jobs as a result of gaining NVQs. Then the situation will arise where people with GNVQs will be seen as deficient in qualifications and will be required to take NVQs. Furthermore, personnel who gain NVQ awards at lower levels and show potential and promise may be preferred to GNVQ qualified applicants in competition for jobs. GNVQ could be under threat, particularly if jobs are difficult to get. The question will be asked, "why spend so much time gaining a vocational qualification where the vocational element is limited, and particularly if there are no jobs at the end of it?' This may mean that it will be judged more as a route to higher education, and it has yet to prove that it can be whilst at the same time not lowering the standard of higher education intakes. GNVQ needs to earn parity with A levels. There is a real danger it may not satisfy these demands nor the vocational. It can be confusing having dual routes in vocational training. At the present time the traditional educational path- way is more well known, better understood and respected, hence the popu- larity of GNVQs. However, this may well change as the NVQ requirements are grounded in functional job analysis, and may, in the end, be more useful to the industry.

A clear factor in the success of NVQ will be cost. This is not as crucial for GNVQ because the cost of educational based courses and assessments is relatively cheap, and the educational world is geared up to this system. At the present time, there are various sources of funding available, for example, through the Training and Education Councils (TEC), and this has been both an incentive for employers and employees to take up the scheme and a means of supporting the programmes. If government funding dis- appeared then the NVQ system would be in jeopardy. However, it would appear that the Government is committed to making substantial funds available for the NVQ system through the TECs.

We understand that some European countries are looking at the NVQ system with some interest, and this may be appealing to those countries with less established vocational qualifications in many industries. If the NVQ model was adopted in Europe with a view to offering comparability of qualifications, then this would strengthen the system. On the other hand it may lead to revisions. There would also be a strong chance that more European Social Fund money would become available.

A revision of NVQ is due in the near future, and a simplification of, and more flexibility in the system and process may well be found to be more acceptable and necessary, as in the case of the National Curriculum and its assessment system (see Dearing, 1994). Such a revision plus the acceptance at managerial levels would no doubt herald the expansion and strengthening of the competence-based model, possibly at the expense of the knowledge-based educational model. However, there is clearly a need for both NVQs and GNVQs and possibly this is the opportunity to merge both philosophies and systems for lifetime education and training, where people can move between both, and both are acceptable and esteemed qualifications.

References

AfC (Association for Colleges) (1994) GNVQ Assessment Portfolio of evidence. London: AfC.

Blackburne, L. (1995) *Times Educational Supplement*, 13 January.

—— (1995) *Times Educational Supplement*, 29 August.

Boswell, T. (1995) *Opinion Business Education Today*, March

BTEC (1994) *BTEC The first decade.* July. London: BTEC.

—— (1994) *GNVQ assessment.* August. London: BTEC.

—— (1995) *Getting GNVQs right*, February. London: BTEC.

—— (1995) *Shaping the future.* May. London: BTEC.

Carroll, B. (1994) *Assessment in Physical Education.* London: Falmer.

Clare, J. (1995) *Daily Telegraph*, August 21.

Collins, V. (1993) 'Who wants GNVQs?', *Business Education Today.* November.

Crowley-Bainton, T. and Wolf, A. (1994) *Access to assessment initiative.* Sheffield: Sheffield Employment Department.

Dearing, R. (1994) *The National Curriculum and its assessment.* Final report. London: SCAA.

Gilling, J. (1994) *Leisure Opportunities*, December: pp 34-35.

FEFC (1994) *National Vocational Qualifications in the further education sector in England.* Coventry: FEFC.

Jessup, G. (1991) *Outcomes NVQs and the emerging model of education and training.* London: Falmer.

Littlefield, D. (1994) 'The trouble with NVQs', *Personnel Management*, Vol. 26, No. 7: pp. 47-48.

McHugh, G., Fuller, A. and Lobley, D. (1993) *Why take NVQs? Perceptions of candidates in the South West*. Lancaster: Centre for the Study of Education and Training, Lancaster University.

Merrick, N. (1993) 'Six years on — a qualified success', *Times Educational Supplement*. 3 December.

Merrick, N. (1994) 'Stores split over value of NVQs', *Times Educational Supplement*. 3 June.

Nash, I. (1994) *Times Educational Supplement*, November 4.

——— (1995) *Times Educational Supplement*, January 13.

——— (1995) *Times Educational Supplement*, July 21.

NCVQ (1991) *Guide to National Vocational Qualifications*. London: NCVQ.

——— (1995) *GNVQ Advanced Leisure and Tourism*. London: NCVQ.

NVQ Monitor (1994) Spring issue.

——— (1995) Summer issue.

OFSTED (1994) *GNVQs in schools 1993/4*. London: HMSO.

O'Leary, J. (1994) *The Times*, November 16.

Preston, S. (1994) *The Times*, August 29.

Pyke, N. (1994) 'NVQs not a sensible use of funds', *Times Educational Supplement*, 26 August.

Ringguth, A. (1993) 'Find your way through S/NVQ', *Hospitality*. No. 139: p. 26.

Sampson, A. (1995) 'Are GNVQs the answer?', *Leisure Manager*, Vol. 13, No. 3: pp. 33-34.

Smithers, A. (1993) *All our futures: Britain's education revolution*. London: Channel 4 TV.

——— (1995) *Times Higher Educational Supplement*, September 1.

Sport and Recreation Lead Body. (1994) *The issues and problems in respect of implementation*. Plymouth: Devon and Cornwall TEC.

Target, S. (1994) *Times Higher Educational Supplement*, February.

THES (1995) Editorial. *Times Educational Supplement*, June 30.

Tyler, D. (1995). *The Times*, March 27.

Tysome, T. (1995) *Times Higher Educational Supplement*, May.

——— (1995) *Times Higher Educational Supplement*, June.

——— (1995) *Times Educational Supplement*, July.

Young, S. (1994) 'GNVQs beat path to degrees', *Times Educational Supplement*, 26 August.

Young, S, (1995) 'Study pushes vocational degrees', *Times Educational Supplement*, 17 February.

Wolf, A. 1995. *Competence-based assessment*. Buckingham: Open University Press.

Leisure Education and Training — Competence Approaches and Quality Issues

David Smith
University College of Ripon and York St. John

Sue Eccles
Airedale and Wharfedale College

Introduction

This paper does not attempt to describe in full the nuances of National Vocational Qualifications (NVQs) and General National Vocational Qualifications (GNVQs) nor does it give basic factual material about these qualifications. For this information the reader is advised to consult publications such as the *Guide to National Vocational Qualifications* (NCVQ, 1991) and other relevant publications (FEFC, 1994a, 1994b, 1995; FEU, 1994). What the paper does aim to do is address the present education environment and the emphasis on the new vocational qualifications and associated competence based assessment.

Our present environment as described in Figure 1 (overleaf) has both controllable and uncontrollable elements. The uncontrollable elements lead on to environmental opportunities and threats whilst the controllable elements reflect organisational capabilities. Many of the uncontrollable elements in education at the moment are associated with 'vocationalism'.

Vocationalism has come to mean the pursuit of attaining and affirming occupational competence, in particular the approaches incorporated within the framework provided by the National Council for Vocational Qualifications (NCVQ). HEQC (1995), in their report Vocational Qualifications and Standards in Focus, state:

> The definition of terms such as 'vocational' and 'vocationalism' is difficult and often contentious, and can easily slip into involving issues of relative status. In this discussion, however, the terms are used to refer to programmes of study and qualifications that are designed to meet the needs of employment. As will become apparent, 'vocational' tends to be a question of degree rather than of kind; and to be influenced by the specificity of the employment in

251

Figure 1   A model of the environment

	C O N T R O L L A B L E	Generic	Historic	Traditional	Functional
Internal **(intra-firm)** **environ-ment**		Culture Structure Resources	Past Perfor-mance	Men (Women) Money Materials Machines Markets Messages Manage-ment	Finance Marketing Research and Devel - opment Purchasing Personnel Manufac-turing

	U N C O N T R O L L A B L E	
Micro environ-ment		**Stake holders** Customers/ Consumers Consumer Organisations Trade Unions Community Government Financial Media Industry Standard Bearers **Industry** **Structure of Industry** **Markets** Substitutes Consumer Suppliers Industrial Buyers Reseller New Entrants Government Competitors International

	U N C O N T R O L L A B L E	
Macro environ-ment		Political Economic Sociocultural Technological Natural /Physical Society International

question. Some qualifications may be intended to provide for employment in a tightly defined role, others for employment in a range of related roles (or broadly-defined industrial field), and still others for employment in general: all might justifiably be regarded as — to some extent — 'vocational'. (HEQC, 1995: p. 2)

In her presentation at a Leisure Education Conference in 1992 (one week after the launch of the Sport and Recreation NVQs), Liz Rick, Director of the School of Leisure and Food Management at Sheffield Hallam University, stated that:

Vocationalism encapsulates a set of values and attitudes concerning educational process and outcomes and is thus used pejoratively or with approval according to the user's beliefs and experience. This may be seen in the apparent juxtaposition of vocational and academic. Phrases such as 'high academic standards' are used with approbation whereas 'merely academic' implies 'of impractical value'. 'Vocational relevance' is a desirable element of the mission of Higher Education (HE), yet the term 'vocational' may be used to imply 'devoid of intellectual content'.

This paper uses the words 'vocational' and 'vocationalism' to imply the principles and processes behind NVQs and GNVQs whilst recognising the comments above, particularly as regards definitional difficulties.

The paper first discusses Further Education (FE) and its present context in relation to vocationalism. Competence approaches and quality issues in FE are addressed. Next, the paper deals with Higher Education (HE) and its present context and some of the implications of vocationalism. This discussions leads on to a proposal for a vocational partnership model between HE/FE and employers for the implementation of an NVQ in HE. Finally, some conclusions are summarised, based on the proposed model.

Further education — context

In Britain from the middle of the 1970s, the concern with equality and equality of opportunities in education was replaced by other issues (Haralambos, 1991). A number of changes have been made to education which reflect a new concern with standardisation and a fresh emphasis on developing a competent and trained workforce:

It is vital to Britain's economic recovery and standard of living that the performance of the manufacturing industry is improved and that a whole range of government policies, including education, contribute as much as possible to improving industrial performance and thereby increasing the national wealth. (Finn, 1987: p. 106)

In a period of accelerating unemployment, and a decline in Britain's economic position, the issue was that education was failing to produce an appropriately motivated and skilled workforce.

In an effort to redress the balance, the government's policies in relation to education and training became known as the "new vocationalism"
(Richardson, Woolhouse and Finegold, 1993: p. 77). The significant events
(adapted from the work of Richardson, Woolhouse and Finegold, 1993: p.
2) which influenced 16-19 education and training policy in England and
Wales, 1987-95 are presented in Appendix 1. The 16-19 reform debate in
England and Wales during the period 1987-95 provides a good platform to
examine the complex interplay of ideologies, ideas and vested interests that
underpin the new vocationalism. However, it is outside the scope of this
study to consider the impact of all the major changes affecting Further
Education. This section, therefore, will concern itself with the issues
relating to vocationalism in the Further Education Sector, and will take
cognisance of the model of the environment presented in Figure 1 (Internal
environment, micro environment and stakeholders, micro environment and
industry, macro environment).

The 1990s brought with it a period of turbulence for the Further
Education Sector. The 1988 Education Reform Act and incorporation in
April 1993 have driven traumatic change through the colleges. The govern-
ance, management and the culture of colleges have been transformed
within a short time span. Control of Further Education colleges moved
away from the Local Education Authority (LEAs), allowing colleges to
become autonomous free standing business units operating within a
competitive market environment with responsibility for self survival.

The Further Education Unit (1991) identified six major changes in
which Further Education now operates:

1. Introduction of National Vocational Qualifications;
2. Education Reform Act;
3. National Curriculum;
4. Increased role of the Training and Enterprise Councils;
5. Increase in links between business and education;
6. Government drive for a Further Education Funding Council.

With the demise of the Local Education Authorities, the Government set up
a new quango, the Further Education Funding Council (FEFC), to
administer and finance the Further Education sector post-incorporation. A
key part of the Further Education Funding Council's brief is to monitor the
quality of the provision within its operating domain.

In recent years, the college's market and product range has changed
significantly to meet the demise of a technologically-based society. With the
demise of the manufacturing base, engineering in some colleges has almost
disappeared, whilst the growth in the service sector has brought with it the
need for professional development in those areas. A shorter working week
and differing patterns of employment has increased leisure time for many,
and has expanded leisure opportunities for some.

The recent legislation (see Appendix 1) has moved the colleges firmly
into a competitive position where strategic planning, operational control

and management of the changes are paramount for their future survival within a volatile environment. One of the results of incorporation has been dramatic changes in the funding of colleges, and most institutions now obtain finance not only from the Further Education Funding Council, the main stakeholder, but from partnerships and contracts with the Training and Enterprise Councils (TECs), Local Education Authorities partnerships with schools, other colleges, governing bodies of sport and other income generating courses and activities. Some colleges, for example Halton college in the North West, are enrolling students on vocational training and drawing down the funding from the Further Education Funding Council. However, the training is being delivered by other agencies, and Halton College's only role in the partnership is to secure the funding and quality assurance. This process has not been without problems and particularly in the quality assurance domain (*Times Higher Education Supplement*: 30th June, 1995).

The experience of the authors of this paper suggests that some faculties within Further Education colleges may attract only 50% of their total funding from the Further Education Funding Council, whilst the remaining 50% of income is generated through work with the TECs, other colleges, franchising arrangements, partnerships with schools and work with industry. The changes in the organisation of the sector has brought with it major implications for industrial relations in the Further Education sector.

New professional contracts have been introduced including a significant redefinition of working conditions which has resulted in down-sizing of the workforce in many Further Education Institutions. This confirms the work of Handy (1985) which suggested that in the future it was likely that organisations would rationalise their workforce and reduce significantly the number of full-time staff and increase the number of part-time temporary staff. His model, known as the Shamrock Organisation (Handy, 1985), pointed to a small core of full-time staff who would support and co-ordinate the work of a large number of part-time staff who would be employed on short term contracts.

As the organisation of Further Education has changed so has the service and product it offers. Curriculum changes have seen the introduction of NVQs and GNVQs along with the development of open learning, the information super highway, learning credits and output-related funding. The context of all this upheaval has been a relentless drive towards a reduction in costs and an increase in productivity. With this in mind, quality and particularly quality in teaching and learning, must be at the top of the agenda of every Further Education college in the sector. Aspects of quality within leisure education will be considered later in this paper.

The major features of the present environment within Further Education is epitomised by vocationalism and the delivery of competence approaches. The presentation of competence models within a vocational context (leisure) is now discussed.

Competence approaches

The central debate in British education today is on the form of the post 16 provision. Post 16 education is influenced by 'A' levels and preparation for higher education, even though 'A' level courses are only pursued by a quarter of the 16 year old cohort, and only one fifth progress to higher education (Richardson *et al.*, 1993).

To bring Britain into line with other industrialised countries, there is a general agreement that there is a need to increase participation in education, and to encourage those in employment to pursue some form of education and training leading to qualifications. After widespread consultation, the National Advisory Council for Education and Training Targets launched an updated framework of National Targets for Education and Training for the year 2000. The revised targets are:

Foundation Learning

1. By age 19, 85% of young people to achieve 5 GCSEs at grade C or above, an Intermediate GNVQ or an NVQ level 2.
2. 75% of young people to achieve level 2 competence in communication, numeracy and IT by age 19; and 35% to achieve level 3 competence in these core skills by age 21.
3. By age 21, 60% of young people to achieve 2 GCE A levels, an Advanced GNVQ or an NVQ level 3.

Lifetime learning

1. 60% of the workforce to be qualified to NVQ level 3, Advanced GNVQ or 2 GCE A level standard.
2. 30% of the workforce to have a vocational, professional, management or academic qualification at NVQ level 4 or above.
3. 70% of all organisations employing 200 or more employees, and 35% of those employing 50 or more, to be recognised as Investors in People.

The government has also set a target to increase the numbers entering higher education by 50 percent over the next ten years (FEU, 1995a) .In the light of the expectation that the numbers gaining 'A' level qualifications are only suitable for a quarter of the population, the expansion into higher education will have to come largely via other routes.

The present framework of qualifications

The existing framework of qualifications in England and Wales comprises three pathways: the academic, the vocational (NVQs) and occupational (GNVQs).

Academic qualifications

'A' levels provide demanding courses of study in a wide range of subject areas providing a good standard of academic ability. The distinguishing factors of 'A' levels lie in their demands for knowledge and cognitive skills. Though 'A' level is associated with traditional academic subjects, courses are now available in vocational areas — for example, business studies, sports studies and theatre studies.

The NVQ philosophy

The introduction of NVQs provides an exciting new challenge. NVQs are candidate centred and can be obtained independently from courses on the basis of assessment of competence. The choice of the units and the speed with which the qualification is achieved is dependent on the candidate's skill and ability. Assessment for NVQs should be available on demand, the request for assessment often being triggered by the candidate. However, there are serious issues in the administration and the delivery of the assessment, and for colleges it plays havoc with the traditional modes of delivery. For industry, it provides concerns regarding the demands of running a business. For the leisure industry and the many small businesses, these concerns are exacerbated.

The qualifications

The titles and content of NVQ qualifications have been specified by the Lead Bodies for leisure which comprise at least nine Lead Bodies associated with the leisure industry — Sport and Recreation; Amenity; Horticulture; COSQUEC; FASTCO; Hotel and Catering; Agricultural Training Board; Arts and Entertainment's Council; Museums Training Institute; and Caravan Industry Training Organisation.

In this paper, the authors concentrate on aspects of the Sport and Recreation Lead Body. The NVQ framework pertinent to the area is presented in Appendix 2.

Whilst developing the standards, the Lead Body was concerned to reflect the requirements of the industry, and the NVQ framework has been derived not from an analysis of education and training programmes, but from an analysis of employment needs, and the standards have been endorsed by them (Jessop, 1990).

NVQs are central to a major new initiative in work based training at present being introduced through the TECs called the Modern Apprenticeship scheme (Employment Department, 1995a). The aim is to attract 16-19 year olds to work based training where individuals learn in the working environment. Drawn up by the Lead Body for Sport and Recreation in 1995, it comprises three parallel but interlinked programmes:

Occupation — at least NVQ 3 Sport and Recreation and all 5 CORE skill areas.

Company — knowledge of the organisation and tailored to meet the needs of the employer.

Sector — knowledge of the relevant industrial sector, underpinned by a broad appreciation of national/international business practice.

The introduction of the new national vocational qualifications has not been without its critics. Some would argue that the qualification frameworks are too narrow and occupationally specific, are mechanistic in nature and train the workforce within a limited range of skills, which are not transferable to other areas of work.

Raggatt's study of NVQs in a number of vocational areas supports the above notion and concludes that an:

> ... inherent weakness of NVQs are that they are too occupationally specific and provide no basis on which workers can transfer the competencies that they develop to different occupational sectors. (Raggatt, 1991: p. 78)

Callender (1992), in a recent study of NVQs in the construction industry, painted a dismal and depressing picture of mechanistic and restrictive training and de-skilling of the workforce. Hyland's (1994) research at Warwick University confirmed the above findings. Jessop (1990) suggests:

> Training needs to be less narrow, concentrating more on adaptability and transferable skills to cope with changing technology, work practices and organisational structures. (Jessop, 1990: p. 19)

Perhaps the introduction of the Modern Apprenticeship scheme with its emphasis on occupation, company and sector will provide the necessary framework for a better trained, higher skilled workforce, which the Government is seeking through its new initiative (Employment Department, 1994).

However, if National Vocational Qualifications are perceived to be too occupationally specific then it is reasonable to regard the introduction of a more broadly based programme as an acknowledgement of the inadequacies and weaknesses of NVQs in this area. The broader vocational and occupational remit of the GNVQs, it would appear, has complimented the narrow and focus of the NVQ and has provided a framework where competencies have been replaced by attainments.

The GNVQ Philosophy

GNVQs were introduced following recommendations from the government's White Paper Education and Training in the 21st Century (DES/ED, 1991).

The GNVQ system has brought together leisure and tourism, which Sampson (1995) would argue have different outcomes and are applicable to different cohorts. Holmes (1995) argues that the marriage of the two courses is a compromise between the two disciplines of leisure and tourism and that students can select optional units which are directly relevant to their vocational needs. However, McWatt (1994) considers that the leisure and tourism GNVQ is too wide and does not meet the quality criteria for leisure education which she defined as including

fitness for purpose;
conformance to standards;

clear standards;

system in place to prevent errors;

getting things right first time.

During the last three years,

have operated as pilot courses. Each year there has been constant changes in the course specification which have brought enormous problems for the delivery centres. Tonks (1994) from the Business and Technical Education Council (BTEC) highlighted some of the issues facing the delivery of GNVQ in Leisure and Tourism. He maintained that GNVQ is not just about developing operational competencies, but is more about delivering educational programmes. He went on to point out that the language surrounding GNVQs is difficult and that students need to be clear about the exact nature of GNVQs and what is required of them on GNVQ programmes.

New course specifications have been produced for 1995 in an effort to ensure that the mandatory units — particularly at Advanced level — are more rigorous and provide sufficient underpinning knowledge. Holmes (1995) would argue that GNVQs are the future, (Employment Department 1993, Employment Department 1994b), and that employers and Higher Education are becoming more accepting of the qualification. Research by the FEU (1995b) confirmed Holmes' work in that 85% of the first cohort of GNVQ Advanced students who applied for a course in Higher Education in 1994 received an offer of a place. The introduction of the new GNVQs has not been without its critics. Richardson, Woolhouse, and Finegold (1993) suggest that the viability of GNVQs still appears uncertain, and that examining bodies are marketing different products. They move on to point out that decisions made by the Department for Education allowing GNVQs to be delivered in schools, has resulted in schools and colleges becoming locked in competition. Sampson (1995) supports the above theory and goes on to point out that schools attract more funding per head for a GNVQ student than colleges, and schools, unlike colleges, are not penalised for students dropping out of programmes. Some would argue that the above causes unhealthy competition between institutions which in the long run does not benefit the student.

The introduction of NVQs and GNVQs has created several concerns in that students are not required to have sufficient knowledge, and the methods of assessing what they understand and can do are simultaneously over-elaborate and unconvincing. Both concerns were seen to stem from the qualifications emphasis on competence — an emphasis which assigns a minor supporting role to underpinning knowledge and core skills, whilst the main emphasis requires lengthy check lists or relatively trivial achievements. It has been acknowledged (City and Guilds, 1994) that the above concerns could be seen to arise from an inherent contradiction in that qualifications that could be described as inherently work based are being delivered in educational settings.

Further Education— quality issues

Information and advice regarding quality abound. There are many quality approaches, models, recommendations and systems available, some more applicable to occupational (GNVQ) and vocational (NVQ) programmes than others. This plethora of exhortations and demands can be bewildering and there is a danger of educational organisations in the FE sector responding reactively in a piecemeal fashion. The FEFC inspection cycle is now half way through and there has been much good work completed by the FEFC and FE colleges to avoid this piecemeal reactive approach. One aspect of quality that is assured in all this change is that FE has a head start on HE as regards quality issues surrounding vocationalism.

Based on the previous comments, the following are the major areas of quality issues, with some examples, that FE has had to address with the introduction of the new vocational qualifications:

1. The differing and not always complimentary quality systems imposed by the various stakeholders. It is not unknown for two Awarding Bodies to have very different approaches to external verification. Instances of an external verification report not matching a FEFC inspector's views have also happened. There are as many unsatisfactory incidences as there are stakeholders.

2. The different assessment methods that are required by the new qualifications. Many FE staff equated the BTEC First, National and Higher National awards with the new GNVQs. They are not the same and some colleges have found difficulty in changing over. Some colleges have hedged their bets, continued with their (proven) BTEC National and run concurrently an Advanced GNVQ with consequent duplication and potential confusion. Some BTEC National Awards have not at present a GNVQ alternative to change to.

3. Closely linked with the new assessment methods is a whole raft of staff development and training issues — from the new assessor awards to a new and important process of internal verification. Internal verification often happened informally, but the new awards require a much more rigorous and structured approach. An advanced GNVQ with, say, 160 performance criteria (activities that require proof of competence) all need assessing and internally verifying. Comments from FE staff suggest that the time to undertake this assessment — although it can vary — is excessive and inhibits staff from actually teaching students.

4. The new qualifications require much more careful tracking and new administration systems. NVQs in particular which are open access and should have a roll on/roll off philosophy with no time for completion have, as already mentioned, caused an about turn in colleges' traditional three term approach.

5. FE colleges are required by FEFC to offer a range of provision reflecting the needs of the community. They are having to differentiate between the full time student, the employed part time student and the unemployed part and full time student. In addition, the student could be enrolling on a GNVQ Advanced, with an 'A' level and NVQ unit. Whilst FE has a tradition of matching courses to student needs, the enormous amount of counselling and guidance now required (even with extra FEFC funding) is a real quality issue.

6. NVQs require realistic work environments (RWEs). In theory, NVQs cannot be assessed in a FE college. Lessons learnt from early attempts to try and access NVQs in RWEs in a college such as a college catering facility (open to the public) have proved that in some instances the FE college can be a RWE. RWEs have also raised the issue of who assesses in a RWE. Often employers have the RWE but no assessors, or the college has assessors but no RWE. The necessity for colleges and employers to work together has caused tension and, depending on the individuals concerned, either (positively) a closer working relationship or (negatively) an unwillingness to cooperate.

7. Linked to the RWEs issue is the employers perception both of FE colleges and their perception of NVQs. The old 'TEC' view by outsiders of the FE college has not necessarily ceased with employers because a college is now autonomous, with a new logo (probably) and a Chief Executive. Despite the enthusiasm for NVQs shown by various organisations, some industries have not been convinced of their worth. Smaller businesses in particular have been especially reluctant. Employers' perceptions of NVQs are central to their success; employers' perceptions of FE colleges as the source of administrative expertise and assessment experience are also crucial. Employers are at the moment inconsistent in their approach which raises questions about the quality of both the provision and infrastructure that provides the vocational awards.

8. Completion and progression for the new awards are less easily analysed. Students completing part of NVQs (a useful and worthwhile exercise in some cases) do not complete the whole NVQ and are sometimes seen as failures or 'wastage'. Similarly, according to recent media reports, GNVQs have a two-thirds drop-out rate. Many students who fail 'n' tests (the externally set tests for GNVQs) are included in these statistics. The retaking of an 'n' test means they are now GNVQ passes but are not necessarily included in the pass statistics. The new vocational awards are assessed differently and yet in statistical analysis are not apparently treated differently from the traditional awards.

Higher education — context

If the main features of the present environment within Further Education is epitomised by vocationalism and the delivery of competence approaches then a key feature of higher education as recipients of students who have undertaken a competence based approach in their education must be to seek to understand this process better. The Higher Education Quality Council's (HEQC, 1995) excellent review document Vocational Qualifications and Students in Focus succinctly suggests:

> HEQC believes that a consideration of the special features of these new qualifications could act as a foil against which higher education might review its own distinctive purposes, the means by which these are achieved, and the standards against which they are judged. (HEQC, 1995: p. 2)

The above quote mentions HE's 'own distinctive purposes'. At the present time HE is, perhaps, even more than FE, in a period of serious self reflection about its role in society. Major changes have occurred in HE, many in parallel with FE, but maybe none as dramatic as those changes being suggested as a result of the vocationalism debate. The Government is to publish a HE green paper before the end of the year. Tysome in the *Times Higher Education Supplement* (THES) reports:

> The green paper is the product of the Government's review of higher education, which has been gathering views on the future size, shape and purpose of the sector and is preparing to look at funding. Responses have signalled enthusiasm for moves towards a more flexible sector supporting 'lifelong learning' while maintaining high standards and protecting academic freedom. (Tysome, 1995a: p. 1)

Gillian Shepherd's recent move to the newly amalgamated Department for Education and Employment has added extra spice to the education and training (vocationalism) debate (Tysome, 1995b).

HE has always been a stronger, larger and more vociferous sector than FE. Whereas FE has the Government funded FEFC to answer to, HE was not satisfied that the comparable HEFC was sufficient and set up its own organisation — HEQC — for quality auditing. Comments made in the THES (30th June 1995; 21st July 1995; 4th August 1995) suggest a general consensus for one single agency. Consensus in HE takes time; implementation can take longer; and with the green paper and a forthcoming General Election, it appears unlikely that a single agency will be implemented before 1997.

Since the Government white paper in May 1991 (DES/ED, 1991) there has been a clouding of the FE/HE provision. FE Colleges have always run some HE provision such as higher national diploma and certificate programmes. With the significant increase in HE student numbers (the target of 1 in 3 18 year olds in HE set in the white paper was reached well ahead of time), the HE institutions have looked to franchise various higher-level work to local and not so local colleges. A not untypical partnership would be for a HE institution to have first year degree students studying at an FE College before progressing to the HE institution. Some HE Colleges have kept traditional FE work as part of their strategic portfolio of programmes, being unable to expand their full-time HE student numbers because of funding restrictions.

What is clear is that HE institutions must work in close partnership with FE colleges as any large scale HE initiative for traditional FE work could, at the worst, destabilise and threaten a smaller and more vulnerable FE college.

Higher education — vocationalism

The new vocational qualifications refer (other than in Scotland) to NVQs and GNVQs (HEQC, 1995). The Employment Department paper 'A Vision for Higher Level Vocational Qualifications' suggests that there are benefits for HE:

> The development of higher level vocational qualifications would help to enhance the role of HE in provision of learning. It would enlarge its opportunities for researching the knowledge relevant to professional practice and strengthen the link between academic and employment. (Employment Department, 1995b: p. 11)

A survey* carried out by the University of East London and reported in the THES of the 30th June 1995 suggested:

- 45% of HE institutions are currently running NVQ programmes.

- 30% of HE institutions are currently running higher** level NVQ programmes.

- More than a third of HE admission heads believe staff at their institution are moderately knowledgeable about NVQs and GNVQs.

- 72. 5% of HE institutions say they accept candidates holding a GNVQ. 43% say they accept applicants with NVQs.

- Approximately a fifth of respondents thought NVQs should be offered at more vocational areas at higher levels.

- The same proportion wanted GNVQs to be offered at higher levels.

(* Survey included questionnaires sent to every UK FE and HE organisation — a total of 625. Response rate for HE was 50%).

(** Higher level vocational qualifications include Level 4 and above NVQs. Level 4 GNVQs are not yet available but are being considered by NCVQ).

Comment

The results of this survey give the initial appearance of a healthy vocational awareness and uptake. However, to take one finding, the 30% of HE institutions that are currently running higher level NVQ programmes is from a response rate of 50%. Assuming more institutions who didn't respond are not involved then this would only give a 15% use of higher level NVQ programmes in HE. In addition, if these 15% are the smaller HE institutions, then in terms of total student numbers involved in higher level NVQs in HE the percentage would be considerably less. The full report (due in the Autumn of 1995) will make interesting reading.

One of the most interesting and contentious areas of debate about vocationalism is in terms of NVQs — the performance v process issue. NVQs 'do not entail programmes of study or training' (HEQC, 1995). Essentially, an NVQ answers the question of what a person is competent to do in a very specific (occupational) way. Many HE degrees have never really been seen as proving competence to do anything — education was academic and study was undertaken for its own sake. Other distinctive characteristics of NVQs contrasted with higher education awards are well documented (HEQC, 1995: pp. 6-8).

The result of the cognitive (academic) versus behaviouristic (vocational) learning theories (Hyland, 1995: p. 240) and the difficulties this causes for HE staff are discussed by Jenkins and Senning (1995) who integrated higher level management NVQs into a traditional HE Department of Management and include:

> Fear of loss of academic standards;
> Not being in tune with contemporary practice;
> New skills and knowledge;
> Ethical reasons;
> Listening to the market or not;
> Fear of centralised systems.

Whatever forces are pushing vocationalism in a positive or negative way, the fact is that it is here and is growing. How does an HE organisation respond and cope with the pressures of a more vocational orientation?

HE/FE/employers—a vocational partnership model

It is possible, if not desirable, for students at an HE institution to be awarded an NVQ without a significant FE or employer contribution, although the lack of an employer relationship raises issues of simulation (NVQ Monitor, Summer 1995) and realistic work environments (RWEs). It is suggested that an HE institution relatively new to competence-based approaches should work with an appropriate FE college with experience and expertise in the NVQ that is proposed and with an employer who can offer RWEs. With partnership as a basic principle, a model for the implementation of an NVQ in HE is represented in Figure 2.

Figure 2   A vocational partnership model for the implementation of NVQs in HE

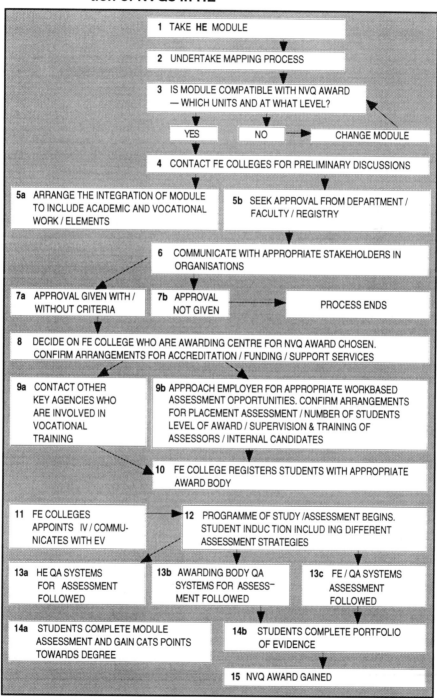

1 TAKE HE MODULE

2 UNDERTAKE MAPPING PROCESS

3 IS MODULE COMPATIBLE WITH NVQ AWARD — WHICH UNITS AND AT WHAT LEVEL?

YES   NO ----> CHANGE MODULE

4 CONTACT FE COLLEGES FOR PRELIMINARY DISCUSSIONS

5a ARRANGE THE INTEGRATION OF MODULE TO INCLUDE ACADEMIC AND VOCATIONAL WORK / ELEMENTS

5b SEEK APPROVAL FROM DEPARTMENT / FACULTY / REGISTRY

6 COMMUNICATE WITH APPROPRIATE STAKEHOLDERS IN ORGANISATIONS

7a APPROVAL GIVEN WITH / WITHOUT CRITERIA

7b APPROVAL NOT GIVEN ----> PROCESS ENDS

8 DECIDE ON FE COLLEGE WHO ARE AWARDING CENTRE FOR NVQ AWARD CHOSEN. CONFIRM ARRANGEMENTS FOR ACCREDITATION / FUNDING / SUPPORT SERVICES

9a CONTACT OTHER KEY AGENCIES WHO ARE INVOLVED IN VOCATIONAL TRAINING

9b APPROACH EMPLOYER FOR APPROPRIATE WORKBASED ASSESSMENT OPPORTUNITIES. CONFIRM ARRANGEMENTS FOR PLACEMENT ASSESSMENT / NUMBER OF STUDENTS LEVEL OF AWARD / SUPERVISION & TRAINING OF ASSESSORS / INTERNAL CANDIDATES

10 FE COLLEGE REGISTERS STUDENTS WITH APPROPRIATE AWARD BODY

11 FE COLLEGES APPOINTS IV / COMMUNICATES WITH EV

12 PROGRAMME OF STUDY /ASSESSMENT BEGINS. STUDENT INDUCTION INCLUDING DIFFERENT ASSESSMENT STRATEGIES

13a HE QA SYSTEMS FOR ASSESSMENT FOLLOWED

13b AWARDING BODY QA SYSTEMS FOR ASSESSMENT FOLLOWED

13c FE / QA SYSTEMS ASSESSMENT FOLLOWED

14a STUDENTS COMPLETE MODULE ASSESSMENT AND GAIN CATS POINTS TOWARDS DEGREE

14b STUDENTS COMPLETE PORTFOLIO OF EVIDENCE

15 NVQ AWARD GAINED

Issues at each stage that arise if the proposed model is used are:

1 & 2   Not all modules in HE are appropriate to be combined with
           an NVQ (HEQC, 1995: §6.11) Some generic modules may be
           appropriate for vocational core skills (HEQC, 1995: §6.26 and
           §9.6; also see Hodgkinson 1995).

3   It is possible to combine an HE module with individual units
           of an NVQ and at different levels. For a recreation manage-
           ment module, undergraduate students may undertake a Level
           2 NVQ (GCSE/'A' Level standard). This difference in levels for
           this vocational area would be acceptable because a graduate
           may commence work as a recreation assistant before moving
           on to supervisory and management positions. Alternatively a
           student — as a result of working towards an NVQ Level 2 in
           Facility Operations — may achieve part-time paid hours
           within their placement (HEQC, 1995: §3.6).

5 a   A semester module in HE would take 15 weeks to complete
           (October–January, February–May). To complete a portfolio of
           evidence for an NVQ Level 2 would require a programme of
           time spent in the work environment to train and be assessed.
           The interface between the education (academic degree study)
           and the training (competence based assessment) would
           require integration.

5 b & 6   There is much informal evidence (HEQC, 1995: §9.3) that HE
           institutions do not have a consistent and structured approach
           to optimise the present expertise of staff in competence-based
           assessment, and lack accurate information on what indivi-
           duals and small groups of staff have as their links and
           expertise in this area.

7a   It is not clear on what criteria an HE institution would use to
           approve or not approve a module associated with an NVQ or
           NVQ unit.

8   The experience and expertise of an FE college is a priority in
           the choice of a college. Ideally the college would already have
           a similar partnership to what is being suggested or a partner-
           ship between itself and an employer for the proposed NVQ. In
           this situation the college would have resolved any teething
           problems with an employer based on the NVQ standards and
           could act as a positive influence for 9b based on previous
           good practice.

9a   Key agencies would include the Training and Enterprise
           Council (who may be able to support the partnership)
           and professional institutions. The link with professional

institutions leads to the issue of integrating occupational competence, professional accreditation and higher educational achievement (HEQC, 1995: §9.7).

9b   Employers have not always been wholehearted in their acceptance of NVQs (HEQC, 1995: 6.14). The agreement of the employer to participate would require clear guidelines of what the implications, responsibilities and benefits of the partnership are.

10, 11 & 12   The experience and expertise of the FE College in student registration, induction and assessment would be invaluable especially for an HE institution with limited knowledge and understanding of the NVQ process. There would also be funding implications.

13 a, b & c   Different assessment processes could 'prove a source of creative tension' (HEQC, 1995: §6.24). The differences inherent in the two processes are the subject of continuing work by the HEQC Quality Enhancement Group (HEQC, 1995: §6.30) and the (ex) Employment Department (HEQC, 1995: §6.34).

14a & b   It is distinctly possible that a students would complete their academic module before their NVQ award. NVQs are not associated with time limits so this would be expected. However, there would be some practical issues to be addressed (see 5a), in that students would not want to extend their portfolio evidence collection over an extended period because of the danger of losing motivation and coherence.

Conclusions

The main conclusions arising out of the present paper are:

1. There is, and will continue to be, an increasing political pressure for a greater emphasis in education on a vocational orientation.

2. There has been justified criticism of NVQs and GNVQs and further changes are likely to be instigated to deflect and respond to these criticisms.

3. The perception of 'A' levels as the 'gold standard' will come under increasing pressure and changes to 'A' levels, however minor, are likely in the long term.

4. The new competence based assessment of NVQs and GNVQs has had a difficult introduction in FE. However many FE staff are neither competent with nor aware of the requirements of the new vocational awards. Hyland (1994) coined the phrase "doomed to succeed" (p. 234) concerning vocational awards — which, considering their history in FE so far, seems particularly apt.

5. Competence based assessment has had a much more limited acceptance in HE and the majority of HE institutions are still debating their
response to the present higher level vocational qualifications.
Similarly, the HE response to the expansion of higher level qualifications at present on offer is open to discussion.

6. There is an increasing emphasis on quality in the education sector but
a danger of duplication with quality assurance systems being based on
several significant stakeholders such as FEFC, HEFC, HEQC, TECs,
NCVQ and Awarding Bodies to name a few of those stakeholders.

The implications for management practice in the education sector are
varied and considerable. The management of change is a key area. Schools,
FE Colleges and HE institutions require an organisation structure that
allows a quick and effective response to the external environment. Leadership is required in positions of senior management. Resource management,
both financial and personnel, in an increasingly competitive environment
constantly requires reviewing. Staff development and training at all levels
of the organisation is needed, and it needs to be focused on a clear vision
for the organisation. Quality (however defined) is central to all activities.
And finally, one of the most difficult but essential strategies required is
that of partnerships — and partnerships not necessarily between equals
but strategic partnerships where each partner recognises the expertise and
strengths of the other(s). Strategic partnerships based on principles of
trust and synergy — principles so often theorised and written about but all
too infrequently implemented in practice.

References

Callendar, C. (1992) *Will NVQs work? Evidence from the construction
industry.* Brighton: University of Sussex, Institute of Manpower
Studies.

City and Guilds (1994) *FE forum series.* London: City and Guilds.

DES (Department of Education and Science), ED (Employment Department) and the Welsh Office (1991) *Education and training for the 21st
Century, Cm1536.* London: HMSO.

ED (1993) 'GNVQs: Winning higher recognition', *Insight No. 27.* Sheffield:
ED.

―――― (1994a) 'Closing the skills gap', *Insight No. 29.* Sheffield: ED.

―――― (1994b) 'Go, go, go GNVQ', *Insight No. 29.* Sheffield: ED.

―――― (1995a) 'Modern apprenticeships', *Insight No. 30.* Sheffield: ED.

―――― (1995b) *A vision for higher level vocational qualifications.* Sheffield:
TEED (Training, Enterprise and Education Directorate).

FEFC (Further Education Funding Council) (1994a) *National Vocational Qualifications in the FE sector in England.* Coventry: FEFC.

———— (1994b) *General National Vocational Qualifications in the FE sector in England. Coventry:* FEFC.

———— (1995) *Assessment in vocational programmes in the FE sector in England.* Coventry: FEFC.

FEU (Further Education Unit) (1991) *Quality matters: Business and industry quality models and FE.* London: FEU.

———— (1994) *GNVQs 1993-1994: A national survey, London:* FEU.

———— (1995a) *GNVQs — vocational qualifications and progression to HE.* London: FEU.

———— (1995b) *GNVQs so far.* London: FEU.

Finn, D. (1987) *Training without jobs.* London: Macmillan.

Handy, C. (1985) *Understanding organisations.* London: Penguin.

Haralambos, M. and Holborn, M. (1991) *Sociology, theory and perspectives.* London: Collins.

HEQC (Higher Education Quality Council) (1995) *Vocational qualifications and standards in focus.* London: HEQC.

Hodgkinson, L. (1995) 'Core skills in HE — experiences from the Open University', *Network* (ED), Edition 2: pp. 3-6.

Holmes, G. (1995) 'GNVQs are the answer', *Leisure Bulletin*, July 27th, Reading: ILAM.

Hyland, T. (1994) 'Silk purses and sow's ears: NVQs, GNVQs and experiential learning', *Cambridge Journal of Education*, Vol. 24, No. 2: pp. 233-243.

Jenkins, H. and Senning, S. (1995) 'Higher education and the dilemma of management development: Soul searching in a Management Department', *International Studies in Educational Administration*, Vol. 23, No. 1: pp. 38-45.

Jessop, G. (1990) 'NVQs: Implications for FE', in M. Bees and M. Swords, (eds) *National Vocational Qualifications and Further Education.* London: Kogan Page and NCVQ.

Mansfield, B. (1995) 'Simulation — a necessary evil or acceptable source of evidence', *The NVQ Monitor*, Summer: pp. 3-6.

McWatt, A. (1994) 'Rationale for leisure education and training', in D. Smith (ed) *ILAM Leisure Education and Training Conference 1994.* York: University College of Ripon and York St. John.

NCVQ (National Council for Vocational Qualifications) (1991) *Guide to National Vocational Qualifications*. London: NCVQ.

Richardson, W., Woolhouse, J. and Finegold, D. (1993) *The reform of post 16 education and training in England and Wales*. London: Longman.

Roggatt, P. (1991) 'Quality assurance and NVQs', in P. Roggatt and L. Unwin (eds) *Change and intervention: Vocational education and training*. London: Falmer Press.

Sampson, A. (1995) 'Are GNVQs the answer?', *The Leisure Manager*, June/July 1995.

Tonks, P. (1995) 'The BTEC response', in D. Smith (ed) *Leisure Education and Training Conference 1994*. York: University College of Ripon and York St. John.

Tysome, T. (1995a) 'Reform signalled in Green Paper', *Times Higher Education Supplement* (THES), July 21st.

Tysome, T. (1995b) 'Merged Ministry triggers alarm', *THES*, July 4th.

Utley, A. (1995) 'College growth probed by FEFC', *THES*, June 30th.

Appendix 1 Events influencing 16-19 education and training policy in England and Wales, 1987-95

September 1986	Introduction of National Vocational Qualifications
March 1987	Higginson Committee convened
June 1988	Higginson Committee reports
July 1988	Education Reform Act receives royal assent
August 1988	GCSEs awarded to 16 year olds — 1st time
December 1988	Department of Employment — creation of TECs
February 1989	Department of Education — call for core studies
August 1989	SEAC report on 16-19 core studies
October 1989	CBI publishes 'Towards a Skills Revolution'
April 1990	Training credits pilot in 11 TECs
June 1990	HMC calls for retention of 'A' levels
December 1990	Government allows schools to offer BTEC
March 1991	Government plans to centralise FE funding
May 1991	Government white paper — Education and Training for the 21st century
July 1991	Ministers pledge to 'world class' education and training targets
October 1991	Queen's speech announces the establishment of an independent FE sector and the abolition of the 'binary' line in higher education
December 1991	Completion of the TEC network
September 1992	Introduction of GNVQs
March 1992	Further and Higher Education Act receives royal assent
May 1994	Competitiveness: Helping Business to Win
November 1994	Introduction of Modern Apprenticeships
May 1995	Government paper: Competitiveness: Forging Ahead
June 1995	Department for Education and Department of Employment merge
July 1995	Review of 16-19 qualifications — Dearing

(adapted from Richardson, Woolhouse and Finegold, 1993: p. 2)

Appendix 2 NVQ framework — Sport and Recreation

LEVEL 1	Sport and Recreation — consists of seven units and is appropriate for new entrants to the industry.
LEVEL 2	Three separate qualifications are available a: Sport and Recreation Facility Operations b: Sport and Recreation Coaching and Activity Delivery Adults c: Sport and Recreation Coaching and Activity Delivery Children
LEVEL 3	Six separate qualifications are available a: Sport and Recreation Coaching Adults b: Sport and Recreation Coaching Children c: Sport and Recreation — Coaching Participants with Disabilities d: Sport and Recreation — Supervision e: Sport and Recreation Development f: Sport and Recreation Outdoor Education
LEVEL 4	Two qualifications which are connected with the Management and Development Charter Initiative a: Sport and Recreation Management (Facilities) b: Sport and Recreation Management (Sports Development) (Sport and Recreation Lead Body — 1992)
PLAY	Playwork is represented at three levels: a. Playwork level 2 b. Playwork level 3 c. Playwork level 4
NEW AREAS	New vocational standards in the following areas are now available or close to being available: a. Sports Therapy b. Spectator Control c. Sports Administration d. Plant Operators e. Safety on Open Water

Missing Services: Leisure Management Textbooks and the Concept of Services Management

Bob Lentell

University of North London

Leisure Management Education — a failing tradition?

Several authors have discussed the problems inherent in the whole notion of leisure management as a professional category. For example, both Henry (1993) and Haywood (1994) cover the tensions set up when the ethos of management is incorporated into a professional self-definition. The issues raised by these authors will continue to be of importance to professionals and their educators.

However, the issue addressed in this paper is rather different from the ones dealt with in those debates. Whatever the drawbacks of 'leisure management' as a category, educators in Higher Education today are confronted with the task of preparing students to compete in the jobs market for 'leisure management' posts, or with the work of delivering in-service education to professionals who see themselves as leisure managers. As the leisure sector becomes more heavily professionalised, several H.E. institutions have established post-graduate leisure management courses. This maturation is testing the conceptual framework of leisure management in the sense that it brings into sharper relief the ability of that framework to sustain analysis and development of corporate policy and strategy.

Thus we are forced to view the debate on leisure management through another lens. The subject of our analysis is not the ability of the leisure management tradition to articulate with the policy or social welfare concerns of the public sector, but its ability live up to its promise to provide the conceptual equipment for management across all sectors. At the risk of overstating the case, the question faced in this paper is if the intellectual tradition of leisure management is succeeding in its own terms. For example, is it able to provide an adequate conceptual framework for such central management functions as leisure operations and leisure marketing? All leisure service organisations have operations to manage, and marketing whilst clearly relevant to the commercial sector, has also gained in significance for public sector providers operating within the 'contract culture'. Operations management and marketing are of critical importance for consideration of other organisational processes, such as those associated with customer and staff relations. They also form essential elements in building a corporate strategy framework for leisure service organisations.

The spur for the research described below has been a growing sense of dissatisfaction with the conceptual underpinning provided by leisure management textbooks available for use in Higher Education. The hypothesis examined is that these textbooks have not yet articulated with the developing fields of services operations management and services marketing.

Leisure management, services operations management and services marketing

The art of managing leisure experiences is an ancient one, certainly as old as the amphitheatre, tavern or circus. Yet the category of 'leisure management' is a recent construct. It is only twelve years since the appearance of the first UK textbook and eleven since the Yates Committee gave official blessing to the notion of 'recreation management'. These past few years have seen an extraordinary development (perhaps an over-development) based upon this leisure management paradigm. There is an active trade press; aspiring professionals study at colleges and universities throughout the UK, academic publishers regularly supply new titles. In this short period a recognisable leisure management intellectual tradition, even an orthodoxy, has grown up.

The aim of what follows is to sketch the development of two other youthful disciplines, namely services operations management and services marketing which are relevant to design and delivery in leisure. It should be noted that the subject is services, not service. That is, the focus is upon service industries rather than upon related, but rather different areas, such as internal customers, customer care and after sales service, which are also important issues for non-service industries.

The origins of operations management lie in the quantitatively based production management which emerged from World War 2. As the discipline spread to include design and all other aspects of the product cycle, the terminology of operations seemed more appropriate. A number of definitions of the subject have been attempted, this author preferring the conciseness of Johnston et al., (1993: p.5):

> Operations management is concerned with the design, planning, operation and control of the use of resources to produce goods and services for customers.

Johnston and his co-authors go on to point out the central problem facing operations managers (p. 5):

> The dilemma, or challenge, facing operations managers is how, with limited resources, to try to meet the needs of their customers in the most cost-effective way.

In a discipline concerned with efficiency and effectiveness, it is not surprising to find strong echoes of 'scientific management'. However, since the 1960s the influence of systems theories has been a significant trend. Thus an organisational system represented in simple form (see Figure 1) underpins much of operations management.

Figure 1   Organisation as a simple process

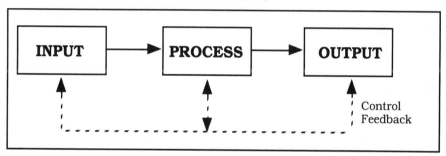

During the 1970s, the growing weight of services within advanced economies prompted the development of a new branch of the discipline. Since the ground-breaking work of Sasser *et al.,* (1978), a new approach to services operations management has grown up. It is now clear that much of what was previously accepted as 'operations' must be seen as specific to 'manufacturing operations'.

The orthodox view of the reasons for the management differences between manufacturing and services has been well rehearsed elsewhere and is summarised by Payne (1993: p. 7):

> Intangibility — services are to a large extent abstract and intangible.

> Heterogeneity — services are non-standard and highly variable.

> Inseparability — services are typically produced and consumed at the same time, with customer participation in the process.

> Perishability — it is not possible to store services in inventory.

In spite of these developments, operations management as a subject remains dominated by its manufacturing heritage. Whilst the literature on services operations is extensive and vigorous, there is as yet only a small, though increasing, range of textbooks available to help students develop their understanding of services operations management.

So in services, the presence of the customer in the production process means that how the service is produced is as important as what is produced[1]. Moreover, it is not possible to produce the service and then sell or market it; marketing must take place before and during production. So an important point is that in services, the production process is a key part of marketing. In a sense, every leisure service user survey which ascertains that many customers found out about the service through 'word of mouth', is a statement of the truth of this fact. A good service product, delivered well, will please customers, cause them to come back and to 'sell' the service to others. One suspects that in many leisure services the de-marketing flowing from faulty or inappropriate operations processes must counter-act the effectiveness of promotional campaigns. Thus for leisure, as in other traded services, operations and marketing are essentially two sides of the same coin.

Palmer (1994) (p. xv) has observed that the marketing tradition developed for consumer goods industries cannot simply be applied to services:

> ...it is now recognised that services can be quite different to goods in how they should be marketed, and some of the tried and tested frameworks for analysis cannot sensibly be stretched to cover services.

Significant steps have been made in the development of services marketing as a distinctive branch. A central ingredient has been the extension of the standard '4P' Marketing Mix, through additional 'Ps' which reflect service operations processes. The version put forward by Booms and Bitner (1981) perhaps has particular applicability to leisure services:

* Product
* Price
* Place
* Promotion
* Participants (Service personnel, customers)
* Physical Evidence (Environment provided by the service outlet plus tangibles which the service involves)
* Process (How the customer is brought to the service and the service is brought to the customer)

Good textbooks on services marketing are now available, which explore the inter-penetration of operations and marketing activities.

It has been convenient for the purposes of this paper to keep separate the subjects of operations and marketing. However they are both present in the new multi-functional discipline of 'services management', which aims to integrate these elements with human resources, financial and strategic considerations. Textbooks such as those of Grönroos (1990), Lovelock (1992) or Fitzsimmons (1994) are also significant in this respect.

Services management has typically conceived of itself as 'different' from Fordist manufacturing. As manufacturing increasingly becomes post-Fordist and the competitive regime undergoes fundamental shifts, it has a tendency to look more like service. This 'servitisation' of manufacturing is prompting a reassessment of services management paradigms (e.g. see Jones and Hall, 1995).

These substantial developments in services thinking have obvious implications for leisure services and for educators of leisure management professionals. In some respects, leisure is one of the purest examples of service, since the service product, the leisure experience, is one of the least tangible. Many leisure services will also score highly on any measures of heterogeneity, inseparability and perishability. In consequence, the additional three 'Ps' of Booms and Bitner's marketing mix have particular relevance for leisure services. What is less clear is how the leisure management tradition has responded.

Method

As a means of assessing these impacts, eighteen UK and seventeen North American leisure management textbooks intended for use in higher education or by management professionals were scanned for service operations management and marketing content. Those texts which deal purely with aspects such as leisure studies or policy were not selected for analysis. Of the texts selected, several deal with leisure management on a sector-wide basis, whilst others deal with a leisure specialism of some kind.

Although a general examination of the texts was made for service operations management and services marketing content, special attention was given to the three conceptual 'markers' referred to above. That is, a special interrogation was made for coverage of the differences between services and manufacturing, for the use of systems models for customer processes and for use of a services marketing mix.

This method gives an indication of the intellectual influences upon leisure management students and their educators. These influences may be transmitted on to the profession through both pre-service and in-service education and training. It cannot be claimed that there is a direct link between textbooks and the professional world-view of leisure managers. However, as leisure management education becomes more established, the significance of the conceptual framework offered by the key textbooks is likely to grow.

Leisure management, services operations management and marketing: a case of parallel development

Of the UK textbooks, amongst the most significant for operations management content are those written or edited by Torkildsen, Badmin, Buswell and Hebden. The volume edited by Mills is also significant as it deals with an issue, quality, which is clearly an operations management concern. Similarly, the texts by Craig, Leadley and Stone, with their focus upon marketing, are also of particular interest here. Other texts, particularly those in the Longman/ILAM series, deal with policy and management for a particular part of the leisure industry.

Torkildsen's (1992) influential and wide-ranging textbook does not unpack the concept of service, or provide service operations concepts. Buswell (1993) sketches in some operations concepts in the introduction to his text attempting to apply these to leisure. However, he has difficulty in applying the operations management systems view to leisure services. He concentrates upon the flow of resources within the service system and therefore loses focus on the customer experience. Lovelock's (1983) classification of services examines the 'nature of the service act' and distinguishes between 'Things' and 'People' and as direct recipients of the service. In other words, we should recognise the differences between those services which consist of actions being performed upon something belonging to the customer from those in which the customer is receiving a treatment of some kind, and in which customers are consequently within the main operating system. One suspects that Buswell has looked to the former type of service (which admittedly form the 'norm' in the services operations literature) to provide a model for leisure which is surely an example of the latter type of service. An alternative system is provided in section five below.

Torkildsen (1993), makes use of the kind of flow charts often used in services operations management, but these hardly develop into a service system view.

Crump and Clowes, writing in the volume edited by Mills (1992), make a useful contribution in the context of leisure marketing. An insightful, though necessarily brief, application of services marketing principles to sport and recreation is provided by Craig (1992). Torkildsen (1992) provides a fifth 'P' — Performance post-purchase — but does not discuss it (each of the other four Ps has its own section). In a rather similar manner, Leadley's (1992) volume explains the four characteristics of services, and mentions the extended services marketing mix, but discounts its significance for leisure. Thus he offers a treatment for leisure services which is essentially identical to that which he provides for leisure consumer goods.

One must conclude that although there are partial exceptions, generally the UK texts have not reflected the great advances made in thinking on services operations management and marketing since the late 70s. In consequence, the way 'leisure management' has conceived of issues such as quality and capacity management, customer relations and programming often seems curiously dated, and the language used is redolent of manufacturing management. Even where the focus is on 'operations' (e.g. Badmin *et al.*, 1992; or Badmin, 1993) or an operations-based topic such as service quality (e.g. Mills op. cit.) the work is open to the criticism that it lacks a credible theoretical framework. Similar problems beset the work of both Stone and Leadley with regard to leisure services marketing.

It is difficult to understand why this neglect of services operations management and marketing should have come about, particularly when one recognises the frequent use of leisure industry examples and cases by the authors of textbooks on operations and marketing (e.g. Voss *et al.*, 1985; Johnston *et al.*, 1993; Palmer, 1994). It may be that there has simply been insufficient time for these ideas to percolate through. Or perhaps leisure management writers have sought to apply more established management principles and disciplines to leisure facilities and services. As a new discipline, leisure management needed to unite the dissimilar conceptual universes of 'leisure' and 'management'. It would be understandable if it was the management mainstream which was trawled, rather than emergent operations management or services marketing theory.

Yet another interpretation is based upon the public/private sector considerations. Services operations management and services marketing developed from consideration of commercial operations; as disciplines they may be, or may be perceived as being, less familiar with the public sector. There are examples of specialists in public sector management building upon these services paradigms in order to develop their own work; this is particularly noticeable in the field of quality management of public services. Perhaps services operations management and marketing have been much less cognisant of the major differences between commercial and public sector services. Leisure management as a professional self-definition in the UK, had its origins in the 1970s 'boom' in provision by local authorities, and remains heavily influenced by public sector management imperatives. Thus it could be argued that in applying these disciplines to it, one has to make a difficult double adaptation, both to leisure and to public service. One notes that hospitality management, and to some extent travel and tourism, where the issues and concerns are often close to those of leisure management, appear to have HE textbooks which better reflect developments in services operations and marketing. Of course, these occupations are primarily rooted in the commercial sector.

Another explanation is that the UK has followed the United States, where leisure management publishing has a somewhat longer pedigree. Modern US textbooks, with one or two exceptions, largely follow in the footsteps of writers such as Meyer and Brightbill (1956), and of Rodney (1964) who pioneered a literature aimed at the substantial public parks and recreation sector. In the North American books examined, one finds scant recognition of operations management as a discipline. No adequate exposition of services operations or services marketing concepts could be found in the books analysed. A standard textbook such as Kraus and Curtis (in its fifth [1990] edition) whilst enumerating some features of operations management and systems models does not allow them to provide a framework for a treatment of, for example, customer relations, or marketing. Similarly the systems models familiar to operations management do not appear in Murphy *et al.*,'s (1991) intriguingly entitled volume.

The marketing section of Kraus and Curtis' book, included for the first time in this edition, is a lucid exposition of the main tenets of the marketing tradition. Consideration is given to some of the issues involved in adapting this tradition to the public sector, but there is no mention of the adaptations necessary in order to adapt it to services.

More encouragingly, some recent papers by US academics have attempted to apply mainstream services quality management ideas to leisure services. Yet this kind of work remains to be taken to the heart of 'leisure management'; service operations management/marketing and leisure management seem to remain on their parallel tracks.

There are reasons for being concerned at this state of affairs. First, the current thinking appears to equate leisure operations management with the technical or day-to-day, and marketing with promotion and selling. The strategic dimension is obscured. This may be connected with the findings of Dibb and Simpkin's (1993) study of leisure services marketing, that leisure service organisations lacked a strategic view of marketing. Second, many concerns which are central both to operations management and services marketing theory, such as quality and customer relations, are peripheral to traditional management concerns. There is a risk that professionals will see these issues as 'fads' rather than as something that should lie at the heart of their professional world-view. Third, public sector leisure managers are facing a whole raft of changes associated with the changing nature of local government. It is difficult to see how they can be best placed to optimise the outcomes for the services they provide without a deep understanding of service processes. Fourth, we live in an age where leisure and recreational provision increasingly inter-penetrates with other forms of activity: holidays are based around sporting pursuits, hotels provide leisure clubs and restaurants provide children's play facilities. There is surely a benefit in leisure management getting out of the ghetto to articulate with the conceptual framework in use elsewhere.

Where to now? Leisure management as services management

Much has been achieved in a comparatively short period through leisure management publishing and through related developments in HE course provision. However, it has been suggested above that the trajectory of this publishing is not one that can sustain the future direction of a HE subject or a professional conceptual framework. It is surely time for a critical reappraisal.

Below are briefly outlined two conceptual models which may have considerable integrative power for the development of leisure management as a branch of services management. Although both models are nearly ten years old now, they seem to have been over-looked by leisure management writers.

One of the features of leisure management is the need for continual development and launch of new service products. This arises not only through the particular influences of fashion and fad upon many sectors of the leisure service economy, but also through the inherently short-lived nature of many leisure service products. A course of swimming lessons, or a cinema film run, come to an end and have to be replaced through the programming process. It is therefore as important for leisure managers at operational level as for those at strategic level to be able to develop service products appropriate both to market conditions and organisational mission. What is required therefore is a means of integrating these within the limits of the operating system.

Heskett's (1986) treatment of services suggests four basic elements of a strategic service vision: target market segments, service concept, operating strategy and service delivery system. It is likely that a change in any one of these will have an effect on the other elements. A service organisation may bring these elements in a harmonious relation through the use of three integrating elements: positioning, value/cost leveraging and strategy/system integration, as shown in Heskett's diagram (see Figure 2). The value of the model shown in Figure 2 for leisure management education is that it offers the possibility of opening up the strategic service discourse (through a discussion of elements on the left of the above diagram) without disconnecting from the operational concerns (on the right of the diagram). In fact the relationship between corporate policy, strategy and operations is much clearer than in the leisure management mainstream texts.

The idea of the service delivery system is as central to marketing-led approaches to services as it is to services operations management. Yet, apart from Buswell (*op. cit.*) attempts have not been made to model this system. In discussions with leisure management professionals, the author has found the work of Johnston and Morris (1987) a particularly fruitful starting point. Johnston and Morris dissent from the orthodox view that intangibility, heterogeneity, inseparability and perishability constitute the defining characteristics of services. They suggest that a key factor is the nature of what is being processed. In manufacturing industries the primary operations are concerned with the transformation of materials into goods; in services they are concerned with the transformation of customers into 'treated' customers. It is the presence of customers within the key processes which give services their special characteristics. Thus a defining

Figure 2

Integrative elements of a strategic service vision

KEY:

Basic elements
representing the key issues which a service organisation must address in order to thrive

Integrative elements
identifying the issues which must be tackled in order that the basic elements can harmoniously articulate

Source: Heskett, 1986

Target Market Segments

What are common characteristics of important market segments?

What dimensions can be used to segment the market?

Demographic?

Psychographic?

How important are various segments?

What needs does each have?

How well are these needs being served?

In what manner?

By whom?

Positioning

How does the service concept propose to meet customer needs?

How do competitors meet these needs?

How is the proposed service difference from competition?

How important are these differences?

What is good service?

Does the proposed service concept provide it?

What efforts are required to bring customer expectations and service capabilities into alignment?

Service Concept

What are important elements of the service to be provided, stated in terms of results produced for customers?

How are these elements supposed to be perceived by the target market segment?

By the market in general?

By employees as a whole?

How is the service concept perceived?

What efforts does this suggest in terms of the manner in which the service is:

Designed?

Delivered?

Marketed?

Value / Cost Leveraging	Operating Strategy	Strategy / System Integration	Service Delivery System
To what extent are differences between perceived value and cost of service maximised by:	What are important elements of the strategy?	To what extent are the strategy and delivery system internally consistent?	What are important features of the service delivery system, including:
Standardisation of certain elements?	Operations?		The role of people?
Customization of certain elements?	Financing?	Can the needs of the strategy be met by the delivery system?	Technology?
	Marketing?		Equipment?
	Organization?		Layout?
Emphasising easily leveraged services?	Human resources?	If not, what changes can be made in:	Procedures?
	Control?		
Management of supply and demand?		The operating strategy?	
	On which will the most effort be concentrated?	The service delivery system?	What capacity does it provide:
Control of quality through:	Where will investments be made?		Normally? At peak levels?
Rewards?		To what extent does the coordination of operating strategy and service delivery system insure:	To what extent does it:
Appeal to pride?			
Visibility / supervision?	How will quality and cost be controlled?		Help insure quality standards?
Peer group control?	Measures?	High quality?	
Involving the customer?	Incentives?	High productivity?	Differentiate the service from competition?
	Rewards?	Low cost?	
Effective use of data?		High morale and loyalty of servers?	Provide barriers to entry by competition?
	What results will be expected versus competition in terms of:		
To what extent does this effort create barriers to entry by potential competition?	Quality of service?	To what extent does this integration provide barriers to entry to competition?	
	Cost profile?		
	Productivity?		
	Morale / loyalty of servers?		

Figure 3 A leisure service operating system

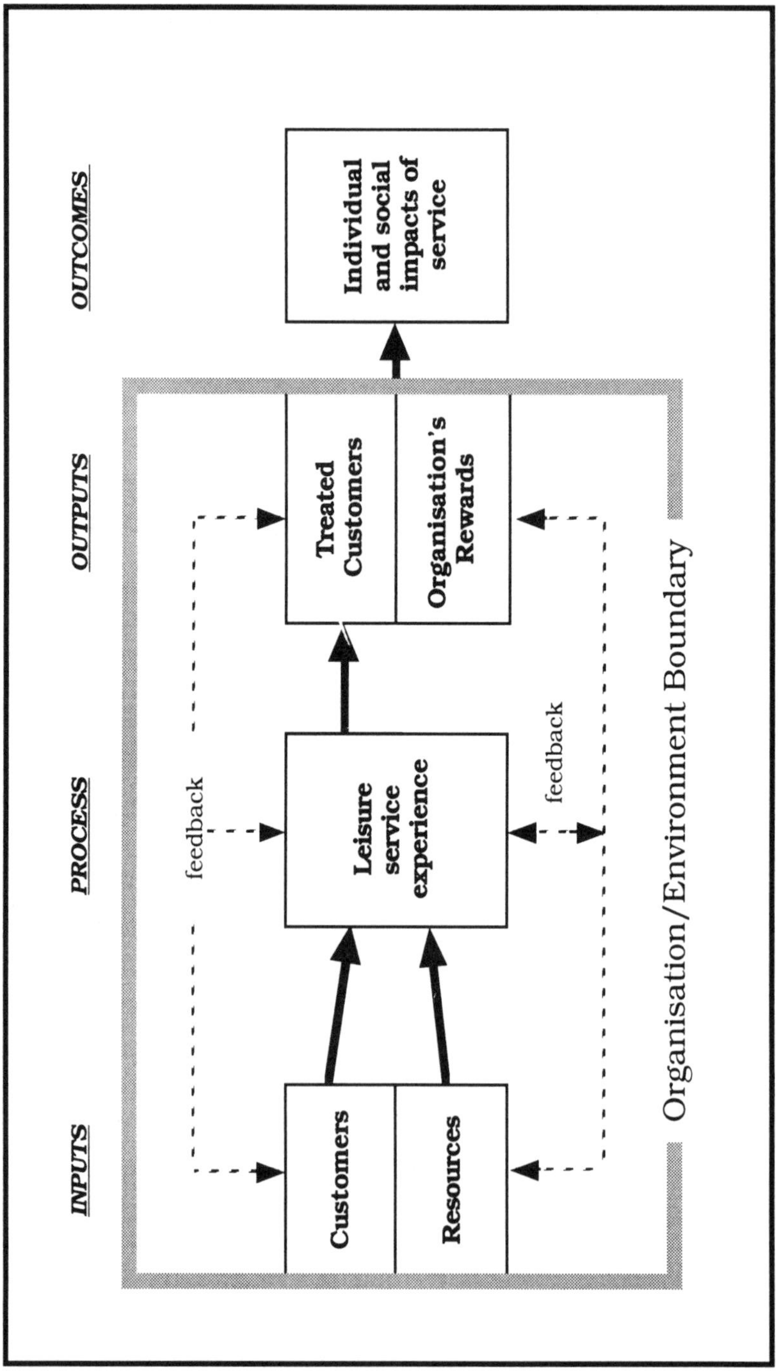

characteristic of service organisations is that they are Customer Processing Organisations. From their work, a simple representation of a leisure service operating system could be developed (see Figure 3).

The benefit of the schema is that it provides a starting place for an exploration of the inter-relationships between desired and actual outcomes, outputs, service processes and variation in inputs (especially in terms of the variety of customers and their expectations).

Some conclusions

Examination of leisure management textbooks reveals a startling lack of recognition of developments within services operations management and services marketing over the last twenty years. In terms of the HE textbook stock, it appears that leisure management as a subject is not well placed to enter into a creative relationship with the emerging cross-functional discipline of services management.

At undergraduate level it may be possible for educators to 'get away with' recommending textbooks which essentially re-work concepts drawn from manufacturing management. However, this approach cannot be sustained at postgraduate level where the focus must be upon policy and strategy issues. Courses will have to draw upon non-leisure specific texts upon services management in order to unpack issues at this level. Two models have been highlighted above which may assist in the unpacking process.

If the textbooks reflect the intellectual development of leisure managers, and there are some pointers that they do, other issues of concern may be identified. A justification for the amalgamation of the diverse conceptual universes of 'leisure' and 'management' into the self-definition of leisure professionals in the UK has been that it identifies a territory which can be protected from the managerial ambitions of other professional groups which have no leisure specific expertise. The growth of the Institute of Leisure and Amenity Management (ILAM), is witness to the success of this approach. However, ILAM remains based in the public sector with far less influence in the commercial sector of leisure, apart from those firms involved in running contracts for local authorities.

It appears that the leisure management textbook stock largely reflects and reinforces the public sector origins of professionalisation. But the long-term success of this professionalisation project

can only be maintained if the management tradition in use is one which can be applied to the problems of the day. If one speculates that 'leisure management' is constrained by the narrowness of the management tradition upon which it draws, then it follows that leadership of leisure service organisations in both the commercial and public sectors will be gained by those operating from more dynamic intellectual perspectives, such as marketing or services management.

Note

[1]   "Customer" is used throughout this paper to denote "external end-user". That is, it is intended to cover those who pay directly to use a service, and those who make no direct payment for the service they receive (e.g. users of an urban park).

References:

Badmin, P. Coombs, M. and Raynor, G. (1992) *Leisure operational management Volume 1 (Facilities)*. London: Longman.

—— (1993) *Leisure operational management Volume 2 (People)*. London: Longman.

Booms B. and Bitner, M. (1981) 'Marketing strategies and organisation structures for service firms', in D. Donnelly and W. George (eds) *Marketing of services, Proceedings series*. Chicago: American Marketing Association.

Buswell, J. (ed) (1993) *Case studies in leisure management practice*. London: Longman.

Crump, S. and Clowes, J. (1992) 'Marketing', in P. Mills (ed) *Quality in the leisure industry*. London: Longman.

Craig, S. (1992) 'Marketing: The principles' and 'Marketing: The marketing plan', in *Sports Council Recreation Management — Facilities Factfile 1*. London: Sports Council.

Dibb, S. and Simpkin, L. (1993) 'Strategy and tactics: Marketing leisure facilities', *The Service Industries Journal*, Vol. 13, No. 3: pp. 110-124.

Fitzsimmons, J. and Fitzsimmons, M. (1994) *Service management for competitive advantage*. New York: McGraw-Hill.

Grönroos, C. (1990) *Service management and marketing: Managing the moments of truth in service competition*. Singapore: Maxwell Macmillan Publishing.

Kraus, R. and Curtis, J. (1990) *Creative management in recreation, parks and leisure services*. St Louis: Times Mirror/Mosby College.

Haywood, L . (1994) 'Concepts and practice in community leisure and recreation', in L. Haywood (ed) *Community leisure and recreation*. London: Butterworth-Heinemann, pp. 26-50.

Hebden, R. (ed) (1992) *ILAM guide to good practice in leisure management*. London: Longman.

Henry, I. (1993) *The politics of leisure policy*. London: Macmillan, pp. 112-137.

Heskett, J. (1986) *Managing in the service economy.* Boston: HBS Press..

Johnston, R. *et al.,* (1993) *Cases in operations management.* London: Pitman

Johnston, R. and Morris, B. (1987) 'Dealing with inherent variability: The difference between manufacturing and service?', *International Journal of Operations and Production Management,* Vol. 7, No. 4: pp. 13-22.

Jones, P. and Hall, M. (1995) 'Now listen! Services operations really are different...sort of', in R. Teare and C. Armistead (eds) *Services management: New directions, new perspectives.* London: Cassell, pp. 174-177.

Leadley, P. (1992) *Leisure marketing.* London: Longman.

Lovelock, C. (1983) 'Classifying services to gain strategic marketing insights', *Journal of Marketing,* Vol. 47, Summer 1983: pp. 9-20.

―――― (ed) (1992) *Managing services: Marketing, operations and human resources.* London: Prentice Hall International.

Meyer, H. and Brightbill, C. (1956) *Recreation administration: A guide to its practice.* Englewood-Cliffs: Prentice-Hall.

Mills, P. (ed) (1992) *Quality in the leisure industry.* London: Longman.

Murphy, J. *et al..* (1991) *Leisure systems: Critical concepts and applications.* Champaign, IL: Sagamore.

Palmer, A. (1994) *The principles of services marketing.* London: McGraw-Hill.

Payne, A. (1993) *The essence of services marketing.* London: Prentice Hall.

Rodney, L. (1964) *Administration of public recreation.* New York: Ronald Press.

Sasser, W., Olsen, R. and Wyckoff, D. (1978) *Management of services operations.* Boston: Allyn and Bacon.

Torkildsen, G. (1992) *Leisure and recreation management.* London: Spon.

―――― (1993) *Tokildsen's guides to leisure management.* London: Longman.

Voss, C. *et al.,* (1985) *Operations management in service industries and the public sector.* London: Wiley.

Part V

Young People, Games and Sport

Team Games in the National Curriculum: The Relevance of Rugby Union Football

Andrew White

North Hampshire Business School, Farnborough

The aim of this paper is to provide a response to the Conservative government's policy of extending, compulsorily, the participation in team games in the National Curriculum to the 14-16 year old age group. Rugby union football as one of the specified team sports is the focus of this response. The paper will begin with an overview of the social development of rugby union football concluding with contemporary processes of commercialisation and the current stage in the transition from amateurism to professionalism. This will assist in identifying the values embedded in rugby union, through the amateur ethos, that appear to form the basis of the attraction of rugby to policy makers. Two issues, the implications of this policy on the construction of gender relations and on the use of schools' physical education as a vehicle for provision will be explored before attention is turned to the likely impact implementation will have on schools and rugby clubs.

Dunning and Sheard (1979) have identified five overlapping stages in the development of modern rugby football, each with more complex rules, organisation and behaviour restraints than the previous stage. They are, chronologically:

i)   from the 14th Century into the 19th Century, a stage of relatively rough, wild and simple games with generally unwritten rules;

ii) from about 1750 to about 1840, when rugby began to emerge as a distinctive game from after being taken up by public school boys;

iii) from about 1830 to 1860, a stage of rapid transition with codification, formal and self-regulation as distinctive features — an 'incipient modernisation' stage. Soccer (Association Football) also emerged at this stage as a specific game-form;

iv) from about 1850 to about 1900 when rugby football diffused into society at large, national associations were set up (the Rugby Football Union (RU) and the Football Association (FA)) and paying spectators were attracted to both games. At this time rugby split into League and Union forms;

v) a stage from about 1900 to the present in which the characteristics of modern sport outlined earlier developed in Rugby Union. Salient features of development during this period were:

• antagonism to professionalism;

• distrust of spectators;

• emphasis on 'player-centredness' and character forming aspects, by an increasingly bureaucratised governing body;

• transformation of the game into a rationalised 'achievement-oriented' pursuit;

• conflict between leading clubs and the 'governing body' (RFU).

During the period from the turn of the century Dunning and Sheard (1979) identify a number of unintended and unforeseen consequences accompanying the expansion of Rugby Union (pp. 232-268). They were:

• the growth of bureaucratic control;

• the development of a rank hierarchy of clubs;

• the rise of gate-taking clubs.

Within these developments the ethos of the game has changed towards 'spectator' rather than a 'player-centred' ethos necessitating ideological changes in attitudes to amateurism. Furthermore the playing of Rugby Union particularly at the top levels and through the 'junior' clubs has become more serious and dedicated leading to a growing 'scientific' management of the playing side, evidence of an emerging professionalisation of functions other than playing the game. Finally the organisation of the game has come to be based on Cups, domestic and international, and league formats, i.e. the institutionalisation of a range of formal competitions.

Throughout this century there is evidence of a limited process of 'democratisation' of Rugby Union. It has tended to diffuse, in playing terms, through the middle-class but has stopped at the boundary between the middle and working classes. It also generally retains its class exclusivity, exceptions in England being Gloucester RFC and to a lesser extent Orrell. Important in this regard is the nature of the values bound up with this middle-class membership and in particular the ethos of voluntary association (i.e. unpaid playing, coaching and administrative duties). This came into conflict with the growing bureaucratisation and professionalisation of the national organisation at Twickenham — processes which were also occurring in the major clubs, financed largely by income from gate-receipts. Dunning and Sheard (1979) suggest that improvements in the facilities and organisation of clubs represent a shift towards professionalism on the grounds that 'player performance' (more accurately the conditions for the execution of player performance) become subject to economic exchange. Thus, whilst there existed official resistance to players receiving direct material benefit, in cash terms this was not so in the case of the clubs, who at the time were becoming unequal in terms of playing strengths and were therefore demanding reorganisation based on leagues. They were perhaps at a stage of 'incipient commercialisation' with bureaucratic and professional structures coming into place.

The stage from the 1960s onwards was characterised by a transition from player-centred to spectator-centred development of rugby and in consequence ideological work by the RFU in the form of a reaffirmation of traditional amateur values. The reasons for this transition were:

- to win back spectators who were switching to Rugby League;
- the competitive tensions generated by the international diffusion of rugby;
- pressure from domestic 'gate-taking' clubs over league and cup competitions;
- the growing dependence of the RFU and major clubs on gate money, revenues from increasing media coverage, and associated advertising revenue and commercial sponsorship.

This spectator-centred development was met with changes in the laws of the game to meet their needs as perceived by both the RFU and media interest. On the level of amateur values however 'accommodating' work needed to be done. Thus in general law changes were justified as being 'in the interest of the player'. However, this was not the only pressure on the amateur ethos. Growing competitiveness was beginning to lead to greater 'seriousness' expressed through increased emphasis on training and coaching eroding the amateur ethos of 'recreational participation'. Dunning and Sheard (1979) present evidence that this development was more or less accepted by players and administrators in the major clubs creating at the very least, opportunities for a process of 'attitudinal professionalism' to develop. At the same time although players may or may not have received payments directly from their clubs it was becoming clear that top players were receiving financial rewards from their position as top class sportsmen. The national RFU then found itself increasingly witnessing an erosion of amateur ideals through demands for competitive playing structures, growing spectator interest in the game and its attendant commercialisation and as an early stage in this process the 'monetisation' of rugby.

Furthermore the growing 'seriousness' of senior club rugby placed emphasis on coaching and training in contrast to the 'recreational' elements. In 1976 the ground the RFU chose to fight on was the introduction of leagues and cups. Indeed the emergence of professionalisation as an issue in the mid-late 1980s can be traced to the debate over the increased competitiveness that the introduction of league structures would bring. Since then leagues have become institutionalised in the organisation of rugby. One would therefore expect the RFU to fight on a major element of the 'amateur ethos' that of player payment.

It is possible therefore to suggest (tentatively) that, with historical roots in previous stages, the development of rugby union is in a sixth stage occurring around the mid-1980s. This stage is characterised by a number of overlapping features notably the re-emergence of the amateur-professional debate, the extension of formal domestic and international competitive structures, continuing global diffusion of rugby amongst a growing but still limited number of countries and an acceleration of the process of commercialisation.

On the basis of the evidence available it is plausible to suggest that there has been an acceleration of the process of commercialisation from around the time of the introduction of cup and league structures in the early to mid-1980s. However this is not to identify this development as a casual factor. The introduction of these competitions can be seen as just as much a result of commercialising pressures as a further stimulus to the process. The commercial activity has been wide-ranging in the search for sponsors, the growth of revenue from TV broadcasting rights, merchandising, corporate hospitality packages and the growth of spectator revenues.

Smith and Williams (1980) draw attention to the social context of this development. In a somewhat deterministic interpretation of commercial influences in Welsh rugby they suggest:

> Sport mirrored a society where market forces predominated: if supply was to keep pace with demand, the spectator appeal of rugby needed to be sustained by making the product more interesting. The provision of increased facilities was one way of obtaining this end; the extension of fixture lists was another. (p. 10)

I would also add *rule changes* to their list which have also added to spectator appeal. During the process of commercialisation all of these strategies have been utilised. The decline in the relative importance of the County and Divisional Championships may point to 'supply' outstripping 'demand'. This section then is an attempt to recognise that development in this particular 'figuration' cannot be detached from the general social framework of social relations in a modern industrial society. Dunning and Sheard (1979: p. 148) draw attention to this connection with commercialisation:

> At a deeper level, however, money and professionalism is what is at stake. In our view, that is necessarily the case for, in capitalist societies, there is an inexorable tendency for sports to be bound up with money values.

Further empirical investigation is needed to assess the importance of economic relations and the relative autonomy of rugby union from capitalist power-relations. It is however ironic that both players and administrators are quoted as regarding the process of professionalisation as 'inevitable', rhetoric one would more usually associate with the proponents of a deterministic form of Marxist historical materialism. There is clearly a symbiotic relationship between commercialisation and professionalisation of this sport — aptly illustrated by the acceleration of the latter process through the competitive battle between media entrepreneurs Packer and Murdoch. It was essentially their intervention that both enabled players to achieve a shift in power-ratios of sufficient magnitude to generate change and exposed the hierarchy of power-relations rugby administrators attempt to reproduce with respect to playing personnel.

Embedded in the social development of rugby and under threat from contemporary processes, are the principles and ethics of amateur sport that appeal to policy makers as a form of social discipline. The Duke of Edinburgh, President of the Physical Education Association, claimed:

> I am convinced that participation in sport, particularly in organised team games, teaches some of the most basic lessons in civilised behaviour. Team games are exercises in structured co-operation .... It is the co-ordination of individual skills and team tactics and the sublimation of individual ambitions for the good of the team that brings success. That is precisely the formula that makes for successful enterprises and communities .... If sport is to be enjoyed by all participants, sportsmanship and fair play really are important factors. (*Guardian*, 7 April, 1994: p3)

The Duke also claimed that games and sports helped young people appreciate the need to abide by the law, apply it fairly and accept the decision of those employed to enforce it as well as how to win and lose gracefully, to be generous in victory and resilient in defeat.

The amateur ideal emerged from the 'sportisation' of pastimes — that is, the development of highly regulated game-contests requiring physical exertion and skill that was associated with and appeared first amongst the landed aristocracy and gentry in the 18th century. These same groups were involved in a parallel 'parliamentarization' process: the resolution of disputes according to regulated behaviours (Elias, 1986). This amateur ideal, a central issue in Victorian and Edwardian sport, became more articulated and fiercely supported at this time, perhaps as a response towards growing professionalisation of particular sports. What then were the processes at work in their social and historical context that came to define the 'amateur' and the 'professional' in the late 1800s and why at this point in English sporting and social history did this distinction emerge as an issue?

The ethos of amateurism, honour, dignified and respectable behaviour, maintaining self control, behaviour in victory and defeat, emphasis on performance and qualities of courage and playing for fun were transmitted first through the most aristocratic public schools and then the Oxbridge Universities by pupils and ex-pupils who were part of the development of 'modern sports' and the 'athletic' ideal (Holt, 1992). These, 'articles of faith' based on gentlemanly behaviour were not universally accepted, particularly by working class amateurs even though they accepted the principles of amateurism of 'fair competition' to common rules, emphasis on competing rather than spectating, the exclusion from the sport of those who profited financially or had an unfair advantage due to their trade and the opposition to gambling.

The 'contested' nature of amateurism gives some clues to an explanation of the social origins of the amateur ethos in sport at this time. Elias (1982) locates the impetus for this development in a wider social process of 'civilisation' of English society components being parallel processes of 'parliamentarisation', and 'sportisation' of pastimes. A further element in the latter process is suggested by Dunning and Sheard (1979). In their study of the development of rugby football they point to the withdrawal of the gentry from folk football and other sports as part of this process. This they suggest was a response to the challenge of increasing bourgeois power, firmly locating the emergence of the amateur ideal and its construction in changes in the social structure which were generating class-tensions between old and emerging social groups. Thus, the theory and practice of amateur sport appears to have emerged out of "the culture of a demilitarised, educated and economically sophisticated English elite" (Holt, 1992: p. 22). However, as Holt points out in his conclusion, this was a contested area with different constructions of amateurism according to social status. These were bound up with a mix of both aristocratic and bourgeois culture with the ethos mainly of aristocratic origin but principles and structures subject to influences from other social groups.

Three points relating to amateurism in English sport need to be drawn out. Firstly it was essentially English: As Stokvis (quoted in Mennell 1992: p. 152) observes:

> Amateurism is originally an English phenomenon. At the end of the nineteenth century Great Britain was the most influential and powerful country in the world ... England's worldwide prestige heightened the esteem in which her sportsmen were held. As a consequence of this the English were in a position to demand that amateur conditions be introduced in other countries also.

Secondly, as Eitzen (1989) and Sandiford (1985) point out, the words 'professional' and 'amateur' can have value laden meanings with the former being a 'praise' word in some occupation contexts and a 'blame' word when used in sport. It also involves not only material security but also in sport 'a yearning for artistic perfection' which transforms play into work. 'Amateur' may also have connotations of incompetence and lack of ability as well as encapsulating a moral code. Within these constructions lies a key to the emergence of the amateur ideal in mid-Victorian England. Those involved in the formulation of the amateur ideology at that time made a clear distinction between 'professionalism' which governed their working lives and 'amateurism' which governed their leisure and attempted to keep the two spheres separate in this context to avoid a level of intensity in sport which would transform play into work. Finally, Gruneau (1983) draws attention to the view that the "concept of amateurism seems to have evolved as a conscious strategy of exclusion in class relations" (p. 170). As a dominant ideology is therefore preserved for some groups a sporting advantage not only over relatively less powerful groups but also over those who, by virtue of their occupation, were deemed to have an 'unfair advantage' in sport. In this way the amateur ideal could also form the basis of wider social differentiation.

Finally, the value of participation in team sport and particularly in rugby union football, arguably a site where the ethos of amateurism has been strong, is being promoted at a time when these values are under significant threat. Rugby is clearly accommodating to processes contouring the development of the game into yet another commercialised, televised sports experience with the emphasis changing from participation to spectacle forcing administrators to confront performance-enhancing drug use amongst players and concerns over violence.

The first issue of relevance in the context of attempts to raise the participation of 14-16 year old young men in rugby is that of the impact on the construction of gender-relations. The approach to this issue in an attempt to contribute to developing the study of men and masculinity (Hall, 1990). It is based on an understanding that 'gender construction' is a process and that, given that there are competing masculinities within and between sports, this contributes to the development of a gender order. A culturally idealised form of masculine character in a particular social and historical setting can come to form a hegemonic masculinity. (Messner and Sabo, 1990). Perhaps this is best explained, albeit anecdotally for the present, with reference to rugby union football. Amongst significant groups of males rugby players are regarded as 'harder' than 'soccer players' who are regarded as being 'harder' than non-contact sportsmen e.g. badminton players. All of these groups are regarded as being physically superior than women participants. In addition, within rugby there is a distinction between the generally physically stronger and more confrontational for- wards, the 'donkeys' or 'fat boys' and the backs who are quicker and more athletic 'the girls'. Even within the forwards there is a hierarchy with front- row forwards ascribed additional status. Manifestations of this type of masculinity based almost exclusively on physical hardness and violence have been identified in rugby football and other contact sports by a number of authors [Donnelly and Young (1985), Dunning (1988, 1990), Grundigh (1994), Messner (1990), Phillips (1987)]. Thus, the particular construction of masculinity prized amongst rugby playing males contours both their relations with other males and with females.

There are however two developments that are effecting subtle changes in the attitudes of rugby playing males to women. The commercialisation of rugby has penetrated into a great many senior and junior rugby clubs and has opened up rugby clubhouses to important sponsors and their guests. In consequence it is much less appropriate for players to indulge in post-match songs relating stories of lobsters hanging from their wives' vaginas or engineers constructing sex machines of such ferocity that they split their spouses in two. However the demeaning and objectification of women is still a significant pattern of behaviour particularly amongst younger males developing their sexual identity. This and other 'rites of passage' for young males are still prevalent in many clubs.

The second feature is the growth in popularity of women's rugby which is at present confined largely to colleges and clubs. Development in this sphere has been rapid over the last 15 years with administrative structures, national leagues, domestic and world cup competitions and sponsorships in place. Comments from women players in the press seem to suggest that rugby provides access to a team-orientated contact sport that is denied them in other traditional 'feminine appropriate' sports and that socially it provides women who are less comfortable with the 'lycra, cosmetics, cattle market' night-club scene with opportunities to interact in a preferred environment. The reaction of the press has been mixed. There have been a number of instances of positive reporting (particularly Sky TV's 'Grass Roots' rugby programme, 20 September, 1994) and photographic images of women performing rugby skills mixed with traditional images of women as 'support' staff at male clubs, as wives or where the focus is on the 'unusual' physique of participants. These mixed messages, in conjunction with the denial of access of 14-16 year old women, restrict the diffusion of women's rugby into younger age groups by reinforcing gender stereotypes. Again, it would seem that the politicians have continued to ignore the earlier recommendations of the final report of the Physical Education Working Group (Department of Education and Science, 1992) with respect to issues of gender relations as constructed in physical education contexts (Hargreaves, 1994: pp. 188-192).

Before speculating on the potential impact of incorporating rugby football as a team sport into the National Curriculum for 14-16 year olds, it is perhaps worth reflecting on the vehicle through which this policy is to be delivered, that is Physical Education in schools. Increased participation in team sports have often been justified on a number of grounds, the most prevalent being the promotion of health and fitness amongst a youth population of 'couch potatoes', the production of national champions and the learning of moral values and duties. However, as Evans and Davies (1986) suggest there needs to be a more reflexive attitude amongst physical education professionals towards their practices and the rationales that sustain them. This I would suggest is of increasing importance in the light of the highly politicised process within which the construction of the National Curriculum for Physical Education takes place (Talbot, 1995). Evans and Davies (1986: p. 19) suggest questions such as:

...into what and whose values and attributes are pupils being socialised? What social, emotional (as well as physical) predispositions are required of pupils in order to take part in and succeed at 'learning' in programmes of Physical Education? What is the relationship between the cultural values which children bring to Physical Education and those which teachers require and transmit in the Physical Education curriculum?... Do schools, and Physical Education within them, reproduce existing inequalities in societies, or does Physical Education offer a medium for lessening the inequalities of opportunity, power and knowledge in our society? Is Physical Education strongly determined by wider ideological economic and cultural forces... or does it have a significant degree of autonomy? What actually happens within the Physical Education curriculum and classroom, in the social relations of teaching and learning?

It is not possible in the course of this paper to address any of these issues adequately, they are complex, conflictual and require much more attention in the way of substantive research. What is worrying is that these issues do not appear to have been addressed at the level of policy formulation. Practicalities of funding and delivery appear to receive more attention than asking the fundamental question — 'why Rugby?', or indeed 'why not Rugby?'! Alderson and Crutchley (1990) go some way in exploring this position with their contention that there is a need to question the educational applicability and value of sporting rules that have been devised by governing bodies, such as the RFU, in different contexts. This, I suggest can apply equally to moral values encapsulated in a sport and to changes in the laws of the game to enhance it's spectator appeal. Julia Bracewell, a former Olympic fencer, member of the Sports Council and a lawyer specialising in sport, reinforces this point when she claims, "I am not sure professional sport is a proper role model any longer" (*Sunday Telegraph*, 12 June, 1994). With respect to the construction of gender relations, Humberstone (1990: p. 201) points out that:

> Male hegemony is produced and perpetuated through the particular images of masculinity constituted by dominant forms of sport prevailing in our society. Sport and physical education (PE) are significant domains in which these dominant forms of masculinity are reported, but they may also be sites of contestation.

Although recognising, on the basis of research at an outdoor-activity centre, that mixed sex-groupings did generate a rethinking of gender by the boys, I would suggest that in rugby football it is less important for young women to demonstrate their physical and technical prowess in relation to men than it is for them to be given the opportunity to participate in types of physical experiences from which they have previously been excluded.

Evaluating the impact of implementing the playing of rugby football in the National Curriculum for 14-16 year olds is necessarily speculative. There is clear evidence that where young people are given a choice of physical activities, rugby football does not feature in the top ten most popular sports (Badminton topped the popularity list). Rugby was the fourth least popular sport followed by Cross Country, Hockey and Gymnastics (*Economist*, 16 January, 1993). Note, in this light, the comment by Ted Wragg that "If you make team games compulsory then you must be prepared for a plethora of sick notes" (*Daily Telegraph*, 4 September, 1994). It is unlikely, given the constraints on teachers' time and the availability of facilities, that the benefits of healthy competition between new rugby playing schools will materialise. Of the 3,000 plus schools affiliated to the English Schools RFU just over 1,000 play competitive fixtures. Offering teachers additional payments to take extra-curricular activities is divisive and devalues the efforts of other subject area specialists, for example, musicians, drama and art teachers, who already undertake such duties. The widening of participation is also likely to generate problems of incorporating social groups unused to the values and ethics of rugby football. At an under-15 club fixture parents with little attachment to or understanding of the game forced the abandonment of a match because of touchline fighting (*Daily Telegraph*, 16 December, 1994). Rugby football is one of the rougher team games and therein lies part of its appeal. However there are implications with respect to violence and injury. Research suggests that men might expect injury every 10 games, women every 17 games and youths every 23 games. Women tend to suffer concussion more than males, but injuries to males requiring sutures are predominately the result of foul play. In this regard 17% of women's injuries, 19% of youths and 33% of men's injuries were due to this feature of rugby violence (*SportCare Journal*, Vol. 1, No. 5: 1994). It is therefore to be expected that the levels and types of injuries sustained by young players will rise if more 14-16 year olds, with relatively low levels of technical proficiency in contact situations in conjunction with increasing physical strength, are forced to participate in this sport.

These deliberations are, of necessity, brief and illustrative, but there is a key assumption that underpins them. It is that the implementation of this policy involves, and perhaps is a product of, a shift in power-relations between groups involved in the figuration of school sports. It involves changing power-balances between state agencies and teachers, between groups of teachers, between teachers and pupils, young males and females, between groups of males and with rugby clubs and governing bodies. The process of implementation and acceptance of rugby football will be conflictual and contested one with outcomes that are unlikely to be intended by policy makers and implementers.

In conclusion, the stance taken in this paper is not one of an unreserved apologist for rugby union football or that of a 'sports knocker' — after all playing rugby is enjoyable. It is an attempt to take a more reflective approach to the incorporation of rugby football into a specific context. It is clear that the choice of this team game has a strong ideological basis. In the light of contemporary concerns over youth behaviours it is possible to hear the echoes of similar concerns of the middle-class proponents of rational recreation as an instrument of social discipline (Holt, 1989: p. 136-141). Elite rugby union players are being drawn into this process with repeated exhortations to curb violent play to 'set an example' to young participants (*Sunday Telegraph*, 12 June, 1994). It is worth, in bringing this paper to a close, to counterpoint this development with a view expressed by soccer player Eric Cantona (1994: p. 102):

> Ah! But what about the importance of setting an example for young people you say to me. My reply to that is I think, one should stop treating the heart and soul of youngsters as clay to be modelled in whatever fashion you like.

References

Alderson, J. and Crutchley, D. (1990) 'Physical Education and the National Curriculum', in Armstrong, N. (ed) *New directions in Physical Education* Vol. 1: Champaign, Ill.: Human Kinetics.

Cantona, E. (1994) *Eric Cantona: My story*. London: Headline.

Donnelly, P. and Young, K. (1985) 'Reproduction and transformation of cultural forms in sport. A contextual analysis of rugby', *International Review for the Sociology of Sport*, Vol. 20, No. 1: pp. 19-37.

Dunning, E. (1990) 'Women and sport: sport and gender in a patriarchal society', paper presented to World Congress of Sociology, Madrid, Spain.

Dunning, E. (1986) 'Sport as a male preserve. Notes on the social sources of masculine identity and it's transformations', in N. Elias and E. Dunning *Quest for excitement*. Oxford: Blackwell, pp. 267-283.

Dunning, E. and Sheard, K. (1979) *Barbarians, gentlemen and players*. Oxford: Martin Robertson.

Elias, N. (1986) 'The genesis of sport as a sociological problem', in N. Elias and E. Dunning *Quest for excitement*. Oxford: Blackwell, 126-149.

Elias, N. (1982) *The civilising process*. New York: Pantheon.

Eitzen, D. Stanley (1989) 'The sociology of amateur sports — an overview', *International Review for the Sociology of Sport*, Vol. 24, No. 2: pp. 95-104.

Evans, J. and Davies, B. (1986) 'Sociology, schooling and physical education', in J. Evans (ed) *Physical education, sport and schooling — studies in the sociology of physical education*. Lewes: The Falmer Press, pp. 11-37.

Grundigh, A. (1994) 'Playing for power? Rugby Afrikaner Nationalism and masculinity in South Africa c. 1900-70', *International Journal of the History of Sport*, Vol. 11, No. 3: pp. 408-249.

Gruneau, R. (1983) *Class, sport and social development*. Massachusetts: University of Massachusetts Press.

Hall, M. Ann (1990) 'How should we theorise gender in the context of sport', in M. Messner and D. Sabo (eds) *Sport, Men and the gender order. Critical feminist perspectives*. Champaign, IL: Human Kinetics, pp. 223-240.

Hargreaves, J. A. (1994) *Sporting females. Critical issues in the history and sociology of women's sports*. London: Routledge.

Holt, R. (1992) 'Amateurism and it's interpretation. The social origins of British sport', *Innovation*, Vol. 5, No. 4: pp. 19-31.

Humberstone, B. (1990) 'Warriors or wimps? Creating alternative forms of physical education' in M. Messner and D. Sabo (eds) *Sport, men and the gender order. Critical feminist perspectives*. Champaign, IL: Human Kinetics, pp. 201-210.

Mennell, S. (1992) *Norbert Elias: An introduction*. Oxford: Blackwell.

Messner, M. (1990) 'When bodies are weapons: Masculinity and violence in sport', *International Review for the Sociology of Sport*, Vol. 25, No. 3, pp. 203-217.

Messner, M. and Sabo, F. (1990) 'Towards a critical feminist reappraisal of sport, men and the gender order' M. Messner and D. Sabo (eds) *Sport, men and the gender order. Critical feminist perspectives*. Champaign, IL: Human Kinetics, pp. 1-16.

Phillips, J. (1987) *A man's country? The image of the Pakeha male: A history*. Auckland: Penguin.

Sandiford, K. A. P. (1985) 'The professionalisation of modern cricket', *British Journal of Sports History*, Vol. 2, No. 3: pp. 270-289.

Smith, D. and Williams, G. (1980) *Fields of praise*. Cardiff: University of Wales Press.

Talbot, M. (1995) 'Physical Education and the National Curriculum: Some political issues', in G. McFee and A. Tomlinson (eds) *Education, sport and leisure: Connections and controversies*. Chelsea School Topic Report No. 3. Eastbourne: University of Brighton, pp. 34-64.

Youth Sport: Motivational Approaches for Coaches

Bill Tancred

Buckinghamshire College of Higher Education

There have been numerous studies relating to young people participating in and dropping out of sport (e.g. Gould, 1982; Lee, 1985; Campbell, 1986; Tancred, 1993). While the results differ slightly from one study to another, it is possible to summarise the major findings as follows:.

- Young people participate in sport for a number of different reasons. The main reasons include fun, excitement, skill improvement, fitness and health, and for friendship.
- Young people have similar motives for participation, but no one motive is common to all individuals.
- Young people have more than one reason for playing sport.
- Young people drop out of sport because the fun element is missing or gone, coach 'dislike', no skill improvement, boredom in training, or the attraction of other activities which promise to be more fun than sport.

Needs of the sports participant

The number of findings from these studies show that while young people have a number of motives for sports participation, they will drop out if their sporting experience does not satisfy these motives (Whitehead, 1988; Thomas, 1988; Ewing, 1991).

It is imperative therefore, that the coach must meet with each individual and find out why they want to participate in the particular sport. Such a meeting will provide the coach with a good understanding of what motivates that individual, and furthermore, allows the coach to structure training and game situations to maintain and enhance motivation. In addition, it is important to hold regular meeting scheduled at the end of training and games, where the participants can express their feelings with the coach in a friendly manner.

Regular observation of each sports participant in training and games can provide the coach with insight into a participant's motivation — for example, asking questions such as "Did you enjoy today's training session? ... why not? ... what could we do to make these sessions more enjoyable?" Such questioning and observation can provide important information which should help the coach develop a realistic success expectancy in the young sports participant.

Motivational approaches

Having identified the motives for sports participation, it is important that they are met. However, the list of successful approaches is long. Ask the experienced coaches what they do and the replies are: "Use anything that stays within the rules of the team and the laws of the land"; "Do anything and everything"; "Use anything that will play on an athlete's psychology and emotional feelings".

Coaches are willing to share their ideas, however, and in what follows there are recommendations from many coaches in the field. These ideas represent actual procedures that have been followed. Some may seem contradictory, but this is because coaches use different approaches to similar situations or similar approaches to different situations.

What a coach does is important, but of equal importance is when it is done. Timing is the key; there is a critical time to act or to use an approach, and one's "gut" feeling may be the best timing device of all. A pat on the back at the right time is better than a hug too early or too late. A few select words at the right moment can do much more than a long speech at the wrong time.

Regardless of the approach used, certain conditions must be present. If sports participants are to be effectively and significantly motivated, they must:.

1   Feel unique or special in some way.
2   Be treated on a personal level.
3   Clearly understand and agree with individual/team goals.

Facilities and equipment

Motivation through facilities and equipment is one sure way to inspire many of the individual and team members. Suggestions from coaches in the field include the following:

1   Have stylish, well-fitted uniforms.
2   Use good safe equipment.
3   Keep facilities/equipment in good repair.
4   Have a large bulletin board placed where it can be easily seen by the sports participants. Keep it covered with interesting, informative and up-to-date material.
5   Post signs and slogans on doors, walls, bulletin boards. Do not use too many or they will be ignored. Change them frequently.
6   Provide music. Have a central system or let the players furnish the music, for example, distance runners may select this week, the sprinters the next.

Recognition

Players and individuals enjoy being noticed and having their accomplishments recognised. A coach does this in practice, before or after a contest and during play; however, having others recognise these feats is a strong motivator. Coaches have used innumerable approaches; these are just a few of the possible ideas:.

1 Establish a "Wall of Fame" where players who were outstanding in the most recent contest will be recognised. Place it on a wall in the hall, corridor, gymnasium, cafeteria, or foyer.
2 Get names in the newspapers, on the radio, on television. Attempt to get recognition for all players, not just the "stars".
3 Have announcements read on the school's public address system before and after contests.
4 Set up a picture-taking day. Post pictures in central parts of the building. Have them available for publicity through the media.
5 Have a town business honour the player of the week.
6 Establish a "Reach your Goal" club. Anyone that reaches a preestablished goal (a difficult one) gets his or her name printed in the "goal" book.
7 Have a pre-season booklet with pictures of team members, data about each one, information about the coaches and schedule (local sponsorship may be available).
8 End the season with a banquet and recognise outstanding players. (An all sports one is good, but one for a single sport may be better.).

Training sessions

Good, well-planned training sessions are great motivators. These daily sessions are conducted to develop a player's skills, mental and physical and improve levels of conditioning. Unfortunately, putting in the time does not guarantee that one learns; motivation is also a necessary ingredient. The coach should manipulate the environmental variables to establish a good learning situation. This is done in many ways:

1 Start and end sessions on time.
2 Have well-planned, useful practices.
3 Make practices enjoyable; this does not mean that they have to be "fun" but they can be.
4 Use a variety of drills.
5 Keep the practice active — do the lecturing and discussing in the dressing room before and after being on the practice field.
6 Post the day's week's, and season's schedules.
7 Play with the athletes; be personally involved in some but not all of the drills. (This is not feasible in all sports.)
8 Direct attention from failure; look at the present and future.
9 Set goals for the day, for the week, for the season.

10 Have competitive events — ladder tournaments, two-on-two, dribble races, challenge matches.

11 Give positive verbal encouragement.

12 Be an enthusiastic coach.

14 Prepare the players mentally and physically.

15 Give the players a day off.

16 Play some other type of game/sport one day; break the routine.

17 Work with all the players.

Player involvement

The game is for the participants. If this is true, they should be involved in the programme in ways other than as players on the field. Most are capable of assuming the responsibilities; if they have a major role in the planning and execution of the teams as well as their own actions, they will possibly be more strongly oriented to team goals. Players can be involved in several ways.

1   Establish a player council to give the players a voice in policies, and allow them to contribute to the over-all programme.

2   Allow players to evaluate coaches at the end of the season.

3   Work with players to set individual and team goals.

4   Have each player state his or her goals (intentions) before the squad members and coaches. Keep a record of these statements and remind the players of their intentions as the season progresses.

5   Graphically chart with the team what the season will be in terms of challenges.

6   Have players lead the warm-up drills; change leaders each day so all get a turn.

7   Encourage players to assume responsibility for preparing themselves mentally and physically for a match.

8   Get player input regarding uniform style.

Personal touch

Good coaches have a "personal touch" when it comes to working with the players. Each player is important and has a special role on the team and should be recognised as an individual. A coach will find ways to let individuals know that they are a cut above the ordinary. In return, the coach will often get a better all-around player:

1   Send a birthday card to each player.

2   Be firm, fair, and friendly to all.

3   Visit with the parents/guardians.

4   Set an example.

5   Keep in touch during the off-season by letter or phone, or call a meeting.

6   Find a place on the team for all who want to play.

7   Be available to help the player at times other than the practice or contest.

8   Recognise success in all areas other than athletics.

9   Attend events in which the player is taking part (i.e. special awards ceremony, fashion show, another sport contest).

10 Recognise the players' birthdays by placing a sign which reads "Athlete of the Day" and posting the names of the players with birthdays on the date.

Feedback

If players' performances are to improve, they must receive information about their performances. This type of feedback reinforces behaviour and serves as a motivator. Many techniques can be used to inform a player if he or she is performing well, reaching a goal, failing to reach a goal, doing better or worse than team mates:

1   Film the game, review the films and the meet with the players individually or in groups.

2   Use video playback during practice.

3   Utilise statistics; e.g. batting average.

4   Evaluate weekly performances of all and talk with each player.

5   Keep close contact during training and games; tell the players what they are doing right/wrong, need to do.

6   Treat each athlete as an individual; give individuals reports on their performances, not always in comparative terms.

7   Be exact with the information; do not just say, "You made a poor pass".

8   Keep the information simple; do not bombard the player with unnecessary information.

Reinforcement

Coaches must approve of properly executed acts or disapprove of improperly executed ones if they are to mould a player's performance. Giving fair treatment to all players is very important. Inconsistency can produce confusion, distrust, and jealousy, so the pleasure or the pain should be distributed equally. There should be no difference in expectations, insofar as regulations are concerned, between the best player and the last one on the bench, or the opening game and the play-off contest. Sport is a place to learn and practice fair play; coaches set the example. Whatever has been decided as an appropriate reward or punishment needs to be awarded as soon as is practical and with an even hand.

1   Look for actions to reinforce; do not take things for granted.

2   Use praise; comment favourably on well-executed actions.

3   Give a surprise, like a watermelon break, if a practice goes well.

4   Reinforce immediately; reward the effort as well as the results.

5   Punish the entire team for one player's mistakes.

6   Praise the good things, but don't do this on every play or action because it will lose its effectiveness.

7   Tell them the good points and what needs to be changed or corrected. Be encouraging.

8   Let the players know that they can contribute to the team; each is important.

9   Threaten the players with extra sprints, a lengthened practice, removal from a game, or demotion, and follow through when the situation demands.

10 Raise voice to emphasise a point.

Preparing for the game

One of the most important, and yet most difficult tasks is to motivate players for a game. A coach should not wait until the hour or the day of the match, but should begin to get the athletes "up for the game" as soon as the last one has ended. It is a mistake to look too far ahead to a future match and overlook a present one; this is a good way to lose unexpectedly. There are coaches who go to almost any extreme to arouse their squads — throw chairs, yell and scream, grab players and shake them, break windows, ram their fists through walls — but most are successful in using much lower key approaches!:

1   Have a good game plan; prepare the players well in advance.

2   Use a positive approach and expect good things to happen.

3   Play music to get them "in the mood".

4   Talk before a game. Use a pep talk, give them an inspired message, read a poem, dedicate the contest to someone, challenge them, tell them an anecdote, give them a personal challenge, threaten them.

5   Bring out new uniforms for the key game.

6   Have team members wear school colours on the day of the game.

7   Enter the field as a unit and have a hot-shot warm-up.

8   Show records of those who preceded them.

9   Give each player a T-shirt that says, "We are the best" or "We can do it".

10 Ask a former player, team leader, popular coach or community leader to give a strong, spirit talk.

11 Tell them a derogatory remark supposedly made by another team.

12 Show films, good ones, of what they have done and how well they have played.

13 Use a scheduled game against a bigger opponent as a challenge; instil a fierce desire in the underdog to defeat the larger, more formidable opponent.

14 Be under control; the coach sets the mood and if he or she gets too uptight and irrational the team will too.

15 Make promises and keep them; if the team wins, or plays well, they get a day off.

16 Have the team sit quietly and think about themselves, about their individual performance and how it fits into the team concept.

Awards/rewards

Like everyone else, players enjoy receiving awards/rewards. "Effort should bring something in return", is a statement made in the American culture. "If you do this, what is it worth?" is the question asked by many athletes. Awards come in many forms — verbal praise, a pat on the back, a short practice period, a trip to a college game, food — but many players like something permanent to show for their "job well done".

1 Award letters, certificates.
2 Give trophies/plaques for special honours.
3 Give a T-shirt to the player the team selects as the Player of the Week.
4 Take top performers to the top meets.
5 Give the top performers the best equipment.
6 Place pictures of the outstanding players of the week in a downtown business establishment.

Rituals

Sporting events are filled with rituals; captains meet in the centre of the playing area for a coin toss, and teams dress in school colours. Teams have rituals too. Old ones are discarded and new ones are established, but the rituals remain to serve as motivators:

1 Have the same players lead the team onto the court for each game.
2 Meet under the goal posts on the home field after each game.
3 Eat lunch together on the day of the contest.
4 Use the same types of warm-up drills prior to each match.

Pride

It is important for a player to have pride — a high opinion of one's own worth and position, and of the team, the school, and the community. Pride is an internal motivator that is not innate but must be developed. The state or feeling of being proud can be very strong, having an enduring influence on an athlete's performance. Those who believe in themselves and what they are doing will put much more effort into the cause:

1 Give each player a T-shirt that says, "...is a member of the lacrosse team".
2 Have the team's captains help design the uniforms.
3 Invite a former athlete back to work with the squad.
4 Remind the team of the school's winning tradition.
5 Invite a well-known athlete or coach from a college or professional team to talk with the squad.
6 Recognise the worth of each player.

7   Work to make the team and members known to the school and community through assemblies, publicity in the local media, services to the community.

8   Expect the coaching staff to show pride in their work and to be proud of the team and individual players.

9   Give all players an opportunity to be somebody.

Team togetherness

The statement "There is no I in team", is a sort of paradox because coach is attempting to develop an individual's self-esteem while asking him or her to be secondary to the total team. It may be expecting too much of players to ask them to like all the others, but it would help if they did try to understand each other and have mutual respect. Generally, teams with compatible members and common goals have greater success than teams with members in constant turmoil:

1   Treat all players, the sub to the star, the same.

2   Stay together at certain events.

3   Dress alike for certain occasions.

4   Develop a positive image by being disciplined, well dressed and well prepared.

5   Set team goals and be proud of reaching them.

6   Have team representatives meet regularly with the coaching staff.

7   Have the players know something about each other.

8   Make seat assignments on the bus and change seating arrangements frequently.

9   Utilise as many players in a game as you possibly can — emphasise that all are a vital part of the team.

10 Have player and coach "get together".

Gimmicks

Using a gimmick to motivate does not mean that one must resort to trickery. A coach uses many tactics and often something new, different, or unusual in an approach pushes the right button in the player. Coaches are always seeking new ways to develop the drive and desire in players, and "little things can mean a lot". Innumerable ones are used:

1   Write a one-word message over the door to the dressing room, i.e. "Determination", "Pride", "Win".

2   Have a living mascot — a student dressed as the team emblem.

Slogans

Many coaches are convinced that slogans and sayings are motivational aids. They post them in their gyms, in locker rooms, over stadium entrances, and in their offices, and they quote them frequently. Some include:.

1   "Neither success nor failure is final".

2   "The difficult I expect you to do immediately, the impossible may take

a little longer".

3   "You are accountable for your behaviour".
4   "Championships do not just happen, they are earned".
5   "Team work is everything".
6   "When the going gets tough, the tough get doing".
7   "The gate to excellence is surrounded by a sea of sweat".
8   "It is not the size of the dog in the fight but the size of fight in the dog".
9   "The only way to win is to work at it".
10 "If everybody does not want it, nobody gets it".
11 "To be average is to be the lowest of the good and the best of the bad. Who wants to be average!".

A change in routine

Frequently a team gets in a slump or hits a dry spell. Players go stale, the zip is gone, and the entire programme seems "snake bit". This is the time to make a change in routine, in programme, or in direction. It often turns out that a simple alteration in procedure can spark a group or bring a team back to their former style of operation. Coaches should not hesitate to do something different:

1   Give them an unexpected day off.
2   Utilise new and different drills in practice.
3   Rearrange the week's practice schedule.
4   Develop a new pre-game routine.
5   Change the schedule if possible; play some different teams or reschedule current opponents on different dates.

Team supporters

All teams have a following of fans, a loyal band of parents and friends who support them in many ways, both financially and psychologically. Not only do they serve the team as scorers, time-keepers, drivers and cooks, but they also serve as motivators for the players. These loyal fans need to be thanked for their efforts and encouraged to continue their support. Many ideas have been proposed and used. Some of the more useful ones are listed:

1   Have coaches visible in the community — join service and civic organisations.
2   Develop a good team reputation by having members being on their best behaviour on trips and in town.
3   Perform at half-time of another event.
4   Be available and make an effort to speak to civic groups.
5   Have free nights for parents, for the fans.
6   Invite parents, girlfriends, boyfriends, representatives of the local media to come to a "picture" day or some special practice day.
7   If the sport is a new one to the area, invite people to an "explanation" meeting — explain and demonstrate the equipment, uniforms, rules.

8   Have an appreciation night for the Head or Principal.

9   Have a Parent's night.

10   Invite parents to a special event, such as the awards banquet, and give them special recognition.

11   Have a "thank you" note printed in the local paper.

During play

A problem facing all coaches is motivating the team or players at a break in the action. So many variables are involved that it is difficult to pinpoint a specific action that should be undertaken. Is the team or individual player the favourite or the underdog; ahead or behind; down or up; angry or complacent? Whatever the situation, the action generally takes the form of a "pep" talk, a game strategy adjustment, or a combination of both. The content and length of the message depend on the nature of the team or individual player and the events that have taken place in the game. Coaches should plan ahead by thinking through possible circumstances and making plans:

1   Use a chalkboard to illustrate the adjustments; players can see much better than they can hear.

2   Emphasise what they did correctly; find something to reinforce, regardless of the contest score.

3   First, get their attention — slam a door shut, kick a bucket, or jump upon a desk or table.

4   Have complete silence when they come into the changing room; they need time to think about past actions.

5   Focus their attention on the upcoming play; the end-of-the-game score is what counts.

6   Get excited. If the team is to get excited, the coach leads the way. Be calm. If the team is to be calm, the coach needs to set an example.

7   Talk coherently — be clear and concise; make a point and then move to the next one.

8   Encourage and instruct rather than demand.

9   Work on individuals; try to get them to spark the team.

10   Define responsibilities so the team members will avoid blaming each other.

11   Give them a fight talk and/or chewing out if they have been playing below par.

12   Use an emotional appeal — win for the player who is hurt, the former player, the spectators who travelled all the way to see them.

13   Tell them what they really need to know just before they return to the playing area so they will feel confident as they return to the action.

Summary

While the recommendations made above are by no means exhaustive, they will help coaches to structure training and games so that young people have the opportunity to participate and enjoy. It is important to bear in mind that young people participate in sports to play, not to listen to the coach talk or watch others perform. Most certainly such attempts could provide less dropping out of sport and provide sport for life for youth today in the UK.

References

Alderman, R. (1978) 'Strategies for motivating young athletes', in W. Staub (ed) Sport *psychology: An analysis of athletic behavior.* Ithaca, NY: Movement publications, pp. 49-61.

Campbell, S. (1986) 'Youth sport in the United Kingdom', in M. R. Weiss and D. Gould (eds) *Sport for children and youths: The 1984 Olympic Congress Proceedings, 10.* Champaign, IL: Human Kinetics Publications.

Ewing, M. E. (1991) 'Achievement orientations and sport behaviours of males and females.' (Doctoral dissertation, University of Illinois).

Gould, D. (1982) 'Sport psychology in the 1980s: Status, direction and challenge in youth research', *Journal of Sport Psychology*, No. 4: pp. 203-218.

Lee, M. J. (1985) 'Moral and social growth through sport: The coach's role'. Paper presented at the First International Congress of the British Association of National Coaches, Birmingham.

Singer, R. (1977) 'Motivation in sport', *International Journal of Sports Psychology*, Vol. 8, No. 1: pp. 78-81.

Tancred, W. R. (1993) 'Children in sport', *Therapy*, Vol. 17, No. 29: pp. 6-7 (February).

Thomas, J. R. (1988) *Physical education for children.* Champaign, IL: Human Kinetics Publications, pp. 10-20.

Tutko, T. and Richards, J. (1971) *Psychology of coaching.* Boston: Allyn and Bacon Inc.

Whitehead, J. (1988) 'Why children take part', *The Institute for the Study of Children in Sport Journal*, Vol. 1, No. 1: pp. 23-31.

Setting the Boundaries: A Critique of Recent Government Initiatives Affecting Sport and Leisure

Sarah Gilroy

Chichester Institute of Higher Education

Introduction

Attending the Recman conference in Birmingham in March of this year I heard Stephen Dorrell, the then newly appointed Minister of State for National Heritage, talk of the government's 'new' strategy for sport. Why, might you ask, do we need a new strategy for sport? It seems that the Department for National Heritage (DNH) is concerned about the impact that the changing nature of work will have on our leisure:

> The challenge facing the Department of National Heritage is to ensure that as we spend less time meeting our basic material needs we devote our energies to activities that fulfil us as human beings. (Dorrell, 1995: p. 2)

This statement reflects the government's paternalist discourse through which they seek to ensure that *we* fulfil ourselves: the implication being that we cannot be trusted to fulfil ourselves in appropriate ways. The DNH argues that one of the key ways through which we can gain fulfilment is through sport — but before you get excited about body surfing or roller blading — it's organised sporting competition that the DNH argues is most beneficial. Beneficial for whom you might ask — if fulfilment is what we're after, does it matter what activity we do?

This government approved form of sport has been embraced not only in John Major's policy document *Sport: Raising the Game* (DNH, 1995) but also in the 'new orders' for Physical Education in the National Curriculum (Department of Education: 1995). This paper examines these recent

315

government initiatives which are designed, according to the *Wolverhampton Express and Standard*, to "... get the Great back into Britain" (14 July 1995). By examining the discourse surrounding *Sport: Raising the Game*, the attempt to reset the boundaries of what is deemed to be appropriate physical activity for young people is explored.

Background to the 'new' strategy

To begin to comprehend why the government now regards sport so highly and why it has sought fit to privilege one particular form of sport above all others we need to reflect on the legacy of the Thatcher years. In the eighties the Conservatives' political agenda centred around the key issues of asserting the state's authority over trade unions, stamping out remnants of socialism, maintaining law and order and reconstructing the country's economic base towards a free-market economy. All of these issues, as I will now briefly illustrate, had to a greater or lesser extent an impact on sport and leisure. Following a clash between the government and the teaching unions many teachers withdrew their goodwill and refused to work outside their contracted hours. For subjects like physical education this meant that teachers were no longer prepared to volunteer the same amount of time to extra-curricular activities such as inter-school competitions as they had previously. The push for local councils to become more market oriented led to the selling off of school playing fields, leaving some schools with nothing more than a tarmac playground for outdoor activities (*Independent*, 15 July 1995). In the push to tighten law and order, young offenders were targeted, along with football hooligans who gained attention particularly following the Heysel Stadium disaster in 1985. The 'problem' of young offenders was part of a wider concern about young people. Youth unemployment rates were high and as Griffin (1993) claims there was a perception that unstructured free time was "... a breeding ground for 'social problems'..." and that young people needed "... to be taught to use this time in 'constructive' ways..." (p. 134). Education and training were to be the linchpins for putting young people back on the 'right' track: learning the 'right' skills, values and attitudes to enable them to be fully functioning citizens.

From the eighties and into the nineties it became clear that in an attempt to roll back the state, the state itself had begun to lose some of its control. Gamble (1994) argues that: "Re-establishing the authority of the state required increasing intervention to force the compliance of other agencies and interests with the wishes and plans of the government" (p. 251). The introduction of a National Curriculum (NC) in state schools following the Education Reform Act (ERA) in 1988 is one example of an intervention designed to meet the needs of the state. Whilst many within the teaching profession supported the notion of a NC (although not necessarily the proposed model), few educationalists could be unaware of the implication of such government intervention. It implied that the teachers, as professionals, could not be left to sort things out for themselves. The recent publication of league tables under the guise of enhancing parental choice was one more step towards a 'free' market economy as schools competed with each other for pupils. Compulsory Competitive Tendering (CCT) within the leisure field was another example of intervention supposedly to improve competition and thereby increase choice to the consumer as well as enhancing the quality of the product. Its impact within leisure is yet to be fully assessed.

Law and order remained a major problem, but one that was increasingly attributed to the decline of traditional family life. Young single mothers were a favourite target of right wing Conservatives who claimed that many young women were becoming pregnant in order to jump the housing queue. In addition to this it was claimed that children were no longer gaining the 'right' moral and social guidance. Schools were culpable, they were not being tough enough on indiscipline and truancy. When Jamie Bulger was murdered by two young boys, education was one of the areas blamed as well as television violence and video nasties such as Child's Play 2. If they had not been truanting, it was alleged, the abduction and murder might never have taken place. Penney and Evans (1994) point out that it was claimed that if there had been more competition in schools then the boys would not have committed such a crime.

The Britain John Major inherited when Margaret Thatcher resigned in 1990 was one in which sport, leisure and physical education were not greatly valued — if status and money invested by the government are used as yardsticks. There was (and is) for example no Minister for Sport, rather there is a sports minister without a cabinet brief. Sport was not ignored and indeed some forms of sport and leisure were seen to be useful insofar as they could help alleviate inner-city deprivation or instil the appropriate values and attitudes in young people, but in terms of any overarching strategy for sport nothing existed[1]. This raises the question of why in 1995 the Conservatives decided to launch *Sport: Raising the Game*. Some put it down to John Major's personal interest in sport and his concern over England's performance internationally, particularly in sports like cricket. Others suggest that it was a palliative to help draw attention away from other more fundamentally problematic areas, for example poverty and unemployment. Examination of the document however reveals something of John Major's expressed reasons and these will now be examined prior to examining the discourse within which the document and media coverage of its launch are framed.

Why we need to 'raise our game'

In the introduction to *Sport: Raising the Game* (DNH, 1995), John Major states that he has always regarded sport (and other aspects of our 'culture and traditions') as being as important as catering for the more material needs (by which I assume he means employment, income and so on), but that it has been ignored and now "It is time for this to change" (DNH, 1995: p. 1). In building his case for *now* being the right time for change he is in effect trying to explain why nothing has been done before despite the fact that the Conservatives have been in power since 1979. He identifies several critical factors which have led to now being the time to change; the first of which is the realisation that "Some of the problems for sport have been created by misguided attitudes and mistaken policies over the last generation" (DNH, 1995: p. 1). Although he does not go on to outline what these misguided attitudes and mistaken policies were, the very focus of the policy document on increasing competition and traditional team games in schools suggests that policies which ran counter to this were wrong. His view of the right way to view sport is clearly enunciated in his introduction to the document. The importance of sport he argues lies in its ability to enrich peoples' lives. It also serves to bind people together between generations and across borders as well as being a source of nationhood and local pride. But what seems to be of particular importance to him are the lessons that young people can learn from sport:

> Competitive sport teaches valuable lessons which last for life. Every game delivers both a winner and a loser. Sports men must learn to be both. Sport only thrives if both parties play by the rules, and accept the results with good grace. It is one of the best means of learning how to live alongside others and make a contribution as part of a team. It improves health and it opens the door to new friendships. (DNH, 1995: p. 2)

In this extract John Major provides an early indication of the extra value attached to competitive team sports, as well as revealing that his is a traditional view of sport as being a male preserve. It is also strongly reminiscent of the claims made for sport in the Victorian era as documented by Mangan (1981) and others.

The second factor is the availability of lottery money. John Major claims that providing funding for sport was one of his main reasons for creating the lottery. Using lottery money he aims: "... to bring every child in every school within reach of adequate sporting facilities by the year 2000" (DNH, 1995: p. 2). The irony is that in setting such a target it draws attention to the fact that some children do not have access to adequate sports facilities. However, when pressed about how many children currently were without suitable facilities he said the government did not know (*Times*, 15th July 1995). Further justification for the policy, John Major argues, comes from evidence from a report by the Secondary Heads Association (SHA) where they document a decline of sport in schools. In his selective use of research findings John Major fails to point out that, according to the *Independent*, the SHA blames the National Curriculum for squeezing sport out of schools (15th July, 1995). Finally, he argues that he wants to help 'our' sports men and women make the most of their talents and lead the world, without having to go and train abroad. This would no doubt mean that athletes like Fiona May (an ex-British athlete who won a medal for Italy at the 1995 World Athletic Championships) would no longer feel forced to go abroad to find suitable support for their sporting ambitions, and Britain would get the credit for their success.

While many would probably agree that there are problems with sport in Britain and that there is a need for an overall strategy for sport there remains the question of whether what has been presented in the policy is the solution. Is John Major correct in his analysis of the condition of British sport and in his remedy for it? To answer these questions we need to scrutinise the assumptions which underpin the policy and its strategies for change.

Assumptions underpinning the policy

We need more competitive sport

One of the first assumptions on which the policy is based is that previous ideas about sport, particularly in schools were misguided. The emphasis on putting traditional games and competitive sport 'at the heart of school life' is evidence of this. Although the policy paper itself makes no direct reference to moves in education in the late seventies and early eighties to de-emphasise competition, it rather generally states: "It is a serious cause for concern that sport no longer commands the place that it once did in school life" (DNH, 1995: p. 6). Media reports were less reticent as this leader from the *Times* illustrates:

> One of the tragedies of the past 20 years is that teachers have stamped upon these natural tendencies [to be competitive]. A whole generation of children has lost out as a result; and so has Britain's sporting status. (14 July 1995)

The *Daily Telegraph* sees the decline of competitive sport as having a major impact on the health of young people:

> Institutionalised mediocrity, enshrined by the absurd theory that competitive sport is an affront to a child's dignity, has produced an indolent, unhealthy generation. (15 July 1995)

Whilst the *Lancashire Evening Telegraph* praised John Major's initiatives it warned that:

> The left-wing element in the teaching profession, who believe there is no room for anything which smacks of competition, must not be allowed to sabotage this move. It is high time our children took up sport again, for the sake of their health and in the interests of British sports prestige. (14 July, 1995)

The blame for the 'decline' in sport in both schools and the international arena is laid clearly at the feet of teachers who were influenced by left wing ideologies and who were mistakenly allowed too much influence over how school sport was run. This blame serves to legitimate further government intervention to modify the National Curriculum through making traditional team games and competitive sport compulsory elements of both curricular and extra-curricular work. The role of the Office for Standards in Education has been increased to include details of the range, time spent and quality of games, including competitive team games in schools and is therefore a logical strategy designed to ensure that there is no 'backsliding' from the push to be more competitive.

What remains largely unchallenged in the media coverage, or in relevant professional publications are the assertions that current practice in PE is problematic (because it is claimed there is not enough competition and traditional games) and that it has damaged Britain's sporting success internationally. This is despite the fact that there has been no evidence brought forward to support these claims. Few of the media comments on the new Orders for PE, or on *Sport: Raising the Game* draw upon teachers' opinions of the proposals, and one which does finds opposition to them:

> I don't see the need for the change in emphasis to games — politicians are harking back to mythical halcyon days. Games don't address the personal development of each child.

> Our job is to turn the pupils on to exercise and sport, make it enjoyable and keep them fit: does it really matter if it's football, hockey or step aerobics? (*TES*, 18 November 1994)

Sport in school has declined. There is less time for PE

The lack of competitive sport in schools is assumed to be part of a general decline in sport in schools both in terms of quantity and quality. What is implied is that it was better in some bygone time. Although no indication is given of when this better time was and why the PE of the past was qualitatively better than it is now.

There is some evidence to support the claim that children are doing less physical education than before. The source most favoured by John Major himself is the SHA's report based on a survey of 1,006 schools. The survey found that curriculum time for PE had fallen for all age groups since 1991. As a result of this few of the schools surveyed were meeting the recommendations of the Conference of Medical Royal Colleges that children should be doing at least two hours of PE a week plus games periods. The most damning finding in the report is that the Heads claimed that it was Department for Education advisers who had encouraged the reduction in PE by suggesting that it needed only 5% of curriculum time (approx. 80 minutes per week) in contrast to the 10% that other NC subjects were given (*Daily Telegraph*, 22 March 1995). Extra-curricular time for PE had been reduced because of the teachers' additional workload created by the NC combined with other factors relating to children's paid employment, teachers' contracts and union disapproval of voluntary activities being undertaken by teachers. The sale of school playing fields was an additional factor thought to be significant, with 11% of schools surveyed reporting that playing fields had been sold or lost since 1991.

No reports of the SHA findings make any reference to 'left-wing' ideas about education or competition as having any bearing on the reduction of PE in schools, yet some media reports favoured this as an explanation of why children do less PE now than they did four years ago.

Children aren't as fit as they used to be

The reduction in time given to PE has fuelled a concern about the health and fitness of young people and led to Iain Sproat making the following claim: "We have the least fit generation we have ever had in this country. All that will change" (*Times*, 14 July 1995). The *Lancashire Evening Telegraph* takes up the same theme and implies that schools have let things slip:

> Now we are told that the current generation of youngsters is the unfittest since the end of the Second World War. Hardly surprising, when so many schools have all but abandoned competitive sports. A few years ago a child had to have a really serious medical condition to be excused what was called Physical Training. (14 July, 1995)

The *Daily Mail* welcomes the policy saying that it: "... comes at a time when countless schoolchildren do nothing more strenuous than slumping in front of a TV or computer screen. They have never been so unfit" (15 July 1995).

Where however is the evidence to support these claims that the current generation of young people are not as fit as their predecessors? There is no longitudinal data re fitness levels so on what basis are these claims made? On the contrary the work of Armstrong and McManus (1994) refute this notion that the fitness of British children is deteriorating and/ or is inferior to children from other countries. They go further and argue that children and adolescents are the fittest section of the population, which does not say much for those who did PT or PE in the halcyon days where competitive team games ruled supreme. Indeed the levels of coronary heart disease amongst the adult population may well lead one to argue that the PT or PE that today's 40-50 year olds did when they were young has not served them particularly well. Interestingly Armstrong and McManus are not in support of moves which force children into compulsory activities such as the daily vigorous exercise recommended by the School Sport Forum.

PE's not as good as it used to be

So whilst there is evidence to support a quantitative decline in PE, particularly in state schools, there is little evidence to suggest that the reduction in time for PE has negatively affected the quality of the child's education, yet in effect this is what is being claimed: less PE equals less effective PE. At a superficial level many would be tempted to agree that more is better, and many PE teachers would want more time for their subject but we need to be careful about focusing on quantity and not considering the quality of the experience. To be able to answer the quality question we need to agree on what quality within the field of PE means. This is at the heart of the revised inspection schedule that *Sport: Raising the Game* (DNH, 1995) outlines for OFSTED[2]. The quality of school PE will be judged on criteria heavily biased towards the inclusion of traditional competitive team games. This does not mean to say that some schools could not choose to do as they do now and include a wide variety of activities both competitive and non-competitive, but there would be limited time left once OFSTED requirements had been met. The policy may serve in practice to squeeze non-traditional activities out of not only the curriculum but also from the extra-curricular programme. To reinforce this notion of quality, schools will compete within the Sportsmark system to be awarded a Gold Star for exceptional achievement. Schools will be allowed to display their awards in prospectuses. Display of the government's new 'kite' mark will show prospective parents and pupils that the school's PE has "achieved a high standard" (DNH, 1995 — covering letter). The 'kite' mark will become like other symbols of approved goods — the lion on the egg, the 'kite' on electrical goods — if the product has it, and you can afford it, you buy it. If the product does not have the 'kite' mark and you can afford to buy one that does, you reject the one that does not have official approval. Accountability is not a bad thing, but what is being proposed is more than that. A particular form of PE is being put forward as the 'right' form of PE and for those not fully aware of the issues, the absence of a sportsmark award will be seen as a lack of quality, whereas it might represent quality but using a different, more broad based approach to PE.

Good sport is traditional competitive team sport

The policy document begins with John Major's letter of introduction which spells out the importance of the initiative: "These new plans are the most important set of proposals ever published for the encouragement and pro-motion of sport" (DNH, 1995: p. 1). His use of the word 'sport' is important here because by implication he is referring to 'all sport'. But this is clearly not the case, as the language gradually changes and it emerges that he does not mean 'all sport' but rather just competitive sport. He comments that: "Competitive sport teaches valuable lessons which last for life" (DNH, 1995: p. 2). Three sentences later there is a further qualification and we learn that it is competitive *team* sport that he regards as being particularly useful. The next page brings the final qualification to what is meant by sport when he states that he is: "determined to see that our great tradi-tional sports — cricket, hockey, swimming, athletics, football, netball, rugby, tennis and the like — are put firmly at the centre of the stage"

(DNH, 1995: p. 3). His opening statements in the document (as quoted at the beginning of this section) are rather misleading for the boundaries he has set for sport in school are very narrow.

At the heart of the new policy is the privileging of traditional competitive team sport over other forms of sport. New sports which it could be argued have grown out of a less elitist context than traditional team sports are not seen as being as good for pupils. Pupils and indeed physical education professionals are not being allowed to make up their own minds about what are worthwhile and useful sports activities. The basis for the privileging of traditional team sports needs to be analysed to consider the legitimacy of the claims being made. What appears to be implied is that firstly competitive sport is more beneficial than non-competitive sport, secondly that competitive team sport is more beneficial than competitive individual sport, and thirdly that traditional competitive team sport is more beneficial than non-traditional competitive team sport.

Despite the fact that evidence to support this type of privileging is conspicuous by its absence in both the document and supportive media reports, John Major, Stephen Dorrell and Iain Sproat have all lauded the moral, social and physiological value of traditional competitive team sports. The document talks of sport providing:

> ... lessons for life which young people are unlikely to learn so well in any other way. Lessons like team spirit, good sportsmanship, playing within the rules, self-discipline, and dedication will stand them in good stead whatever their future holds. (DNH, 1995: p. 6)

John Major is cited in the *Daily Mirror* (15 July 1995) as saying that competitive games build character. In his speech at the Recman conference Stephen Dorrell claimed that:

> Sporting competition is not merely exhausting — it is also a proving experience. It allows participants at every level to test themselves against their peers and measure their improvement. Sporting competition represents a ladder of aspiration — an incentive to improve. (Dorrell, 1995: p. 3)

Whilst Iain Sproat stated that:

> By putting sport back at the heart of school life, it will mean that every child, whatever their abilities, will have a sense that sport teaches lessons that other things at school cannot teach or teach so well: discipline, commitment, team spirit and good sportsmanship. (*Times*, 14 July 1995)

These claims are problematic, firstly whilst many of us from our own experiences could argue that sport can have positive benefits, you similarly do not have to look far in the sporting world for evidence of indiscipline, unsporting conduct, cheating and selfish behaviour. The aphorism that 'sport doesn't build character, it builds *characters*' comes to mind.

Secondly, claims are being made about the special ability of traditional
team sports to aid the social and moral development of the child with
seemingly little consideration of the contribution that non-traditional or
non-competitive or individual sports might make. This is despite the advice
of professionals who have argued that other activities such as dance,
mountain biking, self-defence and ten-pin bowling are equally valuable
(*TES*, 18 November 1994). The *Guardian*'s leader takes up a similar theme
and cautions that:

> Sproat's big five must not be allowed to dominate. Competitive
> team games are fine for those who want competition. But non-team
> games, such as rock climbing or judo, can be just as challenging
> and character-building. (15 July, 1995)

It is also important to ask what 'traditional ' means — traditional for
whom? The sports are traditional for a largely white, male and middle class
section of the population. Given the changing demographic composition of
Britain to what extent is it still valid to adopt an approach which could be
likened to a form of sporting imperialism? Despite many of the same
assumptions being made about the value of sport the parallel launch in
Scotland of *Scotland's Sporting Future* (Scottish Office, 1995) adopts a
slightly different view of team sport. Building on 'Team Sport Scotland' (an
initiative launched in 1991 to promote team sport) which included such
sports as basketball, volleyball and shinty, *Scotland's Sporting Future*
has added swimming, athletics and sport for people with disabilities to the
list. The language in the Scottish Office's (1995) is less strident about
traditional team sport, but given the rise in Scottish nationalism and the
vulnerable position of the Conservatives perhaps this is not so surprising!
For the policies to be successful popular support has to be won as well as
wielding the stick of accountability; the policies have to be seen to be
appropriate for Scotland even if they emanate from an English-based Prime
Minister.

Young people need educating about how to spend their leisure time

The final assumption I want to raise is related to a more general concern,
held by some government ministers about young people. Just as Griffin
(1993) spoke of the perception that unstructured free time was a problem
in the making, so I am arguing that this sports policy is predicated on the
one hand on a view of children as having surplus energy which needs
channelling if they are not to create social problems and on the other on a
perception of children as being inactive and hooked on TV and computers.
The former is echoed in Stephen Dorrell's Recman speech when he argues
that: 'Sporting activity provides an essential outlet for physical and emotional energy. It allows people to let off steam, to release pent-up physical
energy and to enjoy the opportunity to improve skills' (1995: p. 3). Both

points are referred to in the description of Michael Forsyth's comments made at the launch of the parallel policy in Scotland, where he promised:

> ... a sporting strategy which would drag sedentary youngsters from their computer games, keep our youngsters from the streets and the temptation of crime and drugs, and instil a desire for clean living, healthy competition and team spirit. (*Scotsman*, 15 July 1995)

The paternalistic discourse serves to reinforce the boundaries of what is deemed to be acceptable and appropriate behaviour for young people.

'Forget it all for an Instants' — funding the 'revolution'

The naming of sport as one of the five 'good causes' which were initially to benefit from the lottery revenue enabled John Major to put his plans into operation[3]. Indeed he argues that one of his principal reasons for creating the lottery was to transform sport (DNH, 1995). The importance that John Major seemingly now attaches to sport and the degree of financial support given directly by the Conservative government to sport seems somewhat contradictory. Stephen Dorrell for example talks of how he sees sport as an essential part of social policy, but patently it is not such an important part as to put sufficient funds in to support sport development (Dorrell, 1995: p. 4). John Major said that he thought it unlikely that sufficient resources would ever come directly from the taxpayer, and that was why he was advocating the use of lottery money (DNH, 1995: p. 1). If sport is such an essential part of social policy, however, that in itself is a strong argument for it to be supported through taxation, where the contribution would be related to earnings, rather than via the lottery income which early research is indicating is coming largely from lower socio-economic groups.

Also whilst advocating a policy to strengthen sport John Major is at the same time condoning the maintenance of a policy which many claim is eroding a vital physical resource that cannot easily be reclaimed. The policy at issue concerns the government approved selling of school playing fields. Since 1979 5,000 school playing fields have been sold (*Guardian*, 15 July 1995). Despite the concern raised by the National Playing Field Association (NPFA) about the sales John Major argues that he will not change government policy on this: "Playing fields are not sacrosanct and I am not going to impose a blanket ban on any sales" (*Sunday Telegraph*, 16 July 1995). He is also considering making the Sports Council a statutory consultant on any proposed sale of land. This, claims the Director of the NPFA, is an inadequate way of safeguarding school playing fields, particularly when the school population is set to increase by 17% between 1990 and the year 2000 (*Birmingham Evening Post*, 17 July 1995).

It also seems anomalous that the government is attempting to tempt young people away undesirable activity or inactivity via a programme funded by gambling. This is particularly ironic given the concern about the impact of the Lottery Instants game on young people (HMSO, 1995). The Gaming Board for Great Britain noted with interest that the government had set the minimum age for buying a lottery ticket at 16, but for bingo and horse-racing it was 18 (HMSO, 1995). Similarly, it has been noted that the government set up the lottery on grounds more favourable than for other forms of lotteries such as the football pools. The tax rate set by the government is lower for the National Lottery and initially only the Lottery was allowed to advertise, although this has recently been relaxed.

Conclusion

Sport: Raising the Game was welcomed by many involved with sport as it was seen to indicate that sport was at last getting the government support it deserved. However, even a cursory glance at the media coverage generated by the launch would have been enough to indicate that there was not much 'new' about the policy. Prime Ministerial male favourites such as Charlton, Cowdrey, Christie and Underwood were called upon to voice their support for the plans. The launch in the garden of No. 10 Downing Street and later at Millwall Football Club emphasised, as did the document, that this was a traditional version of sport that was being relaunched: it centred around team sport, largely male. In this sense the launch did nothing to dispel the impression created in his introduction to the document through his use of 'sportsmen' and 'sportsmanship' that for John Major sport is male.

Analysis of the document and other material has revealed the absence of any sound educational rationale for the policy whilst at the same time drawing attention to government moves to reset the boundaries of what is considered suitable and appropriate sporting activity for young people. At present it seems highly likely that the government will be successful in its aims. Some opposition has been voiced publicly about the policy although the majority of the quality, tabloid and regional press reported largely supportive comments. The *Guardian* and the *Independent* reported some critical comment both about the ideology underpinning the policy and the practicality of its implementation. The ideology of supporting the elite at the expense of the rest of the participants is questioned, as is the more pragmatic problem of finding extra money to pay staff to cover the additional extra-curricular hours (*Independent*, 15 July 1995). The *Guardian* (15 July 1995) quotes the Education Chair of the Association of Metropolitan Authorities as saying that John Major was: "... guilty of 'blatant hypocrisy' for failing to acknowledge that underfunding of schools damaged sport and other team activities such as drama, dance and music". The underfunding of education and the problems schools would have in resourcing the changes were also highlighted by union and Labour spokespersons. An article in the *Observer* pithily observed that:

> John Major's crusade for school sport announced last week has been widely welcomed — but then a blanket full of holes would be welcomed by someone sleeping on the street. Most experts agree that school sport has been seriously run down over the past 15 years. (16 July, 1995)

The *Guardian* report also challenged some of the assertions made about the decrease in team games, arguing that the proportion of time allocated to them has not changed, but that the time given to PE has been reduced as other National Curriculum subjects have been given priority. The sports academy proposal raised few criticisms probably because few in Britain have sufficient knowledge of its forbear the Australian Institute of Sport (AIS). One exception was an article in the *Independent* (15 July, 1995) written by a reporter in Australia who pointed out that the 'hot-housing' system has its critics and that concern has been shown over the pressure experienced by some youngsters at the AIS.

It is not surprising that the major sports governing bodies are not as yet raising objections to the strategy — to do so would be to commit potential political suicide. One source of opposition could come from within the teaching profession, but with OFSTED's new role the costs of resisting the new policy may be too high. Parents may ultimately be another source of opposition, but the power of the popular appeal of 'Raising the Game' must not be underestimated.

Consultation about *Sport: Raising the Game* with voluntary and professional bodies who have an interest in sport and young people may lead to some changes to the strategy, prior to the white paper being published early in 1996. However, it is doubtful that the assumptions which underpin the current document will be regarded as legitimate areas for discussion. Yet understanding the dynamics of the consultation process is a vital area that needs further research, as is the process by which men and women respond to the document's proposals. Central to these areas of research are issues of power and agency and the translation of policy into practice. Further empirical and theoretical analysis is needed in order to monitor and evaluate the implementation of *Sport: Raising the Game*. Whilst it seems as if the boundaries have been successfully set, the opposition contained and hegemony achieved, we must not underestimate the power of individuals, and groups to resist the imposition of policy by transforming it and somehow making it their own.

Notes

1   Dennis Howell for Labour had, as the only Minister for Sport Britain has had, put forward proposals for a sports strategy but he was

unable to put it into operation following defeat by the Conservatives in the 1979 election.

2   In future inspections OFSTED will have to (DNH, 1995: p. 12):

   i.   inspect and report on the range, time spent and quality of games, including competitive team games, offered as part of the formal PE curriculum;

   ii. report on sporting provision that schools offer to pupils outside formal lessons, during lunch-times, in the evenings and at weekends, paying particular attention to traditional team games;

   iii. report on the pupil participation rates in sporting provision outside formal lesson time and the number of teachers who supervise that provision;

   iv. report on the school's sports competitions programme, both within the school and against other schools; and

   v.   report on the progress made by the school in improving provision in both curricular and extra-curricular competitive games as part of this sporting initiative.

3   On September 26th 1995 the five 'good causes' were expanded to six when it was announced that medical research was also going to be able to apply for lottery funding.

References

Armstrong, N. and McManus, A. (1994) 'Children's fitness and physical activity: A challenge for PE', *The British Journal of Physical Education*, Vol. 25, No. 1: pp. 20-26.

Birmingham Evening Post (1995) 17th July.

Daily Mail (1995) 15th July.

Daily Mirror (1995) 15th July.

Daily Telegraph (1995) 22nd March.

Daily Telegraph (1995) 15th July.

Department of National Heritage (1995) *Sport: Raising the game*. London: DNH.

Dorrell, S. (1995) Speech given at Recman Conference, March 28th.

Gamble, A. (1994) *The free economy and the strong state: The politics of Thatcherism*. London: Macmillan.

Griffin, C. (1993) *Representations of youth. The study of adolescence in Britain and America.* Cambridge: Polity.

Guardian (1995) 15th July.

Department of Education (1995) *Physical Education in the National Curriculum.* London: HMSO.

HMSO (1995) *Report of the Gaming Board for Great Britain.* London: HMSO.

Independent (1995) 15th July.

Lancashire Evening Telegraph (1995) 14th July.

Mangan, J. A. (1981) *Athleticism in the Victorian and Edwardian Public Schools.* Cambridge: Cambridge University Press.

Observer (1995) 16th July.

Penney, D. and Evans, J. (1994) 'It's just not cricket (and not just) cricket', *The British Journal of Physical Education,* Vol. 25, No. 3: pp. 9-12.

Scotsman (1995) 15th July.

The Scottish Office (1995) *Scotland's Sporting Future.* The Scottish Office.

Sunday Telegraph (1995) 16th July.

Times (1995) 14th July.

Times (1995) 15th July.

Times Educational Supplement (1994) 18th November.

Wolverhampton Express and Standard (1995) 14th July.

The Educational Meaning of Tatar Folk Games in Physical Education

Zinaida Kuznetsova and Alexander Kuznetsov

Kama Technological Institute, Tatarstan, Russia

In an important paper describing "some processes concerning the con-struction of National Curriculum Physical Education [in the UK], from the perspective of one member of the Department of Education and Science Physical Education Working Group" (p. 34), Margaret Talbot (1993) stressed the need both for the marshalling of powerful arguments in justi-fication of the place of physical education in schools, and for under-standing the politics of education within which those arguments must be situated. The aim, as she put it, was that physical education professionals could then "... better fight for the curriculum time and resources they needed to deliver the National Curriculum" (p. 34). As Talbot notes, the gathering of such arguments would only take place if the need for it was recognised:

> ... members of the physical education profession must be aware that Physical Education's place in the National Curriculum was not indefinitely assured, and that its future place would need to be constantly established, protected and justified. (p. 34)

This might seem obvious. As Talbot continues:

> The necessity for everyone in physical education to be informed about and to understand the nature of the struggle to ensure physical education's place in the National Curriculum seemed to be so obvious that I had not considered that professional colleagues might apparently prefer to know nothing of the vulnerability of their subject. (p. 35)

So the need to present cogent arguments, and to support them with clear research findings, was stressed. Talbot also remarks on "... the lack of appreciation by many people outside the physical education profession, of either the breadth or the diversity of the subject" (p. 36). As she continues:

> Related to this point is the common and vexed confusion on the relationships between sport and physical education: for many people, including ministers, physical education appeared to be sport. Yet this confusion was not supported by official documentation on physical education, which had long promulgated a progressive, pedagogically based, model of physical education which included activities like educational gymnastics, swimming, athletics and folk games (p. 36)

In this vein, Talbot quoted the aims outlined in *Physical Education Curriculum from 5 to 16.*:

> Physical education in schools aims to develop control, coordination and mastery of the body. It is primarily concerned with the way of learning through action, sensation and observation. [DES, 1989: p. 1, quoted in Talbot, 1993: p. 36)

Talbot's remarks, though directed at the situation in the UK, nevertheless have a broader relevance: physical educationists need to marshal arguments in support of their claims to the general value of their subject(s) in education, basing these arguments in a clear understanding of the nature of the relevant activities. It is in this tradition that the research reported here situates itself.

The aim of this research is:

- to characterize folk games from the pedagogical viewpoint;
- to classify folk games according to age characteristics of the children;
- to produce material for an argument for the inclusion of folk games in a national curriculum akin to the National Curriculum in the UK.

Taken together, these aims constitute one main goal — to increase pupils' learning activity through physical education (specifically, folk games).

A game is a treasury of the human culture: it presents a socially specific, historical means of personal development. Games take different forms, linked with human social development: they constantly evolve and become complicated. The majority of games are chiefly distinguished by their being consciously directed at the achievement of the definite goal.

The notion "game" includes a lot of forms of instantiating folk-lore, each of them promoting all-round development of children: physical, psychical, intellectual. Two important factors are combined in the playing activity of children:

- when children join in the practical activity, they develop physically, becoming used to acting independently;

- they get moral and aesthetic satisfaction from this activity, which can deepen their knowledge of their surroundings.

In these ways, and given cultural diversity, the educational and developmental meaning of folk games is clear.

Physically: different physical qualities are developed by means of the folk games, especially quickness and adroitness. Simultaneously motor skills are acquired and perfected. The movements involved in the playing activity are complex and different, potentially involving all muscle groups. The interplay of moments with rest and intensive actions, placing only a small strain on the musculature, allows the players to complete large volumes of work. The variable character of the loading can be adapted to correspond to the age characteristics of children; and exerts an influence on improving blood circulation and functional-systems-activity respiration.

Culturally: the Educational Department Science Physical Education Working Group studied Tatar folk games and discovered that games differed in terms of both their origin and their content. For example, some games come into existence in a definite situation and disappear together with this situation. These games are individual and unique; they lack traditions. Tatar children have many traditional games (for example, the game "clapping" or 'tag': see below). The rules and the distance of this game change in accordance with time, but its principle is unchanging.

Some games are hundreds, and even thousands, of years old. For example, an outstanding Eastern scientist Machmud Kashgari left interesting data in his *The dictionary of the Turkish language*, written between 1073 and 1074. In that author's description of children's games, we find a game "Ochty, ochty ("fly, fly")" which is played by our children nowadays.

In the 19th century, different classifications of folk games were suggested by Russian and European scientists. I. GutsMuths classified folk games into outdoor and quiet ones; D. Kolotsa classified them into individual, competitive, fighting, amorous, social, etc.; W. Johnson classified games according to the age groups. Some scientists classified games into intellectual and physical, simple and team games. V. Gorinovski classified them into games exerting physiological influence on the players and games used for solving pedagogical tasks. Important classifications of the folk games have also been developed by V. Marts (according to their origin), and by V. Vsevolodski-Gengross (according to typological groups).

A very interesting multi-stage classification of games is given by V. Jakovlev, who grouped them according to the character of the playing team organization, joint children's activities and their aims, typical movements and their varieties. But this classification characterises only the definite games, used mainly at physical education lessons and doesn't permit classification of other groups of folk games, taking into account their diversity of organization forms and types of playing areas.

Thus, there are various and sometimes contradictory classifications of folk games in the pedagogical literature.

Corresponding to the principles of physical education teaching-theory, Tatar folk games can be classified:

- according to characteristic movements and used equipment;
- according to games belonging to different age groups of the population;
- according to organizational forms of using them.

We can consider them in that order. Classified according to characteristic movements and equipment used, Tatar folk games may be subdivided into:

- outdoor games with running and jumping;
- games with throwing;
- games for balance and rotation;
- games played blind-folded;
- circle games;
- symbolic games;
- winter games;
- home games;
- games in the water;
- games with various equipment / toys.

Classified according to the different age-groups involved, Tatar folk games can be divided into *children* and *youth* games (see below).

The third method of classification is represented by the division of games those of *individual* and of *collective* character. For example, a game "clapping" (*Pyatnashki*), or 'tag', is played among boys and girls of 5-12. Two persons or a group of children can play this game. One player lightly 'tags' another by touching him; the latter must catch him up and return the tag, then the players change their roles. If the game continues too long and the person running away is tired, he cries "chur" and stops to have a short rest: he can sit or stand, etc. While he rests the game is stopped. When he moves away from his stopping place, the game is continued. According to the rules and organization forms the game is simple. The main task of the game is to show adroitness and quickness in running; the task of the main player is to 'tag' as soon as possible the running players, and for the runners to be as long as possible 'not tagged'. The game is directed to switching over one action to another one: the change of roles of roles is an essential, educational moment of the game. This game promotes the learning of physical quickness, adroitness and quickness of wit.

Classified according to age characteristics, this game is a *children's game*. According to the classification by organizational forms, this game has a *collective* character.

Classification of folk games according to age-characteristics

Games with complex movements and interrelations are not accessible for pupils 7-9 years old. They like games of imitation, plot or character with running, jumping, throwing balls and different objects. Usually they like to play individual games. For children of 7-9 musical forming of the game is very important. They like games with songs, with reciting. At the age of 9, it is better to recommend games which demand the development and improvement of coordination-movements, organization and behaviour of children.

Higher demands cause greater activity, independence and initiative of the children in playing activities.

By ages 10-11, children have become stronger, have better coordination possibilities. Their quickness, adroitness, hardness are developed; their adaptation to physical loading rises. Games of rather complex contents are accessible for children of this age. Boys prefer games with wrestling elements, mutual assistance. Girls usually prefer quiet games with rhythmical movements and exact actions (with subjects, balls, etc.) The competitive element is vividly expressed in these games. The games become longer and more expressive.

Games for children of 13-15 are rather different. They are shorter in duration but more complicated. These changes are explained by the age-development peculiarities of the children. Their behaviour is distinguished by instability, sharp mood changes, sudden decisions.

Complicated team games are accessible for teenagers. Maturity and independence of thought is shown by children of this age. They are involved in the process of complicated tactical wrestling; they are also interested in relay-races with hurdle clearance, games with wrestling and resistance, rescue and mutual assistance.

Boys and girls of this age often play jointly. But girls prefer games demanding exact and adroit movements, usually found in rhythmical dancing games.

Youths of 16-17 reach a high level of physical development and have much playing experience. Physical fitness takes the first place here. Using of folk games helps to solve this main problem. Youth pay great attention to the tactics and results of their actions. In choosing their tactics and ways of achieving victory they show independence. They prefer to be leaders, team captains. Youths prefer games where they can show strength and adroitness. Different relay-races, games with resistance, complicated coordination tasks are popular among them. Nevertheless we must remember that in this age group the physiological processes of maturation/ development are not complete. That is why we must choose games correctly and regulate the loading.

Conclusion

In order to reach the physical fitness of children and youth (that is, to develop control, coordination and mastery of the body) it is important to use a variety of means of physical development. In accordance with this, great attention is paid to folk games, Tatar folk games particularly, which depict national culture, recall and preserve national traditions and promote the development of the motor qualities and skills.

The Education Department and Science Physical Education Working Group gathered 200 folk games, characterized them from the pedagogical viewpoint, and classified these folk games according to age characteristics of the children. This Working Group provided a two-year experiment in the teaching the folk games to children of different age groups, discussing folk games with teaching staff at Seminars; and recommended folk games as valuable for the National Curriculum Physical Education in Tatarstan. Comparing recommended folk games with the present National Curriculum contents (according to motive structure), the Working Group considers that using folk games in the process of physical education promotes solving educational tasks central to any National Curriculum.

References

Galeev, E., Chanbikov, A. (1975) *Tatarskye Narodnye Igry i prazdniki.* Kazan: p. 93.

Krupskaya, N. (1965) 'Isbrannye pedagogicheskiye proisvedenia', *Prosvesheniye*, p: 143.

Lesgaft, P. (1952) 'Rukovodstvo po physicheskomu obrazovaniu detey shkolnogo vosrasta', No. 2. *Physkultura i sport* (Moskva): p. 120.

Talbot, M (1993). 'Physical education and the national curriculum: Some political issues', in G. McFee and A. Tomlinson (eds) *Education, sport and leisure: Connections and controversies.* CSRC Topic Report No. 3. Brighton; University of Brighton, pp. 34–64.

Validi, D. (1927) "Besneng Yul", No. 3: p. 30.

School Children and Sport

K. Roberts

University of Liverpool

Introduction

This paper discusses some of the findings from three recent nation-wide English investigations into school sport facilities and young people's involvement in sport and other leisure activities.

i.   The first was a set of enquiries during 1994 in which questionnaires were returned by or for a nationally representative sample of approximately 4,400 6-16 year olds, and by 204 of the schools that they attended (Mason, 1995a). These quantitative surveys were complemented by semi-structured interviews with 20 Physical Education (PE) teachers from the schools and 40 of the children and (some of) their parents (Mason, 1995b). This research was conducted by the Office of Population, Censuses and Surveys (OPCS) for the Sports Council and the main purpose was to gather baseline information on schools' sports curricula and children's levels and patterns of participation. From now on these investigations will be described simply as the Participation Survey.

ii. The second investigation was a survey by telephone interview of a representative sample of approximately 1,000 schools (Hunter, 1995). This research was also conducted by OPCS for the Sports Council, the main objective in this case being to provide baseline information on schools' sports facilities and, in particular, the extent to which they were part-used by the wider community and current trends. In the following passages this enquiry is described as the Facility Survey.

iii. The third enquiry was a survey of a nationally representative sample of 3700 11-25 year olds, also conducted by OPCS, in this case on behalf of the Department for Education. The principal purpose here was to investigate young people's involvement in the Youth Service but data on their participation in other leisure activities was also gathered (Department for Education, 1995). This project is described here as the Youth Service Study.

The data collection in all these investigations, and the primary analyses of the findings, were by OPCS, and the detailed findings have been published elsewhere. The present author was an academic adviser to the Participation Survey and the Facility Survey, but this paper comments on and interprets the findings in ways that may or may not accord with the views of the organisations and persons who conducted and sponsored the research. The main reports from all the enquiries present their results systematically. The following passages proceed differently; they sift and select from the findings from each of the investigations to address four questions:

i.   What are the current trends in school sport provisions?

ii. What is happening to team games and other competitive sports in schools and young people's lives more generally?

iii. How much sport do young people play?

iv. What are the main differences by social class and gender?

School sports provisions

The evidence from these recent investigations disarms fears and forecasts of school sport in England being in decline. Several threats have been identified: industrial action by, and loss of goodwill from teachers; parents' safety concerns making them reluctant to allow children to remain at school after hours; the combination of the national curriculum, testing and league tables creating a squeeze on non-core subjects; and budgetary pressures forcing schools to choose between sports facilities, teachers or computers for example.

Despite these potential threats, the Facility Survey found that in general schools had been increasing and enhancing rather than reducing their sports facilities, and the schools expected these trends to continue into the immediate future. Schools had funded recent sports developments in a variety of ways. Local education authorities had been the most common source of funds but other local government departments had also contributed, some schools had benefited from Sports Council grants, some had attracted business sponsorship, and parents had often been involved in fund raising. In 1994 many schools hoped that the National Lottery would become a future source of funds for new or improved sports facilities.

The schools obviously considered sport important and were keen to develop community use of their facilities wherever possible. There was no evidence of schools guarding facilities from outsiders. Whether facilities were made available for community use depended mainly on whether, in a school's view, the community would wish to use what the school could offer. Most schools were keen to open their doors and this was not wholly from fund raising motives; raising a school's profile was usually considered at least equally important. Independent school brochures show that these schools regard their sports facilities as sales features, and in 1994 LEA and grant maintained schools were acting on the same assumption.

The Participation Survey produced congruent findings; schools were extending and enhancing rather than cutting-back on their sports teaching. Ninety-seven percent of the schools offered some extra-curricula sport, and 90 percent of the school informants (usually the PE or head teachers) reported that their schools regarded sport as 'very important'. Most of the remainder said that sport was treated as 'fairly important'. Nearly a half of the schools (47 percent) reported increases in extra-curricula sport during the previous three years whereas only 10 percent reported a decline. These trends were expected to continue, albeit at a slower pace. Twenty-one percent of the schools expected their extra-curricula provisions to be enlarged while just nine percent anticipated a decrease during the next three years.

Competitive team games and other sports

Another fear has been that schools have been neglecting Britain's traditional team games including sports where national success has a purchase in popular culture. Some prominent politicians have voiced this concern, and some sports organisations have expressed alarm at an apparent decline in the numbers of young people taking up and remaining in the sports. Teachers and local (left wing) politicians have sometimes been held responsible for these threats to sports such as rugby and cricket.

Actually the Participation Survey shows that in 1994 team games and other competitive sports were alive and well in England's schools. Neither PE teachers nor their colleagues had turned against Britain's traditional team sports. Nearly all the pupils were playing team games at school during every year in their school lives. The situation was not that team games had been dropped but rather that they had been joined by other activities in broader sports curricula than the traditional games regime. Most pupils were being introduced to a wide range of sports during their school education. Throughout their school lives they would typically play between eight and ten sports in lessons during every school year. The number of sports played regularly (at least 10 times) was, of course, much smaller, typically between two and four. The teachers who were interviewed were aware of the frustrations that could arise from a series of introductions that were too brief to allow pupils to become sufficiently competent to enjoy anything. The pupils themselves who were interviewed sometimes explained that it was impossible to enjoy a sport until one had learnt the rules and acquired the basic skills. All parties were aware that variety could be overdone but the teachers defended their broad curricula as the best way of maximising the number of pupils who would find a sport at which they were competent and which they enjoyed, and who would extend their participation into their out-of-school and post-school lives. The compromise was to let pupils sample a large number of sports while concentrating on a handful which they played regularly.

Virtually all the teachers believed in 'sport for all'. They were more likely to consider it 'very important' to involve as many pupils as possible (50 percent) than to compete against other schools (32 percent) or to win trophies (8 percent), but this did not mean that they were against their pupils learning to play competitive games or succeeding in them. Rather, it appeared that the teachers believed that making success in competitive sports the over-riding objective would exclude most pupils and could deny even star players sufficient breadth of interest and skill to sustain long term sports careers.

The teachers' strategy was succeeding in so far as nearly all pupils were playing some sport in their leisure time. Two-thirds of the young people who were in the final year of their compulsory education were playing at least one competitive team sport at least 10 times per year in lesson time, and those who were not doing so were more likely to be playing other sports regularly than abstaining from any regular sport activity in school. Most pupils were competing at sport regularly both in and out of lessons. The proportion playing team sports regularly out of school was much smaller than the proportion playing in school lessons, but this was not because the majority were avoiding all sport in their leisure; it was because they were more likely to play individual and small group games. The sports that were most likely to be played at least 10 times per year outside school lessons by the secondary pupils were cycling (55 percent of the boys and 38 percent of the girls) and swimming (36 percent of the boys and 42 percent of the girls). Football was played regularly by 55 percent of the secondary school boys. All other sports were very much minority leisure time interests. Among the boys 28 percent played cricket regularly outside lessons, tennis 27 percent, rugby 16 percent and athletics 12 percent. The sports other than cycling and swimming in which the secondary school girls were most likely to participate regularly out of lessons included tennis 24 percent, badminton 15 percent, rounders 13 percent, netball 13 percent, and hockey 9 percent.

Out of school, even more than in lessons, the young people had a choice of sports in which to participate. Among the primary school pupils there were six sports that at least 20 percent played regularly (10 times a year or more) in lessons, and five that were being played this frequently out of lessons. Among the secondary school pupils there were ten and five such sports. Specific sports were therefore competing against each other for the young people's time and attention, and this included the time and attention of the best athletes. With the possible exception of football among boys, there were no sports that could rely on holding the loyalty of potentially gifted players. On the basis of the evidence from this recent research, competition from other sports will be a far more likely reason than the hostility of left wing teachers if cricket, rugby or whatever sports are failing to attract sufficient young talent to compete successfully at world levels. Archery is probably reconciled to being unable to attract all the young people with the physical qualities that could make them excellent. Even men's football may now be facing a similar situation.

Young people's levels of sports activity

How much is enough? Sport participation seems unlikely ever to reach a level in any age group where no-one will find cause to urge 'more'. It is possible to react to the evidence from the recent Participation Surveys with claims that too many young people do too little sport, or to be impressed by the average level of activity.

Most of the young people were playing sport in and out of school lessons. Other recent enquiries have noted that sport appears a near universal leisure activity among young people when researchers probe sufficiently to jog recollections of all the games that individuals might have played, organised and informally, however infrequently (Archer and McDonald, 1990; McCusker, 1985). But there are, of course, wide variations in the amounts that individuals play.

In the Participation Survey 55 percent of the secondary age group were receiving two or more hours per week of PE and games whereas 21 percent had less than one-and-a-half hours. Is less than two hours, or one-and-a-half hours cause for concern? Twenty percent of the secondary pupils were playing seven or more sports at least 10 times per year in lessons whereas 18 percent were playing no sports in lessons this frequently. Similar proportions, 21 and 16 percent respectively, were playing seven or more, and no sport at least 10 times per year out of school lessons. Actually only seven percent were playing no sport this frequently either in or out of lessons. Thirty-five percent of the secondary pupils played sport out of lessons on five or more days a week during term time, 20 percent played for least 10 hours per week during school terms, and 33 percent had played for more than 10 hours per week in their last summer holidays. Young people's, and adults', sport participation levels are distributed normally along a bell-shaped curve. Most are towards the middle. At one extreme a minority are highly active relatively to the norm. At the other extreme another minority is inactive both relatively and absolutely. Twenty-five percent of the secondary pupils in the Participation Survey reported that they played sport on no more than one day per week, and 22 percent claimed to play for less than a hour a week in total, during term time. Fourteen percent said that they had played for less than an hour per week during their last summer holidays.

Clearly some young people could do much more sport. The evidence from the Youth Service Study does not suggest that most young people are so time pressured that they could not increase their sport participation without dropping other things. The 'leisure multiplier' was apparent in this sample's leisure patterns. Those who were involved in any organised form of leisure such as attending youth centres were the most likely to be involved in all the others about which the sample was questioned, including sport.

Nevertheless, before devising programmes and setting targets for bringing the least active in sport up to the current average, and encouraging those who are currently average to become even more active, there are several points to bear in mind. First, the levels of sports participation among young people recorded in the recent investigations are well above the levels described in research that was conducted in the 1950s and 60s. At that time most girls did no out of school sport and most boys did no leisure time sport except football. The norm then was for most young people to be lost to sport, probably for ever, at the end of their school careers. Emmett's (1971) study of 2,683 leavers from 53 schools in south-east Lancashire found that, in the final school year, 30 percent of the boys and 57 percent of the girls did no out of school sport. Football (35 percent of the boys) and tennis (12 percent of the girls) were the only sports played outside school by at least 12 percent of either sex. In the 1994 Participation Survey there were 22 sports that were being played at least 10 times a year outside school lessons by at least 10 percent of the secondary school pupils.

Young people's participation rates may still fall well beneath the requirements for health promoting sport for all but they are much higher than in the past. This is not to deny that most children may be doing insufficient sport to benefit their cardio-vascular health (Cale and Almond, 1992a, 1992b; Thirlaway and Benton, 1993). Nor is to dispute that many young people's health related fitness is sub-optimal. However, if young people's fitness has declined in recent years this must owe more to their diets or their more frequent use of private mechanical transport or something other than a flight from sport. Also, the Youth Service study found that among the 18-21 year olds 82 percent were visiting pubs. And around a third of young people are known to use tobacco products. These features of young people's lifestyles should probably command more attention from the 'health lobby' than their sports participation.

Second, more young people are involved in sport than in any other organised form of out of home leisure. The 'at least once in the last month' participation rates among 11-15 year olds in the Youth Service Study were 47 percent for going to sports and leisure centres (and 56 percent had played sport elsewhere in their leisure time), cinema 42 percent, youth clubs 32 percent, pubs 11 percent, gigs and concerts 8 percent, and arts or culture groups 6 percent. In the 16-plus age group sport was overtaken by pubs and the cinema but maintained twice as many participants as gigs and concerts, and its lead over the Youth Service widened as involvement in these organisations declined with age. In the Youth Service Study sport had a high retention rate in the 16-plus age group. As many 18-21 as 11-15 year olds were going to sports and leisure centres, though playing sport elsewhere declined with age. In their post-school years young people became less likely to play sports casually in streets and parks but their participation in organised, facility based sport did not tail off. The provision of sports centres which are available for everyone appears to have obliterated the 'Wolfenden gap' and reduced the sport give-up rate from its former chronic level in the immediate post-school years. The evidence from the Youth Service Study suggests that whether young people continue to play sport after leaving school may well be strongly related to whether they are already using community facilities.

Third, there will be a natural limit to the popularity of sport which is likely to fall well short of everyone participating frequently. In the Participation Survey the young people were asked a prompted question about what they 'minded' about sport. Approximately a quarter 'minded a lot' when they were hit, kicked, fell over, and had to go outside in bad weather. Far fewer minded getting cold, wet, hot, sweaty or dirty, having to change and shower, or getting their hair wet. The aspect of sport that the young people minded most was 'playing with people who cheat or otherwise break the rules to win'. This was followed by being left out 'because you are not good enough' and 'playing badly'. The converse will be that playing well and being good enough to be picked will be among the rewards, for some, in playing sport. The teachers, parents and children who were interviewed in the Participation Survey made frequent references to how some children were simply better at, and more 'sporty' than others. There is probably no need to digress into the nature/nurture debate to gain agreement that by the time they become teenagers some children know that they are good, and others realise that they are not so good at sport. Of course, the rewards from sport may be made more widely available by giving children a wide choice of activities, matching players with others of similar ability, and providing the option of non-competitive games. The fact will remain that those who are generally less good than most others in their age group will not obtain the socio-psychological rewards of those who can win competitions and bring glory to their schools. 'Sport for all', if it was realised, would not deliver equal benefits to all, which will be one reason why a spread of participation rates is probably inevitable.

Social class inequalities

None of the studies under consideration provide straight-forward evidence on the relationship between young people's sports activity and their social class backgrounds. The Facility Survey did not seek information about the schools' social class intakes, and the Participation Survey did not question the children about their parents' occupations. The Youth Service Study, which was conducted as part of the OPCS Omnibus, did obtain this information but the published report does not relate it to the sample's sport activities. However, the overall levels of sports activity in the Participation Survey, especially among boys (see below), were such that participation could not have been the prerogative of any specific social group.

This implies a change from the situation a generation back when participation was highest among pupils in selective schools, and otherwise among the 'best pupils' (Emmett, 1971; Hendry, 1978). The independent and grammar schools tended to possess the best facilities and, in many cases, a traditional sporting ethos. At that time provision for out of school sport tended to be sparse and spartan. The result was that sport participation after age 15 remained high only among those, mainly at grammar and independent schools, or in the academic streams of non-selective schools, who were continuing in education.

Subsequent trends in education may not have transformed the eventual relationships between social origins and destinations but they have blurred former social divisions. The spread of comprehensive schools has blurred the divide between academic and other pupils. As the Participation and Facility Surveys demonstrate, virtually all schools have now adopted 'sport for all' policies, broadened their sports curricula and involved the vast majority of their pupils. Since the 1970s, and especially since the early 1980s, more young people have been continuing full-time in education beyond age 16. Since the late 1980s higher education has expanded to accommodate roughly a third of the relevant population. Alongside these trends, opportunities to participate in out of school sport have been enhanced through the upgrading and opening of new local authority and voluntary sector facilities. These will be the principal trends that have led to higher levels of sports participation among young people, and from what we know about lifetime sport careers, all other things have only to remain equal for the progress of recent cohorts of young people into adulthood and middle age to boost participation within these age groups (Roberts and Brodie, 1992).

The same trends will have blurred social class divisions in leisure practices. Such recent evidence as is available from investigations that have measured and analysed the leisure implications of young people's social class backgrounds show that leisure differences still exist. Young people on middle class trajectories have higher levels of sports participation than those in working class locations (Hendry et al., 1993; Roberts and Parsell, 1994). In the Participation Survey's home interviews many parents and children commented on the significance of the encouragement that some families had given to their children in the pre-school years. Some young children had been encouraged to play by sports-active parents. While at school the participation of some children had been assisted by their parents' ability and willingness to transport them to and from, and to meet other expenses involved in out of school sport. All these kinds of assistance are certain to be most common in middle class families. However, the main social class differences are no longer in whether young people play any sport but how often. It remains the case that sport participation is related to age, sex and social class, but it is no longer true that all or nearly all participants are young, male and middle class. Playing sport is no longer a hallmark of the country's social, economic or educational elites. The Youth Service Study found that participation in youth clubs and organisations in the 16-plus age group was highest among students and young people in employment but significantly lower among the unemployed. The situation in sport may be similar. A lower working class or underclass may differ qualitatively in its participation levels and patterns from the rest of the youth population throughout which regular sports activity of some type is now the norm.

Gender differences

Sex divisions in sport have probably lessened as young people have taken up more sports, many of which are played by both sexes, but the differences remain stark. The clearest overview of these differences in the recent investigations is probably in the presentation of the Youth Service Study findings. Among this sample of 11-25 year olds, males were only slightly more likely than females to play sport in sport and leisure centres but they were much more likely to play elsewhere (55 percent compared with 23 percent during the previous month). Also, 31 percent of the males against just 13 percent of the females had attended a spectator sports event. The Youth Service Study also found that sex differences were wider in sport than in any other area of the sample's leisure. Sport proved exceptional rather than an example of higher rates of male participation across leisure in general. The study found negligible differences in the likelihood of the sexes attending youth clubs, arts centres, pubs, cinemas, concerts or gigs.

The Participation Survey adds much fine detail. It shows that males and females were participating more or less equally in sport during school lessons. Since most of the schools were co-educational the sexes had the same amounts of timetabled sport and PE. Moreover, the mean numbers of sports played in lessons hardly differed between the males and females in either primary or secondary schools. Nor were there any sex differences in the proportions playing no sports at least 10 times in school lessons, or in the proportions playing seven or more sports this frequently. The girls in co-educational schools were not sitting on the sidelines and watching the boys play. This may have applied in previous years (see Leaman, 1984) but in 1994 the situation was different. Needless to say, the sexes were not always playing the same sports in school, though in the primary schools most of the main sports (those played by the largest percentages) were played by roughly equal numbers of both sexes. This applied to gymnastics, swimming, athletics and rounders. Football was the only major sport in which one sex (boys of course) predominated. In the secondary age group there were more sex differences because more boys' and girls' sports became popular. Rugby and cricket as well as football were played in lessons by many more boys than girls, while hockey and netball became major girls' sports but were played by far fewer boys. However, in the secondary schools there remained many sports which were played by substantial proportions of both sexes. Very few girls played rugby (4 percent)

or football (6 percent) regularly in school lessons, and very few boys played
netball (2 percent), but 23 percent of the boys played hockey and 18
percent played tennis which were both played by more girls, while 19
percent of the girls played basketball which was played by more boys, and
participation in athletics was unrelated to gender.

It was out of lessons where sex differences in sport participation were
widest, just as in the Youth Service Study male dominance was most pronounced in sports participation outside sports and leisure centres. Out of
lessons, in and out of school, the boys played more sports, were the more
likely to participate regularly in seven or more, and less likely to participate
regularly in none. The boys played sport on more days during term time,
for more hours per day, and also spent more time playing sport during
school holidays. These differences existed among the primary and secondary school pupils but were widest at the secondary level. In this respect
sport illustrates a general leisure tendency; sex differences that are evident
in the primary school years become wider with age (Durkin, 1985). In the
primary school age group the sexes played much the same sports out of
school; cycling and swimming were popular forms of leisure time physical
activity and the sexes had virtually identical participation rates in both,
though the boys were more likely to play football and cricket. In the
secondary age group boys outnumbered girls in all the more popular leisure time sports except swimming. There were more boys who cycled,
played football, cricket and basketball, and snooker, pool and billiards
became another set of popular games where males dominated. As explained previously, this higher male involvement is not a pervasive feature
of young people's leisure.

Some writers have criticised sport for its masculine ethos, claimed that
school sport has been pervaded by this culture, and that it has never been
delivered in ways that might appeal to girls (Leaman, 1984; Scraton, 1987,
1992). However, the evidence from the Participation Survey does not suggest that the schools bore a major responsibility for the females' lower rates
of out of school participation. The girls were playing as much sport, and as
many sports, as boys in school lessons, and were being offered a wide
range encompassing sports played mainly by girls and others that were
played by both sexes. The main reason for the girls' lower participation
outside lessons seemed to be simply that they liked sport less than the
boys. The boys were more likely to describe themselves as good at sport, to
say that they enjoyed PE and games lessons, and doing sport in their
leisure time. Girls were more likely to object to getting cold, wet, hit,
sweaty, dirty, kicked and falling over, getting their hair wet, going outside
in bad weather, and having to change, wash or shower. These differences
in the sexes' attitudes and feelings were present among the secondary and
primary school children. Rather than being created or even strengthened
by their school experiences, it seemed rather that the sexes were bringing
their different attitudes into school and a result was that the girls were the
more likely to resent, while the boys were the more likely to enjoy the

similar amounts of sport in which they were required to participate. Out of school, of course, the girls had the option of playing less.

Schools may be sometimes unable to countervail against wider social-ising influences even if they wish to do so. Teachers' views and practices are not always decisive. Trends in school sport may have helped to boost young people's rates of participation and blurred former social class divi-sions, but it does not necessarily follow that gender differences will be equally malleable. School effects in sport will not necessarily be equally powerful whatever the objectives. For example, the Participation Survey found that there was no linear relationship between the importance that teachers attached to sport and their pupils' levels of participation outside school.

References

Archer, J., and M. McDonald (1990) 'Gender roles and sports in adolescent girls', *Leisure Studies*, Vol. 9, No. 3: pp. 225-240.

Cale, L., and Almond, L. (1992a) 'Physical activity levels of young children: a review of the evidence', *Health Education Journal*, No. 51, pp. 94-99.

—— (1992b) 'Physical activity levels of secondary aged children: a review', *Health Education Journal*, No. 51: pp. 192-197.

Department for Education (1995) *Young people's participation in the Youth Service*, London: DoE Statistical Bulletin 1/95.

Durkin, K. (1985) *Gender and the development of leisure interests in adolescence*. London: ESRC.

Emmett, I. (1971) *Youth and leisure in an urban sprawl*. Manchester: Manchester University Press.

Hendry, L. B. (1978) *School, sport and leisure*. London: Lepus Books.

Hendry, L. B., Shucksmith, J., Love, J. G., and Glendinning, A. (1993) *Young people's leisure and lifestyles*. London: Routledge.

Hunter, P. (1995) *Community use of school sports facilities*. London: Office of Population, Censuses and Surveys.

Leaman, O. (1984) *Sit on the sidelines and watch the boys play*, Schools Council Programme Pamphlet. York: Longman Resources Unit.

McCusker, J. (1985) 'Involvement of 15-19 year olds in sport and physical activity', in L. Haywood and I. Henry (eds) *Leisure and youth*, LSA Publication No. 17. Eastbourne: Leisure Studies Association.

Mason, V. (1995a) *Young people and sport — a National Survey, 1994*. London: Office of Population, Censuses and Surveys.

————(1995b) *Young people and sport 1994: The views of teachers and children*. London: Office of Population, Censuses and Surveys.

Roberts, K., and Brodie, D. A. (1992) *Inner-city sport: Who plays and what are the benefits?*. Culemborg: Giordano Bruno.

Roberts, K. and Parsell, G. (1994) 'Youth cultures in Britain: the middle class takeover', *Leisure Studies*, Vol. 13, No. 1: pp. 33-48.

Scraton, S. (1987) 'Boys muscle in where angels fear to tread — girls' sub-cultures and physical activities', in J. Horne, D. Jary and A. Tomlinson (eds) *Sport, leisure and social relations*. London: Routledge.

———— (1992) *Shaping up to womanhood: Gender and girls' physical education*. Buckingham: Open University Press.

Index

Note: No claim is made that this index is either comprehensive or exhaustive. Its modest aim is to provide sign-posts to the extensive range of topics — both discussed in depth and mentioned in passing — in this volume. For example, some authors who have been discussed, quoted and/or extensively cited in a particular chapter are indexed; but no concerted attempt has been made at cross-referencing.